D1171861

THE SOVIET UNION AND THE MUSLIM WORLD 1917-1958

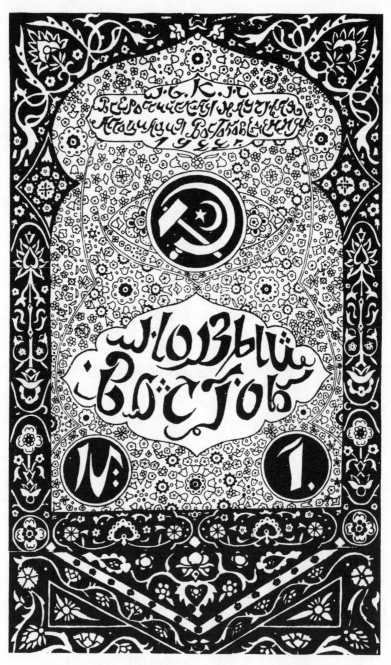

The cover of the first issue of *Novyi Vostok* (1922). The
Muslim crescent combined with the hammer and sickle
indicated the Soviet intent to Bolshevize the Muslim world

THE SOVIET UNION

AND

THE MUSLIM WORLD

1917-1958

By Ivar Spector

Distributed by

UNIVERSITY OF WASHINGTON PRESS   SEATTLE AND LONDON

To Marion

Preface

This work has been written to fill a significant gap in the field of Soviet-Muslim relations. Although many books have been published on the Near and Middle East, including a number of studies of specific countries in that area, and recently some monographs have appeared on the Muslim republics inside the Soviet Union, this marks the first attempt to deal with the Muslim world from the vantage point of the Soviet Union.

Because of the comparative paucity of research in this field to date, it has seemed advisable to place greater stress at this time on those periods when Soviet policy in regard to the Muslim world has been most dynamic, rather than on those in which relations have been largely routine in nature. Thus greater emphasis has been given to the Bolshevik Revolution and the years immediately following it, from 1917 to 1925; and to World War II and the postwar period, when the Soviet regime gave a degree of priority to its relations with Muslim countries that was not characteristic of the thirties. Emphasis has also been given to those Muslim countries with which the Soviet Union was first in closest contact, namely, the border countries of Turkey, Iran, and Afghanistan. Official Soviet relations with most of the Arab countries, with Pakistan, and Indonesia, date either from World War II or the postwar period, and even in recent years the Communist party has ordinarily operated underground in those areas. Among other things, the author has felt that it was necessary, as in Chapter 2, to provide a Soviet definition of the Bolshevik Revolution as it pertained to the Muslim world. The impact of that revolution on Muslim countries is the subject of the subsequent chapters. Chapter 9 is a pioneer effort in the direction of an evaluation of the Soviet cultural impact on the Muslim world--a field to which it is hoped much greater attention will be paid in the years to come.

This study is based largely upon Soviet primary sources. In

this connection, it should be understood that since privately owned publishing houses are nonexistent in the Soviet Union, all newspapers, periodicals, studies from the Academy of Sciences, etc., are carefully supervised and scrutinized and, therefore, reflect at the time of publication official government thinking and policy to an extent completely unknown in the United States. This is particularly true in regard to material dealing with the Muslim world, as Soviet specialists themselves admitted in the first volume of *Novyi Vostok, (The New Orient)*, published in 1922.

A further contribution of this book consists in the inclusion of the first complete English translation of the "Documents of the Programs of the Communist Parties of the East" (Turkey, the Arab countries, and Palestine), as published by the Marx-Engels-Lenin Institute of the Central Committee of the all-Russian Communist party in 1934. These "Programs" are a basic and indispensable text for any study of Soviet relations with the Muslim world. Not only have they never been renounced by the Soviet Union, but recent developments in the Near East seem to indicate that they are still being implemented. Thus they serve as a warning, not only to the West, but also to the Muslim world and to Israel, of the fate in store for the Near East under any Communist regime.

Because of the new alignment in Asia, which is replacing the former political and territorial units, it is clear that the Muslim Orient has it in its power to render one of the greatest contributions both to the Orient and to the rest of the world. As a result of World War II, the Asiatic peoples today may be roughly divided into Muslims and non-Muslims, with the latter greatly outnumbering the former. Although there are approximately four hundred million Muslims, between the non-Muslims and the West they constitute a minority, without organization. If they cast their lot with the Western world, they will create an effective balance against the non-Muslim Orient and the Soviet Union.

This book is the product of many years of study of Russian and Arabic sources, and of courses on Russian expansion and Russia and the Muslim world offered at the University of Washington. Its completion was made possible by a grant from the Rockefeller Foundation for the summer of 1955, by a grant-in-aid from the Social Science Research Council in 1956, and by a grant from the Graduate School of the University of Washington for the summer of 1958. Financial assistance from the Far Eastern and Russian Institute of the University of Washington made possible additional research at the Hoover Library in the summer of 1957.

During a visit to the Near East in the summer of 1958, the author was fortunate in being able to consult in Istanbul General Ali Fuat Cebesoy, commander of the Western forces of the Turkish revolutionists in Anatolia, who became the first ambassador of the Turkish Republic in Moscow early in 1921; and Rauf Orbay, the first prime minister of the Turkish Republic. Both Turkish leaders were close associates of Kemal Ataturk, and are the foremost living Turkish authorities on Soviet-Turkish relations in the crucial period from 1919 to 1921. The author was equally fortunate in meeting Professor A. Zeki Velîdî Togan of the University of Istanbul, a Bashkir leader, who attended the Baku Congress of 1920 incognito and played an important role behind the scenes. In Beirut and Cairo the author likewise obtained important information on Soviet foreign policy in the Arab world.

The author wishes to express his indebtedness to Dr. Witold S. Sworakowski, curator of the Slavic Division, the Hoover Library, Stanford University, and his staff; to Dr. Sergei Yakobson, chief, Slavic Division, the Library of Congress, and his staff; to the Slavic Section, Butler Library, Columbia University; and to the Russian Research Center, Harvard University, for generous assistance in locating and duplicating materials essential to the preparation of this work. He owes a particular debt of gratitude to Professor George E. Taylor, director of the Far Eastern and Russian Institute of the University of Washington, who read the manuscript and offered valuable suggestions; and to Dr. Harold W. Stoke, formerly dean of the Graduate School, University of Washington, for his encouragement and backing during the launching of this project and for continued support during the preparation of the manuscript. Responsibility for all translations from foreign language sources as well as for all judgments rests with the author.

I. S.

Contents

Illustrations

THE SOVIET UNION AND THE MUSLIM WORLD 1917-1958

1. Introduction: Four Hundred Years of Russian Expansion at the Expense of the Muslim World

> But the most wonderful thing in the situation is the resurrection of the old Russian claims. The Bolsheviki are quite evidently developing a policy that has a remarkable trait of continuity with that of the old policy of the Tsars.
> --Baron S. A. Korff, 1923.

> . . . the entire foreign policy of Tsarist Russia was, first of all, an Asiatic policy.
> --Lamzdorf, *Krasnyi Arkhiv*, IV (53) (1932), 4.

By the seizure of Kazan[1] in 1552 Ivan Grozny (1530-84) began the Russian crusade against the Muslim world, which has continued for more than four centuries to the present day. Whereas his main objective was Russian security at the expense of Muslim territory, he nevertheless unwittingly opened the gateway for Russian expansion in a different direction--toward the Pacific. Although Russian colonization and expansion in Siberia was largely the work of adventurers, outlaws, prospectors, etc., in the case of the Muslim world, it was initiated by the Russian government and backed wholeheartedly by the majority of the Slavs in the population.[2] In short, the Muslims, headed by the Turks, became for the Russians a legitimate target. There were no fewer than twelve Russo-Turkish wars between 1672 and 1914. Generally speaking, the four centuries of Russian expansion at the expense of the Muslim world coincide with four hundred years of Turkish domination of the Arab peoples.

When Mohammed II (1451-81) conquered Constantinople in 1453, a strong movement began among Orthodox Russians to overthrow the Tatar yoke and eventually to retake the capital of Orthodox Christendom. It fell to the lot of Ivan III, grandfather of Ivan Groz-

3

ny, in 1480 to overthrow Tatar hegemony in Russia, which had lasted approximately 240 years. Vasily III, Grand Prince of Moscow and father of Ivan Grozny, was tempted by the Holy Roman Emperor with the offer of a kingly crown if he would lead a crusade against the Turks. Since he was confronted with problems nearer home, it was left to Ivan Grozny to begin the counterattack against the Muslims with the aforementioned capture of Kazan.

In the sixteenth century, the Russian state was already conducting a regular trade with the Near and Middle East. During the early part of the century Russian trade in this area was largely in the hands of Turkish contractors, but later direct trade with Iran and Central Asia, in particular with the Nogai Horde, was established. Russia's trade with the East was of greater significance for the economic development of the country than was her trade with the West. To Western Europe, for the most part, the Russians exported raw materials, whereas in the Orient, Russian manufacturers had already found a market. [3]

Although Muslim expansion over a period of several centuries had proceeded at the expense of the territories of Roman Catholic and Orthodox Christendom, Muslim gains were offset in part by the conversion of the Slavs to Christianity--the Poles to Catholicism (966) and Kievan Rūs to Orthodoxy (988-89). The Crusades temporarily stemmed the tide of Muslim expansion and established a tenuous Christian hold on Asia Minor. With the exception of Spain, however, the Christian counterattack made no permanent gains. But the Slavs, particularly the Russians, in the late fifteenth century entered upon a crusade of their own, which persistently drove back the Muslims; and over a period of four centuries they regained South Russia and expanded into the Balkans, the Caucasus, and Central Asia, until Russian expansion itself constituted a threat to the Western world. [4]

While the Rurik dynasty, which experienced the Mongol invasion, inaugurated the counterattack on the Muslim world, it was under the Romanov dynasty (1613-1917) that the greatest gains were made in South Russia, the Caucasus, and Central Asia. It also afforded direct and indirect aid to the Christian Balkan nations at the expense of the Turkish Muslims. The most aggressive policy of the Romanovs occurred in the reigns of Peter the Great (1682-1725), Catherine the Great (1762-96), Nicholas I (1825-55), Alexander II (1855-81), and in the Secret Agreements between Russia and her Allies in 1915 and 1916 under Nicholas II.

It was Peter's ambition to extend Russian boundaries from the Baltic to the Black and Caspian Seas. Due to his preoccupation

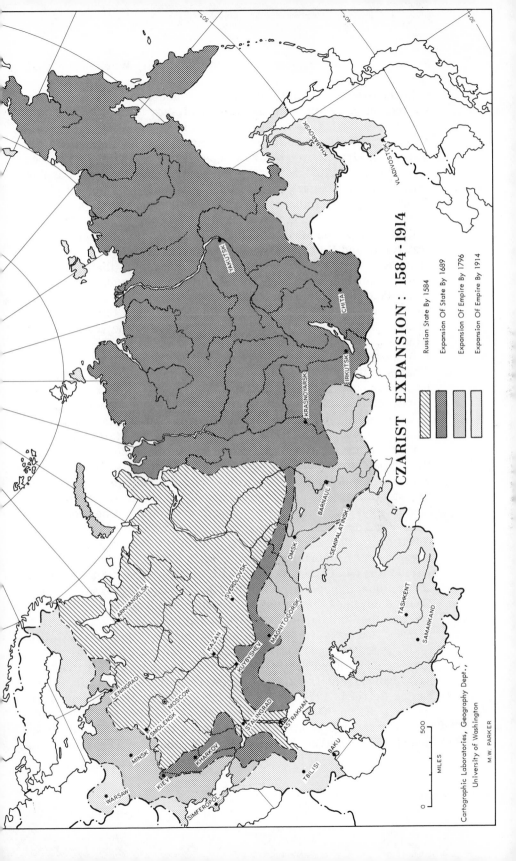

CZARIST EXPANSION : 1584-1914

Russian State By 1584

Expansion Of State By 1689

Expansion Of Empire By 1796

Expansion Of Empire By 1914

Cartographic Laboratories, Geography Dept.,
University of Washington

M.W. PARKER

MILES

0   500

KHABAROVSK

VLADIVOSTOK

YAKUTSK

CHITA

KRASNOYARSK

IRKUTSK

BARNAUL

SEMIPALATINSK

OMSK

SVERDLOVSK

MAGNITOGORSK

TASHKENT

SAMARKAND

ARKHANGELSK

KAZAN

KUIBYSHEV

STALINGRAD

ASTRAKHAN

BAKU

TBILISI

LENINGRAD

MOSCOW

SMOLENSK

MINSK

KHARKOV

KIEV

SIMFEROPOL

WARSAW

with the Swedes under Charles XII, he achieved only temporary success in the south, with the capture of Azov (1696-1700). He set the pattern for his successors, however, by enlisting the support of the Orthodox Balkan Slavs, Rumanians, and Greeks against the Turks. Motivated by a desire to open a route to India, he seized from Persia in 1723 the western and southern shores of the Caspian Sea, including Daghestan, and thus initiated the conquest of the Caucasus, although this territory was relinquished by his successors. The route to India was blocked, not only by Persian Muslims, but likewise by the Muslim Khanates of Khiva and Bokhara in Central Asia, and Peter's efforts to expand in this direction proved unsuccessful. By 1725, according to Vernadsky, "the frontier of the Russian Empire in the Middle East formed an angle from the Altai Range down the Irtysh River to Omsk, and from Omsk to the upper reaches of the Yaik River and thence along the Yaik to the Caspian Sea. The Middle Eastern steppe was at the very Russian frontier."[5]

A significant passage in the memoirs of Catherine the Great indicates that in the middle of the eighteenth century the Russians let slip an opportunity to purchase from the Turks the right to free navigation of the Black Sea, over which so much blood was spilled in later years: "In 1757 or 1758 a favourite of the Sultan Osman offered M. Obreskov, the Russian envoy in Constantinople, free navigation for the Russian Empire in the Black Sea on condition Russia paid about 30,000 ducats. The Russian reply (Count Michel Worontsov was then Grand Chancellor and Count Bestujev in exile) was that owing to excessive expenditure on the war against the king of Prussia, this further expenditure could not be met."[6]

As regards Russian expansion in the Near East, Catherine the Great began where Peter left off. When the Turks in 1768, taking advantage of Catherine's preoccupation with the Poles, declared war on Russia, Catherine had no difficulty in arousing the support of the Russian population against the Muslim aggressor. Under Count Rumyantsev[7] the Russian forces defeated the Turkish army, overran the Crimea, seized Turkish outposts on the Dniester and Danube, and occupied Moldavia and Wallachia. The Russian Baltic fleet, which under Count Alexei Orlov proceeded to the Mediterranean, annihilated the Turkish navy at Chesme. During Russia's naval campaign in the Eastern Mediterranean, Russian forces occupied Beirut in 1772 and 1773 at the invitation of insurgent Arab leaders. From "October 1773 to February 1774, Beirut was effectively under Russian control. 'During this time the Muscovite flag flew over Beirut, the portrait of the Empress (Catherine) was

raised over the principal gate, before which passers-by were
obliged to do reverence . . .' For five months the Russian flag
flew over an Arab population. "[8] As a wartime expedient, the Russian expedition supported the pretensions of Ali Bey, who in 1768
declared Egyptian independence of the Ottoman Empire, and his
ally, Dahir al-'Umar of Syria.

Because of war fatigue on the part of both belligerents and the
Pugachev Rebellion (1773-75), which shook the Russian throne to
its foundations, the Russo-Turkish War was concluded in 1774 by
the Peace of Kuchuk-Kainardji. By this treaty, a landmark in Russian relations with the Near East, Russia obtained control of the
northern shores of the Black Sea from the Bug to the Dnieper and
the right to free navigation of its waters. By exacting a pledge from
Turkey to permit freedom of religion in Moldavia and Wallachia,
Russia emerged as the champion of Orthodoxy in the Balkans. The
treaty of 1774 set the pattern for future international settlements
pertaining to the Black Sea and the Dardanelles, as well as the protection of Orthodox Christians in the Ottoman Empire. The stage
was set for the "Eastern Question" and for the role of Turkey as
the "sick man of Europe" in the nineteenth century.

When the conflict was renewed by the Turks in 1787, the Russian forces under General Suvorov once again defeated them. By
the peace concluded at Yassy in January, 1792, Russia retained the
Crimea (first annexed in 1783) and expanded Russian territory
along the shores of the Azov and Black Seas to include the fortress
of Otchakov. Although Catherine's ambitious plans for the conquest
of Constantinople, India, and Persia failed to materialize, during
her reign the entire north shore of the Black Sea fell into Russian
hands.

Catherine's son Paul (1796-1801), hoping by diplomacy rather
than by force of arms to extend Russian influence to the shores of
the Mediterranean and Adriatic Seas, sought and secured a friendly
understanding with Turkey. In collaboration with Turkey, he undertook to liberate the Ionian Islands from French "tyranny." A Black
Sea squadron under the command of Admiral Ushakov was ordered
to proceed to the Adriatic where, with the backing of a few Turkish
warships, the public support of the Greek patriarch at Constantinople, and the favorable disposition of the local population, the
French were expelled from the islands. A republic was established
in the Ionian Islands, nominally under Turkish control, but in reality a dependency of Russia. Thus Paul's ambition approached realization since a Russian base, from which he could exercise control
over the Orthodox and Slavonic population of the Balkans, had been

secured in the Adriatic. In 1799 the Prince-Bishop of Montenegro, a country which had maintained relations with Russia since the reign of Peter the Great, voluntarily sought an alliance with the Russian emperor, thereby promoting still further his designs in the Adriatic. [9]

As a result of Russo-Turkish collaboration against Napoleon, the first defensive alliance between these two traditionally hostile powers was signed on January 3, 1799. A secret clause in this alliance formally recognized the freedom of passage of Russian ships through the Straits and the closure of this strategic waterway to the warships of other foreign powers. Although Paul subsequently made a deal with Napoleon at the expense of Turkey, his successor Alexander I reaffirmed the alliance by a new treaty in 1805. Once again it was of brief duration since after the victory of Napoleon at Austerlitz (December 2, 1805), the Turks gravitated toward the French, thereby provoking a sharp dispute which terminated in war with Russia.

Wars in the Near and Middle East broke out shortly after the accession of Nicholas I. The first of these was with Persia, where English officers had entered the service of the Shah, and the mullahs preached a holy war against Russia. The Persian forces, which initiated the conflict, retreated before the army of General Paskevitch, who crossed the Araxes, seized the important stronghold of Yerevan, and proceeded to march on Teheran. In alarm the Shah, failing to receive the expected aid from England, hastened to conclude in 1828 the Treaty of Turkmantchay, by which the Russians acquired the left bank of the Araxes and a large part of Armenia, including Yerevan. In addition Persia paid a huge indemnity of thirty-six million rubles and abandoned her claim to the Caucasus. Almost immediately, however, the Muridist revolution, a religious movement, broke out among the Muslim mountaineers in the Caucasus. Under the leadership of able imams and sheiks, the best known of whom were Kazi-Mullah, who was killed in 1831, and Shamyl (1797-1871), who was captured by the Russians in 1859, the revolutionaries maintained a long and stubborn resistance and were not fully subdued until the reign of Alexander II. The conquest of the Caucasus took in all 137 years, from 1722 to 1859.

Scarcely had peace been concluded with Persia when Russia was again involved in war, this time with Turkey. This conflict grew out of the Greek struggle for independence (1821-29). For some time, in conformity with the sentiment of the Holy Alliance, Europe rendered no formal military assistance to the Greek rebels. In Russia, Alexander's opposition to revolution was somewhat compromised by the fact that the Hetairia Philike, a leading Greek revolutionary society, had been founded in Odessa in 1814, and many wealthy Greek merchants of that city extended very considerable financial aid to their rebel kinsmen. Although the possibility of supporting Orthodox Christians against the Turks was an idea that traditionally appealed to Russians, Alexander nevertheless promptly disavowed Prince Ypsilanti, pro-Russian leader of the Greek revolt and, until his death in 1825, refused to intervene actively on the side of the Greeks. However, his more militaristic brother, Nicholas I, who stood for the *status quo* in Western Europe, by no means applied the same principle to Turkey and the Balkans. The ruthless campaign of the Sultan's vassal, Ibrahim Pasha of Egypt, against the Greeks had aroused popular opinion throughout Europe. This led to joint intervention on the part of England, France, and Russia to enforce a diplomatic settlement, and when that failed, their combined fleets destroyed a Turko-Egyptian squadron in the Battle of Navarino in 1827. In the following year Nicholas, acting unilaterally, declared war on Turkey, and the Russian army, supported by the Serbs, almost reached Constantinople. The Treaty of Adrianople, which brought the war to a close in September, 1829, was highly favorable to Russia and marked an important stage in the dismemberment of the Ottoman Empire. By its terms Russia gained possession of the mouth of the Danube and the coast of the Black Sea to Poti. Turkey also acceded to Russia's demand for a protectorate over Orthodox peoples living in Turkish territories and granted commercial privileges to Russian subjects in the same regions. In addition to her concessions to Russia, Turkey agreed to recognize the independence of the Greeks (1830) and to open the Bosphorus and Dardanelles to friendly nations. Moreover certain dependencies of Turkey, namely, Moldavia, Wallachia, Serbia, and the principalities of the Danube, were granted autonomy under Turkish suzerainty.

Nicholas might have exacted far more by the Treaty of Adrianople, but he preferred to moderate his demands and pursue a policy of expansion by peaceful penetration, in conformity with the tactics of Catherine II in the Middle and Far East and those of Paul in the Near East. Thus when Mehemet Ali, the Pasha of Egypt, began hostilities against the Sultan, Nicholas managed to secure from the reluctant Porte an invitation to send Russian forces to Asia Minor to protect Constantinople and the Straits. The unprecedented example of a Russian expeditionary force at the Bosphorus, ostensibly to support the Sultan, startled all Europe. There is reason to believe that Nicholas expected to establish a Russian base on the Bosphorus. [10] Instead, by the Treaty of Unkiar Skelessi (Iskelesi), signed July 8, 1833, the Sultan agreed to an eight-year mutual aid pact with Russia. A secret clause released the Turks from going to the assistance of Russia in exchange for a commitment to close the Straits to the warships of all foreign powers. Although this provision in regard to the closure of the Straits has been interpreted in a variety of ways, the Soviet *Diplomatic Dictionary* (II, 846) still contends that it was applicable "upon the demand of Russia." A literal interpretation of the mutual aid terms seemed to indicate that although the Russians avoided any guarantee of the territorial integrity of Turkey, in the event of an international crisis Turkey was obligated to turn first to Russia for assistance. In any event, the Tsarist foreign minister, Nesselrode, assumed that Russia had obtained for the future a prior right of intervention at the Straits, which would enable her armed forces to be on hand first, and in the greatest strength, either to preserve the Ottoman Empire or to preside over its dissolution. Although the advantages to Russia from this treaty were perhaps more potential than actual, the implementation of its terms would have made a Russian satellite of the Ottoman Empire, with Russia in control of the Straits.

The unilateral policy of Nicholas in regard to Turkey in 1828 and 1833 aroused the fear of Austria and the antagonism of England and France. In spite of the Holy Alliance, Austria found herself increasingly at odds with Russia over the Christian principalities in the Balkans as a result of the Treaty of Adrianople. Since the reign of Catherine II, England had watched, with increasing concern, the expansion of Russia at the expense of Turkey, Persia, and Afghanistan. With the appointment of Viscount Palmerston as foreign secretary in 1830, Anglo-Russian relations began to deteriorate rapidly. France, as the ally of Mehemet Ali, had her own reasons for discomfiture in regard to Russian policy toward Turkey. The groundwork was being laid for the formation of an anti-Russian bloc, which was soon to challenge Russia in the Crimean War.

In order to prevent the formation of such a bloc, on September 18, 1833, at Münchengrätz, the Russians sought and reached an understanding with Austria, by which the two powers undertook to consult one another prior to taking any action in regard to Turkey and the Straits. Having voluntarily limited their freedom of action in the Balkans, the Russians turned their attention to Persia and Afghanistan. In 1837 they had established diplomatic relations with Kabul for the first time. The following year they engineered a Persian-Afghan alliance, with a view to strengthening their strategic and economic position in the Middle East against England, and thereby paved the way for the first Anglo-Afghan War (1838-42). However, the revival in 1838 of Mehemet Ali's pretensions against the Sultan soon engaged the attention of all the major European powers.

In 1839 Nicholas, envisaging an opportunity to collaborate with England in the solution of the Turkish problem, agreed to let the Treaty of Unkiar-Skelessi lapse. In 1840, however, in a move to isolate France, the four great powers--Russia, Prussia, England, and Austria--signed the London Convention, which defined the position of Mehemet Ali in the Ottoman Empire and closed the Straits of the Bosphorus and Dardanelles to the warships of all foreign powers in time of peace. These terms were confirmed by the Treaty of London in 1841, which included France. Still seeking English collaboration, Nicholas visited London in 1844, in order to obtain some assurance of English neutrality in the event of another Russian war against Turkey, or English participation in the dismemberment of Turkey, which he labeled "the sick man of Europe." His visit did little to allay English suspicions of Russian designs on the Ottoman Empire.

The foreign policy of Nicholas I during the breathing spell of the 1840's was characterized by two fixed ideas: (1) a firm determination to stop the spread of democracy and liberalism in Europe; and (2) the acquisition of the Dardanelles and Constantinople. In reality Nicholas achieved neither of his objectives. Not only did he fail to call a halt to democratic and liberal trends in Europe, but that continent became a hotbed of revolution in 1848, the year which marked the appearance of Karl Marx's *Communist Manifesto*. By using Russian troops for the suppression of revolt abroad, Nicholas brought Russia into still further disrepute among Western liberals as a reactionary and autocratic country. In the second place Nicholas' bid for Constantinople and the Dardanelles led directly to the Crimean War (1853-56).

The immediate cause of the Crimean War, however, grew out of the efforts of Napoleon III of France to strengthen French influence and prestige in the Near East, particularly in the Holy Land. [11] He demanded and obtained from Turkey concessions for Roman Catholics living in the Holy Land. He obtained for them also possession of the keys of the Church of Bethlehem, which by the Treaty of Kuchuk-Kainardji (1774) had been assigned to the keeping of the Orthodox Church. Nicholas promptly demanded of the Turks that the treaty be respected and Orthodox rights restored. When Turkey temporized, Nicholas countered with a demand for the recognition of Russian claims for protection over Orthodox Christians throughout the Ottoman Empire, and Russian troops invaded the Turkish provinces of Moldavia and Wallachia to enforce these demands. The Sultan, encouraged by Lord Stratford (Stratford Canning), the English ambassador in Constantinople, to believe that English and French aid would be forthcoming, declared war on Russia on October 1, 1853.

Russia's first move was to dispatch Russian warships to Sinope, where a Turkish squadron was destroyed. Anglo-French naval forces entered the Black Sea, and, after a futile effort to achieve a diplomatic settlement at Vienna, England and France declared war on Russia on March 27, 1854. They were later joined by the ambitious King of Sardinia. Austria and Prussia, from whom Nicholas expected a display of friendship, preserved a hostile neutrality. Russia was thus left alone to face an enemy alignment of the chief powers of Western Europe. In September, 1854, the allied forces landed in Crimea near Eupatoria and laid siege to Sevastopol. The city surrendered after a siege which lacked only fifteen days of lasting a year. Nicholas did not live to see its downfall, for he died on March 2, 1855. It was rumored that he committed suicide by taking poison because he was unable to outlive the defeat of all his plans and the collapse of Russian military power. Peace was concluded in 1856 by his son Alexander II under the terms of the Treaty of Paris.

The Crimean War revealed the backwardness of Tsarist military and naval equipment and Russia's lack of adequate transportation and communication facilities. Russian generals even lacked good maps of the Crimean peninsula. Whereas the Russian fleet was still predominantly a sailing fleet, the ironclad British and French warships were run by steam, and their guns had a range double that of the Russian shore batteries. It must not be forgotten, however, that the Russians not only fought in the Crimea, but had to maintain fronts in the Caucasus and the Baltic while large forces were immobilized throughout the war on the Austrian frontier. Even in the Pacific, units of the Anglo-French fleets attacked the port of Petropavlovsk on the Kamchatka Peninsula in 1854. In spite of this "encirclement, " Russian troops after the fall of Sevastopol won a signal victory against the Turks at Kars in Asia. In the final analysis, the Crimean War demonstrated rather clearly how ineffective was naval power without the backing of huge armies, when pitted against a great land power. At no time did Anglo-French military forces penetrate more than a few miles beyond the Crimean coast. For classic literature on this war, the reader will do well to consult *Sevastopol,* three sketches by Leo Tolstoy, who himself took part in the Crimean campaign.

The defeat of Russia in the Crimean War by no means put an end to Russian efforts in the direction of territorial expansion. It was scarcely to be expected that Russia, which held more than a thousand miles of coastline on the Black Sea, would accept indefinitely the unrealistic provision in the Treaty of Paris that excluded her fleet from that sea and forbade the construction of fortifications along its shores. Russians likewise regarded their exclusion from the mouth of the Danube as intolerable. Alexander II merely awaited a favorable opportunity to dispose of "these two nightmares." Moreover, Anglo-French success in "blocking" Russian expansion in the direction of the Mediterranean in 1856 merely deflected the Tsarist program of expansion to the Middle and Far East, with the result that England, in particular, soon had further occasion for anxiety.

In 1856, shortly after the end of the Crimean War, Prince Alexander Gortchakov, Russian minister of foreign affairs, presented a memorandum to Alexander II which convinced the Emperor that in Europe Russia confronted no major problems; that in Asia, on the other hand, there was in store for her an enormous field of activity; and that, in fact, "the future of Russia lies in Asia." The Emperor's notation on the memorandum read: "I am in complete agreement with this."[12]

The favorable opportunity Alexander sought was afforded by the Franco-Prussian War (1870-71). Under the circumstances it was greatly to Bismarck's advantage to promote discord between England and Russia, while Germany settled her score with France. In October, 1870, therefore, with the prior consent and perhaps even at the instigation of Bismarck, Gortchakov announced Russia's unilateral denunciation of the Black Sea clauses of the Treaty of Paris. In return for the "benevolent neutrality" of Russia during the Austro-Prussian War (1866) and the Franco-Prussian War, Prussia at once refused to join England in any protest against Russian action. As a result, the offensive clauses were formally repealed by the signatories of the Treaty of Paris at a conference held in London in 1871. At the same time, in a face-saving gesture, the powers reaffirmed those clauses which provided for the closing of the Straits to the warships of all nations, except at the invitation of the Sultan of Turkey.

Meanwhile, news of Russian expansion in Central Asia began to arouse concern among the European powers, especially England. After the successful completion of the conquest of the Caucasus in

1859, the Russian army continued its efforts to revive the military prestige of the Tsarist Empire by new victories in Asia and to establish a defensible frontier there. In a rapid succession of victories during the next twenty years the Russians captured the Uzbek city of Tashkent (1865) and made it the capital of the new province of Turkestan; occupied Samarkand (1868), the famous capital of the Empire of Tamerlane; and converted the Khanate of Bokhara into a Russian protectorate. England, greatly alarmed at the strides the Tsarist forces were taking in the direction of India, proposed the recognition of a series of "buffer states," including Afghanistan. Although Russia somewhat tentatively accepted this proposition, the instability of conditions in Central Asia and the absence of a natural frontier led to the occupation of Khiva (1873) and of the Khanate of Kokand (1876), thereby extending Russian frontiers to the mountainous northwest borders of China. Russian forces then proceeded to subjugate the warlike Turkoman tribes in the Trans-Caspian region. Thus Russia carved out for herself a new and rich Asiatic empire. In the wake of Russian armies came Russian merchants and traders. It was not long until American cotton was being cultivated in Central Asia. About the same time Russian relations with Persia assumed a new aspect, when in 1878 the Shah requested the Russian government to undertake the training of the Persian armed forces.

In 1875 the Near Eastern question came once again to the fore, with the outbreak of disturbances in protest against Turkish oppression, first in the Turkish provinces of Bosnia and Herzegovina, and later in Bulgaria. The Bulgarian massacres that marked the suppression of the revolt aroused public opinion throughout Europe and among the Slavic peoples in particular. Although the signatories of the Treaty of Paris had assumed the role of protectors of the Christian peoples under Turkish domination, they failed to take any decisive action in the face of Turkish atrocities. England, having extended loans amounting by 1875 to some £200,000,000 to Turkey, had acquired a vested interest, and although Gladstone made political capital out of the Bulgarian atrocities, Disraeli, the Prime Minister, refused to act in concert with the powers. Bismarck, estranged by Alexander's intervention to forestall a preventive war on the part of Germany against France in 1875, rejected Gortchakov's proposal to call a conference and pursued a policy calculated to embroil England with Russia, thereby fanning the flames of war in the Near East. [13] In 1876 the small Balkan states of Serbia and Montenegro made war on Turkey, and the former placed its army under the command of an able Russian general. The Serbs were, nevertheless, confronted with the certainty of overwhelming defeat when, on April 24, 1877, Russia took unilateral action and declared war on Turkey.

Although the Turkish forces were supplied with up-to-date English equipment, the outcome of the war soon became apparent, as the Russian army continued its relentless march on Constantinople. War hysteria ran high in England, but Disraeli did not wish to fight alone, and his efforts to secure active Austrian intervention proved futile. France was more concerned with the German menace than with Turkey. As Russian troops approached Constantinople, England dispatched a fleet to the Sea of Marmora, and the hostile forces faced one another for a time at San Stefano. Since Austria joined England in threatening to break off diplomatic relations with Russia in the event that Russian troops occupied Constantinople, the Tsar, anxious to avoid a general conflict, halted his army just outside the city. On March 3, 1878, the Turks made peace with Russia by the Treaty of San Stefano.

The terms of this treaty bore witness to the overwhelming defeat of the Turks. They provided for the creation of a new and greatly enlarged principality of Bulgaria, the independence of Montenegro, Rumania, and Serbia, and administrative reforms in Bosnia and Herzegovina. For her share, Russia regained the mouth of the Danube, which she had lost in 1856, together with Batum, Kars, and Ardahan in Transcaucasia, and a financial indemnity. In demanding so much from Turkey, Alexander committed a diplomatic error. He aroused the envy and fear of other powers having interests in the Balkans, namely, England and Austria. Since, in 1875, in response to the urgent appeal of Queen Victoria, Alexander had exerted pressure upon Germany to prevent the renewal of war against France, he had assumed that both England and France would allow him a free hand in the Balkans. This did not prove to be the case. Austria, seeking compensation in the south for what she had lost to Germany, joined England in demanding a European conference to settle the whole problem of peace in the Balkans. For a time a general European war seemed imminent. However, Germany took the initiative through her chancellor, Bismarck, who assumed the role of a "honest broker" and called a conference at Berlin in 1878 to revise the Treaty of San Stefano.

At Berlin, Gortchakov confronted an anti-Russian bloc, with the result that Russia lost by diplomacy a large part of what she had gained by force of arms. The provisions of the Treaty of San Stefano regarding Bessarabia, the Dobruja, and the independence of Montenegro, Serbia, and Rumania were allowed to stand. The territory of Bulgaria was, however, drastically reduced. Macedonia was restored to Turkey, and the remaining region was divided into two parts, namely, Bulgaria and Eastern Rumelia, both of which were reduced to dependencies of Turkey. Austria was permitted to occupy Bosnia and Herzegovina "temporarily, " as well as to station troops in the Sanjak of Novibazar. Since the Russians insisted on retaining Kars, Batum, and Ardahan in Transcaucasia, England took Cyprus as "compensation. "

Thus although Russia, in spite of her complete isolation by the great powers at Berlin, retained her own territorial gains, she once again lost her sphere of influence in the Balkans, and with it her prestige among the Slavic peoples of that area, who felt that their interests had been sacrificed. Alexander II, like Nicholas I before him, had failed to settle the Turkish question by unilateral action. The "defenders" of Turkey, Austria and England, without having fired a shot in the war, participated in what actually amounted to another partial partition of the Ottoman Empire. Bismarck's support of Austria's interests over and above those of Russia at the Congress of Berlin effected a breach in the Three Emperors' League. Moreover Russia's isolation in Europe was still further emphasized by the establishment of the Triple Alliance of Germany, Austria, and Italy (1879-81). As in the case of the Crimean War, Russia turned her back upon Europe and proceeded to concentrate upon further expansion in Asia, especially in the Far East.

Undoubtedly Russia's unilateral action in declaring war on Turkey on April 24, 1877, was precipitated by strong Slavophile sentiment in support of the Slavic peoples under Turkish domination. Many Slavophiles regarded the liberation of the South Slavs as a steppingstone to eventual Russian acquisition of Constantinople. F. M. Dostoyevsky, the most outstanding literary exponent of Slavophilism, in an article published in March, 1877, voiced the sentiment of the majority of the Slavophiles and of the government of Alexander II:

> Yes, the Golden Horn and Constantinople--all this will be ours. . . . In the first place, this will come to pass of its own accord, precisely because the time has come, and even if it has not yet arrived, indeed it is already near at hand; all signs point to this. This is the natural solution, the word of nature herself, so to speak. If it has not occurred before this, it has been precisely because the time was not yet ripe. . . . No matter what happens there--peace, or new concessions on the part of Russia--sooner or later, Constantinople will be ours. . . .
> Yes, it must be ours, not only because it is a famous port, because

of the Straits, "the center of the universe," "the navel of the earth"; not from the standpoint of the long-conceived necessity for a tremendous giant like Russia to emerge at last from his locked room, in which he has already grown up to the ceiling, into the open spaces where he may breathe the free air of the seas and oceans. . . . Our task is deeper, immeasurably deeper. We, Russia, are really indispensable and inevitable, both to all Eastern Christianity and to the whole future of Orthodoxy on earth, in order to achieve its unity. This was always understood to be so by our people and their Tsars. . . .

In brief, this dreadful Eastern Question constitutes almost our whole future destiny. Therein lie, as it were, all our problems, and what is most important--our only exit into the plenitude of history. Therein lies also our final conflict with Europe and our ultimate union with her, but only upon new, mighty and fruitful foundations. Oh, how can Europe at this time grasp the fateful, vital importance to us alone of the solution to this question?--In a word, no matter what may be the outcome of the present, perhaps quite indispensable diplomatic agreements and negotiations in Europe, nevertheless, sooner or later, *Constantinople must be ours,* even if it should take another century![14]

Thus Dostoyevsky summed up the underlying motives of Russian expansion into Muslim territories, especially in the direction of Constantinople. Whereas Russian expansion into non-Muslim territories was motivated by strategic considerations, the urge to the sea, economic factors, etc., in the case of Muslim territories, especially in the Near East, over and above all these factors, Russian rulers elevated Russian expansion to a "mission." Although Dostoyevsky focused attention on Constantinople, for him and for others like him, Constantinople was but a symbol. Since he believed that the Second Advent of Christ would take place under the Russian flag, the implication is that he had in view, not only Constantinople, but the Holy Land. In other words, Dostoyevsky's "mission" included the dismemberment of Turkey and the absorption of the Arab world of the Middle East.

European opposition to the fulfilment of Russia's "mission" in Asia, especially in Muslim Asia, was effectively explained by Nicholas Danilevsky (1822-85), a contemporary of Dostoyevsky and the creator of scientific Slavophilism, in his influential book *Russia and Europe* (1869):

What *role* on the universal stage does Europe assign us, her adopted children? To be the bearers and propagators of her civilization in the East--that is the lofty mission allotted to us, the task in which Europe will sympathize, which she will advance with her blessings, her best wishes, her applause, to the edification and delight of our humanitarian progressivists. Very well. Eastward-ho! then. But stop--*what* East?

We had thought to begin with Turkey. What could be better? There live
our brethren, in blood and spirit, --live in agonies and yearn for de-
liverance. "Whither away? You have no business there," thunders Europe; "that is not the East for *you*; there's more Slavic trash there
than I like, and I'm going to manage them. My Germans have done
such work before. Clear out of there."--We tackled the Caucasus--
that's a sort of East too. Mamma got very mad: "Don't dare to touch
the noble paladins of freedom! much it becomes you to meddle with
them. Hands off!"--For once, thank goodness, we did not obey, and
forgot our Europeanism. There is Persia now; something might be
done there in the way of sowing the seeds of European civilization.
The Germans would not have minded; their *Drang nach Osten* ("East-
ward Push"), scarcely would reach so far; but out of respect to England we had to be checked: "Too near India. Move on!"--To China,
perhaps?--"Well, no. Is it tea you need? We'll bring you all you want
from Canton. China is a wealthy country--we can teach her without your
help. She is smoking our Indian opium like a charm--let her alone."
--But, for mercy's sake, where is *our* East, the East which it is our
sacred mission to civilize?--"Central Asia, that's the place for you,
do not forget it. We could not get there anyhow, besides it would not
pay. There lies your sacred historical mission. . . ."--So then we
shall have gone through a thousand years of labor streaming with sweat
and blood; we shall have built up an empire of a hundred million souls
(of which sixty millions of one race and blood, a thing unequalled in the
world, except in China), --all to tender the blessings of European civilization to five or six millions of tatterdemalions, the denizens of Kok-
and, Khiva, and Bokhara, with two or three millions of Mongolian nomads thrown in--for that is what the high-sounding phrase about--
bearing European civilization into the heart of the Asiatic continent
really amounts to, --an enviable lot indeed, and a mission to be proud
of. In sooth, *Parturiunt montes, nascitur ridiculus mus.* . . .[15]

Under Alexander III (1881-94), Russia, for the most part, stood
aloof from European affairs and ceased to interfere in the concerns
of other nations. This policy of "hands off" had come increasingly
into favor following the Congress of Berlin in 1878. The Emperor
trusted no foreign power, had an especial hatred for England, and
tolerated no outside meddling as a return for his own noninterference. During his reign, Russia but once had resort to arms. This
was the conflict on the Kushk River with the Afghans in 1885. At
its conclusion Russia came into possession of the Merv and Pendeh
Oases.

The Franco-Russian Alliance negotiated under Alexander III
(1891-94), together with the outcome of the Russo-Japanese War
(1904-5) paved the way for better relations with England in the
reign of Nicholas II (1894-1917). In an agreement with Great Brit-

ain in August, 1907, known as the Anglo-Russian Entente, Russia materially modified her claims upon territory in Central Asia, thereby relieving the uneasiness of England in respect to India. By this agreement, Russia recognized Afghanistan as a British sphere; both powers consented to maintain a "hands off" policy in Tibet; and each retained a sphere of influence in Persia--the Russians in the north and the British in the south. A famous cartoon in the English magazine *Punch* portrayed the British lion and the Russian bear mauling the Persian cat. Inasmuch as the Japanese War had all but ruined Russia's pretensions in the Far East, Great Britain had gained most of her objectives, with the exception of Russian recognition of her claim to an exclusive position in the Persian Gulf. Her hostility, therefore, was considerably abated, and the way was paved for a better understanding between the two powers.

Two developments during the opening years of the twentieth century had significant repercussions, not only in the Near and Middle East, but throughout Asia. These were the Russo-Japanese War and the Russian Revolution of 1905-7. The defeat of Tsarist Russia by Japan, an Asiatic power and a comparative newcomer on the international scene, had a tremendous impact upon Asia. From the safe vantage point of Western Europe the relatively unknown Lenin, writing in *Vperyod* (January 1, 1905) on "The Fall of Port Arthur, " immediately hailed the triumph of Japan as the triumph of Asia over Europe: "A progressive and advanced Asia has inflicted an irreparable blow on a backward and reactionary Europe. "

Of still greater importance was the impact of the Russian Revolution of 1905-7 in the Orient. According to Lenin, "without the dress rehearsal of 1905 the victory of the October Revolution of 1917 would have been impossible. "[16] Because of Soviet and world-wide preoccupation with the October Revolution, until recently the role of the Revolution of 1905 vis-à-vis Asia was relatively neglected. The celebration in 1955 of the fiftieth anniversary of the Revolution of 1905 led to the publication in the U.S.S.R. of a veritable avalanche of material on all aspects of the upheaval, with considerable emphasis on its international significance, especially in the Orient. Because these works emanate from Soviet sources and there is a comparative paucity of material in Western languages on the impact of the Revolution of 1905 in Asia, it stands to reason that what has been produced to date is biased and one-sided. Although Soviet writers admit that the 1905 Revolution was a "bourgeois-capitalist" and even a "people's, " as distinguished from a party revolution, nevertheless, they have greatly exaggerated the role of the Bolsheviks as the real power behind the movement. Their main purpose was to make the Russian Revolution of 1905 the starting point for all the national liberation movements in Asia and the pivot around which all of them revolved.

Of all the countries adjacent to Tsarist Russia, Persia, for various reasons, appears to have been the first to experience the full impact of the Revolution of 1905. The appreciable number of Persian students in Russian universities, the traditionally close economic contacts between Russian and Persian merchants, and the large Persian labor force in the Russian Transcaucasian area, especially in the oil center of Baku and in Tiflis, contributed greatly to the rapid dissemination in Persia of information about the events of 1905 in Russia.

According to official tsarist statistics, during the last decade of the nineteenth century from fifteen to thirty thousand migratory workers *(otkhodniki)* bearing passports crossed the border from Iranian Azerbaijan in search of employment in Russia. In the year 1905 alone, when Russian laborers were mobilized for service in the Russo-Japanese War, these migrants numbered sixty-two thousand. The above figures do not include those who slipped across the border without benefit of passport, or those who joined the trek from Gilan and the other northern provinces of Iran. According to the Persian consul in St. Petersburg, by 1910 the number of Persian migratory workers crossing into Russia reached almost two hundred thousand per annum. [17]

In the autumn of 1904 a special Social Democratic Muslim party organization, known as "Gummet" (Power) was created in Baku for Muslim workers laboring in the oil fields. From Baku this organization spread rapidly to other localities throughout the Transcaucasus. In 1905 an organization of Iranian revolutionaries was created in Tiflis. The result was that when these Persian migratory laborers returned to their homeland, they took with them revolutionary ideas, printed propaganda, and weapons to incite strikes and disturbances there. It should occasion no surprise, therefore, that the revolution in Persia followed close on the heels of that in Russia.

In spite of labor participation, the Soviets admit that, as in Russia, the leadership of the Persian Revolution, 1905-11, was in the hands of the middle and upper classes--the clergy, the merchants, and the lesser bourgeoisie. Even the mass meetings held in Teheran, Kerman, and Fars in December, 1905, in protest against the Shah's absolute *rule*, as well as the *best*, * were under the same leadership. Even according to Soviet admission, as yet there was no independent peasant and worker's movement in Iran. The two revolutions followed a parallel course in other respects. Thus, following the Tsar's October manifesto (October 30, 1905) granting a constitution in Russia, came the Shah's decree of August, 1906, bestowing a constitution on Persia. The opening of the first Russian Duma on May 10, 1906, was followed a few months later by the first session of the Persian Mejlis, which Soviet writers have hailed as "the first Parliament in the East." Even the caliber of representation in the Persian Mejlis approximated that in the Russian Duma. Real leadership in both countries was in the hands of men whose views were those of Constitutional Democrats. Their immediate interest was in political change, in the limitation of autocracy by the inauguration of constitutional government, to be followed only gradually by social reform. Even the Caucasian revolutionaries who marched at the head of a mass demonstration in Tabriz on March 26, 1909, bearing the red flag, were content to use the slogan, "Long live the constitution!"[18]

Following the suppression of internal revolt in Russia, the Tsarist government in August, 1907, entered into the Entente with England, which served to strengthen the antirevolutionary forces in Iran. Thereafter, the Shah was able to confine Persian revolutionary activity largely to the northern provinces. Like the Tsar, who dissolved the first Duma on July 21, 1906, and the second Duma on March 5, 1907, the Shah finally dissolved the Mejlis on June 23, 1908. The Anglo-Russian Entente accelerated the collapse of the Persian Revolution of 1905. Its complete suppression was assured by Anglo-Russian occupation of the country in 1911.

The Anglo-Russian "partition" of Iran created a new problem. Instead of constitutional government and social reforms, the quest for national liberation from Tsarist and English "domination" became the prime consideration. In 1912, at the height of the reaction in Persia, there was founded in Gilan an organization called Ittikhadi-Islam (Unity of Islam), the purpose of which was to combat foreign domination. One of its leaders was Mirza Kuchuk-Khan, who became a prominent figure in the uprising in northern Iran following the Bolshevik Revolution of 1917. It was this preoccupation with national liberation that the Bolsheviks were able to take

---

*Originally, a refuge for persons in a sanctuary or consulate, beyond reach of local authorities; today, a kind of sit-down strike.

advantage of in 1917, when they proclaimed the abandonment of all Tsarist rights and concessions in Iran and temporarily, at least, deflected the ire of Persian nationalists against England.

Of particular interest is the Tsarist government's interpretation of the four main factors leading to the Anglo-Russian rapprochement, as summed up during a conference on the Afghan question, held under the chairmanship of A. P. Izvolsky, Russian minister of foreign affairs, on April 14, 1907. (1) The rapid rise of Germany forced England to change her traditional policy toward Russia. (2) The understanding with England made it easier for Russia to find a common understanding with Japan, already an ally of England. (3) The common fear of the development of national liberation movements in the Orient brought England and Russia closer. The Revolution of 1905 had exerted a considerable influence in the Orient and had aroused sympathetic response in a number of oriental countries, especially in Persia. (4) England's fear that she might lose her colonies as a result of revolution, with the consequent loss of prestige involved, impelled her to make concessions to Russian absolutism and to enlist Russian support as a gendarme to help preserve order among the Asiatic peoples. In brief, the fear of revolution in the Orient and the growing strength of Germany in Europe confronted England and Russia with common problems, and led to their collaboration in World War I. [19]

The Russian Revolution of 1905, followed by the Persian Revolution, likewise had repercussions in Turkey, where comparable conditions existed. Russian efforts to limit the power of the Tsarist autocracy, Persian demands for curbing the power of the Shah, revived the aspirations of progressive Turks at home and abroad to put an end to the Sultan's despotic rule. As in the case of Russia and Iran, the leadership of the movement in Turkey rested in the hands of the upper and middle classes--the military, the intelligentsia, and business. In contrast to Russia and Iran, where the objective of the revolutionary movement was the introduction of constitutional government, in Turkey, under the leadership of the Young Turk party, the goal was the restoration of the constitution of 1876, abrogated by Sultan Abdul Hamid II shortly after his accession to the throne.

With the revival of opposition to the Sultan, stimulated by the return of Turkish liberals from Paris and other centers abroad, the Young Turk movement spread throughout Macedonia, Armenia, and Anatolia, with uprisings occurring in Erzerum, Kastamonu, and Trebizond in 1906-7. Caucasian newspapers from Azerbaijan, Armenia, and Georgia were circulated among the population in Anatolia, spreading news of events in Russia. Just as in Russia the Revolution of 1905 had serious repercussions among the Muslim minorities of Central Asia and the Caucasus, so the Turkish Revolution was quickly felt among the minority groups of the Ottoman Empire, including the Arabs. Disturbances occurred from Albania to Yemen. On July 24, 1908, the Sultan was forced to comply with the demands of the Young Turks by restoring the constitution. The promulgation of the Turkish constitution and the opening of the Turkish Parliament led to mass demonstrations in Cairo, with demands for the introduction of a parliamentary regime in Egypt. Failure to extend the privileges of the new regime to the minorities led to an upsurge, especially in Egypt, in favor of national liberation from four hundred years of Turkish hegemony.[20]

As in the case of Persia, the Young Turk Revolution was brought to a premature halt by the return of reaction at home and by a succession of international reverses. The Austro-Hungarian annexation of Bosnia and Herzegovina in 1908 was a blow, not only to the South Slavs, but to the Young Turks. This was followed by the unsuccessful war with Italy over Tripoli in 1911, and the Balkan Wars of 1912-13.

The impact of the Russian Revolution of 1905 was felt even beyond the boundaries of the predominantly Muslim areas of Asia, especially in China and India. It is safe to say that the downfall of the Manchu Dynasty in the Chinese Revolution of 1911 was accelerated by the events of the Russo-Japanese War and the Russian Revolution of 1905. According to Soviet sources, and to Chinese material in Russian translation, the main objective of Chinese revolutionary leaders from 1905 to 1911 was the establishment of constitutional government. Although China had experienced numerous revolts in the past, including the Taiping Rebellion, after 1905 it was the word "constitution" that served as a magnet. Even ultra conservative monarchists sought to induce the Empress-Dowager to accept a constitution in order to save the monarchy. The newspapers *Min Pao* and *Tung Fang Tsa chih* (Vol. II, No. 4) published articles by Chinese monarchists, attributing the Japanese victory to the fact that Japan had a constitution, and Russian defeat to the absence of a Russian constitution.[21]

In other areas of Asia that had not yet achieved independence, such as India, Indonesia, and Korea, the Russian Revolution of 1905 and the counterparts in Persia and Turkey served mainly to stimulate nationalist aspirations for freedom from the foreign "yoke," which manifested themselves in strikes or uprisings against the English, Dutch, and Japanese. Here, too, the leadership, as the Soviets admit, was not proletarian, but came from the upper and middle classes.

In retrospect it appears that the Revolution of 1905 in many respects had a stronger appeal, both inside Russia and abroad, than the October Revolution of 1917. The 1905 Revolution, which emphasized political freedom and constitutional government, appealed to almost all classes and parties, whereas the October Revolution which emphasized social transformation, called for the dictatorship of one class--the proletariat, and one party--the Communists.

The course of European politics was such that Great Britain soon began to fear Germany far more than she ever had feared Russia. The events growing out of the Turkish Revolution of 1908 intensified this fear and also served to cement more firmly the alliance of the Triple Entente against Germany. The aforementioned revolution brought a pro-German government into power in Turkey. In October of the same year, to the consternation of the Triple Entente, Austria suddenly annexed Bosnia and Herzegovina, which she had occupied temporarily in 1878. Although Germany's part in the annexation was clearly discernible, the Russian government was in no position to do anything about the matter, and the Triple Entente accepted perforce the *fait accompli*. The fact was that Izvolsky, the Russian foreign minister, in trying to make a deal with Austria whereby he might secure Austrian support of Russian interests in the Straits, had been completely outwitted by the Austrian foreign minister, Aehrenthal. Worse still, the Bulgars, obviously acting by preconcerted arrangement with Austria, seized this opportunity to proclaim their final independence from Turkey. The upshot of the Balkan crisis of 1908, which has sometimes been termed a dress rehearsal for 1914, was that Pan-Slav sentiment in Russia was thoroughly aroused; Serbia looked to Russia for aid against Austria; and the Triple Entente appeared to be further consolidated by its opposition to the new *Drang nach Osten* on the part of the Central Powers.

In 1910, however, the Germans took advantage of the visit of Nicholas II and Russian foreign minister Sazonov to Potsdam to make an outright effort to detach Russia from the Triple Entente. This they failed to accomplish. Nevertheless, the Russo-German deal pertaining to the Near and Middle East, negotiated at Potsdam and signed August 19, 1911, provided that Germany would seek no concessions in the Russian sphere in Persia, in return for which the Russians undertook to put no obstacles in the path of German construction of the Baghdad railroad in Turkey (Article III) and its extension to Haneken on the Persian border. It was agreed that the

Russians would take the appropriate measures to extend this rail-road from Haneken to the Persian capital at Teheran.

Another move toward German expansion into the Muslim world--this time in Africa--occurred in the summer of 1911. In July the German gunboat *Panther* was sent to Agadir ostensibly to protect German interests in Morocco but in reality for the purpose of securing a foothold there. Powerful Arab leaders of South Morocco were entertained by the officers of the *Panther*, who promised German assistance if the Arabs made an attempt to throw off French control. As in 1905-6, at Algeciras, French diplomacy won the day. France's right to a protectorate in Morocco was recognized, November 4, 1911, but in return she ceded to Germany some 250,000 square kilometers of her possessions in the northern Congo.

There was no reason to believe that the Central Powers would be satisfied with the outcome of the Agadir affair, and European relations became increasingly tense. Inside Russia, German-Austrian diplomacy had long been active in stirring up trouble between the national minorities and the Tsarist regime. For example, Austria sedulously fostered Ukrainian "culture" in her territory of Galicia, from whence it spread to Russian territory and exerted a subversive influence. The purpose of this was to create among Ukrainians a sentiment of good will toward the Central Powers and a desire to separate themselves from Russia. In retaliation for this propaganda, Russia brought about the union of Serbia, Bulgaria, and Greece against Turkey in the First Balkan War, 1912-13. This was intended as an indirect blow against Austria. The Central Powers, however, succeeded in stirring up dissension among these minor powers, which, after defeating Turkey and stripping her of most of her European possessions, divided their allegiance--Serbia turning to the Entente, and Bulgaria seeking the patronage of the Central Powers. In the Second Balkan War (1913), Bulgaria was defeated by the combined action of Serbia, Greece, and Rumania. But the Germans, at the request of Turkey, dispatched a military mission under General Liman von Sanders to Constantinople to reorganize the Turkish army. While Germans dreamed of a Berlin-to-Baghdad railroad, Russians regarded the German interest in the Near East as a direct threat to Russian interests at the Dardanelles. The Balkans remained a veritable powder keg. It required only a slight pretext to cause the mutual hostility to explode, and this was afforded by the events of the summer of 1914. Turkey entered World War I on the side of the Central Powers in October (November N.S.), 1914, thereby closing what might have been an important Allied supply route to Russia.

On the eve of World War I, when General Liman von Sanders was master of Constantinople, England and France began to reconcile themselves to the imperial policy of Russia in the Near East. Turkey's entry into the war, November 12, 1914, on the side of the Central Powers, and subsequent Anglo-French apprehension about the possible withdrawal of Russia from the conflict, paved the way for the so-called Secret Agreement in regard to Constantinople (March 4-April 10, 1915), which was embodied in an exchange of letters among the three Entente powers. In a complete reversal of traditional Anglo-French policy on the Straits Question, this agreement officially recognized the right of Russia to Constantinople, and also provided for the transfer to her of the western part of the Bosphorus coast, the Sea of Marmora, and the Dardanelles, the southern part of Thrace along the line from Enos to Midea, as well as the coast of Asia Minor lying between the Bosphorus, the river Sakaria, and the Gulf of Ismid; finally, the islands of the Sea of Marmora, plus Imbros and Tenedos. [22] This deal was tantamount to the dismemberment of Turkey and together with the Sykes-Picot Agreement (April-May, 1916) it served as a pattern for the Treaty of Sèvres.

The Sykes-Picot Agreement (signed in Petrograd in May, 1916), disclosed in 1917 by the Bolsheviks, substantially extended the understanding reached by England, France, and Russia in 1915, by providing for the disposition of Turkey in Asia, and for the establishment in Arabia of an independent Arab state or a federation of Arab states. Turkish territory allocated to Russia included the provinces of Erzerum, Trebizond, Van, and Bitlis, as well as southern Kurdistan. France obtained the coastal strip of Syria, Adana, and other territory as far as the Russian frontier. To England went southern Mesopotamia, including Baghdad, and the Syrian ports of Haifa and Akka. The Entente powers took advantage of this opportunity to detach Palestine, with the Holy Places, from Turkey, leaving the nature of the regime to be determined by future agreement. By a subsequent agreement in April, 1917, Italy staked out her claim to Adalia and Smyrna. Such was the "promissory generosity" of the Allies toward each other, at the expense of Turkey and the Arabs.

On July 3, 1916, Tsarist Russia concluded a secret treaty with Japan which, strictly speaking, provided for the partition of China between Japan and Russia. [23] Had it not been for the Revolution of 1917, the Tsarist government would have emerged from World War I with enormous territorial acquisitions both in the Near and the Far East. A fate similar to that of Turkey was in store for China.

Small wonder that Tsarist Russia, in the eyes of all Asiatic peoples, especially in the eyes of the entire Muslim world, was viewed as the chief, eternal, and irreconcilable enemy of the whole Orient.

England preserved her solid position in India, thanks not only to her well-organized Indian army, or to her fleet, or to her gold and world influence, not by virtue of her natural barriers and to the impassable heights of the Himalayas and the Karakorum, not because of the grim fortifications of the Khyber and Bolan Passes, but due to the fact that among these mountains and narrow valleys there lived fanatical Muslim tribes who were England's loyal sentinels and guarded these high mountain passes against Tsarist Russia, which was hated by the entire Muslim world. [24]

2. The October (Bolshevik) Revolution and the Muslim World

The Scythians[1]
by Alexander Blok [1918]

Panmongolism! The name, though savage,
yet rings caressful in my ear.

Vladimir Solověv

Mere millions--you. We--teem, and teem, and teem.
  You want to fight? Come on, then--try it!
We're--Scythians--yes! With Asiatic mien
  We watch you, gloating, through our slit-squint eyelids.

For you--long years. For us--alone one hour.
  We, like brute serfs, in blind obedience,
Have held our shield between two warring powers--
  The Mongols and the Europeans!

For years, long years, your ancient furnace forged
  And dulled the avalanches' rumble,
And what a wanton tale of woe was yours
  When Lisbon and Messina crumbled!

A thousand years you've watched this East of ours,
  Amassed and melted down our jewels,
Contemptuously, have counted but the hour
  When you could train your guns on to us!

That hour has struck. Misfortune beats her wings,
  You multiply your insults daily.
The day will come when nothing more remains,
  Not one trace, of your *Paestums,* maybe!

28

Old world! Before you fall in ruins--think,
   While yet you writhe in sweetest torture,
How Oedipus, before the ageless Sphinx'
   Enigma, once, was moved to caution!

So, Russia--Sphinx--triumphant, sorrowed, too--
   With black blood flows, in fearful wildness,
Her eyes glare deep, glare deep, glare deep at you,
   With hatred and--with loving-kindness!

Yes, so to love, as lies within our blood,
   Not one of you has loved in ages!
You have forgotten that there is such love
   That burns and, burning, lays in ashes!

We love them all--cold numbers' heartless heat,
   The gift of heavenly visions in us,
We understand them all--keen Gallic wit
   And gloomy-weighed Germanic genius.

Remember all--the streets of Paris' hell,
   The gentle coolness of Venice,
The lemon groves--their distant, perfumed smell--
   And, smoke-enswathed, Cologne's immenseness . . .

We love the flesh--its taste, its pinkish tone,
   The scent of flesh, too--choking, deathsome . . .
Are we to blame, then, if we crunch your bones
   When our unwieldy paws caress them?

It's nothing new for us to seize the rein,
   To curb our prancing, fiery chargers,
To bend their stubborn will, to break them in,
   And let them know that we're the masters . . .

Come on, then, come!--into the arms of peace.
   Have done with war and all its horrors.
Before it's all too late--now, comrades, sheathe
   Your age-old sword, and we'll be--brothers!

And if not--well, we've nothing left to lose,
   We, too, can be perfidious traitors.
For years, long years, you'll stand--accursed, accused

Of crippled coming generations.

We'll blaze a trail--we'll beat a broad-flung track
   Through the dense woods that fringe, behind you,
The gentle brow of Europe. We'll be back--
   Our Asiatic mugs will find you.

Come on, then--on, unto the Urals. We'll
   Prepare meanwhile the field of battle
Where cold machines of calculated steel
   Shall meet the savage Mongol rabble.

But as for us--we'll no more be your shield;
   Ourselves no longer sword unsheathing,
Through narrow eyes we'll scan the battlefield
   And watch the mortal combat seething.

We shall not turn aside when raging Huns
   Go delving into dead men's pockets,
Turn churches into stables, burn the towns,
   And roast their white-fleshed comrades' bodies . . .

For the last time--Old world, come to! The feast
   Of peace-fraternal toil awaits you.
For the last time--the fair, fraternal feast.
   And our barbarian lyre invites you.

                                    --Translated by Robin Kemball

On the eve of the October (Bolshevik) Revolution of 1917 there were approximately twenty-five million Muslims of Turkic origin in Russia, divided as follows: (1) eastern Muslims--Siberian Tatars, Chinese Uighurs, etc.; (2) southern Muslims--Othmans, Azerbaijanians and Turkmenians; and (3) central Muslims--Tatars, Kirghiz, Bashkirs, and Nogai. For purposes of administration the Muslim population was organized in sixteen regions. [2]

According to Russian authorities, by 1917 the Tsarist government had expropriated the richest Muslim lands in Siberia, Kazan, the Volga area, the Caucasus, the Transcaucasus, the Crimea, and Turkestan. [3] During the two centuries prior to the Revolution it is claimed that the Tsarist rulers deprived the Muslims of 41,675,000 desyatins of land (1 desyatin=2.70 acres), not to mention other forms of wealth. The Crimean Tatars, in particular, bore the brunt of Tsarist persecution, with the result that on several occasions there was a mass exodus to Turkey. At the time of the Russian annexation of the Crimea, Catherine the Great (1762-96) bestowed hundreds of thousands of acres of land on her favorites--Potemkin, Bulgakov, Zubov, Zotov, Katchioni (a Greek), and others, on the ground that the Crimean Tatars, not being members of the nobility, had no right to hold land. In 1791, as a result, approximately one hundred thousand Crimean Tatars left Russia for Turkey. Following the Crimean War, about 1861, several thousands more escaped to Turkey. In 1901, due to the government's Russification policy which the Muslims regarded as a threat to their Islamic faith and heritage, more than fifty thousand Crimean Tatars left Russia. Not content with the expropriation of the private property of the Crimean Tatars, the Russian government took over the *waqf* lands and institutions, thus depriving these Muslims of their community centers, schools, etc. On the eve of World War I, the streets of Turkish cities were literally teeming with Tatar refugees, commonly referred to as *Urus-muhadjiry* (Russian refugees).

Not all Russian Muslims were persecuted as relentlessly as were the Crimean Tatars. In World War I there were 1,500,000 Muslims of various ranks serving in the Tsarist armies. Ironically enough, these Muslims were forced to fight for the victory of the Slavs over the Germans, for the dismemberment of Turkey-- the center of the Caliphate, and for the restoration of the Cross above the Cathedral of St. Sophia in Constantinople. In spite of Muslim discontent with Tsarist rule, on the whole these Muslim troops fought well and proved loyal, at least until 1916.

On June 25, 1916, the Tsarist government mobilized all Kazakh, Uzbek, Kirghiz, Turkmenian, Uighur, and T'ungan males from the ages of nineteen to forty-three for labor duties in the rear of the Russian armies *("nestroyevaya sluzhba")*. This produced widespread discontent directed against local Russian authorities, which soon resulted in a Muslim revolt throughout Central Asia. Although the Tsarist regime succeeded in crushing the uprising in September of that year, strictly speaking, order was not restored until 1921. The 1916 revolt proved to be the forerunner of the *Basmatchestvo,* a movement that plagued the Soviet regime for several years. [4]

The spontaneous revolt of the fourth Duma against Tsarist tyranny in March, 1917, in a sense represented Russia's "finest hour," in that it cleared the way for the establishment of a Russian democracy. The provisional government under Prince Lvov and Alexander Kerensky was heralded by the Russian people, especial-

ly by the Russian minorities, as the dawn of a new era. The October (November N. S.) Revolution of the same year, perpetrated
by the Bolsheviks against the Kerensky regime, was, strictly
speaking, a counterrevolution, imposed by a demagogical minority,
headed by Lenin and Trotsky. The Bolshevik usurpers, who seized
the reins of power, reversed the trend of the Revolution, and substituted a party tyranny beside which the tyranny of the dynasty
paled into insignificance.

From the standpoint of the Soviet leaders like Stalin, however,
the real significance of the October Revolution was that it "ushered
in a new era, an era of colonial revolutions, which are carried out
in the oppressed countries of the world in alliance with the proletariat and under the leadership of the proletariat. "[5] No longer,
according to Stalin, would the countries of the Entente, especially
England, rest secure in their possession of vast colonial areas,
for the October Revolution "dealt blows at the imperialist rear,
at its periphery, " by undermining imperialist domination over colonial and dependent countries. Soviet leaders have never grown
weary of repeating that the emergence of Soviet Russia introduced
a new factor in the relationship of the West to the colonial and dependent East. The October Revolution established "a powerful and
open base for the world revolutionary movement, " namely Soviet
Russia, "a base which it never had before. . . ."[6]

Adoption of the decree on peace by the second All-Russian Congress of Soviets on November 8 (October 26 O. S.), 1917, one
day after the successful Bolshevik seizure of power, marked the
first Soviet venture into the field of foreign policy. Directed to "all
belligerent peoples and their governments, " it called for a "just"
and "democratic" peace without annexations or indemnities, based
on the right of self-determination. It denounced secret diplomacy,
announced the forthcoming publication of the famous "Secret Treaties, " and the determination of the Bolsheviks to conduct all future
Soviet negotiations "completely openly before the whole people. "
Shortly thereafter, the Bolsheviks created a world-wide sensation
by their publication of the Allied Secret Agreements pertaining to
Turkey and the Near East in the government newspaper *Izvestia*
(beginning November 23), followed by their distribution in pamphlet
form for propaganda purposes.

Aside from its domestic significance, the appeal for peace, although broadcast to the world, was designed primarily for the European belligerents and the United States, in whose hands rested
the ultimate decision in favor of war or peace. Since this appeal
was naturally ignored, the hard-pressed Soviet government, which

had promised peace to its own people, pursued other tactics culminating in the opening of armistice negotiations with Germany on
December 2 (November 19 O. S.)

Realizing that they did not have the wholehearted support of the
Russian population, especially of the Slavic element, nor tangible
backing from the European proletariat, the Bolsheviks turned to
the East, in particular to the Muslim East inside and outside the
Russian borders. Although ostensibly anticipating a revolution in
the West, they turned their heavy propaganda artillery toward the
East, where they expected more tangible results. Although many
European workers sympathized with the Bolshevik Revolution, they
were not ready to submit themselves to Russian leadership. In the
Orient, however, the Bolsheviks sensed their opportunity to assume
command. Indeed, within a month of their seizure of power, on
December 5 (November 22 O. S.),[7] 1917, the Council of People's
Commissars of the Bolshevik regime issued the following highly
significant "Appeal to the Muslims of Russia and the East":

> Comrades! Brothers!
> Great events are taking place in Russia. The end of the sanguinary
> war, begun over the partitioning of foreign lands, is drawing near. Un-
> der the blows of the Russian Revolution, the old edifice of slavery and
> serfdom is crumbling. The world of arbitrary rule and oppression is
> approaching its last days. A new world is being born, a world of the
> toilers and the liberated. At the head of this revolution stands the work-
> ers' and peasants' government of Russia, the Council of People's Com-
> missars.
> All Russia is dotted with revolutionary councils of workers', sol-
> diers', and peasants' deputies. Power in the country is in the hands
> of the people. The laboring people of Russia are burning with the single
> desire to achieve an honorable peace and to help the downtrodden peo-
> ples of the world to win their freedom.
> In this sacred cause, Russia does not stand alone. The mighty call
> to freedom sounded by the Russian Revolution is being taken up by all
> the toilers of the West and the East. Exhausted by the war, the peo-
> ples of Europe are already stretching out their hands to us, working
> for peace. The workers and soldiers of the West are already rallying
> under the banner of socialism, storming the strongholds of imperial-
> ism. Even far-off India, the very country which has been oppressed
> for centuries by "enlightened" European plunderers, has already raised
> the standard of revolt, organizing its councils of deputies, casting off
> from its shoulders the hated yoke of slavery, and summoning the peo-
> ples of the East to the struggle and to liberation.
> The empire of capitalist plunder and violence is crumbling. The
> ground under the feet of the imperialist plunderers is on fire.

In the face of these great events, we turn to you, the toiling and underprivileged Muslims of Russia and the East.

Muslims of Russia, Tatars of the Volga and the Crimea, Kirghiz and Sarts of Siberia and Turkestan, Turks and Tatars of Transcaucasia, Chechens and Caucasian mountaineers--all you, whose mosques and shrines, whose faiths and customs have been violated by the Tsars and oppressors of Russia!

Henceforth your beliefs and customs, your national and cultural institutions, are decreed free and inviolable! Build your national life freely and without hindrance. You have the right to do it. Know that your rights, like those of all the peoples of Russia, are being protected by all the might of the Revolution, and by its organs, the councils of workers', soldiers', and peasants' deputies.

Therefore support this Revolution and its authorized government!

Muslims of the East, Persians, Turks, Arabs, and Hindus! All you in whose lives and property, in whose freedom and native land the rapacious European plunderers have for centuries traded! All you whose countries the robbers who began the war now desire to partition!

We declare that the secret treaties of the dethroned Tsar regarding the seizure of Constantinople, which was confirmed by the deposed Kerensky, now are null and void. The Russian Republic and its government, the Council of People's Commissars, are against the seizure of foreign territories. Constantinople must remain in the hands of the Muslims.

We declare that the treaty for the partition of Persia is null and void. As soon as military operations cease, the armed forces will be withdrawn from Persia and the Persians will be guaranteed the right of free determination of their own destiny.

We declare that the treaty for the partition of Turkey, which was to deprive her of Armenia, is null and void. As soon as military operations cease, the Armenians will be guaranteed the right of free determination of their political destiny.

It is not from Russia and her revolutionary government that enslavement awaits you, but from the European imperialist robbers, from those who have transformed your native land into a "colony" to be plundered and robbed.

Overthrow these robbers and enslavers of your countries! Now, when war and desolation are demolishing the pillars of the old order, when the whole world is blazing with indignation against the imperialist usurpers, when any spark of indignation is transformed into a mighty flame of revolution, when even the Indian Muslims, oppressed and tormented by the foreign yoke, are rising in revolt against their subjugators--now, it is impossible to remain silent. Lose no time in throwing off the yoke of the ancient oppressors of your lands! Let them no longer rob your hearths! You yourselves must build your own life in your own way and in your own likeness. You have the right to do this, for your destiny is in your own hands!

Comrades! Brothers!
Let us advance together firmly and resolutely towards a just and
democratic peace.
Our banners bring liberation to the oppressed peoples of the world.
Muslims of Russia!
Muslims of the East!
On this road to the regeneration of the world, we look to you for sym-
pathy and support.
Dzhugashvili Stalin, People's Commissar for National Affairs.
V. Ulyanov (Lenin), President of the People's Commissars.[8]

Under the impact of the Revolution of 1905, several attempts
were made even prior to 1917 to organize the Russian Muslims.
The first Muslim Congress was held on August 15, 1905, in Nizhni-
Novgorod. This was followed by a second congress in St. Petersburg, January 13-26, 1906. Whatever the original motives of the
Muslim leaders, the two congresses clearly indicated that, in spite
of a wide divergence of opinion on many issues, there was no disposition toward secession from the Tsarist Empire. Moreover,
delegates to the second congress, instead of establishing a separate
Muslim party, expressed their readiness to join the Constitutional
Democrats.

In the first Duma, where there were twenty-five Muslim deputies,
no Muslim faction existed. In the second Duma, when their numbers increased to thirty-five, after much effort a Muslim faction
was organized under the chairmanship of Tortchebashev. The
dwindling of their representation to ten in the third Duma and to
six in the fourth Duma rendered any perpetuation of the Muslim
faction impractical.

The fact is that many Muslims, especially the more articulate
leaders, had a vested interest in the regime, some having acquired
wealth and titles, others having become army officers during the
Russo-Japanese War. These Muslims had no desire to organize a
radical political opposition, especially one that veered toward atheism and revolution. This disposition toward conservatism was
characteristic of the military, clerical, and business elements
among the Muslims. Prior to 1917 the majority of the Muslims in
Russia appear to have been concerned primarily with the attainment
of local cultural and religious autonomy. Police records indicate
the existence of Muslim secret societies, especially in Kazan,
which attracted a radical minority, but did not represent the leading spokesmen of the Muslim population.[9] The revolt of 1916 among
the Muslims of Central Asia was the result of Tsarist withdrawal,
due to wartime conditions, of certain traditional privileges enjoyed

by them and of arbitrary action on the part of the local bureaucracy. [10]

World War I and the Russian Revolution had brought to the surface the surging unrest among the Muslim peoples of the Tsarist
empire, already aroused in some measure by the Revolution of
1905. By 1916 the Tatars along the Volga, the Kazakhs in Central
Asia, the Muslim inhabitants of Khiva, Bokhara, and Turkestan
either showed the signs of revolutionary ferment or were in open
rebellion against the Tsarist regime.

Under the Kerensky regime, efforts to organize the Muslims on
an all-Russian scale, in order that they might assume their responsibility under a representative form of government, came
from the Muslims themselves. [11] It was the Muslim faction in the
fourth Duma that in April, 1917, took the initiative in calling for
the All-Russian Muslim Congress which opened in Moscow on May
1, with the reading of the Koran. [12] At this congress approximately
one thousand delegates made far-reaching decisions in regard to
the emancipation of Muslim women, the establishment of a new religious administration, and the adoption of a federal democratic
republic along national territorial lines as the form of government
best suited to the needs of Muslim peoples. The second Muslim
Congress in Kazan in July, controlled by the Tatars, proceeded to
implement the minority opinion at the Moscow conference in favor
of Muslim cultural autonomy. In the summer of 1917, similar
Muslim congresses were held by the Bashkirs and Kazakhs at Orenburg, by the tribes of the northern Caucasus at Vladikavkaz, and
by other Muslim groups. At all these gatherings the emphasis was
on political or cultural autonomy, rather than on independence.
Thus, before the Bolshevik Revolution occurred, the Russian Muslims, left free to pursue their own objectives, had already made
considerable progress in the direction of religious and cultural administration of Muslim affairs on a state-wide basis. The Bolsheviks, on the contrary, with the "Appeal to the Muslims of Russia and the East, " clearly indicated that the government was seizing the initiative, that it intended to control the Russian Muslims
and to assume leadership of the Muslims abroad.

The Soviet "Appeal" to the Muslims, who were thought to be
sympathetic to the Revolution, was an outgrowth of Soviet weakness elsewhere and represented a desperate effort to break through
"capitalist encirclement. " Moreover, its remarkable display of
Soviet tolerance toward the Muslim faith was in marked contrast
to Soviet persecution of the Russian Orthodox Church, regarded as
an agent of counterrevolution.

Although the Council of Commissars could well afford to make extravagant promises to the Muslim world in December, 1917, it was by no means in a position to implement its pledges at that time or in the months to come. The Soviet government did follow up its December "Appeal to the Muslims" with the establishment on January 19, 1918, of a Commissariat for Muslim Affairs, headed by a Tatar, to handle domestic relations with the Muslim peoples. Local Muslim commissariats were set up, not only in areas where Muslims were predominant, as in Central Asia, but also in such thickly populated Slavic centers as Petrograd, Archangel, and Perm. The Soviet government at this time made a number of symbolic gestures toward the Muslims, indicative of its desire to prove its goodwill toward Islam. For instance, it presented a copy of the "Holy Koran of Osman, " formerly in the State Public Library, to a Muslim congress meeting in Petrograd. Many historic and religious monuments confiscated by the Tsarist regime were returned to the Muslims of Central Asia, the Crimea, and the Caucasus. The Bashkir Karavan-Sarai Mosque in Orenburg and the Sumbeki Tower in Kazan were among the historic buildings restored to the Muslims as a dramatic propaganda gesture. In November, 1918, a regional Muslim congress meeting in Moscow set up a Central Bureau of Muslim Communist organizations for the purpose of disseminating propaganda in all the languages of the Muslim peoples. A second congress of Muslim Communists, held in Moscow just one year later, in November, 1919, passed resolutions calling for the formation of Communist parties in the countries of the East, and for their integration in the Comintern.

In retrospect, we may safely say that the main purpose of the Council of Commissars in 1917 was to create the impression that the Bolshevik Revolution, as distinguished from the March Revolution, had as its mission the liberation of the Orient, in particular of the Muslim Orient. In fact, the Bolsheviks made many of their own Muslims believe, at least temporarily, that it was the hand of Providence that brought about the Bolshevik Revolution. Russian Muslims even spread propaganda to the effect that the Soviet regime would be established on the principles of the Koran and the Shariat. Many ignorant Muslims compared Mohammed with Lenin and the Koran with the teachings of Bolshevism. [13]

A careful analysis of the "Appeal to the Muslims" and of other literature pertaining to the period suggest that the Soviet government believed the success of the Bolshevik Revolution to be contingent upon its alliance with the Muslim Orient. In other words, the success of the October Revolution and the liberation of the Muslim world were regarded as inseparable and interdependent. One could not be achieved or endure without the other. This position was substantiated still further by a resolution of the seventh All-Russian Congress of Soviets on December 5, 1919:

> In greeting the representatives of Soviet Turkestan and Soviet Bash-kiria, the seventh All-Russian Congress of Soviets of workers, peasants, Red Army soldiers and Cossack deputies, regards their presence not only as proof that a feeling of solidarity with the toiling masses of the U.S.S.R. has penetrated the Muslim toiling masses, but that the conviction has penetrated the Muslim East that the R.S.F.S.R., located as it is between capitalist Europe and the peoples of Asia enslaved by imperialism, is their stronghold in their struggle for liberation from national oppression.[14]

Moreover, since the Bolsheviks could secure neither recognition nor help from the West and confronted opposition at that time from Russians at home, it was logical enough for them to appeal to the largest of the Russian minorities, the Muslims, who constituted about 10 or 12 per cent of the population, and through them to the Muslims of the world.

It is significant that, even prior to the October Revolution Lenin, speaking before the third session of the All-Russian Congress of Workers' and Soldiers' Deputies (June 3-16, 1917), said:

> . . . if the revolutionary democracy in Russia were a democracy, not in word but in deed, then it would start moving the Revolution forward, and not towards agreements with capitalists, not towards discussions of peace without annexations and indemnities, but towards an outright declaration that she considers any annexation criminal and murderous. Then it would be possible to avoid the imperialist aggression threatening with destruction thousands of millions of people over the partition of Persia and the Balkans.[15]

Lenin, who by no means voiced the majority opinion at this congress, by this statement created the impression among the representatives of the "annexed" minorities that he favored not only cultural and religious autonomy, but outright independence for all minorities on the ground that every annexation was "criminal and murderous." Since the Muslim minorities had already achieved a modicum of religious and cultural autonomy, the injection by Lenin of their right to independence opened before them a new horizon, at a time when the real purposes of the Bolsheviks were still unknown. Lenin's pronouncement may have led them to assume that the Bolsheviks stood for independence of Muslim peoples inside Russian borders, in addition to the liberation of those under the domination of the "imperialist colonizers." The subsequent Bolshevik "Appeal to All the Muslim Peoples of Russia and the East" on December 5, 1917, which promised only religious and cultural autonomy to the Muslim minorities in Russia, clearly indicated that once they were in power the Bolsheviks had no intention of granting independence to these monorities.

In the light of what happened later, Lenin looked upon national movements as a force suitable for exploitation in the struggle for power. We know his attitude toward the Jewish Bund, the Caucasian Socialists, and toward the exponents of the Renner-Bauer formula in the Russian Social Democratic movement. Richard Pipes has summed up his position as follows:

> Lenin's theory of national self-determination, viewed as a solution of the national problem in Russia, was entirely inadequate. By offering the minorities virtually no choice between assimilation and complete independence, it ignored the fact that they desired neither. Underestimating the power of nationalism and convinced without reservation of the inevitable triumph of class loyalties over national loyalties, Lenin looked upon national problems as something to exploit, and not as something to solve. But as a psychological weapon in the struggle for power, first in Russia and then abroad, the slogan of self-determination in Lenin's interpretation was to prove enormously successful. The outbreak of the Russian Revolution allowed the Bolsheviks to put it to considerable demagogic use as a means of winning the support of the national movements which the revolutionary period developed in all their magnitude. [16]

The "Appeal" of the Council of People's Commissars likewise marked a turning point in the attitude of Muslims toward Russia. As a result of Bolshevik denunciation of Tsarist imperialism and renunciation of Tsarist claims on Constantinople and the Straits, as well as of all treaties that infringed on the sovereign rights of adjacent Muslim states, Muslim hatred of Russia was mitigated, at least temporarily. Stalin, who, as commissar of nationalities, was particularly concerned with the problems of colonial and dependent peoples, emphasized this in an article in *Pravda,* November 7, 1923, on "The October Revolution and the Question of the Middle Strata":

> . . . the fact that Russia, which formerly served as the symbol of oppression in the eyes of the oppressed nationalities, has now, after it has become socialist, been transformed into a symbol of liberation, cannot be described as a mere chance. Nor is it accidental that the name of Comrade Lenin, the leader of the October Revolution, is now the most cherished name of the downtrodden, browbeaten peasants and revolutionary intelligentsia of the colonial and semienfranchised coun-

tries. If formerly Christianity was considered an anchor of salvation among the oppressed and downtrodden slaves of the vast Roman Empire, now things are heading towards a point where socialism can serve (and is already beginning to serve!) as a banner of liberation for the many millions in the vast colonial states of imperialism. [17]

Since Russia, by denouncing all Tsarist special privileges and territorial claims on the countries of the Muslim world temporarily, at least, became "a symbol of liberation" for the oppressed colonial and semicolonial peoples, it was logical that England in the eyes of many Muslims should supersede Russia as "the symbol of oppression." Prior to World War I, England controlled the largest area of Muslims, and at the conclusion of that conflict she appreciably extended rather than diminished the area, which stretched from Egypt to India. It stands to reason, therefore, that England became the main target of Soviet propaganda. This propaganda took deep root among Muslims and other Asiatics.

A message from the Indian National Muslim League in Delhi, published in *Pravda* and *Izvestia,* November 17, 1918, reflected the new climate of opinion and likewise assumed that the Revolution could achieve no permanent success without the liberation of India from British rule:

Leaders of the Russian Revolution! India congratulates you on the great victory you have won in the interests of democracy throughout the world. India marvels at the noble and humanitarian principles you promulgated when you took power into your hands. India prays that Providence will strengthen you and make you persevere in these high ideals. At the same time, India is apprehensive as to the duration of your success: for as long as England holds 350,000,000 Indians in a condition of enslavement, we think that you will not achieve the realization of your world aims.

For the sake of the success of your noble tasks, India warns you against friendship with England. You must choose one or the other: in a dirty neighborhood it is difficult to keep one's own home clean. You ought to know that England will not brook, alongside her most important colonies, a democratic Russia founded on the principles you have promulgated. Bear in mind that England will not stop, no matter how difficult and incredible the efforts, in her determination to strangle your new socialistic republic. If you wish to achieve success, although that will require many years, you must not permit any compromise. The independence of India must be a part, even the main part, of your program, no matter how difficult it may seem to you at first glance. No domination of democracy is possible in this world without the liberation of India and a complete liberation of India means the destruction

of British imperialism. You, yourself, know better what constitutes
the policy of Russia.

Sincerely yours,
The Peoples of India.

This message clearly indicated that, in spite of the identification
of Soviet interests with those of the peoples of the Orient, there
were still many who feared an Anglo-Soviet entente reminiscent
of the Anglo-Russian entente of 1907, which was achieved at the
expense of the countries of the Middle East. Hence the warning
against any compromise with the colonizer, especially with England, which has been the theme song of the nationalists, not only
of India but of the Muslim East, from that day until the present.
From the Indian standpoint, any *modus vivendi* with England would
enable that country to maintain its supremacy over India. With the
vast reserves of Indian manpower at her disposal, England would
never permit the existence of Soviet "republics" adjacent to her
colonial preserve. Thus in 1918 the success of the October Revolution was said to be contingent upon the independence of India.

M. N. Roy, an Indian delegate at the second congress of the
Third International in July, 1920, likewise insisted that the success of the revolutionary movement in Europe was "absolutely
dependent" on the rise of the revolutionary movement in the East,
and that it was "a fundamental thesis" that the destiny of world
communism was dependent on the triumph of communism in the
East.[18] Roy's thesis was challenged, not only by Lenin, but by
another Oriental Communist, Sultan-Zade, delegate from Persia,
who maintained that the social revolution would not come from the
East, nor would it free Europe. According to him, the Comintern
must go to the aid of the toiling masses of the Orient "to facilitate
for them the process of social revolution."[19]

In view of their identification of the Bolshevik Revolution with
Muslim liberation, Soviet leaders revised the traditional concept
of the Eastern Question, which, to the average person under the
Tsarist regime meant the partition of the Ottoman Empire, including the Russian threat to Constantinople, the Dardanelles, and
the Bosphorus. The "Appeal to the Muslims" appeared to remove
the threat of Russian expansion at the expense of Turkey and the
Muslim world. Not only did the Soviet government publicly renounce the secret treaties by which the Tsarist regime paved the
way for further annexations, but it redefined the Eastern Question
as one which involved Soviet aid for the liberation of enslaved peoples from domination by "England, France, the United States, and

other capitalist countries. " Moscow was to become "the Mecca and Medina of all enslaved peoples. "[20] Moreover, the Soviets broadened still further the scope of the Eastern Question, by including therein the problems of oppressed colonial peoples everywhere--not merely in Asia:

The Orient is not only the oppressed Asiatic world. The Orient is the entire colonial world, the world of oppressed peoples, not only in Asia, but also in Africa and South America; in short, the entire world on whose exploitation rests the might of capitalist society in Europe and the United States. European and American capitalism draws its chief strength, not from industrial European countries, but from their colonial possessions. [21]

The extent to which the Soviet government identified the interests of the Soviet regime with those of the new Orient was clearly indicated by M. Pavlovitch, when he said: "A war against any of these countries of the Orient is a war against the U.S.S.R., just as a war against the U.S.S.R. is a war against the Orient. "[22] Thus in the Soviet interpretation of the October Revolution one can easily detect the signs of a new Soviet imperialism, which later developed on a global scale, and which now constitutes a threat not only to the West but to the Orient itself.

This chapter, strictly speaking, presents the Soviet definition of the October Revolution of 1917 with respect to the Muslim world. The record of Soviet relations with the Muslim countries of the Near and Middle East from 1917 to 1958, which reveals the impact of the October Revolution on the Muslims, is the subject of subsequent chapters.

3. The First (Baku) Congress
of the Peoples of the East, September, 1920

The Dispute
by M. Yu. Lermontov
(This poem was widely quoted at the Baku Congress.)

Once, while in listening circles sat
  Their tribe in converse close
Between Kazbek and Old Mount Shat*
  A great dispute arose.

"Take care!" the grey-haired Shat began
  To Kazbek towering near:
"Brother, you are enslaved by man--
  His work will cost you dear.

"About your rocky ledges steep
  His smoky sails will cling;
Through all your wooded gorges deep,
  His axe will loudly ring.

"Deep in your stony breast he'll tear
  A fearful road one day,
Seeking for gold and copper there
  With iron spade and tray.

"Already caravans explore
  Your lofty turrets' blue,
Where only mist-wraiths hung before
  And lone Tsar-eagles flew.

---

*Mt. Elbruz.

43

"Mark me, these men are wise, and though
   Their first rush may have ceased--
Take care! It is an Orient flow--
   The teeming, powerful East!"

"The East shall not affright my ease, "
   Kazbek made answer fair:
"Already nine long centuries
   The race of men sleeps there. "

"And dozing in the nargileh's smoke,
   Stretched on a flowered divan,
Beside the fountain's pearly cloak,
   Low slumbers Teheran.

"And scorched by God, there underneath
   Jerusalem's desert skies,
Voiceless and motionless as death
   A lifeless country lies.

"Beyond, forever lost to shade,
   Beside the serried pile
Where the dead Pharoahs' bones are laid
   Washes the yellow Nile.

"And there the Bedouin clean forgets
   Raids for his tents of gold;
And counting stars, sings songs and lets
   His fathers' deeds be told.

"Yes, all the seeking eye sees here
   Sleeps and is glad of rest:
No, I have no great need to fear
   The Old, decrepit East. "
                    --Translated by Alexander
                      Welikotny and C. E. L'Ami

     The above verses, written by the Russian poet, Mikhail Yure-
vitch Lermontov (1814-41), undoubtedly epitomize the thinking,
not only in Russia, but throughout the Western world, in regard to
the Orient, especially the Muslim Orient, about the middle of the
nineteenth century. Little did the poet laureate of the Caucasus

realize that within less than a century, the East that "sleeps and is glad of rest" would awaken to become one of the focal points of world strategy. The present rise of the Orient, especially of the Muslim world, is the result, not of evolutionary growth from within, but of the impact of the West, of two world wars, and of the Russian Revolutions of 1905 and 1917.

As previously indicated, the "Appeal to All the Muslims of Russia and the East" of the Council of People's Commissars of the Bolshevik regime was issued within a month of the October (November 7) Revolution of 1917. Subsequent events prevented the Bolsheviks from taking effective measures to implement this call to revolution. The German-dictated Treaty of Brest-Litovsk (March 3, 1918), which recognized the independence of the Ukraine, Poland, Finland, Esthonia, Latvia, Lithuania, and Georgia, and surrendered to Turkey the Transcaucasian provinces of Kars and Ardahan, including Batum, virtually dismembered Russia in Europe. Immediately thereafter, the Bolsheviks were placed on the defensive by the intervention of Great Britain, France, the United States, Turkey, and Japan to stem the tide of revolution and to support the White Russian armies engaged in Civil War with the Communists. The counterrevolutionary forces of Denikin and Kolchak, as well as those of the British and French invaders, made regular communication with the Muslim East for some time impossible.

The Bolsheviks attributed to the Red Army (established February 23, 1918) and the Third International (organized March, 1919)[1] the real credit for turning the tide against the foreign invader and the White armies. The political and psychological warfare conducted by the Third International led to mutiny in April, 1919, among the French troops at Odessa in the south and among the American forces at Archangel in the north, followed by the early withdrawal of both French and American occupation forces. The White armies of Denikin were undermined by widespread defection among the war-weary troops. Along the southern periphery, the Denikin slogan of "Russia: One and Indivisible, " which served to rally the Tsarist nationalists, aroused only fear and dismay among the minorities, including the Muslims. Indeed, the Bolsheviks attributed part of their success against Kolchak, Denikin, and Wrangel to the sympathy and support of "the oppressed masses of the borderlands of former Russia" (Stalin). In April, 1920, the Soviets reoccupied Baku, revolutionary center of the Caucasus, following the departure of the English (August, 1919). By the summer of 1920, the remnants of Denikin's army under General Wrangel were making their last stand in the Crimea. The Polish forces that invaded the Ukraine in April, at the instigation of Wrangel, were by midsummer driven to the gates of Warsaw by the Red Army.

By July, 1920, therefore, the Soviet regime was confident of victory over the White armies and foreign interventionists and reasonably sure that the war-weary Russians were in no position to offer a serious challenge to Soviet authority. The first congress of the Third International had been summoned in 1919, at a time of dire emergency for the Bolshevik regime, to devise ways and means for the successful defense against counterrevolution and foreign invasion. The second congress, summoned in July, 1920, as a result of foreign withdrawal and the disintegration of domestic opposition was ready to assume the offensive. In Turkey, the "revolutionary core" of the East, the Nationalist forces of Kemal Pasha were already challenging the Entente powers. In neighboring Iran, a Soviet republic had been established in Gilan, and there was upheaval in Khorassan. Georgia, although its independence was recognized by a treaty signed with the Soviets on May 7, 1920, was still regarded as the "kept mistress of the Entente," and the Bolsheviks feared that the theater of Entente military operations had been removed from Russia proper only to be re-established in Transcaucasia.

The second congress of the Comintern thereupon determined, first, to instigate strikes, riots, and subversion in Europe and America, especially in those countries that had led the foreign intervention, in order to discourage any repetition of the invasion of Russia. Second, it planned to attack the colonial periphery, "the Achilles' heel of imperialism," to deprive the Entente of its sources of raw materials and fuel. The summons to Baku was therefore a summons to the Muslim world to organize a counterattack against the foreign invaders of Russia, in order to expel them from the lands adjacent to the Soviet republics, including Turkey, Iran, Armenia, and Mesopotamia.

In 1908, twelve years before the Comintern issued its summons for a Congress of the Peoples of the East at Baku, a prominent Crimean Tatar by the name of Ismail Gasprinsky conceived the idea of holding an all-Muslim congress in Egypt to consider the ills that beset the peoples of the Muslim world, to exchange ideas, and to propose remedies to ensure the progress and welfare of Muslims everywhere. The invitation to this congress, a copy of which fell into the hands of the Russian police, was published in Egypt in Arabic, Turkish, and Persian. [2] Although owing to the course of events the Cairo congress failed to materialize, the search for at least a semblance of Muslim unity had begun. Instead of holding such a congress in Cairo, the Comintern chose Baku, where the Muslims would meet under Soviet rather than under Egyptian auspices.

Professor A. Zeki Velîdî Togan

Whereas the "Appeal to All the Muslims of Russia and the East" of December 5, 1917, was issued by the Soviet government (Council of People's Commissars, R. S. F. S. R.), the summons to the Baku Congress of 1920 came from the second congress of the Third International or Comintern, July 19 to August 7, 1920. It was addressed exclusively to the peasants and workers of the Orient, in particular to the Iranians, Armenians, and Turks, and called for the Bolshevization of the East. The main purpose of the Council of People's Commissars in 1917, as we have seen, was to identify the October Revolution with the liberation of the peoples of the East. The invitation to these peoples to come to Baku, issued by the Third International, was more aggressive in tone, its main purpose being to create the machinery needed to implement the Sovietization of the Muslim world. It summoned the "faithful" Muslim proletariat in order to bring about a jihad, or holy war, against the colonial powers, especially England.

The idea of convening a Muslim congress originated with A. Zeki Velîdî Togan (Velidov), a prominent Bashkir from Muslim Central Asia, who in 1919 was with Karl Radek, a well-known Bolshevik intellectual, and a group of Turkish officers in Moscow. According to Togan, this congress was to have been summoned by the Muslim peoples themselves, not by the Russians or the Third International, and, in accordance with his recommendation, it was to be held in Baku. General Ali Fuat Cebesoy, the first ambassador of the Turkish Republic in the Soviet Union, credits Radek with the plan for a Muslim congress, to be held in Moscow. Radek, with the object of arousing the leaders of the Muslim world against the West, planned to use the former Turkish leaders of the Sultanate, including Enver Pasha and Jamal Pasha, to entice Muslim delegates to Moscow. General Cebesoy managed to convince Enver Pasha that the congress should be held in Ankara, Turkey, far removed from Soviet pressure. Before any agreement was reached with Ankara, the impatient Bolshevik leaders summoned Muslim delegates to Moscow, some of whom responded, but failed to locate Enver Pasha, and nothing was accomplished. Faced with this debacle, Radek and his associates appear to have selected Baku as a compromise gesture. The Bolsheviks then stole the show by having the Third International summon the Muslim peoples to the Baku Congress, with the result that neither Togan, the Bashkir leader, nor Enver Pasha participated officially in the proceedings.

The following document is a translation of the invitation extended by the Third International to the peoples of the East to come to Baku, as published in *Izvestia*, July 3, 1920:[3]

The Communist International to the Enslaved Peoples of Persia, Armenia, and Turkey

The Executive Committee of the Communist International summons a congress of the workers and peasants of Persia, Armenia, and Turkey, to convene on August 15, 1920, in Baku.

What is the Communist International? It is the organization of the revolutionary toiling masses of Russia, Poland, Germany, France, England, and America, awakened by the thunder of the World War and impelled by hunger, who have revolted in order to work, not for the rich but for themselves, and to take up arms, not against their own suffering and poverty-stricken brothers but in order to use them for their own defense against the plunderers. These toiling masses have understood that their strength lies only in union and in organization, that this is the only guarantee of their victory, and thus last year a strong organization was established in the form of the Third International. The latter, in spite of all persecution by capitalistic governments has become within one and one-half years the soul of all the revolutionary workers and peasants of the whole world, who long for liberation.

Why, then, does the Communist International now summon a congress of the Persian, Armenian, and Turkish workers and peasants? What does it offer them? What does it want from them? The workers and peasants of Europe and America, who are struggling against capitalism, appeal to you because you, like them, are suffering under the yoke of world capitalism, and because you, like them, are forced to fight the world plunderers, because your joining the workers and peasants of Europe and America will accelerate the destruction of world capitalism and guarantee the liberation of all workers and peasants throughout the world.

Peasants and workers of Persia! The Teheran Kajar government and its hirelings--the provincial khans--have plundered and exploited you for centuries. The land was seized by the lackeys of the Teheran government; they control this land; they are imposing taxes and levies on you at their discretion; and after having drained the country of its vitality and reduced it to poverty and ruin, they sold Persia last year to the English capitalists for £2,000,000 sterling, so that the latter could form an army in Persia which will oppress you even more than heretofore, and so that this army should squeeze from you still heavier taxes and duties for the Khans and the Teheran government. They have sold to England the rich South Persian oil resources, thereby facilitating the plundering of your country.

Peasants of Mesopotamia! The English have declared your country independent, but 80,000 English troops are on your territory, plundering and killing you and violating your wives.

Peasants of Anatolia! The English, Italian, and French governments have kept Constantinople under the fire of their guns; they have imprisoned the Sultan, have forced him to agree to the dismemberment of purely Turkish territory, and have handed over Turkish finances to foreign financiers, in order to facilitate the plundering of the Turkish people impoverished by six years of war. They have occupied the coal mines of Heracles and your ports; they are sending troops to your country, destroying your fields, enforcing their laws which are alien to the peaceful Turkish peasant, trying to convert you into their beasts of burden to carry all kinds of loads. Part of your beys and effendis have sold themselves to the foreign capitalists; another part calls you to arms, in order to fight against foreign invasion, not allowing you, however, to take the power into your own hands in your own country, not allowing you to use the land and the fields bestowed by the Sultan on various parasites, not allowing you to cultivate them for your own use. And tomorrow, when the foreign capitalists reach an agreement with your oppressors over more lenient peace terms, your present leaders will avail themselves of this in order to impose on you new chains, as is being done by the landowners and former bureaucrats in regions effectively occupied by foreign troops.

Peasants and workers of Armenia! For many years you have been the victims of foreign capitalists, who talked a great deal about the massacres of the Armenians by the Kurds, who called upon you to fight the Sultan, and who extracted for themselves more and more benefits from your struggle against the Sultan. During the war they not only promised you independence, but they also induced your teachers, merchants, and priests to demand for themselves the land of the Turkish peasants, in order to bring about a perpetual struggle between the Turkish and Armenian peoples, from which they would derive perpetual profit, because as long as this strife between you continues the foreign capitalists will extract profits for themselves, threatening Turkey with the peril of an Armenian revolt and the Armenians with Kurdish pogroms.

Peasants of Syria and Arabia! The English and French have promised you independence, but now their troops have occupied your country, imposing upon you their own laws; and you, after liberating yourselves from the Turkish Sultan and government, have now become the slaves of the Paris and London governments, the only difference from the Sultan being that they will keep a stronger hold on you and will plunder you more effectively.

You yourselves understand this very well. The Persian peasants and workers have revolted against the traitorous Teheran government. The peasants of Mesopotamia are rebelling against the English army of occupation, and the English press reports the losses the British army sustained in its battles with the revolutionists near Baghdad.

Peasants of Anatolia! You are urgently called to the colors under Kemal-Pasha, in order to fight the foreign invasion, but at the same time we know that you are trying to form your own national party, your own peasants' party, which would be able to continue the fight in the event that the Pashas should conclude peace with the rapacious Entente.

In Syria, they are unable to establish peace, and you Armenian peasants, whom the Entente, in spite of all its promises is starving, the better to keep you in its clutches--you understand more and more that the hope for salvation through the capitalists of the Entente is quite absurd. Even your bourgeois government of the Dashnaktsutyun party, of these lackeys of the Entente, is forced to appeal to the workers' and peasants' government of Russia, asking for the conclusion of peace and for help. Now we see that you begin to understand your own needs, and we therefore turn to you, as representatives of the European proletariat, using the vast amount of experience accumulated in our own struggle for the purpose of helping you in the cause of your liberation. We say to you: the time when European and American capitalists were able to suppress you by force of arms--this time has passed once and for all. Everywhere in Europe and America the workers are taking up arms against the capitalists and are waging a bloody struggle against them.

If we are still unable to defeat world capitalism, nevertheless the capitalists no longer have the power to dispose at will of their peoples' blood. For two and a half years the Russian Revolution has been fighting the whole world. French, English, and American capitalists have tried by every means--by force of arms, by starvation--to defeat the Russian worker and peasant, to put a noose around his neck, and to make him a slave. They did not succeed. The Russian workers and peasants have defended their regime stoically, have organized their own army, and have totally defeated all the reactionary armies supported by the capitalists of the Entente.

Workers and Peasants of the Near East! If you organize yourselves, if you form your own workers' and peasants' regime, if you arm yourselves and join the Russian workers' and peasants' army, you will defeat the English, French, and American capitalists, you will liberate yourselves from your oppressors, you will secure freedom, you will be able to organize a free, peaceful republic of toilers, you will use the riches of your own land in your own land in your own interests and in the interests of the rest of toiling humanity, which will be glad to come to your assistance. About all this we want to talk with you at the congress.

The Executive Committee of the Communist International, representing the English, French, American, German, and Italian workers, will come to Baku to discuss with you the question of how to unite your forces and those of the European proletariat for the struggle against the common enemy.

Make every effort to reach Baku in the greatest possible numbers by September 1. You formerly went through deserts to the holy places; you now cross mountains, rivers, forests, and deserts, in order to meet one another, to discuss how to free yourselves from the chains of slavery, to form a fraternal union, and to begin a free, equal, and brotherly life.

We turn, first of all, to the workers and peasants of the Near East, but we shall be glad to see among them the delegates and representatives of the oppressed masses living at a greater distance--the representatives of India, as well as the representatives of the Muslim peoples who are developing freely in alliance with Soviet Russia.

On September 2, thousands of Turkish, Armenian, and Persian workers and peasants should peacefully unite in Baku for the liberation of the Near East.

Let the Congress say to your enemies in Europe, America, and in our country that the time of slavery has passed, that you are rising, and that you will be victorious.

Let this Congress say to the workers of the entire world that you are defending your rights and are joining the mighty revolutionary army, which is now fighting against all injustice and plunder.

Let your Congress give strength and faith to millions and millions of the enslaved throughout the world; let it instill in them confidence in their own strength and let it hasten the day of their final victory and liberation.

The Executive Committee of the Communist International:

Zinoviev, President

K. Radek, Secretary

For the British Socialist Party: W. MacLaine, Tom Quelch

For the Factory Committee of England: Jack Turner, G. T. Murphy

For the French Delegation to the Communist International Congress:

A. Rosmer, K. Delinières, J. Sadoul
For the Italian Delegation to the Communist International Congress:
Bombacci, A. Graziadei
For the Communist Party of America: A. Fraina, A. Stoklinsky
For the Communist Labor Party of America: A. Bilan
For the Spanish Labor Federation: Angel Pestaña
For the Central Committee of the Russian Communist Party: N. Bukharin, V. Vorovsky, A. Balabanova, G. Klinger
For the VTSPS (All Russian Soviet of Trade Unions): A. Lozovsky
For the Communist Party of Poland: Yu. Markhlevsky (Karsky)
For the Communist Party of Bulgaria and the Balkan Communist
Federation: N. Shablin
For the Communist Party of Austria: Reussler
For the Communist Party of Hungary: Rakoszy, Rudnyansky
For the Communist Party of Holland: D. Wynkoop

According to Bolshevik claims, and their figures are subject to question, 1, 891 delegates answered the summons. Of these, 1, 273 were said to be Communists, 266 nonparty, 100 failed to indicate their affiliation, and 55 were women.[4] All the Muslim peoples of Soviet Russia and those linked by treaty relations with it, were represented. In addition to the Turks (235 delegates), Persians (192), and Armenians (157), specifically summoned by the Third International, there were Chinese (8), Kurds (8), and Arabs (3), as well as Georgians (100). Some of the delegates representing other Muslim countries were already in Soviet Russia as exiles, including Mustapha Subhi, a member of the Presidium, and Enver Pasha of Turkey, who did not appear in person before the Congress. It was in all a motley assembly, too heterogeneous for effective action. Three official languages--Russian, Azerbaijani-Turkish, and Persian--proved altogether inadequate, and additional translations into standard Turkish, Kalmyk, Uzbek, Chechen, etc., were necessary. The three official delegates of the Third International, Grigory Zinoviev, Comintern president who served as chairman, Karl Radek, a prominent Bolshevik intellectual, and Bela Kun, erstwhile leader of the short-lived Communist regime in Hungary, set the tone of the conference. Apparently the Comintern at that time saw nothing anomalous about sending three Jews on a mission to win the Muslim and Armenian peoples to the Soviet cause!

It was no accident that Baku was chosen as the site for the first Congress of the Peoples of the East. Addressing a meeting of the Baku Soviet of Deputies and the Azerbaijan Congress of Trade

Unions on August 31, 1920, on the eve of the congress, Karl Radek explained:

It is no accident that we chose the city of Baku when we planned the Congress of the Peoples of the East. Here in Baku, where for many years Persians, Turks, and Tatars worked, here in Baku where capitalism ravished and exploited them, and where, at the same time there came to them the socialist idea, and it found a general response in their hearts.

We know how here in Baku was born the socialist revolution, and how from here went forth the idea of the struggle against Russian Tsarism, and how the workers, having returned to Persia carried with them the idea of this struggle, not only against Tsarism, but against capitalism, for the liberation of all peoples from any yoke. We are convinced that this city of workers, in which there existed unheard-of bourgeois luxury on the one hand and the darkest life of the workers on the other--that this city will become the arena of international revolution, that from here will emanate an electric current of political consciousness, that here will be installed the banner of the struggle for the liberation of the East, which the Communist International entrusts to the Baku proletariat, experienced fighters for the liberation of the workers of mankind. [5]

No doubt one reason Baku was chosen for the congress was because it was readily accessible to the Muslim peoples of Soviet Russia, and to the Persians, Turks, and Arabs to the south. What Zinoviev failed to mention was that the Soviet government undoubtedly hoped by this means to consolidate Soviet power among the Muslim minorities, much of whose territory had been occupied without much difficulty by the English, French, and Turks during the period of foreign intervention. There was still widespread disaffection among anti-Soviet forces in the area. Indeed, in the city of Baku itself, Communist power had been re-established as recently as April, 1920. Even while the congress was in session at Baku a serious revolt erupted in Daghestan.

The high watermark of unity among the delegates appears to have been reached during Zinoviev's fiery summons of the Muslims to a jihad, or holy war--primarily against English imperialism--which was delivered as the keynote speech at the opening of the congress. A holy war against English imperialism was something that Arabs, Turks, Persians, and other Muslims could understand and which they could wholeheartedly endorse. The record indicates that the Zinoviev address was punctuated by "stormy applause" and "prolonged hurrahs." The aroused Muslims, convinced by Zinoviev that they were participating in one of the most important events in history, in a frenzy of excitement rose from their seats and, brandishing their swords, daggers, and revolvers, swore to undertake the fight against imperialism. It is of interest to observe that the one delegate to sound an anti-American note at Baku was the American, John Reed of the state of Oregon, best known as the author of *Ten Days That Shook the World*. In his attack on United States policy in the Philippines, Central America, and the Caribbean Islands, he undertook to warn the assembled delegates that "the peoples of the East, the peoples of Asia, had not yet experienced the power of America."

If the official record is not distorted, the three representatives of the Comintern held the whip hand at the congress. A plethora of speeches, for the most part prepared in advance of the sessions, and involving endless repetition of Comintern principles, gave a cut-and-dried aspect to the performance and left little opportunity for discussion, even if the babel of languages had permitted the free interplay of ideas. Indeed, there was more than one indication that the Comintern leadership railroaded its decisions through the congress. When the list of forty-eight candidates for the proposed Council of Action and Propaganda in the East, intended to carry on the work of the congress after the delegates dispersed, was presented, a lone Persian delegate raised his voice in protest, but it was drowned in the ensuing hubbub, and the list was declared to have been passed "unanimously." The two manifestoes issued by the congress, "To the Peoples of the East" and "To the Workers of Europe, America and Japan," were approved "in principle," without the delegates having any opportunity to see or discuss the text of the messages. Zeki Velîdî Togan (Velidov), later protested to Lenin, Stalin, and Trotsky that Zinoviev and Radek treated the representatives of the Eastern nations "like anti-revolutionary peasants."[6] Togan, who was present incognito in Baku, and who wished to salvage something from the congress for his fellow Muslims, busied himself behind the scenes by formulating resolutions for the delegates. According to him, Zinoviev recognized that someone was providing resolutions with uncanny regularity, but remained ignorant of their real authorship.

The Baku Congress afforded an opportunity for the recruitment of revolutionary forces designed to spearhead the Communist revolution in other Muslim lands. Mustapha Subhi, who had organized Communist Turkish prisoners of war for the Central Bureau of the Eastern Peoples, a subdivision of the Commissariat of Nationalities, moved his headquarters to Baku in May, 1920, in advance of the congress, and in September held a conference of Turkish Communists there. Subhi and his cohort proceeded to enter Turkey in November, ostensibly to join the Turkish struggle for liberation in Anatolia, but actually to promote communism there. Armenian Communists were likewise accused of using the congress to gain adherents, who shortly thereafter went to Armenia to displace the Dashnak (Menshevik) government already established there. Little wonder that on their return to their respective countries many of the delegates were cast into prison as Communist agitators and had no opportunity to disseminate the Baku gospel!

According to Soviet thinking, only the Third International was capable of liberating the Orient, especially the Muslim East. Strictly speaking, the Second International was regarded as an agent of imperialism, concerned primarily with the workers of Europe and their problems, rather than with the "Eastern Question." The Orient was remote and constituted a problem for their governments.

The Second International, by its very nature, was incapable of supporting a revolutionary movement among the oppressed peoples of Morocco, Algiers, Tunis, Asia Minor, Persia, India, Egypt, etc. In particular, it was incapable of assuming the initiative in the matter of revolutionizing the Black and Yellow continents. Even in regard to such a simple matter as propaganda for the dissemination of the ideas of liberation among the long-suffering masses of Asia and Africa, the Second International neither desired nor does it desire to understand the East from this standpoint. Of course, in words the leaders of the Second International permitted themselves to criticize the colonial policy of their governments, and from time to time even published in Paris, London, or Berlin books and brochures on these themes, such as those of Charles Dumas. But these gentlemen have never translated all these books into native languages, and they wrote on colonial themes only to attract attention to themselves in the metropolis and in parliamentary circles in general, or in the Socialist party in particular. In reality, all these staunch defenders of the natives supported the colonial policies of their governments. When news reached them about the Armenian pogroms in Turkey, the European Socialists willingly organized demonstrations, organized huge meetings of protest against the bloodthirsty Sultan. But when the French government year after year sent new forces to Morocco and slaughtered Muslim tribes, the Socialists of the Second International preserved silence. The English Socialists assumed the same attitude with regard to atrocities in India, to the strangulation of Persia, to the enslavement of Egypt, to the massacres and bloody orgies of the English forces on the Black Continent.[7]

Referring to the leaders of the Second International, Joseph Stalin further emphasized their lack of awareness of colonial problems:

These . . . Socialists did not even assume that the abolition of national oppression in Europe is unthinkable without the liberation of the colonial peoples of Asia and Africa from imperialistic oppression, that the former is organically interwoven with the latter. The Communists were the first to reveal the connection between the national question and the colonial question, to formulate it theoretically and to make it the basis of their revolutionary practice.[8]

According to Pak Dunshun, delegate from Korea to the second congress of the Third International, the complex question of the revolutionary struggle of enslaved peoples was foreign to the ideologists of the Second International. Not until the October Revolution in Russia was it possible to secure a response from the peoples of the East: "The great victorious October Revolution in Russia first bridged the chasm between the proletariat of the West and the revolutionary East; Soviet Russia became the connecting link between the two formerly separated worlds."[9] In other words, the very existence of Soviet Russia and its national policy made it possible for the Third International to do what was impossible for the Second International.[10]

In his closing speech at the Baku Congress, Zinoviev stated what was, in his opinion, the foremost achievement of this first great gathering of the peoples of the East:

In recent years, the bourgeoisie has been afraid that the workers of the West would rise in revolt, but as regards the peoples of the East, right up to the present it has been complacent; and at the very moment when it was sleeping sweetly on a soft cushion, when it was certain that from this quarter nothing unexpected lies in wait, at this moment the oppressed peoples of the East are assembling at this congress, are organizing and are acting with unprecedented and amazing, with an uplifting spirit of unity. . . . This is what is most significant at our congress.[11]

To the president of the Third International, as he faced this large assembly of the "old decrepit East," hitherto of no concern either to Kazbek or to the Western bourgeoisie but now assembled and working in apparent harmony under Communist leadership, it appeared that a miracle had occurred--the East had awakened and was organized. Ostensibly this was a great achievement and it could well have marked a turning point in Soviet-Muslim relations, had the Third International not made the fatal mistake of attacking Islam and Muslim religious institutions. It was one thing to attack organized religion in the Soviet Union, but quite another to apply the same epithets and slogans to the Muslim world, where conditions were entirely different. Even the most stalwart Muslim adherents of the Third International were not yet conditioned for an attack on their faith. Thus the achievements of the Baku Congress were virtually annulled by Zinoviev when under his chairmanship delegate Skatchko labeled the Muslim clergy parasites and oppressors who should be deprived of their lands:

> The clergy, which has seized enormous areas of land . . . declare that these lands belong to God, and therefore they are inviolable . . . but, comrades, this is a lie and a fraud! Even according to the Shariat, the land can belong only to the one who tills it and thus the clergy who have seized the land, as . . . in Persia, were themselves the first to violate the basic law of the Muslim religion; they are not the defenders of this religion, but its distorters. They are as much parasites and oppressors as the feudal landowners, but they are also hypocrites, who hide behind a white turban and the Holy Koran the fact that they are parasites and oppressors. Comrades, this holy mask must be torn off and the lands belonging to them must be ruthlessly confiscated and given to the toiling peasantry. [12]

Rumors spread that after this speech local Muslims gave vent to their displeasure and disillusionment by hurling garbage at Zinoviev.

Evidently Zinoviev failed to heed Lenin's warning at the eighth congress of the Communist party in 1919, when the latter said:

> What can we do with regard to such peoples as the Kirghiz, Uzbeks, Tadjiks, Turkmenians who, up to the present time, are under the influence of their mullahs. In Russia the population, after long experience with their priests, helped us to overthrow them. . . . Can we approach these peoples, and say: "We will overthrow your exploiters"? No, we can't do that, because they are entirely under the domination of their mullahs. Here we must wait the development of the nation in question and the differentiation between the proletariat and bourgeois elements, which is inevitable. [13]

Although Lenin, Stalin, and others had warned the representatives of the Third International to be cautious in their approach to the Muslims, especially in regard to religious issues, these warnings were ignored at the Baku Congress. Zinoviev, president of the Executive Committee of the Third International, evinced very little knowledge of the Muslim Orient. His utterances revealed more heat than light on the subject. Casting caution to the winds, he brushed aside likewise the warning of K. Troyanovsky who in 1918 in his book, *Vostok i Revolyutsia,* explained that "Muslim unity consists, not in territorial or other ethnographic foundations. It rests almost exclusively on spiritual and cultural foundations, on religion, which for the Muslim is theology, ethics, jurisprudence, and the supreme terrestrial power that is the state. Islam is an extraterritorial power. "[14] Hence any attack on Islam is an attack on Muslim life as a whole.

Zinoviev not only attacked Islam, directly and indirectly, as well as its leaders and institutions, but he committed another unpardonable blunder. He attacked Turkey, which the Soviet government intended to use as its key agent to win over the rest of the Muslim world, especially the Near and Middle East. To win adherents to the Turkish cause, Kemal Pasha had promised the masses that Turkey was waging its war to retain the caliph. [15] But at the Baku Congress, Zinoviev, referring to Turkey, complained: "What the government of Kemal is doing in Turkey is not communism. You must not support the power of the Sultans. . . . On the contrary, you must break up and destroy the faith in the Sultan, just as the Russian peasants destroyed the faith in the Tsar. The same thing will happen in Turkey and throughout the Orient when the real black soil peasant revolution breaks out. "

This, in no uncertain terms, was an appeal for a Soviet revolution in the Muslim world, with all its implications. The importance of the Baku Congress is that it marked a turning point by reviving the suspicions of Muslims against the Soviet Union, which the Soviet government had been taking such pains to eradicate. Zinoviev not only alienated the Muslim elements, but in his unbridled zeal he antagonized Turkey, without which the Soviet Union could never expect to win the Muslim world. The Baku Congress did accomplish its purpose of stirring up the Muslim peoples, but not in the manner envisaged by the Soviets. It destroyed the illusion that the Soviet Union might become the Mecca and Medina of the Muslims. The threat to Islam was clear, even to the most ignorant mullahs, who had been comparing Lenin and Marx with Mohammed. No matter how much Muslims outside Russia detested colonialism and all it stood for, they feared even more the antireligious propaganda that emanated from the Baku Congress. A few Muslims may have been conditioned for this, but not the bulk of the delegates, and these few upon their return found that they were unpopular among their own people. Thus the Baku Congress served as an eye opener to the most "progressive" Muslims on the kind of "liberation" the Third International had in store for them. [16]

Accurate information concerning the Baku Congress is exceedingly limited. The basic primary sources are the stenographic record of the sessions, together with the manifestoes and other material published following the Congress in the official journal of the Comintern. [17] The Soviet press, no doubt for very good reasons, practically ignored the congress *(Izvestia,* September 19, 1920). In all probability, the Soviet government, which was on the eve of emerging victorious from the Civil War and foreign intervention, preferred to leave to the Third International the summoning of the Muslim and Armenian peoples to a counterattack against the invaders. Foreign newspaper reports on the congress need to be handled with caution, since they were in no wise firsthand accounts of the sessions. The world's journalists were not invited to cover a congress devoted to the incitement of social revolution in colonial and semicolonial countries and to the struggle for national liberation on the part of Muslim countries, whose lands, as in the case of Turkey, were occupied by English, French, Greek, Italian, or other foreign armies. Finally, the vast majority of the delegates to the Congress, still far from being articulate on the broader issues involved, were not the kind who kept diaries and published memoirs. They came to listen and to get their instructions from the leaders of the Third International. The columns of their hometown newspapers were ordinarily closed to them and, as previously indicated, many landed in jail, instead of returning as heroes to their native lands.

Commenting on the Baku Congress some three months later, the Red Army newspaper *Krasnaya Gazeta* (December 10, 1920) claimed that in the Communist Manifesto at Baku the Muslims found a new Koran which would lead them to the promised land. The editorial on the congress continued, as follows:

> Over Baku we waged a great struggle with England, which sought to deprive us of fuel. Now Baku is on our side and we have every opportunity to supply not only England but the whole Entente with a new kind of fuel, which in the very near future will generate a great deal of heat. Instead of oil, the gentlemen imperialists will feel the flame of a revolutionary conflagration in the East.

A few other comments in the same vein appeared in *Petrogradskaya Pravda* (September 4, 1920) and *Zhizn' Natsional'nostei* (September 16 and October 27, 1920).

The Baku Congress approved in principle the issuing of an "Appeal (Manifesto) to the Peoples of the East" (see Appendix A), the text of which was not passed by the delegates or included in the official records of the congress. This document, obviously drafted for use as an instrument of propaganda throughout the Muslim world, was directed entirely against England, the country regarded by the delegates as the one great imperialist power which had emerged from World War I with the strength and intent to dominate the "oppressed" peoples of the East. It summoned them, one and all, to a holy war against England, as the only means of achieving their liberation from political subjugation and economic exploitation. In its attack on Islam, this document was even more hostile than were the addresses of Zinoviev and company before the assembled delegates. It is extremely doubtful whether the congress, had its members been afforded an opportunity to hear and discuss the text, would have given the following antireligious passage the stamp of its approval:

> Peoples of the East! Many times you have heard from your governments the summons to a holy war; you have marched under the green banner of the Prophet; but all these holy wars were deceitful and false, and served the interests of your selfish rulers; but you, peasants and workers, even after these wars remained in serfdom and destitution; you won the blessings of life for others, but you yourselves never enjoyed any of them.
>
> Now we summon you to the first genuine holy war under the red banner of the Communist International.

In brief, this manifesto urged the Faithful to substitute the red flag of revolution for the green banner of the Prophet, the Third International for Islam, Lenin for Mohammed. The price of liberation from England was the repudiation of religion--of Islam.

The only machinery established by the Baku Congress was its provision for a Council of Propaganda and Action to convene once in three months in Baku to implement the policies of the congress. Apparently this council, comprised of forty-eight members representing more than twenty nationalities, proved cumbersome for it took no significant action and was soon abandoned. The council included six representatives of the Comintern (Pavlovitch, Ordzhonikidze, Yeleyeva, Kirov, Stasova, and Skatchko), and even one representative of the Eastern Jews (Sephardic) by the name of Ostrovsky. [18]

Smarting under the failure sustained at the Baku Congress of 1920, which was primarily a gathering of Soviet Muslims and those of the Middle East, the Comintern a year later turned to the Far East. During the third congress of the Communist International (June-July, 1921) the decision was reached to hold a Congress of the Toilers of the Far East. Whereas the invitation to Baku was issued by the Third International and signed, for the most part, by its European members, the summons to the Far Eastern congress was issued by the Asians themselves. [19] Its preliminary sessions were held in Irkutsk in November, but the congress proper took place from January 21-27, 1922, in Moscow and Petrograd. As at Baku, Zinoviev on January 23, delivered the keynote address to the

assembled delegates, this time tactfully admitting Comintern
ignorance of the Orient. Since this congress coincided with the
Washington Conference (1921-22), from which the Soviets were excluded, the latter became the main object of attack. Whereas at
Baku the main target was England, in Moscow it was the United
States. Either because the Comintern had learned its lesson at Baku, or because religion did not occupy the same place among the
peoples of the Far East as it did among the Muslims, Zinoviev and
his cohorts did not mar the congress by virulent antireligious propaganda.

Thirty-five years after Baku, the next congress of the peoples of
the East--the Asian-African Conference in Bandung, Indonesia, in
April, 1955--was held without benefit of the Communist International or the Western democracies. The delegates of the twenty-
nine independent nations were in striking contrast to those of the
motley assembly of colonial, semicolonial, and strife-torn countries represented at Baku in 1920. Although much water had run
under the bridge between Baku and Bandung, some major issues
remained the same, namely, colonialism and religion. It is significant that the Bandung delegates, like those at Baku, were unanimous in their opposition to colonialism. In the Muslim environ-
ment of Indonesia, however, there was no attack on religion, only
an appeal for tolerance. On the contrary, the numerous references
to religion in the plenary sessions by President Sukarno of Indonesia, Sir John Kotelwala, prime minister of Ceylon, and others,
indicate that the Bandung assembly was fully conscious of the significance of religion in the Orient. Even the premier of Red China,
Chou En-lai, whose delegation included a pious Imam representative of the millions of Chinese Muslims, expressed the hope that
"those with religious beliefs will respect those without," and announced that the days of instigating religious strife should have
passed. [20] In this connection, it should be noted that in 1956 when
President Sukarno of Indonesia visited the Soviet Union, he openly affirmed in his speech to the Uzbeks of Central Asia that one
of the five principles on which the Indonesian state was founded
was "belief in God and respect for all religions" (*Pravda-Izvestia,*
September 6, 1956).

In the light of the treatment of the religious issue at Bandung,
we can better appreciate Zinoviev's fatal mistake at Baku, which
sounded the deathknell to the schemes of the Third International in
the East. It was perhaps symbolic that the Baku Congress closed
with a funeral ceremony. [21] Although the delegates intended to
make it an annual event, actually it had no successor. Due in part

to the blunders at Baku and to the course of subsequent events, this was the first and last Congress of the Peoples of the Middle East to be held under the auspices of the Third International.

4. The Soviet-Turkish Rapprochement, 1917-25

Now the Turkish Revolution is returning the Dardanelles to the Turkish toiling masses and through them to the world proletariat, which includes also the Russian. Thus, what Russian imperialism failed to realize by virtue of centuries of intrigue, now as a ripe plum will fall to the Russian working class.
--Yu. Steklov, "Turetskaya Revolyutsiya," *Izvestia*, April 23, 1919.

The Turkish Revolution, 1918-22, of which Mustapha Kemal Pasha (Atatürk) became the recognized leader, was a direct outgrowth of Turkey's military defeat in World War I, of foreign occupation by English, French, and Greek troops, and of the October Revolution in Russia. The October Revolution, accompanied by the Soviet decree on peace, publication of the Allied Secret Agreements, and Soviet abandonment of all Tsarist territorial claims on Turkey, opened up the prospect of an early end of the war and a peace without dismemberment for the hard-pressed Turks. The peace of Brest-Litovsk went even further, by providing for Turkish territorial acquisitions--the return of Kars, Ardahan, and Batum, seized by the Russians in 1878. Turkish armed forces proceeded to invade the Transcaucasus, took possession of Kars and Batum, and in September, 1918, overextended their lines of communication by the occupation of Baku. The sudden collapse of Germany caught them unprepared and left them face to face with disaster. By the truce signed by Turkey and England at Mudros on the island of Lemnos, on October 30, 1918, Allied forces occupied the Turkish forts at the Straits and their warships gained access to the Black Sea. The uncompromising terms exacted by England included the surrender of Turkish garrisons in Arabic

63

countries (Iraq, Syria, Hejaz, and Yemen), the evacuation of Turkish forces from Iran and Transcaucasia, the immediate demobi-
lization of the Turkish army, Allied control over Turkish communications, and the right of the Allies to occupy Batum, Baku,
or any part of Turkey deemed essential to Allied security. Although the Sultan and his government remained in Constantinople,
the spontaneous resistance of the Turks to the Allied occupation
soon assumed the proportions of a political and national revolution in Anatolia, of which Kemal Pasha became the leader in 1919.

When news of the Turkish Revolution reached the Soviet Union,
the Soviet government and the official Soviet press regarded it as
a counterpart and an elongation of the October (Bolshevik) Revolution. It was welcomed with enthusiasm by the editor of *Izvestia*
"as the first Soviet Revolution in Asia."[1] Of immediate importance to the hard-pressed Soviet government, then confronted by
civil war and foreign intervention, was the strategic position of
Turkey. Revolutionary Turkey was expected to protect the exposed
Russian flank in the Caucasus and to serve as a bulwark likewise
for revolutionary Hungary. Even more important, however, was
the fact that Soviet leaders appear to have sensed an opportunity
to make use of revolutionary Turkey, not only as an ally against the
Entente powers, but as the vanguard of Bolshevik Revolution in the
Muslim world, especially in the Near and Middle East. In the words
of Stalin at the tenth congress of the Russian Communist party, in
March, 1921, "Turkey, the most politically developed country
among the Muslim peoples, raised the banner of revolt and rallied
around itself the peoples of the East against imperialism."[2]

As previously indicated, in its "Appeal to the Muslims of the
East" on December 5, 1917, the Soviet government completely
abandoned all Russian claims to Turkish territory: "We declare
that the secret treaties of the dethroned Tsar regarding the seizure
of Constantinople, which was confirmed by the deposed Kerensky,
now are null and void. The Russian Republic and its government,
the Council of People's Commissars, are against the seizure of
foreign territories. Constantinople must remain in the hands of the
Muslims."[3] Although Soviet leaders reiterated this renunciation
time and again and even boasted about it, at least until 1947, there
is reason to believe that the Turkish Revolution of 1918-22 produced
a sudden "about-face" in their attitude. Of special interest to the
historian and diplomat is an article by Yu. Steklov on "The Turkish
Revolution," published in the official government newspaper *Izvestia* on April 23, 1919, which has been completely overlooked
in the evaluation of Soviet-Muslim relations:

The famous question of the Dardanelles now assumes a somewhat different color. Russian imperialism of the Tsarist and bourgeois period continually dreamed about these Dardanelles. German imperialism intended to seize these Dardanelles. But actually it was Anglo-French imperialism that took possession of them. And recently we learned that American imperialism is stretching out its greedy hand for them. Now the Turkish Revolution is returning the Dardanelles to the Turkish masses and through them to the world proletariat, which includes also the Russian. Thus, what Russian imperialism failed to realize by virtue of centuries of intrigue, now as a ripe plum will fall to the Russian working class.

There can be no better proof that the Soviet regime had never really abandoned the traditional Tsarist designs on Constantinople and the Straits. It merely expected to receive them on a platter instead of by conquest. Just two years earlier, in May, 1917, Bolshevik leaders had forced the resignation of Miliukov, minister of foreign affairs in the provisional government, because he refused to yield an inch on the matter of Russian claims to Constantinople under the secret treaties of the Entente powers. Due to Bolshevik pressure, the provisional government, following the removal of Miliukov, publicly called for a peace without indemnities and without annexations. Of course, the Soviet government expected to fall heir to Constantinople and the Straits, not as a result of the secret treaties of 1915-16, but because of a "Soviet" revolution in Turkey. Steklov nevertheless gloated over the prospect that the Soviet regime was about to win what Tsarist imperialism had long failed to accomplish. In the light of Soviet action in respect to its Muslim neighbors, especially from 1919 to 1921, it is clear that Steklov was not indulging merely in revolutionary clichés. Even as late as 1921, M. Pavlovitch, editor of *Novyi Vostok*, revealed Soviet designs on Turkey that were virtually the same as those of Steklov:

> Not until the entire Black Sea is in Soviet hands, and over Constantinople is raised the red Turkish banner or the banner of the Soviet Federation of the Black Sea States--the Ukraine, the Caucasus, Turkish Anatolia--will these states begin to lead a peaceful life and be able to devote themselves to creative and constructive work.[4]

Whether the Turks knew of or simply overlooked the public acknowledgment of Soviet designs in the Soviet press, it is difficult to say. They were undoubtedly aware of Communist propaganda in Turkey, the purpose of which was the ultimate overthrow of Kemal Pasha's regime. In spite of the efforts of the Sultan, the Germans, and later, allied censorship, news of the revolutionary upheaval in Russia had spread quickly throughout Turkey. As early as March, 1917, in Ushe, one of the remote villages of eastern Anatolia, the overthrow of Tsardom was celebrated.[5] In various parts of the country Turkish peasants, craftsmen, and even merchants welcomed the Revolution because it signified an early end to the war in which Turkey faced disaster. Following the October Revolution, Russian and Turkish troops fraternized on the Caucasian front. In the months after the military collapse of Turkey, peasant agrarian discontent was reflected in the mushrooming of local soviets in Anatolia.[6] The first steps in Soviet foreign policy, the "Appeal by the Council of Commissars to the Muslims of the East," the decree on Turkish Armenia, and the withdrawal of Russian troops from Persia created an impression among the hard-pressed Turks. Students at Istanbul University, to the horror of their professors, demanded that Lenin be awarded the Nobel Peace prize.[7]

Turkish prisoners of war returning from Russia following the Bolshevik seizure of power were already indoctrinated with the Communist virus, while those returning from Germany were influenced by Spartacist ideology. They helped to organize trade-unions in Istanbul. A leading Turkish Socialist, Mustapha Subhi, who had been interned in Russia during World War I, played a prominent role in the indoctrination of "thousands" of Turkish prisoners of war.[8] He edited a Turkish propaganda organ, *Yeni Dünya (The New World)*, first in Moscow and then in Baku, and took an active part in the Baku Congress before returning in November, 1920, to Turkey to organize Communist groups. These groups, together with some formed earlier (1918-19) in Anatolia and in Istanbul, led to the creation of the Turkish Communist party in 1920.[9] Weak as it undoubtedly was, even according to Soviet admission, it was instrumental in distributing quantities of Communist literature in the Turkish language, thereby promoting dissension at a critical period in the country's history. M. Sultan-Galiev, one of the top Muslims in the Soviet hierarchy, in an article on "The Political Parties in Turkey" (*Izvestia,* May 19, 1920), openly acknowledged Soviet responsibility for the activities of these Turkish Communists: "The Turkish Communists consist of a group of underground workers, former Turkish prisoners in Russia. This group is not particularly large, but works very intensively."

More recently a Soviet historian[10] has listed the type of literature that these Turkish prisoners from Russia distributed in Turkey. It included the biography of Lenin, the program of the Russian Communist party, the constitution of the R. S. F. S. R., the theses and address of Lenin on "Bourgeois Democracy and the

Dictatorship of the Proletariat, " delivered at the first congress of the Third International, Karl Marx's *The Communist Manifesto,* a pamphlet on *What Is the Soviet Power?,* and other works of Communist propaganda. During this critical period of the Turkish Revolution, according to Soviet sources, the Anatolian press regularly carried articles and general information about the Soviet republics, and the provincial sheets spoke of Lenin as "the pride of mankind" and "the sun and pride of all peoples. "

One particularly brazen example of Soviet interference in Turkish internal affairs was the direct appeal by the Soviet foreign minister, Chicherin, to the workers and peasants of Turkey on September 13, 1919. [11] Attacking the "ill-fated" Turkish Parliament as an assembly of "exploiting pashas, " he called upon Turkish workers and peasants to join with Russia in driving off "the European robbers, " to destroy the venal pashas and unprincipled and irresolute political parties, and to take the affairs of the country into their own hands. A very urgent and pressing letter from the director of public instruction in Erzerum on September 25, to his colleagues in Ankara, claimed that Chicherin's letter was causing trouble:

A very bad impression . . . has been produced and has moved the population to revolt and resist, from the fact that the notorious letter written by Tchitcherin has to a certain extent contributed to the failure of military operations; that the Army, under the pretence of an Armenian-Bolshevist alliance, has shown a certain lack of courage, whilst the Armenians, having been emboldened by this letter of Tchitcherin's, have tyrannized over the Mohammedan population, and that no success has been reached in coming to a satisfactory understanding with the Reds. . . . [12]

Much of the deep-rooted agrarian discontent, which in many parts of Turkey had resulted in spontaneous pro-Soviet demonstrations by the peasantry in 1919, found more organized expression, after the establishment of the Grand National Assembly in 1920, in the formation of the Green Army, which pledged its support to the Turkish Revolution. Kemal at first encouraged the Green Army, in spite of its heterogeneous membership, which represented all shades of Turkish opinion from communism to Pan-Islamism, and made effective use of it in the struggle for Turkish independence. The Marxist leaders active in its midst, its manifest influence over the partisan detachments in the interior of Anatolia, and the growing insubordination and hostility of some of its officers toward the Nationalist leadership aroused great uneasiness among the Kemalists in the autumn of 1920. By this time there was more than one indication that the Green Army was taking advantage of the

Greek invasion, which had begun in May, 1919, to stab Kemal Pasha in the back. Kemal first tried to infiltrate its ranks with his own trusted supporters. On the eve of Turkish military action against Armenia, Kemal attempted unsuccessfully to liquidate the Green Army. Its final defeat by the Kemalists on January 10, 1921, was, according to Soviet sources, regarded as equivalent to the defeat of the Greeks in Inönü on the same date. Indeed, the Green Army partisans at times proved more troublesome to the Kemalists than the Greeks and required the diversion of more Nationalist troops to hold them in check. The Soviets preferred to account for the defeat of the Green Army by asserting that it lacked proletarian leadership.

No doubt the Turkish government was forced to put up with Soviet subversive propaganda, for the time being, even when it was explicitly and openly acknowledged in the Soviet press, or when Soviet leaders like Chicherin blatantly interfered in the domestic affairs of the country to promote a Soviet revolution. Confronted by foreign occupation and the prospect of the dismemberment of their country by the Entente victors, the Turks may have regarded Communist infiltration as the lesser evil, to be dealt with under more favorable circumstances. In retrospect we may safely say that during the Turkish Revolution and for some time thereafter, the character of Turkish relations with the Soviet government was contingent upon the policy of the Entente toward Turkey. In other words, whenever the Turks were hard-pressed by the Entente and threatened with dismemberment of their country, they turned inevitably, even though reluctantly, to the Soviet Union for support. On the other hand, in proportion as the Entente powers eased their pressure and displayed a willingness to compromise, the Soviet-Turkish rapprochement cooled off appreciably.

In order to suppress the Turkish Revolution, English troops occupied Constantinople in force on March 16, 1920. [13] Cutting himself aloof from the Ottoman government in Constantinople, Kemal Pasha called for the election of a Turkish Grand National Assembly, which held its opening session in Ankara on April 23, 1920. Henceforth, to all intents and purposes, there existed two Turkish governments, that of the Sultan in Constantinople, and that of Kemal Pasha at Ankara. According to the Turkish leader, "the first decision arrived at by the Grand National Assembly of Turkey was to send an Embassy to Moscow. "[14] On April 26, Kemal Pasha hastily dispatched a note to Lenin asking for the establishment of diplomatic relations and appealing for Soviet aid to revolutionary Turkey in its struggle against imperialism. [15] Headed

by Bekir Sami Bey, Turkish minister of foreign affairs, and including Yussuf Kemal Bey, minister of economy, as well as Fouad-
Sabit, a Turkish Communist, the delegation left Ankara on May
11, 1920, with the object of establishing diplomatic relations between Soviet Russia and Turkey. Judging by the caliber of the delegation, the Kemalist regime felt the need of Soviet support. On
May 9, the reading of the Soviet "Appeal to All the Muslim Toilers
of Russia and the East" (December 5, 1917) before the Turkish
National Assembly produced a demonstration in favor of Soviet
Russia. [16] Shortly thereafter the first unofficial Soviet representative, a Bashkir by the name of Manatov, reached Ankara. Clearly
the Entente powers, with their disclosure in May of the Allied peace
terms for Turkey, had the Turkish Nationalists with their backs
to the wall. In June the Greeks launched a major general offensive
against the Turks, which increased the danger of their predicament.

Within two weeks of the public acknowledgment in *Izvestia* (May
19, 1920) of Soviet fifth-column activities in Turkey, Chicherin
boldly replied to Kemal Pasha:

> The Soviet government takes cognizance of the decision of the Grand
> National Assembly to coordinate our activities and your military opera-
> tions against the imperialist governments, with lofty ideals as to the
> liberation of oppressed peoples. . . . In order to establish friendly re-
> lations and a durable friendship between Turkey and Russia, the Soviet
> government proposes the immediate establishment of diplomatic and
> consular relations. . . . It is following with the liveliest interest the
> heroic struggle which the Turkish people are waging for their inde-
> pendence, and in these difficult days for Turkey, it is happy to lay a
> sound foundation of friendship, which should unite the Turkish and Rus-
> sian peoples.

The actual date of the establishment of diplomatic relations between the R. S. F. S. R. and Kemalist Turkey is not entirely clear,
but June 2, 1920, the date of Chicherin's reply to Kemal Pasha,
is the date recorded in the Soviet *Diplomatitcheskii Slovar (Diplomatic Dictionary)*. [18]

Uniting the Turkish and Russian peoples was easier said than
done. Once diplomatic relations were established, neither the Turks
nor the Russians appeared to be in a hurry to cast their lot with
one another by concluding an alliance. Negotiations were begun following the arrival of a Turkish diplomatic mission in Moscow on
July 11. According to Kemal Pasha, "Although certain essential
points in the Treaty that Russia wanted to make with our Government had been agreed to on the 24th of August, the actual signature
to the Treaty was postponed on account of certain details about

The three that made the Turkish Republic--Rauf Orbay,
Mustafa Kemal Atatürk, and General Ali Fuat Cebesoy

which no agreement had been arrived at, concerning some matters
that affected the situation."[19] On June 2, Chicherin had suggested
Soviet mediation in regard to the settlement of Turkish-Armenian
and Turkish-Persian border problems--a recommendation that Kemal appears to have accepted in principle in his reply of June 20.
It seems hardly likely that Zinoviev's attack on Turkey at the Baku
Congress in September was conducive to the settlement of existing causes for disagreement. In any event, the active resumption
of negotiations did not occur until the final defeat of General Wrangel's armies, culminating in the Soviet occupation of the Crimea
by November 15, 1920. In December, with the sovietization of Armenia, the Russians, for the first time since the Civil War, had
a common frontier with the Turks.

General Ali Fuat Cebesoy and Rauf Orbay, who took active parts
in the conduct of Turkish negotiations with Soviet Russia and England respectively, attributed the Soviet-Turkish deadlock in the
summer of 1920 to two factors: (1) Soviet reluctance to disrupt the
early stages of Anglo-Soviet negotiations by making a deal with the
Turks; (2) Soviet insistence on self-determination for the eastern
cities of Anatolia, to which the Turks would not agree. The Soviets, according to Cebesoy and Orbay, took the initiative to break
the deadlock by asking for the appointment of an important Turkish
representative to resume negotiations. General Cebesoy, the num-

ber two man in the government of Kemal Pasha, was selected and left Ankara in November, 1920. Due to the disruption of communications resulting from the Civil War in Russia, he did not reach Moscow until February 27, 1921.

It was Turkish reaction to the Treaty of Sèvres (August 10, 1920) that induced the Kemalist government to turn once again to Soviet Russia. This treaty provided for the dismemberment of the Ottoman Empire. In this respect, it was comparable to the Treaty of Brest-Litovsk (March 3, 1918), imposed on the Russians by the Central Powers. Ironically enough, the Allies sought to accomplish in regard to Turkey what the Central Powers did to Russia, and what Tsarist Russia had long dreamed of accomplishing in Turkey.

In brief, the Treaty of Sèvres deprived Turkey of all her Arab possessions--Hejaz, Syria, Palestine, and Mesopotamia. Western Thrace, eastern Thrace as far as the Chatalja line, Imbros, Tenedos, and a number of other Aegean Islands were ceded to Greece. On the coast of Asia Minor, Smyrna was placed under Greek jurisdiction with a plebiscite scheduled to take place after five years. Italy was assigned the Dodecanese Islands, including Rhodes. Turkey was forced to recognize the independence of Armenia, the Armenian-Turkish boundary to be settled by arbitration by President Woodrow Wilson. Turkey lost Kurdistan east of the Euphrates, whose fate was to be decided by England, France, and Italy. The Straits, assigned by the secret treaties of 1915-16 to Russia, were to be internationalized, with Constantinople remaining in Turkish hands. In addition to the drastic territorial settlement, Turkish military power and Turkish finances were to be subject to Allied control, the capitulations were to be maintained, and Turkey undertook to observe certain rules and regulations toward her national and religious minorities. By a separate agreement, Britain, France, and Italy divided the lost Turkish territory into spheres of influence for themselves.

Kemal Pasha's proclamation to the people of Anatolia in protest against the Treaty of Sèvres showed clearly enough that in these desperate circumstances, he was willing to accept aid from any source, including Communists:

> Brethren in Islam, Communist Comrades! A horrible injustice is about to occur. The Great Powers are strangling the new Muslim victim, which is on the brink of destruction. But we will die with weapons in our hands, defending the territory of our fatherland, for which we made bold to claim our rights. Our peasants will defend their land, their hearths, and their villages against the ravishers, and they can

die assured that the day is near when all Islam, having united with communism, will avenge them. [20]

The Turkish newspaper, *Istikbal* (September 1, 1920), openly discussed the feasibility of a Soviet-Turkish alliance:

> The most vital question of the day is the alliance between revolutionary Russia and Turkey, which strives for independence. . . . But it must be said that in the past we could never have thought of a rapprochement with Russia, for the distinguishing feature of the Russian Tsarist government was its antipopular character and its determination to destroy Turkey. . . . After the overthrow of Tsardom, truth triumphed and a Russo-Turkish rapprochement has become a reality. The Turks, like the Russians, understood the benefit to be derived from a rapprochement of the two peoples.
>
> Events have helped even more to bring us closer. If the Allies had not forced the Turks to take up arms to defend their independence, a Russo-Turkish rapprochement would not have developed so rapidly. The Russo-Turkish rapprochement came into being as a result of the threat to both states. [21]

It stands to reason that after the Treaty of Sèvres the Turks had nothing to lose, and possibly much to gain, by turning to Soviet Russia, which was successfully combating domestic opposition and foreign intervention by the same Entente powers that Turkey confronted. Undoubtedly the final Soviet defeat of the White armies, backed by the Entente powers, in November, 1920, encouraged further resistance on the part of the Turkish Nationalists to the Entente-dictated Treaty of Sèvres. Belatedly, on November 29, 1920, Kemal Pasha dispatched the following telegram to Chicherin, the tone of which appears to indicate the high watermark of the Turkish-Soviet rapprochement:

> I have the honor to acknowledge receipt of your letter of July 2 [June 2 ?], 1920 . . . and to express to you my sincerest gratitude for your flattering appreciation of the struggle which we are waging against the coalition of Western imperialists.
>
> It affords me great pleasure to inform you of the admiration felt by the Turkish people for the Russian people, who, not content with breaking their own chains, for more than two years have been waging an unequal struggle for the liberation of the entire world, and with enthusiasm enduring unheard of sufferings in order that persecution shall perish forever from the earth.
>
> Our nation fully appreciates the great sacrifices the Russian nation has undergone for the sake of the salvation of mankind, inasmuch as it has, itself, for centuries struggled to defend Muslim countries which are the object of the lust of the European imperialists. I am deeply

convinced, and my conviction is shared by all my compatriots, that on that day when the workers of the West, on the one hand, and the subjugated peoples of Asia and Africa on the other, understand that at the present time international capitalism makes use of them for mutual destruction and enslavement for greater profit for their masters, and on that day when consciousness of the criminality of colonial policy penetrates the hearts of the toiling masses of the world--then the power of the bourgeoisie will come tc an end.

The high moral authority of the government of the R.S.F.S.R. among the workers of Europe, and the love of the Muslim world toward the Turkish people, afford us assurance that our close alliance will suffice to unite against the Western imperialists all those who have heretofore supported their power submissively due to patience and ignorance. [22]

Under the pressure of the Treaty of Sèvres, judging by the content of the above telegram, it appeared that Kemal Pasha spoke one language to the Turkish masses about the retention of the caliphate, whereas he wrote to Chicherin as if he were a comrade in revolution. He clearly wished at this moment to pick up the threads of Soviet-Turkish negotiations as of June 2, 1920, before they had bogged down and ended in deadlock in August. If the Soviet government and the Comintern had not interfered in Turkish internal affairs by spreading subversive Communist propaganda, there might have been effected at this time a Soviet-Turkish alliance, which would have been the equivalent of an alliance between the Soviet Union and the Muslim world. Fortunately this did not occur. The Turks stood in dire need of Soviet assistance to defy the Treaty of Sèvres and preserve Turkish independence. They made use of the Soviets until they were able to wring concessions from the Western Allies at the Lausanne Conference of 1923.

In spite of the exchange of friendly sentiments by Soviet and Turkish leaders, there existed deep distrust between them. As indicated above, only their common predicament brought them together. On the very day following the receipt of Kemal Pasha's telegram of November 29, Stalin expressed his suspicion of a possible shift in Turkish policy[23] in the direction of the Entente.

"Kemal and his government," according to N. Rubinstein, "pursued a two-faced policy in regard to the Soviet Union. They were generous in their assurances of utmost goodwill." While Kemal talked goodwill in the telegram, "the Kemalist government was reconnoitering the ground for treacherous schemes with the imperialists, the USA, England, and France, seized Armenian ter-

ritory, and stalled in regard to signing the treaty" (that of March
16, 1921, which was initialed in Moscow, August 24, 1920).[24]

Although Soviet historians are quick to condemn Kemal Pasha
as a hypocrite,[25] they neglect to mention that the Soviet government with one hand extended military aid to Turkey and with the
other doublecrossed the Turkish government by efforts to organize
the Turkish Communist movement, with the object of overthrowing
the Kemalist regime. Neither country trusted the other, although
circumstances forced them to collaborate on the international scene.
Barely two months after his appeal to Chicherin, Kemal Pasha took
steps to rid himself of the Communist menace at home by seizing
the notorious Subhi and sixteen members of his Communist cohort
at Erzerum. They were cast into the Black Sea off Trebizond in
January, 1921, as a warning of the fate that awaited others of their
persuasion. Chicherin's inquiries merely produced word that the
Communists had possibly met with an accident at sea.[26] Not even
this incident produced a breach between Turkey and Soviet Russia,
when it was manifestly in the interests of both countries to reach
an agreement.

At the close of 1920 and early in 1921 there was sharp disagreement between the Kemalist and Soviet regimes over Soviet-Turkish
territorial boundaries. When Soviet military success in Georgia led
to the establishment of the Georgian S. S. R. on February 21, 1921,
the Kemalist government demanded the cession of the districts of
Artvin and Ardahan and proceeded to occupy Batum (February 28).
The Entente powers, already seeking a *modus vivendi* with the
Turkish Nationalists, looked optimistically for another deadlock
in Soviet-Turkish negotiations, or even for open conflict between
the two adversaries.

The London Conference of the Entente powers with Turkey and
Greece was in session from February 23 to March 12, with the object of reaching a settlement in the Near East. The representation
there of Kemalist Turkey, as well as the "legitimate" Turkish
government in Constantinople, amounted to a *de facto* recognition
of the former. Although the head of the Nationalist delegation,
Bekir Sami Bey, sought to obtain better terms by pledging that
Turkey would join the anti-Soviet front, the Entente powers were
not yet prepared to scrap the Treaty of Sèvres and the conference
ended in stalemate. Bekir Sami Bey's proposals were disavowed
by Kemal Pasha, and the Turkish foreign minister was forced to
resign. According to Kemal Pasha, Turkey could not enter into
confidential relations with countries that had not abandoned the
Sèvres Treaty: "The Sèvres Treaty is such a death sentence for the

Turkish nation that we demand its very name shall not be mentioned by anybody who calls himself our friend. "[27]

Once again when the Turkish Nationalists had to choose between the Sèvres Treaty and a Soviet "alliance," they chose what was regarded as the lesser evil. It was in the midst of Turkish efforts to reach an understanding with the Entente powers in London and the Soviet-Turkish dispute over the boundaries of Armenia and Georgia that the negotiations of the Kemalist government with Soviet Russia were resumed. On February 18, 1921, a Turkish delegation headed by Yussuf Kemal Bey arrived in Moscow. Opening the Moscow conference on February 26, Chicherin emphasized the Soviet role in the Turkish struggle against foreign intervention:

If for the past six months the Turkish situation has changed radically, along with the heroism evinced by the Turkish workers and peasants against the foreign invaders, a considerable part of the credit should be given to the friendly relations existing between Russia and Turkey, which strengthened the position of the latter. These friendly ties must be reinforced by a formal treaty. [28]

Under the direct supervision of Lenin and Stalin, [29] the negotiations progressed to a successful completion. Yussuf Kemal Bey as early as March 1 indicated that the goal was in sight: "Turkey has chosen the right road. All her circumstances point to the road leading to Russia! . . . Before us are two peoples, who do not wish to submit to capitalist domination. These two forces must act together. . . . The Sèvres Treaty leaves nothing to Turkey and she cannot accept it. "[30]

On March 16, 1921, Turkey and the R. S. F. S. R. , recognizing that they shared certain principles of "the brotherhood of nations and national self-determination, taking note of their solidarity in the struggle against imperialism, as well as of the fact that any difficulty created for one of the two nations worsens the position of the other," finally signed a "treaty of friendship and fraternity. "[31] This treaty established a boundary settlement between the two countries, by which Kars, Ardahan, and Artvin were ceded to Turkey and Batum was restored to Russia (Georgian S. S. R.). It included a pledge by each contracting party against interference in the internal affairs of the other (Article VIII). Taking cognizance of "the points in common between the movement of the Eastern peoples for national emancipation and the struggle of the workers of Russia for a new social order," Turkey and Russia agreed to recognize "the right of these peoples to freedom and independence" and to a government of their own choosing (Article IV). The troublesome Straits Question was to be settled by a conference of the Black

Sea powers, with the proviso that there should be no infringement of Turkish sovereignty and that Constantinople should remain in Turkish hands. In brief, the Moscow Treaty normalized relations between Turkey and the R.S.F.S.R., although contrary to opinion in some quarters, it contained no pledge of joint action against the Entente powers. [32] The Soviet government undertook to take steps toward the conclusion of similar treaties between Turkey and the Transcaucasian Soviet Republics (Armenia, Azerbaijan, and Georgia), which was carried out on October 13, 1921. On January 2, 1922, during M. V. Frunze's mission to Ankara, the Ukrainian S.S.R. likewise entered into treaty arrangements with Turkey. [33]

In spite of their criticism of the Kemalist government, Soviet leaders recognized that this treaty strengthened the international position of the Soviet government. From the Soviet point of view, this treaty, together with similar treaties concluded with Persia and Afghanistan in the same year, was greatly instrumental in strengthening the cause of peace, served to encourage the national liberation movement in the Near and Middle East (Article IV), "paralyzed" the Allied intervention in Transcaucasia, and in general weakened the position of the Allied camp. Even when Soviet leaders suspected that the Turks were using the R.S.F.S.R. in order to make better terms with the Entente, they justified the military aid extended to Turkey on the ground that the Turks were fighting Soviet battles and that Turkish defeat of the Greeks spread dissension among the Allies. These were the two factors which, in their estimation, brought about a rapprochement between Turkey and the R. S.F.S.R., and led to the treaty of March 16, 1921. [34]

The Moscow Treaty likewise strengthened the Turkish position vis-à-vis Greece and the Entente powers, thereby making it possible for the Turks to make a better deal with England and France at Lausanne. A Soviet authority in this field, A. F. Miller, assesses the significance of the treaty as follows:

> The Moscow Treaty was a decisive factor in strengthening the international position of the new Turkey. Relying on this treaty, which signified *de jure* recognition of the government of the Grand National Assembly, the Kemalists acquired greater international prestige than heretofore. From a practical point of view, the Moscow Treaty enabled the Turks to count on the increase of that aid which, after the victory of the Soviet regime over the interventionists and White Guards, could now be extended in ever-growing quantities. [35]

Soviet sources on the Turkish Revolution invariably emphasize the role of Soviet "material" as well as "moral" aid in the Turkish struggle for independence. The nature and amount of that ma-

terial aid is largely veiled in obscurity. Donald E. Webster[36] as-
serts that the Reds were in no position to furnish aid to the Turks,
even after the defeat of the White armies. Louis Fischer, who
had the advantage of personal contact with Soviet leaders in this
period, especially with Chicherin and the Soviet Foreign Office,
has cast a little light on an obscure subject. L. Karakhan, deputy
commissar of foreign affairs, told Fischer in person that following
the Treaty of Sèvres, when Kemal organized a regular army in
Anatolia against the Greek invaders, Soviet Russia "helped Kemal
with much cannon, money, arms, and military advice."[37] Later,
in December, 1921, when Mikhail Frunze, commander-in-chief of
Soviet forces in the Ukraine, visited Ankara to negotiate a treaty
between the Ukraine and Turkey, he arranged for "heavy shipments
of Russian munitions and for the mapping out of a detailed campaign
against the Greeks in which, if need be, Red officers would participate." During the course of his journey, Frunze located in Trebizond large quantities of Russian matériel, including equipment,
wagons, telephones, steamships, rails, and locomotives abandoned
by Russian troops during their retreat and desertion following the
outbreak of the Revolution. Experts of the Denikin army estimated
the value of the equipment at seventy million rubles. Although this
territory was under Turkish jurisdiction from February, 1918, to
March, 1919, there appears to be no record of Turkish utilization
of the equipment, much of which was useless by the time Frunze
passed through Trebizond in the winter of 1921.[38] After Frunze's
departure Aralov, the new Soviet envoy to Turkey, joined Kemal
Pasha on the Turkish front, addressed the Turkish troops, and
distributed "thousands of comfort bags" among them as a propaganda gesture.

As late as 1922, according to Fischer, there was a divergence
of opinion among Soviet leaders as to the advisability of providing aid for Turkey--Lenin and Trotsky were in favor of such action, whereas Stalin, Ordjonikidze, and other Georgian and Caucasian leaders, with Batum in mind, were reluctant to build up
Turkish military power.[39] The proponents of aid emerged victorious, and the Turkish Nationalists appear to have received military
equipment captured by the Red armies from the White forces under
Yudenich, Denikin, Kolchak, etc., although there was until recently no precise indication as to the actual extent of this military
aid. In his report to the Grand National Assembly, Kemal Pasha
himself was very reticent in regard to Soviet-Turkish relations in
general, devoted only one sentence to the fact that the Moscow

Treaty had been concluded, and made no comment whatsoever in regard to Soviet military assistance.

Fortunately, General Ali Fuat Cebesoy, commander of the western forces of the Turkish revolutionaries in Anatolia, and first ambassador of the Turkish Republic in Soviet Russia, was in possession of specific data on Soviet aid to revolutionary Turkey that is unavailable from other sources. In an interview in the summer of 1958 in Istanbul, the General declared that Soviet Russia provided the beleaguered Turks with substantial aid, as follows: ten million gold rubles, thirty thousand Russian rifles with one thousand rounds of ammunition for each rifle, thirty thousand bayonets, from two hundred and fifty to three hundred machine guns with ten thousand cartridges for each gun, some cavalry swords, from twenty to twenty-five mountain cannon, and a large number of hand grenades. Altogether, according to the General, the Soviets supplied enough arms to equip three Turkish divisions. Among other things, the Soviet government deposited in Berlin one million Russian rubles to the credit of the Turks, who were thereby enabled to secure replacements for German weapons obtained before and during the first World War. In 1916, when the Germans took large numbers of Russian prisoners on the Eastern front, they provided their Turkish allies with from fifty to sixty thousand weapons seized from these prisoners. Kemal Pasha's forces later obtained from Soviet Russia the necessary replacements for these Russian weapons. General Cebesoy and Rauf Orbay, the first prime minister of the Turkish Republic, agreed that Soviet aid helped the Turkish revolutionaries both materially and psychologically, but that it was not available in sufficient quantities to prove decisive. Tsarist arms abandoned by the retreating White armies, according to them, went to the Sultan's forces, and were of no use to Kemal Pasha.

Although, on the one hand, the Soviets appear to have rendered moral and material aid to the Turkish Nationalists, on the other hand, they disseminated Communist propaganda hostile to the Kemalist regime and organized Communist detachments, or partisans led by Communist sympathizers, to harass the Turkish armed forces. At one moment, the Kemalists feared the dismemberment of Turkey by Greece and the Entente powers, and the next moment they faced being stabbed in the back by pro-Soviet partisans. This is somewhat reminiscent of the position of the Soviet regime during and after the Revolution, when it confronted foreign intervention and civil war at one and the same time. Both countries faced foreign intervention, in part from the same sources.

The domestic opposition to the Soviets was directed toward the restoration of the Tsarist regime or the establishment of a constitutional government, whereas Kemal faced the possibility of being superseded by the Communists and their sympathizers. According to Soviet sources, the Kemalist government at times had to use more soldiers against the partisans than against the Greek invader. [40] It is not surprising that, as soon as he was able to check the Greek advance, Kemal Pasha set about in earnest to remove the Communist menace. The ban on the Turkish Communists, which had been temporarily lifted from March to October, 1922, while Kemal Pasha was conducting a major campaign against the Greeks, was renewed once the Turks had driven the Greeks into the sea, and no longer stood in dire need of Soviet aid.

Renewed persecution of the Turkish Communists was music to Entente ears, and the Soviet press suspected that this was the real motive behind it. According to *Izvestia* [41] (November 14, 1922), "The Kemalist government tries, by persecuting Communists, to earn the good will of the imperialist powers." This was in accord with the similar procedure of the Ankara government prior to the London Conference of February-March, 1921.

As the Soviets assessed the situation, the Turks in recent years had considerably strengthened their position on the home front by the development of strong Turkish upper and middle classes, replacing tne minorities (Greeks, Armenians, etc.), and thereby making it possible for them to present a united front in matters of diplomacy. A former diplomat, writing in *Izvestia,* explained the situation for the benefit of the Soviet public:

> In Turkey profound changes have taken place. In Turkey a native middle class has been born, full of energy and enterprise, one which wishes to remove from its path the old middle class of the Turkish cities, which was of foreign origin and of a different faith. . . . The Turk in former times took no part in the productive work of the middle class. This he delegated to the Greeks, Armenians, or to Westerners who were protected by extraterritoriality. [42]

As a result, the Soviets recognized the weakness of the Communist party in Turkey and urged it to follow the leadership of the Turkish middle class in support of the nationalist movement. Even during the summer of 1922, G. Astakhov, in an article on "Shifts in the Ankara Mejlis and their Meaning," revealed the futility of relying on the Turkish Communists: "Only now does the Communist party of Turkey begin to revive. It has in Ankara its own committee and publishes a daily, *Eni Heyat [New Life].* . . . In any event, we cannot think of seizing power, nor is there any chance for the Communists to exercise any serious influence over the regime. "[43] Even the Turkish Communists admitted that the greatest deterrent to the spread of communism in Turkey was religion, and that it would be a long time before much headway could be made. In other words, Islam was the real bulwark against communism in Turkey. This was explained by M. Pavlovitch, one of the leading Soviet authorities on the peoples of the East, as early as 1921: "The Turkish people, due to historical reasons of adherence to religion, cannot at this moment entirely accept the Communist program: it will require a long and stubborn struggle to push them in that direction. "[44]

The fourth congress of the Comintern, meeting in Moscow from November 5 to December 5, 1922, although unanimous in its denunciation of the persecution of the Turkish Communists, after much discussion decided in favor of continued support for the time being, of Kemalist Turkey in her struggle for national independence. Turkey was still "the outpost of the revolutionary East, " and the Kremlin dream of using the Turks as the vanguard of Soviet revolution in that part of the world had not entirely faded.

It is perhaps worth noting that the Turkish reforms of Kemal Pasha have many counterparts in Russian history, both under the Tsarist and Soviet regimes. In Turkey, such reforms as the adoption of the Latin script even for the Koran, the abolition of the caliphate, the transfer of the capital to Ankara, the secularization of the state, and the emancipation of Turkish women were achieved, relatively speaking, by peaceful means. Comparable changes in Russia, both under the old and new regimes, have been accompanied by violence, revolt, and concentration camps. Whether this was due to the Turkish temperament, or to other factors, it is difficult to say, but it undoubtedly served to preserve the independence of the Turkish Republic. It is highly improbable that such reforms could have been achieved peacefully in other Muslim countries.

Kemal Pasha, having outwitted the Communists in Turkey, was equally successful when he turned to the international arena. His victorious campaign against the Greeks in 1922 led the Entente powers, especially England, to retreat from their now manifestly untenable position based upon the Treaty of Sèvres and to come to terms with the Turkish Nationalists while Kemal Pasha could still serve as a bulwark against communism in the Near and Middle East. Following the armistice concluded at Mudania on October 11, the danger of outright conflict between the victorious Turks and the

English occupation forces was removed, and negotiations were instituted for the conclusion of peace at Lausanne.

Allied plans to bar Soviet Russia from the Lausanne Conference evoked such vigorous protests from Chicherin that provision was made on October 27 for Soviet participation in discussions relative to the Straits Convention.[45] At the Lausanne Conference in the winter of 1922-23, Chicherin appeared as a leading champion of Turkish interests, much to the annoyance of England's Lord Curzon, and even to the occasional embarrassment of the Turkish delegation under Ismet Pasha. The duel between Curzon and Chicherin was well matched. Soviet backing and Chicherin's advice undoubtedly strengthened the Turks, especially during the period of deadlock over the restoration of the capitulations. But the Turks unqualifiedly repudiated their Soviet ally on the matter of Turkish sovereignty over the Straits, which the Russians with the recent experience of the intervention in mind, insisted should be closed in peace and war to warships, armed vessels, and military aircraft of all countries except Turkey. The historic roles of Britain and Russia in regard to the Straits were thus reversed. Had Chicherin succeeded, the Soviet government would have been able to deal with the Turks alone in matters pertaining to the strategic passage through the Dardanelles and the Bosphorus, a situation very much to Soviet advantage. Confronted with this possibility, the Turks at Lausanne even appeared to welcome the prospect of Entente participation in the control of the Straits to offset Soviet naval strength in the Black Sea, although that strength was more potential than real at the time. England under Curzon's leadership was therefore successful in separating Turkey from Russia on this issue, although to do so required concessions to Turkey, especially in the matter of capitulations. The Straits Convention, concluded with the Treaty of Lausanne, July 24, 1923, was not ratified by the Soviet government.

Thus Turkey emerged from the Lausanne Conference independent of both the Soviet Union and the Allies. In making the necessary concessions to Turkey, no matter how great their reluctance, England and France proved farsighted. They took the wind from the Soviet sails. The Lausanne Conference helped Turkey to re-establish herself as a republic and as a non-Communist state. Since the outcome was most unfavorable to the Soviets, the Soviet press tried to divert attention from this situation by claiming that the Turks owed their victory to the very existence of the Soviet Union and to Soviet support. Chicherin himself, in an article on "The Lausanne Conference and the World Situation,"[46] pointed out that

the victorious struggle of the Turks had led at Lausanne to the capitulation of all the world powers before little Turkey, weakened
by twelve years of war. "The victory of Turkey, " Chicherin continued, "is our victory. . . . Why did the world powers make the
greatest concessions to little Turkey? Because they were afraid of
Soviet Russia. "

Yu. Steklov, the editor of *Izvestia,* in his summation of "The
Results of the Lausanne Conference, " for that official mouthpiece
of the Soviet government on July 13, 1923, followed a somewhat
similar line of thought and interpreted Lausanne as a victory, not
only for the Turks, but for all the peoples of the East: "If the Turkish peoples have succeeded . . . in defending their rights against
Entente imperialism, then they are indebted to the existence of the
Soviet Republic, and, although it was not present at the Lausanne
Conference . . . all the oppressed peoples of the East should know
this very well. The stronger Soviet Russia is, the more profitable
for them. "

Just as the Baku Congress of 1920, by attacking Islam and
preaching the Bolshevization of the Near and Middle East, alienated
the Muslim peoples from the Soviet regime, the Lausanne Conference of 1923 marked a decisive turning point in Soviet-Turkish
relations. By scrapping the Treaty of Sèvres at Lausanne, England
and France set Turkey free from impending bondage within the
Soviet orbit. Although they did not meet all Turkish demands, they
nevertheless removed the trap that Soviet diplomacy had carefully
set for the Kemalist regime. By so doing, they were likewise greatly instrumental in stemming the tide of militant communism of the
pre-NEP vintage in Iran, Afghanistan, and the Arab countries. The
blunders committed by the Third International at Baku, namely,
the attack on Islam and the use of subversive propaganda, were
repeated in Turkey. The loss of Turkey as the key Soviet agent for
the spread of revolution in the East signified the loss of Soviet
leadership in the Muslim world.

In 1925 the Mosul question and the Locarno Pact contributed to the
revival of the Soviet-Turkish rapprochement. After Lausanne, the
English and the Turks were at loggerheads over the disposition of
the oil-rich Mosul area, on which no settlement had been reached.
The problem was aggravated in February, 1925, by a revolt of the
Kurdish tribes in southeastern Anatolia under the leadership of
Sheikh Said of Palu, who protested the establishment of the Turkish Republic (April, 1924), demanded the restoration of the Shariat,
and land reforms. Although the revolt was ruthlessly suppressed
by the end of April, it was one factor that induced the Turks to

reach a settlement with England the following year (June, 1926). Meanwhile the Mosul dispute, which in 1924 was submitted to the League of Nations, on December 16, 1925, was settled in favor of Iraq, with the proviso that the British mandate over that country should continue for twenty-five years. The following day the Turkish foreign minister rushed to Paris to conclude a deal with the Soviet Union.

Although the Soviet government was repulsed by Turkish action at Lausanne and Turkish efforts for closer relations with the Western powers, it viewed with apprehension the signing in October, 1925, of the Locarno Pact, which, from the Soviet standpoint, constituted the formation of an anti-Soviet bloc and a possible prelude to the renewal of foreign intervention in Russia. Since both Turkey and the Soviet Union remained outside the League of Nations, it occasioned no surprise that once again they should make common cause in time of emergence. Thus on December 17, the Soviet and Turkish foreign ministers signed a treaty of friendship and non-aggression, which was tantamount to an alliance. By this treaty, Turkey and the Soviet Union agreed to remain neutral in the event that either was attacked by a third power, or by a combination of powers (Article I). Each undertook to enter into no alliance and to make no political agreement directed against the other contracting party (Article II). This treaty, concluded for ten years, was extended and supplemented on several occasions until, as we shall see, it was denounced by the Soviet Union on March 19, 1945, as an outgrowth of World War II. Its basic value for the Soviet Union consisted in the assurance it provided against aggression from the Straits in the event of war between Russia and the Western powers, and it ensured Turkish neutrality during the Soviet-German conflict of World War II. The Turks, for their part, derived immediate profit from the alliance, which greatly facilitated the settlement of their Mosul dispute with England in 1926.

5. Soviet Russia, Iran, and Afghanistan

I. IRAN

The Persian revolution may become the key to a general revolution in the East.
--K. Troyanovsky, *Vostok i Revolyutsiya* (Moscow, 1918), p. 47.

In the minds of the leaders of the October Revolution, Iran[1] ranked next to Turkey in importance. At times, because of its geographical location, Iran even took precedence over Turkey in Soviet strategy. In fact, prior to 1921, Turkey, Iran, and Afghanistan, because they were Muslim states and had a common frontier with Soviet Russia, and because all of them, for the time being, recognized England as a common enemy, were treated as a unit by Soviet diplomacy. The control of these three Muslim states was tantamount to the domination of the Near and Middle East and a threat to "colonialism" throughout Asia. Soviet leaders labored long and hard to create a chain of vassal states along the southern periphery of revolutionary Russia, both as a measure of defense against foreign intervention and as a prelude to the Bolshevization of India and the East.

Konstantin Troyanovsky's book *Vostok i Revolutsiya,* published as early as 1918, clearly revealed the handwriting on the wall as far as Iran was concerned. This "natural basin" was for him a primary objective of Soviet policy because it was the gateway to India, "the citadel of revolution in the East, " which only the Bolsheviks were in a position to open. According to Troyanovsky:

The Persian revolution may become the key to the revolution of the whole Orient, just as Egypt and the Suez Canal are the key to English

domination in the Orient. Persia is the "Suez Canal" of the revolution.
By shifting the political center of gravity of the revolution to Persia,
the entire strategic value of the Suez Canal is lost. . . . The political
conquest of Persia, thanks to its peculiar geopolitical situation and
significance for the liberation movement in the East, is what we must
accomplish first of all. This precious key to all other revolutions in
the Orient must be in our hands, come what may. Persia must be ours!
Persia must belong to the revolution![2]

With the exception of the revolution, there was nothing new in
the Soviet blueprint for Iran which had not been envisaged by Peter
the Great, General Kuropatkin, and other Russian imperialists of
the Tsarist era. For a time it appeared that Lord Curzon's night-
mare of Russian power established on the Persian Gulf might become reality under the Soviet regime.[3]

As far as Iran was concerned, the Soviet government inherited
from Tsarist Russia and the provisional government the following
situation: (1) the Anglo-Russian Treaty of 1907, which divided Iran
into British and Russian spheres of influence, with a neutral zone
between them; (2) the occupation during World War I of northwest
Iran by Russian military forces; (3) the extraterritorial rights and
other special privileges accorded Russian citizens by the Treaty of
Turkmanchai in 1828; (4) numerous Tsarist concessions in Iran; (5)
restrictions on Iranian sovereignty in matters pertaining to the
Caspian Sea.[4]

The Bolshevik "Appeal to All the Muslims of Russia and the East"
(December 5, 1917), as already indicated, condemned Tsarist imperialism in Iran and declared that "the treaty partitioning Persia
is null and void." It likewise promised that "as soon as military
operations cease, the armed forces will be withdrawn from Persia,
and the Persians will be guaranteed the right of free determination
of their own destiny." Shortly thereafter, Trotsky, Soviet commissar of foreign affairs, in a note of December 19 (December 6,
O.S.), to Assad Khan, Iranian *chargé d'affaires* in Petrograd, proposed immediate negotiations for the evacuation of imperial Russian troops from Iran, on condition that the Turks withdraw simultaneously.[5] This was in line with the armistice agreement between
the Central Powers and the Bolsheviks concluded at Brest-Litovsk
on December 15 (December 2, O.S.). The Treaty of Brest-Litovsk
later confirmed (Article VII) the "political and economic independence and the territorial integrity" of both Iran and Afghanistan.[6]

On January 4 (December 23, 1917, O.S.), 1918, Trotsky informed the Iranian government of the Soviet evacuation program,
which was to begin at once with the withdrawal of those Russian de-

tachments that served no military purpose, and of the Russian military mission training the Iranian Cossack brigade.[7] According to Trotsky, there should be no delay: "The greatest speed is necessary in this matter in order to wipe out as quickly as possible the effects of the acts of violence perpetrated by Tsarist and bourgeois Russian governments against the Persian people." Shortly thereafter, on January 14, 1918, Trotsky officially reassured the Iranian government of Soviet renunciation of the Anglo-Russian Convention of 1907, and of all other conventions infringing upon the independence of Iran.

Having actually begun the evacuation of Russian troops from Iran in December, 1917, the Soviet government completed the withdrawal in the summer of 1918. The "vacuum" created by the departure of Russian and Turkish troops was promptly filled by the English who, ostensibly to forestall the Turks in Transcaucasia, included all of Iran in the British sphere, moved in limited numbers of British and White Russian troops, and intervened from this vantage point in revolutionary Transcaucasia. In June, 1918, the English occupied Resht and Enzeli (Pahlevi) in the Caspian area, overthrew the local Soviets, and proceeded to occupy the oil center of Baku in advance of the approaching Turks.

The subsequent Anglo-Iranian Treaty of August 9, 1919, to all intents and purposes, transformed Iran into a British protectorate. According to this treaty, Great Britain obtained control over the key branches of the Iranian administration through the appointment of advisers to the Treasury, of officers to reorganize the army, of experts to revise the tariff, by assistance in the matter of railroad construction, and a loan of £2,000,000 sterling.

When the terms of this treaty became known, the Soviet government on August 30, 1919, appealed to the Iranian people over the head of the Iranian government of Vossuq-ed-Dowleh, by denouncing English policy and reaffirming Soviet renunciation of all Tsarist infractions on Iranian sovereignty. Chicherin, in what may have been a rehearsal for his "notorious" appeal to the Turkish people two weeks later, made every effort to arouse the country against the English, representing Soviet Russia as the sole support and only friend of the Iranian people:

> At this moment when the triumphant victor, the English robber, is trying to lasso the Persian people into total slavery, the Soviet workers' and peasants' government of the Russian Republic solemnly declares that it does not recognize the Anglo-Persian Treaty which carries out this enslavement. . . . [It] regards as a scrap of paper the shameful Anglo-Persian Treaty by which your rulers have sold themselves and

sold you to the English robbers, and will never recognize its legality. [8]

Chicherin promised that the hour was near when the "valiant revolutionary Red Army will march across Red Turkestan to the frontiers of a still enslaved Persia. "

The Anglo-Iranian Treaty was a "triumph" for the diplomacy of Lord Curzon, English foreign minister, who had long regarded Russian encroachment on Iran as a major threat to British possession of India. Sincere as he undoubtedly was, Curzon failed to understand what his biographer has taken pains to point out, that in 1919 the roles of Britain and Russia in regard to Iran were reversed. [9] The Iranians were not, as in the closing decades of the nineteenth century, looking to England for support against the Russian enemy. For a time, at least, the Bolshevik Revolution, accompanied by the complete renunciation of Russian interests in Iran and the withdrawal of Russian troops, left the English, as the sole occupants of the country, the major threat to Iranian independence.

In spite of English pressure for the speedy ratification of the Anglo-Persian Treaty, this Iranian version of the Treaty of Sèvres was never ratified by the Mejlis, due to widespread opposition from Iranian nationalists and effective Soviet propaganda. In protest against it the Iranians, like the Turks after the Treaty of Sèvres, turned to Soviet Russia for support against England and for a treaty based on "equality" of the signatories. With England in control of Iran and Soviet Russia isolated from Iran by White Russian forces and those of the intervention, treaty arrangements were not within the realm of possibility. There were many difficulties in the way of establishing official contacts, the misadventures of Ivan Osipovitch Kolomiitsev[10] being a case in point. Upon recommendation of the Soviet government that an official representative be dispatched to Teheran, Shaumyan, Soviet commissar extraordinary in the Caucasus, selected Kolomiitsev, who reached the Iranian capital on June 30, 1918. The Iranian government, allegedly under pressure from the English, refused to recognize the Soviet mission on the technical ground that Kolomiitsev had no documents signed in Moscow. In the summer of 1919, when Kolomiitsev, equipped with the appropriate documents, attempted to return to Teheran as the official Soviet representative, he was captured by White Russians and shot on the island of Ashurad. Widespread Communist activity in the northern provinces of Iran proved to be another obstacle toward the establishment of closer relations between Soviet Russia and Iran.

According to Soviet sources, under the impetus of the October

Revolution there came an upsurge in the national liberation movement in Iran. In northern Iran, especially at Resht and Enzeli
(Pahlevi), the Shah's governors were removed and local Soviets
were established by Russian soldiers who had gone over to the side
of the Revolution and by representatives of the local population.
In connection with the Iranian Revolution (1917-20), the importance
of Central Asiatic Russia, and especially of Baku, should not be
overlooked. At the second congress of the Comintern (July-August,
1920) Sultan-Zade, an Iranian delegate, maintained that the experiences of the Russian proletariat in Kirghizia and Turkestan
showed what could be accomplished where no industrial proletariat existed, and that the same could be accomplished in Iran, Egypt,
and India.[11]
        While there were undoubtedly many local factors contributing to
the unrest in northern Iran, such as agrarian problems, bureaucratic corruption, and hostility to foreign occupation, the strongest impact emanated from Baku in adjacent Azerbaijan. Baku was
a revolutionary school for workers, farm hands, and a miscella-
neous assortment of people who went there to work in the oil fields.
That is one reason why it was chosen by the Third International for
the first Congress of the Muslims of the East in September, 1920.
Iranian migrant workers, returning to Iran from Baku and Central
Asia, where they had witnessed or even taken part in revolutionary
activities, played an important role in the spread of Soviet ideas in
their homeland. These migrants were responsible for the organization of the first so-called Iranian Proletarian party, A'delyat (Justice), which in 1920 was transformed into the Communist party of
Iran. [12] The choice of the name "Justice" was psychologically as-
tute, since among the Muslims it was more powerful than any of
the customary revolutionary slogans. To the average Muslim, justice is an all-inclusive term which symbolizes the solution of all
problems, and it is a cardinal point in Islam.
        A'delyat was organized by Kafar-Zade in Baku immediately fol-
lowing the overthrow of the Romanov dynasty (February, 1917) and
quickly spread throughout Turkestan, the Caucasus, and into Iran.
Upon the initiative of the Turkestan Regional Committee, the first
A'delyat party congress was summoned at Enzeli on July 23, 1920,
at which time its name was changed to that of the Communist party
of Persia. The Enzeli Congress was attended by forty-eight delegates from Iran, Turkestan, and the Caucasus. As at the Baku
Congress several weeks later, the main target was England. Some
of the delegates who had worked in revolutionary circles from ten
to fifteen years expressed their preference, under existing cir-

cumstances, for the principles of the Russian Revolution of 1905 in the direction of constitutional government, instead of coming out for the doctrine of social transformation set forth by the October Revolution. They likewise called for the exploitation of the national movement in Persia.

Sultan-Zade, a prominent delegate from Turkestan, who later attended the Baku Congress, explained during the second session in Enzeli why the Persian Revolution should be modeled after the 1905 Revolution rather than after the Bolshevik pattern. According to him, the October Revolution drew its main support from the Russian peasantry, which constituted about 90 per cent of the population. In Iran, however, out of a population of fifteen million, only about half were peasants. In addition there were around three million nomads, three million merchants, and approximately one million belonging to the nobility and clergy. Iran, he felt, was not yet ripe for the Soviet structure.

The revolutionary movement in the Iranian province of Gilan, under the leadership of Kuchik Khan, was in many respects typical of the course of the revolution elsewhere in northern Iran. No doubt Lenin, at the second congress of the Comintern (July-August, 1920) had Gilan in mind when he confidently asserted: "At the present moment the flag of the Soviet is beginning to be raised throughout the Orient, in Asia" (*Petrogradskaya Pravda*, July 21, 1920). The leadership of the rebellion was essentially middle-class rather than proletarian, including tradesmen, small landed proprietors, and intellectuals. Because of this composition and in order to secure a united front, the Communist program subordinated local issues in order to concentrate on the one objective common to all--the expulsion of the English from Iran. Once having achieved a modicum of unity by driving out the English, the next step was to be an attack on the feudal landowners--another issue on which there was general agreement among the middle-class leaders. The third step in the program was to be the capture of Teheran, the capital, and the overthrow of the Shah's regime. This was, in a nutshell, the program outlined by the Third International for the revolution in the Near and Middle East. The real social revolution in Iran was to follow, and not to precede, these three prerequisites. However, under pressure from Ekhsanulla Khan, Pishevari, and other extremist elements among the followers of Kuchik Khan, including Russian advisers who held key positions in his government, the revolutionaries ignored this basic program, which was prepared with backward Near Eastern conditions in mind, and tried to achieve everything at once. In other words, they tried to effect in Gilan a

full-fledged Bolshevik program, with wholesale confiscation of
enterprises, prohibition of private trade in the bazaars, attacks on
the Muslim clergy and on Muslim social customs. There followed
a virtual reign of terror against the middle class. This terrorist
program broke the united front so painstakingly fostered among the
leaders and led to the rejection of all revolutionary leadership by
the more moderate and conservative elements, the most articulate
members of the population.

Although the Third International was working hard to justify the
Bolshevik regime in Russia, it was completely opposed to Bolshevik revolution in Iran at this stage. This was indicated at the
Baku Conference, where "the traitorous policy of the Iranian Left-
ists" was criticized. Thereafter the Central Committee of the
Communist party of Iran was reorganized under the leadership of
an Iranian member of the Baku Presidium, Haidar Khan Amouqli,
a friend of Stalin, who had spent many years in the Baku oil fields,
and who became one of the founders of the Communist party of Iran.
Since this change proved ineffective in winning the support of the
moderates in Gilan, another reorganization took place in March,
1921, upon the initiative of the Central Committee of the Communist
party in the city of Fumen. Ostensibly a reconciliation was effected
at this congress among Kuchik Khan, Ekhsanullah, and Haidar
Amouqli. A new government was formed, in which Kuchik Khan
became president of the Sovnarkom and commissar of finance,
Haidar Amouqli assumed control of foreign affairs, and Hali Kur-
ban became commissar of military affairs.

The main purpose of this reorganization was to appease the middle and upper classes, but it came too late. By this time Kuchik
Khan was convinced that the Third International wished to use him
only as a tool to effect the ultimate Bolshevization of Iran. Being a
patriot, although not of the stature of Kemal Pasha in Turkey, he
subordinated the welfare of the Party to the welfare of Iran. He definitely broke with his Bolshevik colleagues, foreign and native,
on September 29, 1921, when during a conference in Fumen, his
forces attacked and routed them, putting a number of Communist
leaders to death, including Haidar Amouqli. Kuchik Khan's detachments then destroyed the Communist regimes in Resht and
Enzeli. Obviously, he was determined to wipe out communism in
northern Iran. However, this interparty strife paved the way for
action on the part of the Shah's armies, which had no difficulty in
occupying the whole of Gilan. Kuchik Khan himself, instead of being
regarded as a hero, was put to death and his head presented to the
Shah. Essentially a supporter of the *via media*, Kuchik Khan in the

end was regarded as a traitor by both the Communists and the Iranian government. Needless to say, a note of caution should be sounded as to the use of Soviet sources on the career of Kuchik Khan. Many works appearing in English have largely accepted the Soviet estimate of this Iranian nationalist. In this connection, it is significant that Major-General L. C. Dunsterville, who led an English expedition through Gilan to Enzeli in 1918, recognized Kuchik Khan as "a high-minded enthusiast," whose main objective was "Persia for the Persians."[13]

Soviet action in regard to Gilan affords one more indication of how the Soviet government failed to live up to its promises of "friendship" and "noninterference" in the internal affairs of other countries. Although the predicament of Iran was such that a Soviet-Iranian alliance against England was well within the realm of possibility, once again, as in the case of Turkey, the Bolshevik menace became even greater than the threat from the English invader. In reply to Iranian protests over Soviet incursions at Enzeli and in Gilan, Moscow disclaimed all responsibility, asserting that the new republic of Azerbaijan, over which it had no control, had acted on its own authority. Today, however, the Soviets attribute their failure in Gilan, Khorassan, and south Azerbaijan to provocative and tactless leftist elements who took premature action in confiscating Iranian lands and attacking the Muslim religion.[14]

In the spring of 1920, several factors contributed to the renewal of Soviet and Iranian efforts to reach an understanding. After the restoration of Soviet authority in Baku at the end of April, Iranian merchants began to insist on the resumption of trade and diplomatic relations with Soviet Russia. The withdrawal of the British in May from Enzeli and Resht in advance of Soviet troops weakened British prestige and rendered even less likely the ratification of the Anglo-Iranian Treaty of 1919. The advance of Soviet Azerbaijan forces into Gilan and the subsequent proclamation of the Soviet Republic of Gilan on May 20, 1920, aroused apprehension in Iranian government circles, but it may have indicated the need for an understanding, especially in view of the fact that Iranian protests to Moscow and to the League of Nations produced no results.

On May 5, 1920, Vossuq-ed-Dowleh asked the Soviet government to establish normal diplomatic and trade relations and to conclude an "equal" treaty based upon the earlier Moscow proposals. He was even ready to recognize the Soviet Republic of Azerbaijan. However, according to Soviet sources, the Iranian government refused to guarantee the safety of Soviet representatives upon their arrival in Iran.[15] Not until the following October did the Iranian representative, Mushaver-ol-Mamalek, Iranian ambassador at Constantinople, arrive in Moscow to begin negotiations with the Russians.

Soviet-Iranian treaty negotiations, which began in November, 1920, were not completed until the advent of Reza Khan to power in February, 1921. Meanwhile, the special council summoned by the Shah to expedite ratification of the Anglo-Iranian Treaty met on December 13, 1920. The English, already forced by the Communists to withdraw from Enzeli on the Caspian Sea, now threatened to abandon northern Iran entirely, leaving the country open to Soviet occupation, unless the Anglo-Iranian Treaty was speedily ratified. In spite of English pressure, the council postponed a decision on the Anglo-Iranian Treaty pending the outcome of Soviet-Iranian negotiations in Moscow, which were then nearing a successful conclusion. On December 3, the council approved the draft of the basic terms of the Soviet-Iranian Treaty, with minor amendments. News spread that the Soviet government had abandoned the capitulations, the restoration of which was stipulated in the unpopular Anglo-Iranian Treaty. English efforts to offset the Soviet-Iranian negotiations, under these circumstances, proved unavailing.

The Soviet-Iranian Treaty was concluded in Moscow on February 26, 1921, as the first official act of the new government of Seyyid Zia ed-Din and Colonel Reza Khan, who had seized power by army *coup d'état* five days earlier. The new prime minister, Seyyid Zia, [16] had been active in the preparation and conclusion of the Anglo-Iranian Treaty of 1919, and he praised this treaty in a brochure published in 1920 in Baku, where he was a member of the Iranian delegation which conducted negotiations with the anti-Soviet Mussavatist (Muslim Democratic) government in Baku prior to the restoration of Soviet authority. The main purpose of Reza Khan, an Iranian counterpart of Kemal Pasha, was to free Iran from both English and Soviet interference and to introduce drastic reforms, which in the Muslim world are known as secularization. Just as Kemal Pasha used the Russians to offset English and French encroachment, Reza Khan first used the English to help him consolidate his power. The treaty of friendship between Iran and the R.S.F.S.R. on February 26, 1921, enabled him in turn to force a British withdrawal from Iran and to abandon the Anglo-Iranian Treaty of 1919. On the heels of the departure of the last British troops from Iran in May, 1921, Kuchik Khan's forces, with the support of Soviet advisers and reinforcements from Soviet Azerbaijan, began their march on Teheran, which failed miserably. Chicherin promptly repudiated any Soviet connection with this effort and according to

Louis Fischer, Soviet leaders abandoned Kuchik Khan and withdrew their forces from Iran by September, 1921. [17] The collapse of the Gilan Soviet Republic followed.

The second official act of the new regime was the repudiation of the treaty with England, on the pretext that the Mejlis had failed to ratify it. Soviet historians claim that Seyyid Zia did everything possible to prevent the ratification of the Soviet-Iranian Treaty. One even goes so far as to say that he annulled the Anglo-Iranian Treaty to create confusion, to paralyze the national democratic movement, and to prepare the ground for a new agreement with England. [18]

Commenting on the Anglo-Iranian and Soviet-Iranian treaties, one Soviet writer summed up the situation as follows:

> The October Revolution is one of the most important events in the history of contemporary Persia. . . . England wanted to impose upon Persia the famous treaty of 1919, but the emergence of the Soviet power and the Soviet forces on the Persian boundary, and the appearance of the Red Fleet at Enzeli . . . and, finally, the Soviet-Persian Treaty of 1921, not only annulled all the successes achieved by England, 1917-19, but it brought about a serious shift in the balance of power between English imperialism and Persia. After the Soviet-Persian Treaty of 1921 there could be no talk of ratifying the Anglo-Persian Treaty of 1919. [19]

The difference between the Soviet-Iranian Treaty of 1921 and the abortive Anglo-Iranian Treaty of 1919 was as great as that between Lausanne and Sèvres for the Turks. Having reiterated their intention of abandoning Tsarist policies and declared once again that all Tsarist treaties with Iran were null and void (Articles I and II), having with minor adjustments on both sides restored the Russo-Iranian boundary of 1881, the R. S. F. S. R. restored to Iran numerous concessions and properties of the Tsarist government, including roads, railroads, telegraph and telephone lines, church properties, etc., and canceled Tsarist loans. Each contracting party agreed to refrain from intervention in the internal affairs of the other and to prohibit hostile organizations and groups from operating on the territory of the other. The Iranians secured the right to free navigation on the Caspian Sea.

The full significance of Articles VI and XIII, which did infringe upon the territorial sovereignty of Iran, and constituted a serious potential threat to Iranian independence, was not apparent until World War II. Article VI provided as follows:

> If a third party should attempt to carry out a policy of usurpation by

means of armed intervention in Persia, or if such Power should desire to use Persian territory as a base of operations against Russia, or if a foreign Power should threaten the frontiers of Federal Russia or those of its allies, and if the Persian Government should not be able to put a stop to such menace after having been once called upon to do so by Russia, Russia shall have the right to advance her troops into the Persian interior for the purpose of carrying out the military operations necessary for its defense. Russia undertakes, however, to withdraw her troops from Persian territory as soon as the danger has been removed.

Article XIII further provided: "The Persian Government, for its part, promises not to cede to a third Power, or to its subjects, the concessions and property restored to Persia by virtue of the present Treaty, and to maintain those rights for the Persian Nation."[20]

When the Iranian government in November, 1921, in apparent violation of Article XIII, granted an oil concession formerly held by a Georgian of Russian nationality to the Standard Oil Company of New Jersey in the five northern provinces of Iran, vehement protests from the Soviet government led to the annulment of the concession. The same fate befell the Sinclair Oil Company in a similar venture in 1923.

Iran protested the vagueness of the above-mentioned and other articles in an exchange of notes on December 12, 1921, and received assurance that Article VI applied only to "preparations for a considerable armed attack upon Russia or the Soviet Republics allied to her," such as might be organized by White Russian émigrés, with the active assistance of foreign powers, and not to verbal attacks on the Soviet Union by Russian émigrés or Persian groups. Article XIII, according to the Russians, was not intended "to place any restriction upon the progress and prosperity of Persia."[21]

Article VI did serve as a basis for Soviet intervention in Iran, August 25, 1941, to forestall German occupation in World War II. Both articles nevertheless proved of direct service to Iran, Article VI by facilitating British withdrawal, and Article XIII by preventing the concessions and properties restored by Russia to Iran from reverting to any other foreign power. R. Radmanesh, representative of the People's party of Iran at the nineteenth congress of the Communist party of the Soviet Union in Moscow (1952), referred to the Soviet-Iranian Treaty in glowing terms:

The Soviet-Iranian Treaty of 1921 is the first equal treaty concluded by a great power with Iran. This treaty has not only given the Iranian people enormous economic and political advantages, but it has not infrequently led to the frustration of various imperialistic schemes directed against the national independence and vital interests of the Iran-

ian people. This treaty has been, is, and will be one of the basic factors of our national independence. [22]

One reason the Soviet government was prepared to make major
concessions to Iran at this time was that the prevalence of famine
made peace abroad a virtual necessity. These concessions came on
the eve of the introduction of the New Economic Policy, which
stemmed the tide of militant communism at home and abroad. The
Russian treaties with Iran, Turkey, and Afghanistan were designed to erect an effective southern barrier against further English
intervention. The text of the Iranian treaty, especially Article II,
suggests that the Soviet leaders still hoped to make a lasting impression on the peoples of the Orient. This they might well have
accomplished, had it not been for the subversive propaganda activities that belied the fine phrases of the treaties. This treaty
nevertheless formed the basis for all later agreements between the
U.S.S.R. and Iran and served to restore peace and order in the
midst of chaotic conditions on both sides of the border. The Soviet-
Iranian Treaty, and those with Turkey and Afghanistan concluded in
the same year, together with major religious, social, and economic
concessions made by the Soviet government to the natives of Central Asia, [23] had a pacifying effect in a very troublesome area in
the Soviet Union.

With the conclusion of the Soviet-Iranian Treaty, the Soviet government appears to have abandoned any immediate prospects for the
establishment of a Soviet regime in Iran. According to the *Year
Book of the Comintern* for 1923, which devoted more space to Iran
than to any other Muslim state of the Near and Middle East, there
were in 1922 no more than two thousand Communists and Socialists
in Iran, only one Communist newspaper, and altogether only twenty
thousand Iranians connected with trade-union organizations. [24] This
insignificant number, less than half of the 4,500 Communists Sultan-Zade had boasted of in *Pravda* (July 16, 1921), was a clear indication that communism had failed to make headway among the
poverty-stricken masses in Iran. Even as early as October 22,
1920, according to Chicherin (*Izvestia*, November 6, 1921), the
Central Committee of the Communist party had resolved that an
Iranian revolution would not be possible until the complete bourgeois development of the country had occurred. Rationalizing this
failure, Soviet leaders concluded that Soviet interests did not require an Iranian revolution. Writing in 1923, Karl Radek explained:

For the Soviet government it is completely unnecessary to create in

Persia artificial Soviet republics. Its real interests in Persia consist in the fact that Persia should not become a base for an attack on Baku. If the Persian government obligates itself to demand the withdrawal of the English forces, and England rejects this demand, in spite of the promise of Lloyd George, then the Red forces will make their appearance in Persia, not as conquerors but as allies. If the Persian government adopts this course, dictated by its own interests, then the form of government in Persia, the solution in Persia of the agrarian question (the labor problem barely exists there) will be exclusively the business of the Persian people, of the spiritual influence of the Persian Communists, the majority of whose responsible leaders understand very well that the revolutionary movement in Persia will for a long time be possible only in the form of a peasant movement and that at this time communism may go for a short distance on this road along with the democratic intelligentsia. [25]

On October 1, 1927, the Soviet Union and Iran signed a Treaty of Guarantee and Neutrality, which reaffirmed the provisions of the Soviet-Iranian Treaty of February 26, 1921. According to Soviet sources, this treaty enabled Iran to proceed with the abolition of the capitulations in 1928, as well as to pass legislation for an autonomous customs tariff.

II. AFGHANISTAN

The struggle of the Afghan Emir [Amanullah Khan] for the independence of Afghanistan is objectively a revolutionary struggle, in spite of the monarchical outlook of the Emir and his followers, for it weakens, disorganizes, and undermines imperialism.
--J. V. Stalin

The Soviet government and the Comintern lost no opportunity to convince the Soviet peoples and those of the Near East that not only Turkey and Iran, but likewise Afghanistan owed its freedom and independence to the October Revolution. In April, 1919, inspired in part, at least, by the Bolshevik Revolution, Amanullah and his "Young Afghans," who by means of a palace revolution had seized power the previous February, denounced Afghanistan's treaty obligations with England. Amanullah's first manifesto declared that Afghanistan must become a free and independent country, enjoying the rights of every sovereign state. Since the English government was by no means persuaded to accept the Afghan *coup d'état*, Amanullah turned to Soviet Russia for assistance. The initial Afghan attitude toward the new Soviet regime may have been conditioned in part by a brochure on *Bolshevism in the Koran,* by the Hindu revolutionary leader Barkatulla, published in Persian, Afghan, and Arabic.

As a result of the Second Anglo-Afghan War of 1878-81, Afghanistan had lost its independence. [26] Thereafter its foreign policy was wholly directed by the British government through the British viceroy in India. In addition to this humiliating treaty arrangement, in 1893 Afghanistan, under British pressure, was forced to accept a modification of its boundary with India in favor of the latter, known as the Durand line. The culture and economy of the country remained at a low level. There were no railroads, only one major highway leading to India, one printing shop, and no factories other than a military arsenal. Amanullah, influenced no doubt by the "Young Turks" and the Iranian revolutionaries, as well as by the Russians, intended to cast off English domination and introduce many needed reforms in this backward country.

Confronting the threat of hostilities with Great Britain, Amanullah on April 7, 1919, addressed identical letters to Lenin and Chicherin, informing them of his accession to the throne and of the independence of Afghanistan. He proposed the establishment of diplomatic relations. [27] On May 27, when Lenin and Chicherin replied, in line with the provisions of the Treaty of Brest-Litovsk, with unconditional recognition of the sovereign rights of Afghanistan to independence and indicated their willingness to establish diplomatic relations, the Third Afghan War (May-June, 1919) with England was already under way. As in the case of Iran and Turkey, the Soviets insist that Afghan success in this war was due to the October Revolution. Because of the removal of the Russian threat in the north, the Afghans were able to concentrate all their forces against the British. Actually the English were not defeated, but were handicapped by an uprising in the Punjab. Both sides appear to have been satisfied to terminate the conflict. On August 8, 1919, in Rawalpindi, India, an Anglo-Afghan truce was signed, by which England recognized the independence of Afghanistan in domestic and foreign relations. The Afghans were forced to accept the Indian boundary of 1893, which left some three million Afghans in India.

Although a Soviet representative, Ya. Z. Surits, arrived in Afghanistan during the summer of 1919, due to foreign intervention in Russia and Soviet difficulties in Central Asia, it was October before an Afghan mission, headed by Mohammed Vali Khan, arrived in Moscow to enter into treaty negotiations with Soviet Russia. A recent interview with Mirza Mohammed Khan, a member of this mission, by a *Pravda* reporter (*Pravda,* December 18, 1955) during the much-publicized visit of Bulganin and Khrushchev in Kabul, throws additional light on the conditions under which Soviet-Afghan relations were established. According to Mirza Mohammed Khan, in 1919 it took the Afghan delegation thirteen days to travel from Tashkent to Moscow. With civil war raging on all sides, they had to tear down fences and old buildings to provide fuel for their locomotives. In Moscow the diplomatic corps consisted of the representatives of only three states which at that time recognized the Soviet regime. Nevertheless, as the Afghan delegate explained during his reminiscences, Soviet recognition of Afghanistan's independence constituted valuable moral support for his country at the very time England embarked on the Third Afghan War. In his unforgettable interview with Lenin, the Soviet leader expressed like appreciation for the friendly act of the Afghan government, which, according to him, was the first to recognize the Soviet regime.

In England, where the mission of Mohammed Vali Khan had gone first, the Afghans were told to negotiate directly with the British viceroy in India. An Afghan appeal to the recently established League of Nations produced no immediate results. The Soviet regime, on the other hand, received the Afghans warmly and, sensing its opportunity, entered into treaty negotiations without delay. As in the case of Turkey and Iran during the period of the intervention, Afghans infiltrated Central Asia, with the intent of extending the borders of Afghanistan. They caused sufficient trouble that the Soviets were willing to enter into treaty arrangements to put an end to border problems. Moreover, as Stalin pointed out, "The struggle of the Afghan Emir [Amanullah Khan] for the independence of Afghanistan is objectively a revolutionary struggle, in spite of the monarchical outlook of the Emir and his followers, for it weakens, disorganizes, and undermines imperialism."[28]

Writing to Amanullah on November 27, 1919, Lenin called for trade and friendly agreements "for a joint struggle against the most rapacious imperialistic government on earth--Great Britain." Referring to Afghanistan as "the only independent Muslim state in the world," he indicated in phraseology that has a familiar ring in view of Soviet references to Turkey, that the Afghan people confronted "the great historic task of uniting about itself all enslaved Mohammedan peoples and leading them on the road to freedom and independence."[29]

Actually Amanullah displayed no more haste in completing treaty relations with Soviet Russia than was shown by Kemal Pasha in Turkey. Afghan sympathy with the fate of Bokhara and Afghan designs on Turkestan were apparently among the factors which induced the Emir to hesitate. Once the truce was signed with England, Afghanistan was under no pressure to come to terms with Moscow. Ivan Maisky,[30] in his study of Soviet foreign policy during these years, has indicated that there was friction at this time between Afghanistan and the R. S. F. S. R. A Soviet source,[31] which makes no attempt to account for the procrastination, states that the discovery in June, 1920, of an English plot to assassinate Amanullah Khan strengthened the desire of the Afghans for a rapprochement with Soviet Russia. It therefore appears that the renewed threat of English intervention revived Soviet-Afghan negotiations. On September 13, 1920, a preliminary draft of the Soviet-Afghan Treaty was signed in Kabul.

Writing to Lenin the following December, Amanullah acknowledged his familiarity with "the high ideals of the Soviet government in connection with the national liberation struggle of the peoples of the East, " and asked for the speedy conclusion of a treaty of friendship:

> Taking into consideration that the objectives of the Soviet government are directed toward the elimination of imperialist policy all over the world, and especially toward the liberation of the peoples of the East from the despotism of the world imperialists and toward the establishment of such a regime as would let all peoples decide their fate as sovereign states, and motivated by this we should like, as speedily as possible, to regulate the relations between our imperial government and the government of the republic of the Soviets. . . . These clarifications and this information have strengthened and confirmed, as never before, our hopes and our faith in the action of your government. Soviet policy consists in extending to the Asiatic peoples prerogatives which the other powers do not wish to give them.[32]

Alarmed by the turn of events in the latter part of 1920, the British government through one of its agents in Afghanistan, in January, 1921, tried to shelve the Soviet treaty by substituting for it the draft of an Anglo-Afghan Treaty, which would have required the Afghans to accept certain English political demands and to restrict themselves to the establishment of trade relations with Soviet Russia. In spite of the efforts of the Afghan Anglophiles, the treaty between the R. S. F. S. R. and Afghanistan was concluded on February 28, 1921, two days after the Soviet-Iranian Treaty, and was ratified in August of the same year.

The Soviet-Afghan treaty[33] reaffirmed the independence of Afghanistan, provided for the establishment of regular diplomatic relations, the opening of consulates, promised Afghanistan "fi-

nancial and other material assistance, " and the restoration of
frontier areas which belonged to Afghanistan in the nineteenth century. A supplementary article, of particular interest in that it affords a preview of the tactics pursued on a much larger scale by the
Soviet Union today in the Middle East, provided for Afghanistan an
annual Soviet subsidy of one million rubles in gold or silver, the
construction of a telegraph line on the Kushk-Herat-Kandahar-Kabul
route, and Soviet technical experts and other specialists for the
assistance of the Afghan government.

Immediately following the Soviet-Afghan Treaty and while negotiations were still in progress for the Soviet-Turkish Treaty,
there was signed in Moscow on March 1, a Turko-Afghan Treaty,
obviously designed to fit into the projected Soviet system of alliances with Muslim lands on the southern Soviet border. This
treaty, a first-class propaganda instrument, having recognized
that "thanks to the Almighty, " the oriental world was at last awakening, credited Turkey with having been "the guide of Islam" and
"an example" in regard to the caliphate. The treaty recognized the
complete independence of both Turkey and Afghanistan, as well as
"the emancipation of all oriental nations and their right to freedom
and independence. " Each of the contracting parties undertook to
support the other against "an imperialist state which follows the
policy of invading and exploiting the East"--an obvious reference
to England. It is significant that this treaty, too, no doubt in conformity with the wishes of Afghanistan, specifically recognized the
independence of Khiva and Bokhara (Article II). It likewise provided
for the establishment of diplomatic and consular relations, as well
as for the sending of Turkish military and educational missions to
Afghanistan for at least five years. The fact that this treaty was
signed in Moscow under Soviet auspices indicated that all three
countries involved had one objective in common--collaboration
against English intervention.

As in the case of Turkey and Iran, Soviet Russia made concessions to remove the threat to her southern frontier. The Soviet-
Afghan Treaty placed the Afghans in a favorable position to secure
like concessions from England. In the Anglo-Russian Trade Agreement of March 16, 1921, Afghanistan was referred to as "the independent state of Afghanistan. " Alarmed by Soviet conquest of
Bokhara and other Soviet successes in Central Asia, the Afghans
signed a treaty with England, November 22, 1921, which recognized
Afghan independence and existing Afghan boundaries, as in the case
of the Soviet treaty provided for the exchange of diplomatic representatives and the establishment of British consulates in Afghan-

istan. The treaty prohibited the opening of Soviet consulates at Ghazni and Kandahar close to the Indian frontier--a setback for the Russians.

The sending of Fedor Fedorovitch Raskolnikov (Ilin) as the first Soviet minister to Afghanistan, 1921-23, clearly indicated that the Soviet government planned to make use of its treaty arrangements to establish in Kabul a key propaganda center for activity against the British in India. Raskolnikov, a Bolshevik since 1910, had been acting commissar of the Red Navy (1918) and commander of the Caspian flotilla (1919) which drove the British from Enzeli, in northern Iran. Having some pretensions as a scholar, he became a member of the board of directors of the Scientific Association of Orientalists. Lord Curzon, in his ultimatum to Soviet Russia of May 2, 1923, accused Raskolnikov of "exceptional zeal" in conducting propaganda activities against the British in Afghanistan, as well as of supplying arms to the rebellious tribes of the Indian northwest frontier, and demanded his recall. [34]

Since the Afghans continued to take advantage of the *Basma-tchestvo* revolt against Soviet authority, the Soviet government on August 31, 1926, at Pagman, entered into a Treaty of Neutrality and Nonaggression with Afghanistan, by which each contracting party agreed to refrain from interference in the internal affairs of the other. This pact, according to Soviet interpretation, [35] put an end to the frequent raids into Soviet territory on the part of Afghan sympathizers with the *Basmatchi* movement, [36] and also marked a new step in strengthening friendly relations between the U.S.S.R. and Afghanistan. The Pagman Treaty was renewed in 1931. During his European tour in 1928 Amanullah visited Soviet Russia, where this so-called "Socialist King" received a royal reception from the Soviet Socialist regime, and a gift of two tractors. Although shortly after his return to Kabul, Amanullah was overthrown, his successor pursued the policy of using Russia to offset English influence.

The treaties concluded with the three Muslim states in 1921 proved conclusively the failure of Soviet propaganda to make any appreciable headway among the Muslims outside Soviet territory. The Soviet regime intended to make Central Asia the stepping stone from which to win over all Muslims to the Soviet side. In retrospect, we may safely say that the Baku Conference and the subsequent Soviet propaganda accomplished just the opposite. Instead of being on the offensive, the Soviets were forced to assume the defensive. The *Basmatchestvo* was not solely a local movement, but also a kind of counterattack inspired and guided from the outside, especially from Turkey and Afghanistan. In other words, the impact of the Muslims outside Soviet territory on the Muslims inside was much stronger and more effective than any impact of the Soviet Muslims abroad.

It was during this period that, with a burst of self-criticism, the Soviet press and periodicals began to explain Soviet failure in the Muslim world as due to Soviet ignorance of that world. The impression is given that, impelled by starvation and chaos at home, the Soviets took stock of the situation, became aware that someone had blundered, and decided, even at cost to themselves, to restore peace on the southern frontier and to study the Orient before resuming an aggressive policy in that area. Although communism is ordinarily thought to breed on chaos and confusion, in this case the chaos and confusion created by these neighbor states threatened to wreck the Soviet government so that it was willing to come to terms and make concessions. As yet, inadequate recognition has been given to the role of Turkey, Iran, and Afghanistan, weak and divided though they were, in stemming the tide of communism in the Muslim world. They met Soviet aggression with territorial claims of their own against the Soviet regime. Soviet aggression had to contend with Turkish, Iranian, and Afghan invasion. Even as recently as February 13, 1956, *Pravda* revealed that in the summer of 1955 "a band of diversionists" crossed the Central Asiatic border in an attack on the Soviet Union. Islam confronted Soviet atheism and emerged the victor, acquiring in the process a strong anti-Soviet bias.

Throughout Russian history, the rebellion of minorities constituted no real threat to the overthrow of the Tsarist regime. Revolution had to come at the center, not at the periphery, if it was to prove successful. But in the case of the Soviet government, which at this time was not yet firmly in the saddle, rebellion and disturbance along the southern border very nearly succeeded in bringing about its downfall.

One of the basic Soviet propaganda tactics vis-à-vis the Muslim world, that for national independence, backfired as far as the Soviet Muslims were concerned. For Turkestan (Central Asia) national independence did not mean casting its lot with Russia, even with a new Russia. We find that even during the initial stages of the Russian Revolution, in spite of the transformation of the rest of Russia, the Petrograd *Izvestia* (March 18, 1917) complained that Turkestan alone held aloof:

Throughout Russia the sun of liberty has risen. The hirelings of the old regime have everywhere been replaced and the administration of the country has been placed in the hands of the provisional government. In Siberia the governors-general have been arrested; in the Caucasus the vice-regency has been abolished, and commissars have been sent to the northern and southern Caucasus to transfer the administration to new hands. Only Turkestan remains aloof from all these changes.

Even under the Soviet regime, it is clear that the Muslim population did not accept the Soviet definition of sovereignty. A striking example is to be found in the case of Bokhara:

> In Bokhara, there is a strong political movement under the slogan, "For a Great Bokhara," which was set forth by the Emir in order to save his power. This idea is a very clever one. It is possible to popularize this among the natives on the ground . . . of the national and religious fanaticism of the Islamic population of Turkestan, which, by the way, comprises about 95 per cent of the entire population.

In other words, Soviet propaganda for the national independence of the Muslim peoples of the East was a two-edged sword. It did stir up the colonial and semicolonial Muslim peoples, but it likewise left its imprint on the Soviet Muslims, especially on their intellectuals, who could not reconcile themselves to the fact that they had freed themselves from the Tsarist regime only to become an integral part of the Soviet state.

It should be understood that even in the early stages of the Revolution, it was the religious and national factors, rather than the avalanche of materialistic propaganda about raising living standards, that were of primary significance to the Muslim peoples outside and inside the Soviet borders.

6. The Communist Programs for Turkey and the Arab Countries

> To free the entire Muslim world from European colonial policy, and to enable it to develop freely and independently, this was his (Lenin's) sincere and ardent wish. He regarded this as the first stage in the movement toward the rebirth and liberation of the toiling Muslims from their domestic oppressors. . . .
>
> --N. Narimanov, *Izvestia*, January 25, 1924.

The treaties of 1921 between Soviet Russia and Turkey, Iran, and Afghanistan afforded clear and unmistakable proof of the failure of the Soviet government and the Third International in their efforts to Bolshevize the Muslim Orient. Before launching another attack on the citadel of Islam, the Soviet regime required a breathing spell in foreign, as in domestic affairs. The above-mentioned treaties provided such a respite, in which Soviet leaders could take stock of the situation, account for their failure, and make more adequate preparations for the future.

Although many reasons were advanced to explain the failure of their mission to communize the East, including lack of organization, there was one which ran like a scarlet thread throughout Soviet literature and the press, namely, Soviet ignorance of Asia in general and of the Muslim East in particular. To remedy this situation, it was decided to launch an extensive and intensive study of the Orient. Accordingly in January, 1922, acting upon the instructions of Lenin and Stalin, the All-Union Scientific Association of Oriental Studies was established in Moscow. Several periodicals soon made their appearance, devoted to the national and colonial problems of the East, the most important of which were *Novyi Vostok (The New Orient)*, the official organ of the association, *Zhizn Natsionalnostei (The Life of the Nationalities), Revolyutsion-*

nyi Vostok (The Revolutionary East), and *Materialy po Kolonial-
nym i Natsionalnym Problemam (Materials on Colonial and National Problems)*. Branches of the association were formed in such
centers as Tashkent, Baku, Tiflis, and even abroad--the first foreign center being in Teheran. In addition to the Institute of Oriental Studies of the Academy of Sciences of the U.S.S.R. established
in Leningrad (transferred to Moscow in 1950), new centers for the
study of oriental problems made their appearance, especially in
Central Asia. Some leading orientalists of the Tsarist regime took
an active part in this educational venture, including Academicians
V. V. Bartold, former editor of *Mir Islama*, B. Ya. Vladimirtsov,
and I. Yu. Kratchkovsky.

One of the most influential Soviet specialists on Asian countries
during this period was M. Pavlovitch (Mikhail Lazarevitch Veltman,
1871-1927), head of the Scientific Association for Oriental Studies.
Even his pseudonym had significance, as was often the case with
Russian revolutionists, for he regarded himself as a new Paul, the
disseminator of Lenin's ideas in the Orient. Pavlovitch's main contribution to the study of the East was made as editor of eighteen
volumes of *Novyi Vostok*, to which he contributed numerous articles
and editorials from 1922 to 1927. The name of the new journal he
seems to have appropriated from a German periodical, *Der neue
Orient*, published in Berlin. As Soviet publicist and historian, Pavlovitch was not held in high esteem by the leading Tsarist scholars,
still working under the Soviet regime, who were inclined to regard
him as an upstart, and whose contribution he looked down upon,
since it was mainly in "the fields of linguistics, geography, arche-
ology, and literature" rather than "a systematic scientific study of
the East," emphasizing politics, economics, and ideology. Whether
or not he opened new vistas in oriental scholarship, he was, in the
first place, greatly responsible for making the Russian Social Democrats (Bolsheviks) conscious of the Orient. It was one of his main
objectives to open a new epoch for Marxists, whose ignorance of
Eastern languages and of the contemporary East he deplored and
hoped to overcome by the training of new cadres of Asian scholars
versed in Marxist principles. Second, he wrote extensively on India, Persia, and China for the benefit of the Turks, Indians, and
other Eastern peoples, in order to provide them with literature "in
the Marxist spirit" about the revolutionary movements in their own
and neighboring countries. Not only did he glorify the October Revolution vis-à-vis the Orient, but he was one of the pioneers in re-
interpreting the Revolution of 1905 and its impact on the East, anticipating by almost thirty years those Soviet writers who took real

Mikhail Pavlovitch, editor of *Novyi Vostok*

cognizance of its significance only in 1955. "In the life of the Asian peoples," according to Pavlovitch, "the Russian Revolution [of 1905] played the same tremendous role as the great French Revolution formerly played in the lives of Europeans." Likewise in many other respects he established patterns of thinking and tactics which are being followed even today by the Soviet regime in its dealings with the Orient.

On a different level, but likewise designed to train Communist cadres for the revolution in the Orient, was the Communist University of the Toilers of the East, established in Moscow by Stalin under the auspices of the Commissariat of Nationalities. Essentially a propaganda center, it provided a four-year curriculum where oriental students were indoctrinated in the principles of Marxism, where they received training in revolutionary tactics, and studied oriental customs and languages. Branches were established in Central Asia, especially in Tashkent, in Irkutsk, and in Baku. In 1922 the university claimed an enrollment of seven hundred students, representing fifty-seven nationalities.

As a result of this intensive study of the Orient and the re-examination of colonial questions at the sixth congress of the Comintern in 1928, several conclusions were reached, which provided the basis for the new Communist programs for the Muslim world. Whereas, in 1917, the Soviet government made one, all-inclusive appeal to the Muslims of Russia and the East, they now discovered that the same yardstick would not suffice to measure the problems that confronted the variety of peoples, cultures, and economies of this vast area. According to P. Kitaigorodsky,[1] one of their specialists:

> The East is extremely heterogeneous. It is impossible to measure with the same yardstick the Persian bourgeoisie, which is not yet industrially minded, and the Indian bourgeoisie, which has already had a taste of the tree of knowledge of industrialization. In precisely the same way, we ordinarily apply the general term "national bourgeoisie" in Syria, Turkey, Algeria, Tunis, and even in Morocco, forgetting that in all these countries the specific weight of the bourgeoisie in the economy and management of the country is not everywhere decisive, that bourgeois-capitalist relations have not yet penetrated everywhere, and if they have, not infrequently national capital plays quite an insignificant role. Therefore, it is necessary to find out what stage of development national capital has reached, what is its strength in the economy of the country, and what positions it has already succeeded in winning from the dominant financial capital of the metropolis.

To insure the success of their struggle to win the colonial and dependent peoples of the East, Soviet leaders changed their tactics, and instead of a quick decisive victory they envisaged a prolonged struggle in which the revolutionary movement would pass through three distinct stages. (1) The colonizing power would be expelled by means of an intensive national liberation movement--in other words, a campaign against colonialism which, in their opinion, would create a united front of all classes except the direct agents of imperialism. (2) Once national independence was achieved, the local Communists must conduct a campaign among the workers and peasant masses to the effect that political sovereignty was not enough--that complete liberation involves a social as well as a political revolution. The liberated state must therefore pass to the control of the workers and peasants. (3) The final stage involved the seizure of power by the Communist party.

In the preliminary stage, realizing that the Communist parties in the East, even when well-organized, constituted a small and weak minority, the Soviets directed them to join the struggle for national liberation. To justify this unorthodox step, Karl Radek (*Pravda*, November 22, 1922) cited well-established European precedents:

> As is known, Marx in 1847 advised the Young Communist movement in Germany to support the national democratic movement of the bourgeoisie, and even advised the revolutionary elements in Poland to support those elements of the landowning class that stood for peasant reform. The Communist International likewise advised the Turkish Communists to support the national movement in Turkey, which is directed against foreign imperialism.

Stalin pointed out that the struggle waged by Egyptian merchants and bourgeois intellectuals for Egyptian independence "is objectively a *revolutionary* struggle, despite the bourgeois origin and bourgeois title of the leaders of the Egyptian national movement, despite the fact that they are opposed to Socialism . . ."[2] In discussing the tactics to be pursued in regard to national liberation, Stalin emphasized that "the peasantry represents the basic army of the national movement, and without a peasant army there is not and cannot be a strong national movement."[3]

The teaching of Lenin and Stalin became the key to all Communist thinking and action in regard to the liberation of the Orient. The first task was to get rid of the colonial power, England being the main target. Soviet leaders realized this could only be accomplished by a united front within the country, together with moral and material aid from the outside. As early as 1918, K. Troyanovsky, thinking along these lines, defined Islam as a cultural movement, the only factor of unity among the Muslims, and he was concerned about how best to utilize this cultural movement to the advantage of the Soviets. He concluded that it must be used in the interest of national independence--that first there must be unity, and then national independence.[4]

During the struggle for "complete" liberation, Lenin and Stalin taught the Communist party to emphasize the supremely important fact that the toiling masses of the countries of the Orient were living under a twofold yoke: an external yoke (the imperialist colonizer) and an internal yoke (their own landowners and capitalists).[5] When Soviet-Turkish collaboration was at its peak, prior to the Lausanne Conference, *Pravda* instructed the Turks that "the task of the Turkish Communist party is to unite Turkish workers around a strong center, so that it might be able to defend itself from a twofold yoke--foreign and native; and in the hour of decisive battle of the proletariat with the international bourgeoisie, to be ready to fulfill its mission.."[6] In other words, it was the task of the Communist parties in colonial and dependent countries to make it crystal clear to the masses that national liberation from colonialism was not enough. While they might rid themselves of the external or political yoke, there would still remain the internal or social yoke. Unless they could cast off both, their liberation would not be complete.

Once the first stage--that of national independence--was accomplished, Soviet leaders believed that the second stage, the overthrow of the internal yoke, would be a far easier task. It was one thing to fight a mighty colonial power, such as England, and quite another to fight a practically disarmed and inexperienced land-owner-merchant governing class. To accomplish the latter required only a small, but well-organized Communist group, with aid from the outside. Thus the *Klassenkampf* was to follow the achievement of national independence. This became and has remained the classic Soviet method of approach to national liberation, especially in the Orient.

In 1948, for instance, when Zionism was already outlawed in the Soviet Union, the Soviet government supported the independence of Israel in the belief that Israel without Great Britain would be weaker than Israel under the wing of the British Empire. In like fashion, the Communists have supported India in 1955 against Portugal in the dispute over Goa, while, at the same time, they plot the eventual overthrow of the Nehru regime and claim that Indians are only now fighting for their "complete" independence. In 1955, while Nehru was being dined and wined in Moscow and the red carpet was being rolled out for him, an article appeared in *Pravda* (May 10, 1955), by a Soviet correspondent writing from India, who more than implied that the Indian Communists hoped to take over the Indian government by peaceful means. This was overlooked by our press, which apparently took no advantage of the situation to show the Indians what the Soviet regime really had in store for them. In retrospect, great credit should be given to the Turkish regime of Kemal Pasha, which managed to forestall all Soviet designs on its internal structure, in spite of achieving national independence with Soviet aid.

The extent to which the Communist thesis on national liberation has penetrated the thinking of non-Communist national revolutionary leaders in other countries is evinced in Gamal Abdel Nasser's philosophy of revolution in *Egypt's Liberation:*

I can now state that we are going through two revolutions, not one revolution. Every people on earth goes through two revolutions: a political revolution by which it wrests the right to govern itself from the hand of tyranny, or from the army stationed upon its soil against its will; and a social revolution, involving the conflict of classes, which settles down when justice is secured for the citizens of the united nation. [7]

The third and final stage, as indicated above, is the seizure of power by the Communist party, by peaceful means, if possible, or in the case of a country adjacent to the U.S.S.R., by outside help, if necessary. In the Muslim East this stage has not yet been reached, although the Soviets almost succeeded in northern Iran following World War II.

The results of approximately a decade of study of the Muslim East, with a view to the promotion of a successful Communist revolution there, are to be found in the *Documents of the Programs of the Communist Parties of the East*. Because of their authenticity and historical importance, a complete and unabridged translation, the first to appear in English, is presented in this chapter. They not only sum up Communist achievements in the 1920's in Turkey, Egypt, and other Arab lands, including Palestine, but make Communist activity in that area today more meaningful, and they provide a key to future Communist action there. Although in some cases the first stage of the Communist program--that of national independence--has been achieved since the publication of these programs by the Marx-Engels-Lenin Institute of the Central Committee of the all-Russian Communist party (b) in 1934, Communist strategy and tactics are nowhere else so clearly revealed.

MARX-ENGELS-LENIN INSTITUTE OF THE CC OF THE ALL-RUSSIAN COMMUNIST PARTY (B)

Proletarians of All Countries, Unite!

DOCUMENTS OF THE PROGRAMS OF THE COMMUNIST PARTIES
OF THE EAST

Edited By

L. Madyar
P. Mif
M. Orakhelashvili
G. Safarov

PARTY PUBLICATION

Moscow   1934

TURKEY

In the labor movement in Turkey there has long been a socialist organization, especially in Constantinople, Salonika, and Eskishehir. The fact that these parties went over to the side of the Entente definitely exposed them, and their influence on the Turkish laboring class vanished.

From 1919 to 1920 three factors simultaneously gave rise to the Communist movement in Turkey. In Istanbul, Ankara, and Baku, Communist groups were organized, which rallied around them the really revolutionary workers and intelligentsia, whose task it was to organize and to lead the struggle of the Turkish proletariat and peasantry against the imperialists, national bourgeoisie, and landowners.

During the rise of the national liberation movement in Anatolia the Communist party did not yet exist. The "Communist People's Party," which was created later, an organization of the petit bourgeois intelligentsia isolated from the proletarian centers which were occupied by the forces of the Entente, assumed the character of a petit bourgeois peasant party. Hence the compromise of the Party with the "Green Army" (a revolutionary organization of poor peasants hostile to the Kemalists).

During this entire period, a group of Turkish theoretical Marxists (a group of the Third International), established in 1919, carried on serious and fruitful work in the ranks of the working class in Constantinople. This group laid the foundations for the revolutionary movement of the Turkish workers, organized the first trade-unions on the basis of the class struggle, endeavored to secure solidarity and unity between the toiling masses subjected to the yoke of imperialist occupation and the militant workers of the anti-imperialist front. *It was this group that constituted the main core of the Communist party of Turkey, which was formed after the victory in the war for independence.*

In spite of the cruel blows of the White terror, which inflicted heavy losses on the Party, the Party continued to develop, steadily being transformed into a purely proletarian party, now numbering in its ranks 90 per cent of the workers.

The imperialist war, the national liberation movement, and the overthrow of the Sultanate, forced Turkey in the direction of further capitalistic development. The working class, which, in the years of the war for national liberation was, from a numerical and organizational standpoint, weak and could not, as a result of the occupation of the industrial centers by the imperialists, assume the leadership of this movement, now has grown into an independent force, whose task it is to lead the toiling masses of Turkey in the forthcoming battles for a revolutionary democratic dictatorship of the working class and peasantry for socialism.

The Kemalist Revolution has not solved the basic problems of the bourgeois democratic revolution in Turkey. The mighty agrarian movement, which developed during the years of the war for national liberation, was scrapped by the Kemalists in the course of the Revolution. "The Kemalist Revolution is a revolution of the top national business bourgeoisie, which emerged in the struggle against the foreign imperialists and was directed, in its further development, basically against the peasants and workers, against the very possibility of an agrarian revolution" (Stalin). Neither has the Kemalist Revolution brought the anti-imperialist struggle to an end, having left in the hands of foreign capital the key economic positions in the country. In subsequent years the Kemalist bourgeoisie, defending its role as the independent exploiter of the toiling masses of Turkey, took serious steps in the direction of capitulation to the imperialists. The class nature of the Kemalists forced them both to oppose the imperialists and to capitulate to them, doing the former and the latter in the class interests of the Turkish national bourgeoisie.

Thus, there runs like a scarlet thread through the program of action of the Communist party of Turkey the idea that "the struggle against the Kemalist People's party is inseparable from the struggle against imperialism, which strives again to bury the political independence of Turkey, achieved in a revolutionary struggle. " It is precisely for the purpose of this struggle that the Communist party regards, as its basic task, "the organization of the Turkish working class, uniting it into an independent political force, and transforming it into the leader of the entire mass struggle, " thereby creating "virtually the only real stronghold against the new imperialistic enslavement of Turkey and paving the way for the establishment of the dictatorship of the workers and peasants in accordance with the Soviet pattern. " This dictatorship of the workers and peasants "inflicts mortal blows upon its most dangerous imperialist enemies and the reactionary semifeudal lords, confiscates and nationalizes the big enterprises belonging to imperialist capital and the agricultural estates belonging to the big landowners and religious institutions. " Only this dictatorship is in a position to guarantee and to accelerate the transition from the bourgeois system to the direct building of socialism. The allies of the Turkish proletariat in this struggle are the poor, as well as the middle-class masses of the peasantry, but not all the peasantry. The kulak, and in particular the kulak class in the areas where capitalism is most developed, is in the camp of the Kemalists.

The basic features of the Party's program of action were first formulated in 1925 at the Party Congress. On the basis of the directives of the congress, the Bureau of the Central Committee of the Party abroad worked out a program of action which was confirmed by the Party Conference in 1926.

But this program of action of the Communist party of Turkey, under the conditions which accompanied the further development of Kemalism and in view of the approach of a new round of revolutions and wars, already seemed inadequate. As a result, in 1929 the CC of the Party broadened and defined more exactly the Party's program of action, and worked out the special thesis of the Communist party of Turkey. Both these documents laid the foundation for all future work of the Communist party of Turkey.

Program of Action of the Communist Party of Turkey

1. The Communist party of Turkey, a section of the Communist International, on the basis of the specific conditions prevailing in Turkey wages a struggle against imperialism and the domination of the bourgeoisie and landowners for the U.S.S.R., for the international proletarian revolution and communism, and for the replacement of the existing bourgeois domination by the Soviet system. By a systematic organization of the workers, farm hands, and semiproletarians of the city and village, by developing the class struggle against all kinds of oppression and exploitation, and by uniting under the leadership of the proletariat the basic masses of the peasantry, the Communist party is creating *virtually the only real stronghold against the new imperialistic enslavement of Turkey and is paving the way for the establishment of the dictatorship of the workers and peasants in accordance with the Soviet pattern.* Only this dictatorship can accomplish the national democratic revolution and guarantee its victory; on the other hand, only this dictatorship is in a position to guarantee and to accelerate the transition from the bourgeois system to the direct building of socialism in alliance with the U.S.S.R.

2. The Communist party of Turkey wages an irreconcilable and persistent struggle against the Kemalist "People's party," which is in power. Having begun in the early period of the national liberation revolution as the guide of the bourgeois leadership, this

party[1] thereafter began to convert revolutionary victories into a foundation for the domination and enrichment of the new Turkish, predominantly business bourgeoisie, which came to replace the old big business bourgeoisie and the bourgeoisie of the national minorities, tied up with imperialism. The struggle against the Kemalist party has as its primary purpose, the *exposure* of the antipopular character of this party, its evolution in the direction of compromise with foreign imperialism, and its reactionary attempts to suppress the class struggle of the masses of workers and peasants in the interest of a bourgeois dictatorship, which is powerless to halt the growth of class conflicts.

3. This struggle against the Kemalist People's party is *inseparable* from the struggle against imperialism, which strives again to bury the political independence of Turkey, achieved in a revolutionary struggle against imperialism, which craves to make of Turkey a tool in the struggle against the U.S.S.R. Imperialism finds support for its objectives, so long as it retains control over a number of key economic positions, which the Kemalist bourgeoisie was not capable of doing, nor could it liquidate them; so long as it relies on the reactionary strata of the landowners, the old bureaucracy, and the old big business bourgeoisie allied with imperialism, whose power could not be broken by the Kemalist bourgeoisie which opposed the struggle with the landowners and the economic agents of imperialism; so long as the bourgeoisie, itself, which is in power, helps him (Kemal) with its conciliatory proclivities and its policy of suppressing the class struggle of the masses. The Communist party of Turkey organizes the mass repulse from below of imperialistic attempts to enslave the country. The Communist party of Turkey assembles, educates, and unites the masses of workers and peasants in the struggle for a genuine revolutionary dictatorship of the proletariat and peasantry. The Communist party of Turkey draws the masses into this decisive historical struggle, relying on their vital class interests, on their hatred of imperialism and its hirelings, and on their sympathy for the country which is building socialism.

4. The foremost task of the Communist party of Turkey is the *organization of the working class* of Turkey, in order to protect its immediate and daily economic and political interests, to weld it into an independent political force, and to transform it into the

---

[1]The Kemalist People's party. --Ed. [The footnotes in this translation are those of the original document, and not those of the translator.]

leader of the entire mass struggle. In an effort to suppress all manifestations of the class struggle of the masses, Kemalism has directed its main blows against the proletariat and its Communist party. Under the pretext of national unity, Kemalism brutally persecutes labor organizations, fights against strikes, arrests Communists, and causes provocation. The Communist party of Turkey regards as the basic prerequisite of its activity the organization of the broad masses of workers in defense of their immediate interests. The struggle for the dictatorship of the working class and peasantry against imperialism and for the U.S.S.R. cannot count on any success without such a mass organization of the proletariat, first of all in industries through factory and foundry committees, and in the trade-unions, and thereafter also in the ranks of the Communist party of Turkey. The Communist party of Turkey directs the entire struggle of the workers and farm hands against their exploiters, organizes the laboring youth, and stirs up a movement among the unemployed. The entire program of action of the Communist party of Turkey must concentrate, in the first place, on complete freedom for the class struggle, and on winning this struggle by means of a mass struggle from below.

5. The Communist party of Turkey unites the peasant masses in the struggle for *complete and immediate abolition of all the vestiges of feudalism and land (land and water) usury.* In an effort to broaden and strengthen its support in the countryside Kemalism, which abolished the *ashar*[2] only under the pressure of the revolutionary peasant movement, at present protects in every way possible the shunting of the feudal and semifeudal economies of the big landowners and the *aga*[3] to capitalist rails at the expense of merciless exploitation and expropriation of the peasant masses by the landowners, industrial and usurious capital, taxes, and imperialism. The fusion of the kulaks and usurers strengthens these tendencies. The Communist party of Turkey endeavors to achieve confiscation without compensation of all feudal and semifeudal property, including the property of the aga (both land and implements), and its transfer to the jurisdiction of committees of peasants and farm hands. The Communist party of Turkey organizes strikes of farm hands, tenants, and the struggle of the peasants for the immediate seizure of the landowners' property. The Communist party of Turkey exposes the compromising and treacherous role of

---

[2] A tithe, one-tenth of the crop taken by the government. --Ed.
[3] Kulak. --Ed.

Kemalism toward the landowners, and strives to bring about closer cooperation between the proletariat and the peasantry in their struggle to create a militant union of workers and peasants.

6. As regards the urban *petite bourgeoisie*, this stratum manifested the greatest vacillation, even in the struggle for independence and its discontent, caused by the ruination of craftsmen and small business under the blows of competition from foreign and Turkish industry and trade, state monopolies, and the general economic crisis, often veers toward reaction. The Communist party of Turkey, conducting its work primarily among the semiproletarian elements of the *petite bourgeoisie*, defends their interests as workers, and endeavors to attract them to the side of the workers and peasants.

7. The Communist party of Turkey advances a number of transitional political demands. Their purpose is to bring the masses directly into the revolutionary struggle on behalf of their interests, to demonstrate to the masses of the worker and peasant class that only their militant preparedness and organization can, on the one hand, prevent a new imperialistic enslavement of Turkey, and, on the other hand, extricate the country from a state of vegetation in the interests of the top bourgeoisie who monopolize the gains of the revolution.

8. The Communist party of Turkey struggles for a general amnesty for all Communists, workers--participants in the revolutionary movement, for all revolutionaries rotting in Kemal's prisons, and for soldiers and peasants, persecuted for forest, fiscal, tax, and other crimes.

9. The Communist party of Turkey strives to achieve the immediate confiscation of all movable and immovable property belonging to the old dignitaries of the monarchial political apparatus and to the old politicians, who conduct any kind of activity whatsoever in favor of the restoration of the Sultanate.

10. The Communist party of Turkey strives to achieve for the workers, peasants, and soldiers--those eighteen years of age or over, irrespective of sex, religion, and nationality--the right to elect their representatives and to be elected to all legislative, municipal, or communal assemblies, and to recall these representatives, and to deprive the clergy, landowners, usurers, speculators, etc., of the right to vote. At the same time, the Communist party of Turkey exposes Parliament to the masses as the tool of the Kemalist dictatorship, and explains and demonstrates to the masses by experience and practice that it is not the parliamentary struggle, but only the revolutionary democratic dictatorship of

workers and peasants that is capable of solving the problems confronting the proletariat and basic masses of the peasantry.

11. The Communist party of Turkey struggles for the election
and recall of judges and all responsible officeholders by voting.

12. The Communist party of Turkey demands, as the most reliable means for the preservation of independence and revolutionary gains, the arming of the workers and peasants, the abolition
of professional armies and their replacement by workers' and
peasants' militia, and the right of electing their own commanders.

13. The Communist party of Turkey recognizes the right of national minorities, without any reservation, freely to determine
their destiny (self-determination), even to the point of complete
secession. It opposes by every means the policy of the People's
party, which is directed toward the compulsory assimilation and
Turkicization of national minorities and the persecution of Christian and Jewish minorities. It explains to the toiling masses of these
minorities the treacherous role of their leaders and their bourgeoisie, part of whom have gone over to the Kemalists and part of
whom openly sold themselves to the imperialists.

The Communist party of Turkey strives to achieve, in the interest of equal rights for the national minorities, complete freedom
to speak in their native tongue and to cultivate this language, the
liberation of peasants and nomads from feudal enslavement by their
semifeudal overlords, and partition of the latter's land and livestock without compensation in favor of the peasants and nomads.

The Anti-Imperialist Struggle

14. The Communist party of Turkey is the irreconcilable foe of
imperialism and all its native agents (big landowners, big bourgeoisie of all nationalities, clergy of all faiths, counterrevolutionary strata of the bureaucracy--those who have retired or are still
in the service, etc.). It assumes the leadership of any struggle
directed against the social forces personifying the domination of
imperialism and the return to the old order of dependence and "capitulation."

15. The Communist party of Turkey struggles against all forms
of clericalism, which prepares the cultural prerequisites for imperialist penetration, and it demands the expulsion of Catholic and
Protestant missionaries, the closing of schools of which they are
in charge, and the confiscation of their properties.

16. The Communist party of Turkey demands the confiscation of
all enterprises (navigation, mines, railroads, ports, big indus-

trial enterprises, banks, etc.) belonging to the imperialist capital or controlled by it.

17. The Communist party of Turkey, with every means at its disposal, opposes the attempts of foreign capital to obtain new concessions and once again reduce Turkey politically to the level of a semicolony.

18. The Communist party of Turkey demands the complete cancelation of state and municipal debts and the abolition of the rights of the imperialist creditors to make use of the income of certain customhouses.

19. The Communist party of Turkey conducts daily and intensive propaganda against the inevitable threat of an anti-Soviet imperialist war, and an energetic campaign to demonstrate to the population the inevitable necessity for the Turkish nation, in the event of such a war, to fight side by side with the armies of the world proletariat against the armies of world imperialism. The Communist party of Turkey, with all its strength, struggles against the contrary tendency as criminal treachery to the cause of national independence and to the most vital interests of the toiling masses of the city and village.

20. The Communist party of Turkey struggles against any foreign policy which seeks a rapprochement with imperialist powers. The Communist party of Turkey wages a struggle for a political and economic alliance with the U.S.S.R., for only by the closest collaboration between the U.S.S.R. and the workers of Turkey can the independence of Turkey and the free economic development of the country be guaranteed. At the same time, the Communist party of Turkey stands for a close alliance with the national liberation movement of the colonies and semicolonies oppressed by imperialism and for the support of these movements.

21. Although the Communist party of Turkey is convinced that within the framework of capitalism no reforms whatsoever can seriously mitigate the dire need of the workers, it assumes the leadership of all their battles for the improvement of their material condition, in order to prepare them for the great, decisive battle, the purpose of which is the overthrow of the bourgeois dictatorship.

22. The Communist party of Turkey demands the immediate implementation of the following:

(a) Complete freedom to organize local factory and foundry committees, trade-unions, national trade-union organizations, a general confederation of labor, revolutionary parties and all other revolutionary organizations, which strive to protect the interests of the working class; the recognition of the right of trade-unions and factory and foundry committees to represent the workers before the employers and governmental authorities, and to conclude collective agreements; the right of national labor organizations to join international labor organizations.

(b) Complete freedom of the press, coalitions, demonstrations, and collective cessation of work (strikes) for the workers and peasants.

(c) An eight-hour working day (six hours of work underground), forty-two hours per week, double pay for overtime and night work, a weekly day of rest with pay, an annual four weeks' vacation with pay, etc.

(d) Sanitary working conditions, labor safeguards for women and children, a six-hour day for all teen-agers under the age of eighteen, abolition of night work for women, equal pay for equal work, prohibition of child labor under the age of fourteen.

(e) Preventive measures, insurance against sickness and unfortunate accidents, compensation for labor victims, social insurance, factory hospital funds, pensions without deduction from earnings, etc., state aid to unemployed at the expense of employers, inspection of labor under the control of labor organizations.

(f) The construction of adequate housing for workers in the vicinity of foundries, mines, etc.

23. The Communist party of Turkey struggles to secure for the workers and low-salaried employees of those enterprises (railroads, tobacco monopolies, etc.), which the Kemalists considered it necessary to convert into state monopolies, the right on an equal basis with other workers to defend their interests by all means, including strikes, against the capitalist entrepreneur--the state.

The Peasantry

24. The Communist party of Turkey supports the struggle of the peasants, with the object of securing for each peasant a minimum amount of land, adequate for the existence of himself and his family. The Communist party of Turkey wages a struggle for the liberation of the peasants from harsh exploitation and oppression by big landowners and by well-to-do and influential peasants. With this purpose in view, the Party demands the confiscation without compensation of their large estates and possessions, implements and livestock, and the transfer of these lands without compensation to the jurisdiction of committees composed of farm hands, day labor-

ers, and seasonal workers, lower and middle peasants. The Party strives to achieve, among other things, the allotment gratis to poor and middle peasants of lands belonging to the state and to religious communities.

25. The Communist party of Turkey struggles for the annulment of usurious debts and mortgages which ruin the peasantry, and for the liberation of the peasants from the perennial threat of forced sale at auction of their lands and domestic animals to defray debts and taxes.

26. The Communist party of Turkey organizes into trade-unions the farm hands and, in general, all the landless and those who have suffered from the exploitation of the propertied peasant class, leads their struggle for immediate demands against the landowners and rich peasants, strives to insure contact between them and industrial workers, and helps them to take advantage of all the privileges which were won by the latter. With this purpose in view, the Communist party of Turkey wages propaganda for the creation of peasant committees by the peasants themselves and for their conversion into peasant unions during the upsurge of the mass movement, and it supports the peasantry in their organization. At the same time, the Communist party of Turkey strives to achieve the organization of farm hands into independent class trade-unions.

27. The Communist party of Turkey demands complete freedom for the toiling masses to organize themselves around revolutionary organizations of every kind, which permit them to defend their interests against the capitalists, landowners, and the bourgeois state.

Economic Questions

28. The Communist party of Turkey struggles against the economic policy of the Kemalist dictatorship--a policy which is tantamount to the support of big capitalist enterprises and mixed Turkish and foreign corporations by money subsidy at the expense of the state budget, by exempting them from taxes, and by creating monopolies.

29. The Communist party of Turkey holds that only the closest economic collaboration with the country which is building socialism --the U.S.S.R., where the victorious proletariat carries out the Five-Year Plan, can guarantee the free economic development of the country and the abolition of key positions in the hands of the imperialists. Only the closest political and economic collaboration with the U.S.S.R. can safeguard craftsmen and small storekeepers,

etc., from the competition of the capitalist countries which ruins them.

30. The Communist party of Turkey advocates and works for the creation of consumers' cooperatives for the workers, organizing fractions there, and struggles by all means to prevent them from becoming an organic and integral part of national capitalism. As regards peasant cooperatives, which, at the present time, represent bases for the support of the landowners and kulaks in the countryside, the Communist party of Turkey does not refuse to work in them, in so far as they include poor and middle-class masses.

Tax Problems

31. The Communist party of Turkey resolutely campaigns against the existing tax system, which more and more strives to shift to the backs of the broad masses of needy consumers the great part of the tax burden, replacing the majority of the direct taxes with indirect levies. It campaigns chiefly, on the other hand, for the introduction of such taxes as would directly strike the most well-to-do social strata.

32. The Communist party of Turkey struggles against various taxes levied on the peasant's immovable property and on his draft animals, which the Kemalists levied in the place of the tithe, and which constitute, to the utmost degree, a heavy burden for the lower-income peasants. It demands the abolition of all these exactions and all kinds of forced labor, and their replacement by a single progressive income tax on all the income of the landowners and big peasants, as well as the liberation of the poor and weak middle peasantry from any levies whatsoever.

33. The Communist party of Turkey struggles against the present tax on earnings, large or small--a tax which literally ruins the craftsmen, small businessmen, and low-paid employees, workers, etc., and demands its replacement by a progressive tax on the entire property and income of the capitalists and big *rentiers*, and the liberation of the working class from any tax on earnings.

34. The Communist party of Turkey demands the introduction of a progressive inheritance tax.

35. The Communist party of Turkey struggles for the abolition of all indirect taxes, such as city taxes, excise taxes, and various other kinds of levies, which increase the cost of food and housing for workers and for the urban pauper class.

Public Education

36. The Communist party of Turkey demands for the children of the workers, peasants, and for all the poor of the population free public schools, controlled by workers' and peasants' committees, and insurance that these children have an opportunity to graduate from these schools (clothing, footwear, books, food, etc.).

37. The Communist party of Turkey fights against the monopoly of the Kemalists over all cultural activity, and against the ban on workers and peasants opening night schools for illiterate adults, free from any kind of bourgeois control, and against the ban on the study of revolutionary Marxist literature, as well as on giving the toiling youth a revolutionary education.

38. The Communist party of Turkey demands an increase in the number of trade schools and the democratization of higher education to enable students of proletarian and peasant origin in grade and high schools to complete their scientific education in the higher schools of learning.

Youth

39. The Communist party of Turkey devotes particular attention and energy to its work among the young intelligentsia in the ranks of the workers and peasants, and, in general, among all the young elements of the poorer classes. By paying special attention to activity among young workers and by strengthening the Turkish Communist Union of Youth, and by actually guiding them, the party increases the influence of the Communist ideology on the toiling youth, and thus provides the labor movement with new revolutionary elements.

40. The Turkish Communist Union of Youth, which is guided by the directives of the Communist party of Turkey, constantly and fearlessly struggles for the dissemination of the Party slogans and those of the Communist International, and for their implementation in all social circles (*petite bourgeoisie,* lower and middle peasantry, the poorest masses of the national minorities, and youth organizations in general, etc.), which might be likely to join the revolutionary movement of the proletariat; and it strives to instill in the hearts of the youth an ineradicable hatred of imperialism and capitalist exploitation. The Turkish Communist Union of Youth leads the struggle for the partial demands of the youth, tying them up with the ultimate purpose of the movement.

41. The Communist party of Turkey, through its Komsomol organization, wages systematic Communist propaganda among the youth. The Communist party of Turkey carries on its work in the army.

The Women's Movement

42. The Communist party of Turkey conducts systematic propaganda among the working women of Turkey. In the first place, it endeavors to infiltrate and to strengthen its influence among the masses of women workers and among the poorest peasants. The Communist party of Turkey sets forth economic and political demands, which reflect the interests of working women, as, for instance, the complete emancipation of working women, politically, and as regards their daily lives, equal pay for equal work, the introduction of special legislation to protect women's labor, the prohibition of night work and work in enterprises detrimental to the health of women, the protection of motherhood and childhood, etc.

By strengthening its influence among the masses of working women, the party attracts the best of them into its ranks, endeavors to organize them under the slogans of the leftist labor movement, making them sympathizers of the Communist party organization, by inducing them to participate more actively in the class revolutionary battles of the proletariat and the peasantry.

43. The Communist party of Turkey fights against the bourgeois, nationalist, political, religious, women's organizations, which spread their influence among the masses of working women, by exposing the class content of their slogan, so-called equal rights, under the conditions existing in a capitalist society, and by setting forth in contrast their own class slogans, in the interest of proletarian and peasant women.

The Task of the Workers' and the Peasants' Government

44. As soon as the workers' and peasants' bloc seizes power under the leadership of the proletariat, directed by its vanguard, the Communist party of Turkey, an urgent task will confront the workers' and peasants' government, organized on a Soviet basis--that of defense against counterrevolutionary attacks by its class enemies. The workers' and peasants' government must immediately begin the disarmament of the big landowners and big bourgeoisie, the destruction of the counterrevolutionary armies, and the arming

of the workers and peasants. Thus will be formed the nucleus of the Red Army and revolutionary militia.

45. The Communist party of Turkey carries on among the toiling masses of the people constant organizational, propagandistic, and educational work, with the object of accelerating and bringing to fruition the tasks of the bourgeois democratic revolution, making it possible to shorten the period of transition from a democratic dictatorship of the workers and peasants to a dictatorship of the proletariat, and to prepare the working class from an organizational and ideological standpoint for this historic mission.

46. The dictatorship of the workers and peasants inflicts mortal blows on its most dangerous enemies--the imperialists and the reactionary semifeudal lords: it confiscates and nationalizes big enterprises (water and land transport, mines, industrial enterprises, telephones, banks, etc.) belonging to foreign financial capital, farms and estates (with all livestock and machinery belonging to big landowners and religious institutions), cancels state debts, etc.

47. Every attempt on the part of the national bourgeoisie to oppose the execution of the revolutionary program of the workers' and peasants' government and to sabotage the national industry involves the confiscation and nationalization of enterprises belonging to the national bourgeoisie. In any event, the workers' and peasants' government establishes workers' control over big enterprises, achieving this through factory and foundry committees.

48. All nationalized enterprises, and all those enterprises which belong to the state and the municipalities, are transferred to the jurisdiction of the Soviets for reorganization, and are run by them with the participation of the trade-unions. The confiscated estates are transferred to the jurisdiction of the Soviets.

49. The land, the forests, the mines, and the waters, which formerly belonged to the state, are likewise transferred to the Soviets and managed by them.

50. Credit through the agricultural bank is extended exclusively to the poor and middle peasantry. Under the directorship of this bank a wide net of credit cooperatives should save the peasantry from exploitation by usurious capital. The workers' and peasants' government frees the peasants from all debts of a usurious character. The poor peasantry is exempt from all taxation. In proportion as the basic masses of the peasantry become convinced by their own experience that small economy will not deliver them from need and poverty, the Communist party of Turkey works for the development of a movement for the organization of collective econ-

omies, and the workers' and peasants' government in every way promotes the conversion of peasant economies into all forms of collectivization and cooperatives. The Communist party of Turkey mobilizes the broad masses of the peasantry, draws them into the cooperative movement and into the management of cooperatives.

51. Foreign nationalized banks, in particular, the Ottoman Bank, are transferred to the workers' and peasants' government. Foreign trade is monopolized.

52. Consumers' cooperatives are encouraged by every possible means. The Communist party of Turkey insures the active participation of the masses in their construction and management.

53. Maximum protection of labor: the Communist party of Turkey must strive to insure to Turkish workers all the privileges enjoyed by the workers of the U.S.S.R.

54. In the principal industrial cities, the palaces, the dwellings of the landowners, the houses from which they derive an income, the hotels, and large storehouses are confiscated and transferred to the local Soviets, which insure their management. Those which are not converted into museums, administrative institutions, or schools, are handed over to the labor organizations.

55. The workers' and peasants' regime grants the right of self-determination, including the right to secession from the state, to national minorities living in compact masses (the Kurds, the Laz). The Communists among these national minorities are obliged to conduct propaganda for the international solidarity of the workers, and in view of the fact that the dominant classes of the national minorities, part of which have assumed the guise of Kemalists and part of which have sold themselves to the imperialists, drive the toiling masses under the yoke of imperialism, the Communists must struggle for a fraternal union between the workers of the national minorities and Turkish workers and peasants. At the same time, the Turkish workers' and peasants' regime, organized in the form of a Soviet republic, strives for an alliance with the toiling masses of the now oppressed national minorities in the form of a federation of Soviet republics for the struggle against imperialism and the feudal lords.

56. The workers' and peasants' government nationalizes all printing shops, all dailies and periodicals, big cinemas and theatrical enterprises, radio, etc., transferring them to the Soviets and using them for the general and political education of the broad toiling masses of the city and countryside. Thus it prepares the cultural prerequisites for socialist construction by carrying out the political propaganda of Marxism and Leninism.

57. The workers' and peasants' government reorganizes completely the institutions of public education, in order to make it genuinely possible to struggle against the backwardness in which the masses of the people are held, and to extract from the very depths of these masses the future cadres of the proletarian dictatorship. The Communist party of Turkey subjects to constant control that part of the student body which is a remnant of the old regime, exposes to the public opinion of the working class any attempt at the propaganda of bourgeois chauvinism, and mercilessly suppresses such attempts.

Published in the Turkish language in the illegal organ of the Communist party of Turkey, *Inkilap Jolu (The Road to Revolution)*, Nos. 3-4 (1931).

Published for the first time in the Russian language.

THE ARAB COUNTRIES

In 1920 a Socialist party was organized in Egypt. In 1923 it changed its name to "The Communist Party of Egypt," and became a section of the Communist International. In 1924 it carried out (with the aid of the revolutionary federation of labor, which was under its influence) a number of mass strikes and demonstrations in Alexandria. In the same year, the National Reform government of Zaghlul Pasha, which came to power, banned the party, arrested and tried its leaders. The Party was driven underground. In subsequent years, the work of the Party was weak, limited to the publication of Party organs, leaflets, and desultory action; and partly because until 1931 there were in the Party leadership undesirable elements, who occupied themselves with intrigues and squabbles, and who were subsequently excluded from the ranks of the Party and Communist International, it achieved no success in the area of work among the masses.

The program of action of the Communist party of Egypt, published after the removal of the old leadership, gives an analysis of the class forces in Egypt and lists the most important tasks of the anti-imperialist revolution in the country, pointing out the close connection of this struggle with the antimonarchist and antifeudal revolution in Egypt, and calling upon the masses to break away from the national reformists and traitorous Wafd by exposing this basic party of the Egyptian bourgeoisie and landowners.

The program of action points out a whole series of partial demands, around which it is necessary to weld the workers of Egypt,
and it lists the basic demands of the peasantry. It gives the objectives of the Party on most important questions confronting the
trade-unions and the agrarian movement. The program of action
of the Communist party of Egypt plays a great role in restoring and
improving the Party and serves as a lever for the development of
its work among the masses.

The Communist party of Syria was founded in 1924, but was not
taken into the Communist International as a section until 1928. The
Party did not openly enter the political arena until 1930. However,
during its brief existence, it has already achieved some success.
The Party actively participated in the strikes of the Syrian workers
and in the mass movement against French imperialism; and, of
late, it has become active among the trade-unions. In particular,
the Party demonstrated its great revolutionary activity in the
strikes of the chauffeurs and printers (1933).

A resolution adopted at a joint session of the Syrian and Palestinian Communist parties on "The Work of the Communists in the
Arab National Revolutionary Movement" sets forth the slogan of
unification of the Arab countries in their struggle for independence.
The resolution shows that the persecution of the Arab countries by
imperialism is accompanied by their dismemberment, in which they
are parceled out by force among the imperialist powers. Analyzing
the causes of this partition and the necessity of the participation of
the Communist party in the national revolutionary movement, the
resolution sets forth the slogan of unification of the workers' and
peasants' republics of the Arab countries. It has great significance,
not only for the program of Palestine and Syria, but for all the
Arabic countries in general.

The Communist party of Palestine was founded in 1919. In the
beginning it experienced a prolonged factional struggle. It was tak-
en into the Communist International in 1924. The Party, by carrying out a whole series of anti-imperialist and anti-Zionist activities,
assumed a basically erroneous position on the Palestine national
question, that is, on the question of the role of the Jewish national
minority in Palestine with regard to the Arab masses. As a result,
the Party did not carry out practical work among the Arab masses
and remained a particularistic section, which worked only among
the Jewish workers. This isolation was reflected in the position
of the Party during the Arab revolt of 1929, when the Party was
cut off from the mass movement.

After two appeals to the Party by the Executive Committee of the

Communist International, at the end of 1930 the seventh Congress of the Communist party of Palestine convened. This Congress adopted a number of resolutions, which corrected the errors previously permitted and served as a basis for the reorganization and Arabization of the Party.

The Tasks of the Communists in the All-Arab National Movement (Resolution adopted at the Conference of the Communist parties of Palestine and Syria in 1931)

1. One of the most important tasks of the revolutionary struggle for liberation against imperialism in the huge area of the Near East is the solution of the Arab national question. The masses of the people in all Arab countries are under the yoke of imperialism. In one form or another, to one degree or another, all the Arab countries are deprived of political independence. Palestine, Transjordania, and Iraq are mandates wholly subject to the domination of English imperialism; Syria is governed by French imperialists; Egypt is under the heel of British domination, and the "independence" of that country, declared in 1921, is an insult to real independence, due to the fact that the most important, key political positions are in the hands of English imperialists; moreover, the English remain the dictators of the Sudan; Tripoli is a colony of the Italian imperialists; the French regime dominates Tunisia and Algeria, and as for Morocco, it is partitioned between French and Spanish imperialists. Yemen, Hijaz, and the Nadj, although they are not directly subjected to imperialist domination, are deprived of the prerequisites for an independent existence, and, encircled and hounded by the colonies of the imperialists, are forced to submit themselves to the dictates of imperialism.

    The entire system of imperialist domination over the Arab peoples is based, not only on their outright enslavement and subjugation, but on the fact that they have been split up arbitrarily into parts at the command of world imperialism. This division of the Arab peoples among the English, French, Italian, and Spanish imperialists reflects the prevailing balance of power among these imperialists and is so adjusted as to perpetuate their domination. It is in the most crying contradiction to the vital interests of the Arab peoples. The political boundaries dividing them have been established and maintained forcibly by the imperialists, who thus carry out the principle of "divide and rule." These boundaries artificially weaken the masses of the Arab peoples in their struggle against the foreign yoke for their political independence and national unification in accordance with the free decision of the masses of the people.

The gist of the Arab national question consists in the fact that the English, French, Italian, and Spanish imperialists have dismembered the living body of the Arab peoples, hold the Arab countries in a state of feudal fragmentation, deprive each and every one of these countries of the prerequisites for an independent economic and political development, and block the national political unification of the Arab countries.

Syria is arbitrarily broken up into five parts, each with a different government, different laws, etc. The English have seized the Sudan by force. By converting all the Arab countries into agrarian and raw material appendages to corresponding metropolises, and by distorting and hampering the development of the productive forces and their general development, imperialism thereby strives to preserve and to perpetuate their enslavement. The feudal elements thus become predominant, whereas the development of the capitalist elements, for the most part, is confined to the creation of a business bourgeoisie, which is more or less tied to the feudal landowners, its function being to dispose of the products of the metropolis and to pump out the raw materials for the metropolis. Thus imperialism preserves the medieval feudal monarchies (Egypt, Morocco, and Tunisia), creates new semifeudal monarchies (Iraq, Transjordania), relying upon various petty "dynasties," or creates its own imperialist colonial regime without the aid of its monarchial agents (Palestine, Syria, Tripoli, Algeria), combining oppression and plunder with mandatory government in the name of the League of Nations.

2. What is general and decisive for all Arab countries is the fact that, alongside the key political positions accupied by the imperialists, foreign and financial capital holds in its hands all the decisive key economic positions. The biggest banks, factories, railroads, ports, navigation, mines, the most important irrigation systems, the key positions in foreign trade, the state debts, etc., are in the hands of foreign financial capital. Moreover, the majority of the imperialist plunderers of the Arab countries have seized the best lands (in Morocco, Algeria, Tunisia, Tripoli, Egypt, Syria, Palestine), and the English imperialists have employed counterrevolutionary Zionism to seize and plunder the lands in Palestine. The Arab fellahin and the Bedouins[4] are crowded onto the poorer land

---

[4] Fellahin--peasants; Bedouins--pastoral tribes. --Ed.

and are deprived of land and pasture. Imperialism makes use of its key political and economic positions for the merciless exploitation of the Arab masses.

In oppressing and exploiting the workers, the imperialists rely on reactionary monarchial cliques, on feudal and semifeudal landowners and sheikhs, [5] on native bourgeois compradores, [6] and on the higher clergy. What is characteristic, general, and decisive for the agrarian system of the Arab countries is that a large part of the land, livestock, and pasture, not yet seized by the foreign owners of *latifundium*, planters, banks, colonists, or the state, are in the hands of feudal and semifeudal landowners, sheikhs, and the church. The fellahin and Bedouins are subjected to the worst forms of feudal exploitation *(khamis, [7] metayage)*. Against the background of feudal exploitation of the peasantry, under conditions of the development of goods and money relations, imperialistic plunder of the land, the disintegration of the communities, the plunder of communal lands by landowners and by the imperialist colonial regime, and the crowding of the Bedouins from their pasture, usury flourishes on a grand scale. Extremely high taxes, which, in part, are still in kind (ashar[8] in Syria, Palestine, etc.) constitute an additional burden on the already unbearable situation of the basic masses of the people. The various areas of the Arab countries are at different stages of economic development and class struggle. In Syria, Palestine, and Egypt, the struggle for national independence and national unification of the Arab peoples, on the basis of people's governments, inevitably is fused with the struggle for an agrarian peasant revolution, directed against the imperialist usurpers and their agents (Zionists in Palestine) and simultaneously against the local feudal landowners. In Iraq, there still prevails feudal, tribal, and patrimonial ownership, which is being subjected to seizure on the part of plantation companies of the top local feudal lords and business bourgeoisie, acting under the control of imperialism. Here the center of gravity of the agrarian movement lies in the mobilization of the masses of the people for the struggle against the usurpers, against the background of

---

[5]Sheikh--the head of a tribe, village, etc. , combining spiritual and civil power. --Ed.

[6]Concerning compradores, see footnote, p. 16. --Ed.

[7]Ostensibly a fifth, but actually a larger part of the crop, exacted by the landowners for their benefit. --Ed.

[8]See footnote, p. 150. --Ed.

the struggle with imperialism and its immediate assistants. To a still higher degree this applies to such countries as Tripoli and Morocco, where the basic mass of the population is still chained to the nomadic mode of life and to the feudal patrimonial system, and where the urban centers cannot extend their revolutionary influence. In northern Algeria there exists, more or less, an established colonial domination, with cruel exploitation of the local sedentary population and a relatively important development of the cities and capitalist relations. In southern Algeria, there are still nomadic tribes, not yet subdued by the French imperialists. Under a backward social economic order, the peasants often begin to constitute an independent force only during the process of the disintegration of semiprimitive communities and patrimonies. An exact account of all the specific variations of these conditions is absolutely necessary for an accurate statement of the problem of the relationship between the anti-imperialistic and agrarian peasant revolutions of the Arab peoples. The Communist parties and groups of the Arab countries must devote special attention to the study of these conditions and make use of them in the interest of the revolutionary struggle.

3. The struggle for the liberation of the Arab peoples and for the destruction of the imperialist yoke, which dominates in the most diverse forms, in accordance with the various stages of development in different countries, has already enveloped all the Arab countries. In Morocco, and in southern Algeria and Tripoli, the national liberation struggle manifests itself in almost continuous armed uprisings of the tribes against French, Italian, and Spanish imperialism. In Tunisia the Destour,[9] meanwhile, succeeded in heading the mass indignation and then left it leaderless. In Egypt, the postwar development is characterized by a wave of national struggle, which has led more than once to mass outbreaks. In Syria, the armed uprising of 1925 was crushed, but by 1929 there was a new wave of anti-imperialist struggle. In Palestine, mass indignation against British imperialism and its agency, counterrevolutionary Zionism, has more than once resulted in armed uprisings against the British imperialists and Zionists. In Iràq, the national movement against the English mandate does not subside. In the struggle of the Wahhābis,[10] under a peculiar religious guise

---

[9]Reform Party of Tunisia.--Ed.
[10]A militant Arab tribe under the leadership of Ibn Saud.--Ed.

there were certain elements of struggle against the agents of British imperialism, etc., etc.

What is characteristic of all these movements is that they have evoked the most lively response and sympathy all over the Arab East. In spite of the artificial political boundaries, in spite of the feudal fragmentation, and in spite of the fact that the movement was directed now against English, now against French, now Italian or Spanish imperialism, the national struggle in any one Arab country reverberated, in one degree or another, in all the Arab countries from Palestine to Morocco.

The striving of the Arab masses toward national unification with political boundaries established, not at the command of the imperialists, but on the basis of their own free decision, is inseparable from their endeavor to liberate themselves from the yoke of English, French, Italian, and Spanish imperialism. The Arab masses feel that in order to cast off the yoke of imperialism they must unite their forces, relying on a common language, historical conditions, and a common enemy. Their fusion in the revolutionary struggle against imperialism and the scope of the struggle indicate that the Arab peoples have all the prerequisites to cast off the imperialist yoke, to achieve national political independence, and to create a number of Arab states, which, thereafter, of their own free will, could unite on the basis of federal principles.

4. The conversion of the Arab countries into agrarian and raw material appendages to the metropolis and the divergence of their economic systems result in the fact that the formation of the classes of capitalist society and the development of the elements of national sovereignty proceed very slowly and irregularly. The imperialists take complete advantage of this situation in their own interests, by grouping under their leadership the reactionary feudal elements and by attempting to make of the Arabic countries strong bases for their imperialistic and aggressive policy of usurpation. In particular, the English imperialists make use of their domination of Iraq, Palestine, and Egypt, to protect the approaches to India, to prepare for a war against the U.S.S.R., and to develop their interests in the eastern Mediterranean. The French imperialists endeavor to convert the Arab population of their colonies into cannon fodder for a future imperialist war and intervention against the U.S.S.R. The feudal landowners and the top feudal lords in all areas of sedentary population finally have gone over, more or less, to the side of imperialism. In the ranks of the Arab bourgeoisie and of the landowners tied up with it, national reformism prevails, and assumes more openly the character of counterrevolution and

capitulation. The bourgeoisie and the bourgeois-landowning elements are incapable of a revolutionary struggle against imperialism. They veer more and more in the direction of a counterrevolutionary deal with it within the framework of limited pseudocon-
stitutional concessions, which only disguise the imperialist domination. The mass movement in the summer of 1930 in Egypt quite
clearly revealed the traitorous essence of the Wafd, [11] which removed the slogan of "independence" and tries only to obtain a constitution, which demonstrates that it fears the awakening of the
peasant masses more than complete capitulation to imperialism
(agrees to sign an Anglo-Egyptian treaty). The position of the Kutlat el Watani[12] in Syria is determined by playing the role of the
opposition, absolutely refusing to take part in any revolutionary
activities and in any real struggle. Many of the former leaders in
the uprising of 1925 are now sitting quietly at the feet of the French
generals. The Kutlat el Watani is preparing a deal with the French
oppressors. In Palestine, the Arab Executive Committee[13] has
entered upon the road of traitorous competition with Zionism in
bargaining for concessions from English imperialism in exchange
for a guarantee of "peace and quiet" for the Arab masses. National
reformism turns more and more to counterrevolution and capitulation, in proportion as, on the one hand, especially under the influence of the world industrial and agrarian crisis, the dissatisfaction and indignation of the toiling masses increase; the more
so, that it (i. e., national reformism) does not meet with adequate
opposition to the traitorous national interests on the part of the
broad masses of the Arab workers and peasants, who, as yet,
have been unable to organize themselves adequately and to oppose
their bourgeois and bourgeois-landowning reformism with their
own revolutionary platform. In Iraq, the National party appeals to
the League of Nations, but actually it does not wage a struggle
against the English usurpers, but confines itself only to phrases.
In Tunisia, the remnants of the Destour went over to the French
imperialists. In Algeria, bourgeois-landowning national reformism demands only the granting of French citizenship to the Arabs.
The bourgeois and bourgeois-landowning national reformism op-

---

[11]See the Program of Action of the Communist Party of Egypt, pp.
170-82 of the current collection. --Ed.
[12]"The National Bloc," the National Reform party of Syria. --Ed.
[13]The top leaders of the National Reform movement in Palestine.
--Ed.

poses imperialist domination only within the framework of the exploiting interests of the local bourgeoisie and landowners. They themselves want to exploit the masses of workers and peasants. However, in so far as their immediate exploiting interests, especially in a situation of crisis and imperialistic pressure on the colony, are at variance with the general national interests, they openly betray the general national interests and help imperialism in its struggle against the masses. The traitorous counterrevolutionary nature of national reformism has not as yet been adequately revealed to the broad masses of workers, peasants, and urban *petite bourgeoisie*. National reformism in the Arab countries does not go beyond the political boundaries, established by imperialism, which artificially divide the Arab peoples. It capitulates before the feudal monarchs, who are tools of imperialism, and refuses to struggle against imperialism on an all-Arab scale. The peculiarity of the present stage is that, whereas in all Arab countries national reformism openly capitulates to imperialism, the masses of the workers, peasants, and urban *petite bourgeoisie* are more and more energetically drawn into the struggle for their everyday interests, into the national liberation struggle. The fact that counterrevolutionary national reformism has not been exposed before them to any appreciable extent, thereby threatens grave consequences, since this would make it easier for new counterrevolutionary treason and for blows from an ambush. Now, as never before, over against the capitulation and counterrevolution of national reformism there must be juxtaposed an *all-Arab revolutionary anti-imperialist front* of the broad masses of workers, peasants, and urban *petite bourgeoisie*, a front which relies on the development of the workers' and peasants' movement, and which draws from it its strength.

5. In a number of Arab countries, the working class has played and is playing an increasing role in the national liberation struggle (Egypt, Palestine, Iraq, Algeria, Tunisia, etc.). In some countries, following their destruction the trade-union organizations of the working class are in the process of formation or restoration, although the majority of them are in the hands of the national reformists. Labor strikes, demonstrations, active participation of the workers in the struggle against imperialism, the withdrawal of some strata of the working class from the national reformists, are a signal that the young Arab working class has entered upon the struggle for its historic role in the anti-imperialist and agrarian revolution, in the struggle for national unity. In sev-

eral countries, Communist parties have already been organized and are in the process of formation.

The world industrial and agrarian crisis, in one way or another, has enveloped all the Arab countries, having hit with particular force the workers and the peasant masses. The decline in earnings and unemployment are worsening the poor living standards of the proletariat, which are bad enough without that, and this drives it along the road to revolutionary class struggle. The ruined poor and middle peasants and workers, who are perpetually in need, and who are laid off, the representatives of the urban pauper class and the broad strata of the *petite bourgeoisie,* who are at present greater in number than heretofore, feel the yoke of imperialism and begin to rise for the struggle in the name of national liberation. Imperialism endeavors to cast on their shoulders all the consequences of the crisis and to square accounts at their expense. However, the new wave of peasant indignation against the unbearable claims of the landowners, usurers, and agents of imperialism, tends to unite the workers in their struggle for their daily bread; in protest against the imperialist yoke, all Arab countries dismembered by English, French, Italian and Spanish jackals of capital, are uniting in the struggle for national unity and national independence. Under these conditions, the growing struggle of the Arab masses against imperialism is, together with the revolutionary struggle in China, India, Indo-China, etc., in Latin America, and Black Africa, the most important moment in the crisis of the entire imperialist colonial system.

In Syria, Palestine, and Egypt, where the working-class movement has more or less taken shape, where Communist parties have been organized, where the peasant movement has reached an appreciable degree of maturity, where further development of the anti-imperialist struggle is unthinkable without a consistent and systematic struggle against national reformism--there the urgent and immediate task of the Communist parties is an agrarian peasant revolution and the organization of their work in accordance with the aims of anti-imperialism and antifeudalism. The overthrow of the imperialist yoke, the confiscation of all concessions, enterprises, constructions, plantations, and other possessions of the imperialists, complete national political independence (plus the abolition of the monarchy in Egypt and the restoration of political unity in Syria), the confiscation of the land of all feudal landowners and colonial usurpers who live on unearned income, an eight-hour working day, and social insurance of workers at the expense of capitalists, freedom of organization for the toilers, and a workers' and peasants' government, a struggle for the liberation of the Arab peoples and their free and voluntary union--such are the main demands which define the content of the anti-imperialist and anti-feudal revolution. The delimitation of and struggle against national reformism must be based on such a foundation. Among the partial demands which should be set forth are the following: the reduction of the working day to eight hours, an increase in wages, unemployment insurance at the expense of the capitalists, freedom of workers' and peasants' organizations, annulment of the indebtedness of poor and middle peasants to usurers, landowners, and banks, discontinuation of payments for leasing land, withdrawal of all the armed forces of the imperialists, and a free popular vote on the question of political self-determination (in Egypt, about the monarchy and the Anglo-Egyptian Treaty; in Syria and Palestine, about the mandate of the League of Nations). In more backward countries, such as Iraq, Tunisia, Tripoli, Morocco, the existing Communist groups there must endeavor to organize and to bring about the spontaneous rise and growth of the anti-imperialist movement, connecting it with the struggle against the top reactionary feudal lords and national reformists, with the struggle of the workers and peasants for their everyday needs. In Algeria, which is a completely enslaved French colony, the center of gravity of the work must be shifted to the development of a struggle for the organization of Arab workers against starvation, colonial norms of pay and general labor conditions, and to a struggle against colonial plunder of Arab lands. The unifying slogans of the anti-imperialist struggle for all the Arab countries must be: (1) Down with imperialism in Arab lands; (2) Complete national political independence of Arab countries, and free decision by them on the question of their political system and boundaries; (3) A voluntary federal union of the liberated Arab peoples within the framework of an all-Arab workers' and peasants' federation of the Arab peoples, on the basis of a union of the working class, the toilers of the city, and the peasantry.

The slogan of the All-Arab Workers' and Peasants' Federation of the Arab peoples could and should be set forth, not in the sense that the working class makes as the condition for its participation in the anti-imperialist national liberation struggle the outright victory of the working class and the basic masses of the peasants. It should be interpreted in the sense that, by waging a struggle for national liberation under all and any circumstances with greater firmness and consistency, the proletariat at the same time explains to the masses that there can be no lasting victory for na-

tional and political independence without an agrarian peasant revolution and the establishment of a workers' and peasants' government, at least in the more developed Arab countries (Syria, Palestine, Egypt, and Algeria). The Communist parties will be able
to lead the broad masses of workers against the bourgeoisie, the
peasant masses against the imperialist usurpers, landowners, and
usurers; they will be able to elicit the support of the poor in the
city and the masses of the *petite bourgeoisie,* only when they simultaneously act as leaders and organizers of the struggle against
imperialism for the national liberation of the Arab countries. Hegemony over the working class cannot be realized without a persistent proletarian struggle for Arab national independence and
freedom.

The Communists are duty bound to wage a struggle for national
independence and national unity, not only within the narrow and
artificial boundaries created by imperialism and the dynastic interests of certain Arab countries, but on an all-Arab scale, for
the national unification of the entire East. In overcoming the artificially created boundaries, the anti-imperialist revolutionary
movement must find its strength, must achieve a genuinely revolutionary range, must become the center of gravitation for the
broadest masses. This will also facilitate the struggle against the
influence of the reactionary clergy. No such situation should be allowed as the isolated outbreak of a revolutionary anti-imperialist
movement in Egypt, Palestine, or in any other Arab country, without the support of the other Arab countries. The Communist parties are called upon to act as organizers in the struggle for national
liberation and for an anti-imperialist revolution on an all-Arab
scale.

The relationship with the *petite bourgeoisie* and national revolutionary groups which wage, albeit with great hesitation, a struggle
against imperialism, must follow the rule: To proceed separately,
but to strike together. Occasional temporary agreements with them
for militant action are permissible, provided their vacillation and
inconsistency are criticized, thereby preserving the complete ideological and organizational independence of the Communist movement. The Communist parties must try to attract to the side of the
anti-imperialist struggle, not only the workers and peasants, but
also the broad strata of urban *petite bourgeoisie.* Besides taking
stock of all specific conditions of the struggle, the Communist
parties must bear in mind the fact that the sharpening of contradictions among imperialists, which inevitably leads to world conflict, creates a particularly favorable soil for a new upsurge of the

Arab national and revolutionary movement. Both the strategic position of the Arab countries and the efforts of the imperialists to make use of the Arab peoples as cannon fodder for a new world carnage, and for the intervention against the U.S.S.R. --all this lends a special significance to the anti-imperialist struggle of the Arab masses.

6. A bold and resolute setting forth of the slogan for the national liberation of all Arab peoples is especially necessary because, in spite of the quite firm and clear decisions of the Communist International, the questions of the struggle for the liberation of the Arab masses from the yoke of imperialism, both English and French, as well as world imperialism in general, have not yet occupied their proper place in the work of the Communist parties of Syria, Palestine, and Egypt. Some Communist groups and individual Communists in Iraq, Algeria, and Tunisia are devoting even less attention to this question of primary importance. Opportunism, especially Rightist opportunism, which capitulates before the great powers and the national bourgeoisie on the national question, is one of the main handicaps to the development of the Communist movement in Arab countries. In Palestine, the Communist party experienced its gravest crisis in connection with the Arab uprising in 1929, when the Party found itself isolated from the Arab masses, as a result of Zionist deviation, which hampered the Arabization of the Party. It took one and one-half years to secure the indispensable prerequisites for the Bolshevization of the Party, and even so it did not occur without opportunistic efforts, under anti-Bolshevik slogans, to block the Arabization of the Party. In Egypt, the Party found itself completely isolated from the masses, at the very time the mighty, spontaneous outbreak of the mass movement was in full swing. Not only was it unable to expose the traitorous counterrevolutionary conduct of the Wafd and to create a revolutionary counterpoise to it, but it even permitted the crudest anti-Bolshevik errors on the matter of the irreconcilable struggle against imperialism and its reactionary monarchial agency by detaching itself from the mass anti-imperialist movement. In Syria, the Rightists opportunistic elements openly rose up in opposition to any declaration by the Communist party to the workers' and peasants' masses as to its mere existence, and to the fact that the Communist party began, under its own banner, the struggle against French imperialism. In Tunisia and Algeria, by the way, the Communist organizations are also growing weak, because of the fact that the Communists have been unable to present to the masses the question of the struggle against French imperialism. Without overcoming oppor-

tunism, and especially arrant Rightist opportunism on the Arab national question, Communist parties cannot develop in Arab countries.

Leaving in force the decisions concerning the tasks of the Communists in any one Arab country, the following steps are necessary in order to strengthen the activities of the Communists in all Arab countries:

(1) To develop an extensive mass campaign as to the aims and tasks of the anti-imperialist Arab national liberation movement, tying it in with the regular tasks of the workers' and peasants' movement in the corresponding countries.

In waging a struggle for the overthrow of the imperialist yoke in each separate country, it is necessary to weave in this slogan with the struggle for a free decision by the Arab popular masses on the question of national self-determination, and along with this, for the Communists to carry on propaganda for national unity in the form of an all-Arab workers' and peasants' federation.

(2) For this purpose, it is necessary to hold large and small meetings, and wherever possible demonstrations, to issue special leaflets, to organize anti-imperialist committees to assume the initiative in the struggle, whose representatives are chosen from the factories and foundries, and from the rural and urban working population.

(3) To create a general press organ, for the time being, for the Communist parties of Egypt, Syria, Palestine, and the Communists in Iraq. To establish a more regular and lasting contact for the exchange of experience and to coordinate the work in the early stages among the Communist parties of Egypt, Syria, Palestine, and the Communists in Iraq, bearing in mind the fact that in the future it will be necessary to secure the over-all collaboration of the Communists of Tripoli, Tunisia, Morocco, and Algeria. Having taken special measures to organize and to unify the Communists in Algeria, Tunisia, and Morocco, the future course must be to detach the organization of all these countries from the French Communist party and make them independent units.

Published in Japanese
in the journal, *Marxism*
(Tokyo, March, 1928).

PROGRAM OF ACTION OF THE COMMUNIST PARTY
OF EGYPT

I. *National Injustice, Enslavement of the Toilers, and the Economic Crisis*

Egypt is actually a colony of English imperialism, although it conceals its domination behind a tattered curtain and a reactionary monarchy. The monarchy of King Faud, supported by a bureaucratic and police gang, by big landowners and compradores' capital, [14] helps English imperialism to strangle and plunder the country. With the aid of this monarchy, English imperialism masks its claws. The English mailed fist hangs over the head of the Egyptian people. The English usurpers hold the Suez Canal. In their hands are all the keys to the wealth of the country. They have thrown around the neck of Egypt a heavy noose of debt. They have seized the Sudan. They own the banks. They have converted Egypt into a slave-labor cotton plantation. Egyptian industry is developing only on a *small* scale, *slowly* and *weakly*. The bulk of the masses of the population is tied to the land and to the production of cotton, which is not being manufactured in Egypt, but goes to English factories, only to return to Egypt again in the form of expensive textiles. The Egyptian lackeys and hirelings of foreign imperialism are pitiful pawns. The English bosses openly give orders to Faud and his underlings. They hire and fire Ministers and run the entire state apparatus. The Egyptian people bears on its shoulders *a twofold yoke--English imperialism and an arbitrary monarchy of lackeys and thieves.*
Worst of all is the lot of the workers, peasants, and urban poor. This system of national shame and injustice, of slavery and poverty, is supported by inhuman exploitation and oppression of the toilers. The Egyptian worker works eleven, twelve, and even fourteen hours a day. For this exhausting labor he receives from five to six piasters. [15] Women and children work under still worse conditions. The absolute power of the boss has no limits. Over the worker always stands an overseer with a whip, prodding him as if he were a slave. Contractors--*"muqawilin"*--are in charge of hiring the workers and they rob them. These butchers--*"ra'is*

---

[14] See footnote on page 16. --Ed.
[15] A unit of Egyptian currency worth, according to the gold standard, ten copecks, but now six copecks.--Ed.

firqah" (overseers) beat and torture the workers, deprive them of their earnings, and hold them up to ridicule. For their brutal crimes, such as raping female workers, they go unpunished. Fines plague the workers at every step. They work under the most horribly unsanitary conditions, and after just a few years the worker becomes an invalid. The factory stores rob the workers. From fifteen to twenty persons live in one tent. Where the Arab receives pennies, the European worker gets five times as much. All laws are aimed against the workers: for "incitement" against the absolutism of Faud and his English ravishers, there is a five-year jail sentence, for organizing a strike--two years, for taking part in a strike--one year or six months. There are no laws providing for sickness, disability, unemployment insurance, and the protection of labor. Everywhere the police spies hound the class-conscious workers. Workers' organizations independent of the police and capitalists are mercilessly persecuted.

The lot of the peasant masses of fellahin is no less burdensome. The fellah labors from dawn to dusk, but he has to give up his last penny to pay for rent and taxes. He grows cotton, but cotton prices are dictated by the foreign masters of Egypt and by the world market. The fellah is barefoot, poor, and hungry. Even the "highest" prices are of no help to him; they only increase the wealth and power of the exploiters and leeches, landowners and usurers, speculators and second-hand dealers, bureaucrats and police gangsters. Cotton, which is being grown by the arduous labor of the poor fellahin, accounts for more than four-fifths of Egyptian exports. *More than half of all the land under cultivation* belongs to the landowners, and more than seven-tenths of the fellahin possess only *one-tenth* of all the land. Ruination leads the toiling fellahin to such extremities that they abandon the land and wander hither and thither. But in the city they can find neither work nor food. The few factories and shops always have a long queue of people looking for work. Those who have no identification are deported from the cities and returned to slavery, to their previous exploiters. The fellah is ruled by the landowner. In the eyes of the fellah, any policeman or any bureaucrat is all-powerful. He is ordered about by the *'umdah,* [16] who, being both an administrator and a usurer, rides herd over the fellah. He is in charge of the seed reserves, the fertilizers, and credit. He is kind to the kulak, who is close

---

[16]The local representative of the state in the village (appointed by the government). --Ed.

to him, but he shows no mercy to the poor and middle-class toiling fellah. Whereas the masses of the fellahin, who increasingly fall into slavery to the usurer and landowner, struggle and starve on insignificant plots of land, the great wealth of the land and all the huge irrigation projects belong to the imperialist usurpers. There is no justice or national freedom in Egypt; the Egyptian people is subjected to foreign imperialism and its sycophants. Worst of all is the plight of the poor worker, who has no fixed working hours, has no holidays, lives in a state of semistarvation, and cannot utter a protest.

A *severe economic crisis* has been raging for the past three years. Tens of thousands of unemployed are without bread and work. Every worker on the railroad, at the port, at the factory, and on the plantation is under threat of being thrown out into the street. Everywhere there is severe unemployment, and the masses of the unemployed cannot be satisfied with the pitiful scraps, which are served in several so-called charitable restaurants in Cairo and Alexandria, created as a blind. The last insignificant plots of land, together with everything on them, to the very last shirt, are taken away from the fellahin. The capitalists, the landowners, the usurers, the police and bureaucratic gangsters, and the imperialists take advantage of the crisis to rob even more and to tighten their stranglehold on the workers, peasants, and the urban poor. They try to transfer all the burdens of the crisis to the shoulders of the workers. Cotton is being sold for almost any price, and the death noose and taxes are drawing tighter around the neck of the peasant. Faud temporarily cut the rent by one-third, but cotton prices declined more than twice as much. Everywhere the fellah's property is being sold at auction, and entire villages are being deserted. In the cities, new masses of refugees are begging alms. In the countryside, as in the city, there is no work, no bread. As for the poor and destitute toilers, there is no justice or law for them. The courts work for the benefit of the landowners and usurers to squeeze out taxes, which go to pay tribute to the imperialists, for the maintenance of police and bureaucratic gangs, and sinecures for the concessioners, big landowners, and usurers. English imperialism strips Egypt of gold through indemnities, demanding payment of debts in gold, while the value of the English pound has declined one-third. The burden of taxes and ruination grows.

The enslavers of Egypt, namely English imperialism and its hirelings, the police-bureaucratic monarchy of Faud, the big landowners and big business, who grow rich on deals with foreign capital, *strive to extricate themselves from the crisis at the expense of a new and unprecedented ruination and enslavement of the toilers of Egypt.* They try to cut the price of Egyptian cotton even further, in order that English cotton manufacturers, bankers, stock companies, and the owners of irrigation projects, can make bigger profits. The fellah will have to continue to pay ruinous tribute to the landowner, usurer, foreign usurpers, and the government gang; he will have to pay them even more than heretofore. Therefore he and his family will have to suffer and starve still more, working for the parasites and the usurpers. This is their purpose!

They are trying to establish conditions, as in former times, in which the whip of the "ra'is firqah" cracked over the heads of the workers of the cotton-cleaning plants, tobacco and cement factories. They are trying to establish conditions under which the labor of the workers will bring even less pay than now. They want to make an even greater mockery of the lack of national and political rights of the Egyptian people. Egypt is under their heel and will serve more and more as a factory for the preparation of a new bloody imperialistic carnage, for new hangmen's executions by the imperialists of the enslaved peoples (first of all, the Arab peoples), *for an attack on the Soviet Union*--the country of complete national freedom and victorious socialism. Again they will drive the fellahin and working battalions by force; again they will requisition cattle and bread from the fellahin; again they will collect by force for the English Red Cross. English bombers from Egypt will fly to the boundaries of the fatherland of all toilers and enslaved people, to the U.S.S.R., sowing death and destruction.

This is the way out of the crisis for which the imperialists crave. The myrmidons, clustering around Faud and Sidki Pasha,[17] are trying to achieve the same thing. Al-Ittihad, the party of the court hirelings, the top bureaucracy, and big feudal lords, Hizb al-Sha'b, the party of the millionaire compradores and cotton exporters, Ahrar Dastur, the party of the business and usurers' bourgeoisie and stock exchange speculators--all these are parties which conceal behind their labels and promises their slavish kowtowing to English imperialism and to the blackest reaction.

The Wafd is the party of bourgeois, landowning, counterrevolutionary, national reformism. It unites the rich capitalists, lawyers, speculators, and liberal landowners, who, for fear of a people's revolution, favor a deal with the enslavers of Egypt, and count on

---

[17]Egyptian Prime Minister and dictator from 1930-33, leader of the "Hizb al-Sha'b" party. --Ed.

receiving some small remuneration in return. This is the party
which deceives the entire population, the party of national treason.
It haggles over small unessential returns from the imperialists
and the Faud gang, in order to strengthen the situation of the capitalists and landowners at the expense of the workers and peasants.
It fences itself off from the camp of Faud and Sidki Pasha, and actually makes use of the national liberation movement of the masses
of the people to disorganize the revolutionary struggle, and to wan-
gle concessions in favor of the bourgeoisie and landowners. The
Wafd Party not only opposes any real struggle for Egyptian independence, for the overthrow of the monarchy, for the confiscation
of the landowners' possessions, and for an eight-hour working day,
but it likewise *attempts to assume leadership of the mass movement,* in order to weaken and crush this movement, and to betray
and sell it. The entire history of the Wafd since 1919 is the history
of its struggle against the revolutionary workers, peasants, and
toilers in general. When the Wafd was in power, all independent
class-conscious workers' organizations and all revolutionary organizations were destroyed. The Wafd made a deal with English
imperialism, having sold it the liberty and independence of Egypt
as early as 1930, but this deal was not signed because of disagreement on formalities over the question of the Sudan. The Wafd was
ready to make any kind of deal with imperialism, provided it bore
a constitutional label. This is a party opposed to the people and with
a counterrevolutionary policy, a party which, in the words of Nahas
Pasha, [18] declared its readiness to fight the U.S.S.R. in the interests of English imperialism. The false phrases of the Wafd help
imperialism and the monarchy to stifle and to crush the people's
movement. For many years the Wafd pretended that it works for
the independence of Egypt, trying to deceive the masses with promises. When English imperialism used the Faud monarchy as its
screen, the Wafd began to cry that it wages a struggle for "constitutional liberty." *It didn't dare* to call upon the masses, even
in the struggle for the overthrow of the decrepit monarchy. Now
the Wafd again pretends to oppose English imperialism. *In reality,
however, together with the imperialists and their hirelings in
Egypt,* it seeks a way out of the crisis in the direction of further
subjugation and enslavement of the masses of the people. It is precisely *to camouflage* this that it spreads "opposition" phrases.

The Hizb al-Watani party, which in 1919 expressed the dissatis-

---

[18] Leader of the Wafd following the death of Zaghlul Pasha. --Ed.

faction of the broad masses of the *petite bourgeoisie,* but which drifted to the support of the Faud gang, has lost its former influence.

The toiling masses of Egypt, led by the working class, now as never before, must ask themselves why the countless victims sacrificed in the struggle for the liberation of Egypt from imperialist slavery and the landowners' and usurers' cabal, in the struggle for the fundamental improvement of the condition of the workers' and peasants' masses, has not produced the desired success? There can be only one true answer. The masses of the workers, peasants, and city toilers sincerely and unselfishly entered the struggle, but they were led by foreign, traitorous, counterrevolutionary forces, who on each occasion directed their blows away from the imperialists, and on each occasion brought them under the blows of their enemies.

The only revolutionary way out of the present critical situation the workers can find is the revolutionary struggle against imperialism, against reactionary monarchy, against the landowners and usurers, against the counterrevolutionary bourgeoisie of national reformism. They will find their revolutionary way out in the fusion and union of all the workers *under the leadership of the revolutionary proletariat, under the leadership of the Communist party of Egypt.*

II. *The Struggle for the Revolutionary Way out of the Crisis*

The national reformist bourgeoisie has, of course, interests at variance with those of English imperialism, in so far as they clash in dividing the loot, which is squeezed out from the majority of the workers of the country. But the national reformist bourgeoisie, led by the Wafd, completely supports imperialism in the struggle against the revolutionary movement of the working class, the peasants, and the urban toilers. The Wafd is afraid of the revolutionary victory of the workers and peasants, and with all its strength and means, endeavors to block it. It sees therein the main threat, inasmuch as this victory will signify both the overthrow of the imperialistic yoke and the confiscation of all the land of the imperialists, the crown, the landowners, and the *waqf*[19] in favor of those peasants and farm hands who till it, and a eight-hour working day, as well as an appreciable improvement in the living standards of all

---

[19]Church lands belonging to the Muslim clergy. --Ed.

workers. Gone will be the fat incomes from cotton speculation and joint-stock companies; the power of the landowner will be swept away, the power of the usurers will be undermined, the influence of the 'umdah, on whom not only the Faud gang but also the Wafd rely, will disintegrate. The Egyptian capitalists and the "liberal" landowners want the kind of "freedom" for Egypt which would bring no freedom for either the worker or the fellah. They need the kind of "independence" for Egypt, under which they can play the role of a buffer and also the role of hirelings between the imperialists and the oppressed and exploited masses.

There can be no successful and victorious revolutionary struggle without a complete and irrevocable break with the Wafd, without a very sharp and merciless struggle with them. *Between the camp of the Wafd and the camp of the People's anti-imperialist and agrarian-peasant revolution lies an impassable gulf.* To overthrow the imperialist yoke it is necessary to break and destroy the influence of the Wafd on the masses, its influence on the workers, peasants, and *petite bourgeoisie.* Between the camp of the Wafd and the camp of imperialism and its monarchial hirelings there is a strong bond, supported by their rivalry in currying favor from English imperialists.

The working class is the most progressive and revolutionary class of the Egyptian people. It is united by working at big capitalist enterprises and its members become class-conscious revolutionaries because the class struggle educates and teaches them to oppose hired slavery and capital. This struggle places it in the vanguard of the struggle against foreign enslavers and the cabal of landowners and usurers. Over its head cracks the whip of the overseers and police of its masters, it is deprived of the most elementary human and civil rights because the entire country is languishing in colonial slavery, because its brother fellah does not know any other lot than forced labor for the landowner. The working class is not split up or scattered as are the peasant masses. It alone is capable of leading the majority of the Egyptian toilers on the independent road of revolutionary struggle under the leadership of its own Communist party, which has fused and united it under the banner of revolution. It alone can completely expose the deceit and counterrevolutionary policy of the capitalists, who exploit it and at the same time, under the label of the Wafd, call themselves "friends of the people's liberty." The working class is the class which, throughout the world, leads the workers, not only toward liberation from the power of imperialism, monarchy, and landowners, but toward the complete elimination of any ex-

ploitation of man by man. The working class created the first socialist state in the world, the U.S.S.R., where, completely and to
the very last detail, the right of all peoples to national self-determination has been realized, where tens of millions of workers,
having expelled the capitalists and the landowners, are building a
new life--socialism.

Only a continuous and *fraternal alliance of the working class and
the peasant toilers under the leadership of the proletariat* will be
able to insure the victory of the people's revolution. In the struggle
against imperialism, against landowners and a reactionary monarchy, against the counterrevolutionary policy of the Wafd, the
workers and peasants have common interests.

*The direct and immediate purpose of the anti-imperialist and
antifeudal revolution* in Egypt is the overthrow of the imperialist
yoke and the reactionary monarchy, the winning of complete independence for Egypt, *an agrarian-peasant revolution,* an eight-hour
working day, and a radical improvement in the condition of the
workers, the establishment of the revolutionary and democratic
dictatorship of the working class and peasantry in the form of a Soviet workers' and peasants' government. This revolutionary victory
will help in the future struggle of the working masses under the
leadership of the proletariat for the dictatorship of the proletariat
and socialism, for the abolition of the classes, and complete public
ownership of all means of production. In all corners of the globe,
there is taking place *a struggle of two systems*--that of the bloody,
decrepit, and dying capitalism and socialism, which has an in-
destructible foundation in the U.S.S.R. The present world economic crisis has hit particularly hard the countries enslaved by
imperialism, which is an outgrowth of the ever-increasing and
sharpening crisis of world-wide capitalism, which cannot exist
without colonial enslavement of the majority of mankind. Over
against this world of exploitation, oppression, parasitism, speculation, and colonial pillage is a new world, the U.S.S.R., which
in 1931 completed the building of the foundation of a socialist economy.

Imperialism seeks to extricate itself by an attack on the working
class, a new subjugation of colonies, and provocation of war against
the U.S.S.R. The seizure of Manchuria by Japanese imperialism
and the general attack by the imperialists on China signify an attempt for a new partition and complete enslavement of China, and
preparation for intervention against the U.S.S.R. The Chinese
workers and peasants, led by the Communist party of China, have
already created a number of Soviet areas and their own Red Army.

Following their example, the workers of Indo-China and India prepare themselves for the decisive conflict with imperialism.

The Egyptian workers and peasants do not want any longer to drag their slave chains and vegetate in a state of semistarvation. Their struggle for their liberty and independence, for land for the peasants, and an eight-hour working day for the workers, is indissoluble and constitutes an integral part of the common struggle of all the toilers and oppressed against imperialism, against the new enslavement of colonial peoples, against the threat of a new world carnage, against the threat of anti-Soviet intervention. By fighting for their vital cause, the Egyptian workers and peasants are fighting for the liberation from imperialism of all the Arab peoples, and for their own militant alliance with them.

The victorious struggle of the Egyptian working class is possible only by uniting its vanguard in the ranks of the Communist party of Egypt. Only the support by the entire working class of its class party will insure the Egyptian proletariat the leadership of the majority of the toilers. Because of temporary weakness in the workers' movement in Egypt, police provocateurs and petty careerists have succeeded in disorganizing the activity of the Communist party of Egypt, and have detached it from the workers and from the revolutionary mass struggle. Communists, who hold themselves aloof from the workers for fear of being arrested, are not Communists, but miserable cowards and traitors, who put to shame the cause of the workers.

But to the Egyptian workers their own cause, the cause of labor, is dear, the cause of the Communist International. The workers of Port Said, of Suez, Cairo, and Alexandria, the workers of Bulaq, who built barricades in 1931, and *thousands upon thousands of proletarians, farm hands, and poor, class-conscious fellahin cannot fail to succeed in organizing their strong, militant proletarian party* to lead the struggle for an anti-imperialist and agrarian-peasant revolution, for a Soviet regime of workers and peasants, which will create the prerequisites for the further strengthening of the revolution and for the future struggle for the dictatorship of the proletariat and socialism.

They need a militant Communist party of the masses. They need a militant program for a people's revolution. We call upon them to raise the banner of their Party, and led by their Communist vanguard chosen from among the most unselfish proletarians and poor fellahin, to go among the *masses* to organize the workers and peasants to repulse the rapacious imperialists, landowners, usurers, and counterrevolutionary bourgeoisie, in the struggle for a

revolutionary way out of the crisis. The Communist party is necessary to unite and organize the broad masses of workers and toiling peasants in the struggle for their vital class interests against
imperialism, the landowners, and the capitalists. It is also necessary in order to unite and direct the whole struggle of the working class and its ally, the *toiling peasants,* for a conscious revolutionary purpose. The Communist party is necessary, first of all,
to the progressive workers, in order to struggle consciously and
to lead the struggle of the broadest toiling masses. The Communist
party is the only party struggling for the interests of the toilers.
Without it, they are handed over into captivity to their enemies,
who deceive them with baits and promises. The Communist party
of Egypt must become a part of the world proletarian party and of
the most progressive elements of the toiling peasantry. All over
the globe there is taking place the clash of two worlds--socialism,
which wins and liberates, and capitalism, which decays, dies, and
butchers. The workers of the colonies and semicolonies can cast
off the rusty chains of colonial slavery and of the cabal of landowners and usurers only by a fraternal and unbreakable alliance
with the country of victorious socialism and with the international
proletariat.

The Egyptian proletariat, the toilers, and exploited peasants do
not have to wait and beg for favors from above. Their program is
the program of revolution, which demands unselfishness and sacrifices but which, at the same time, leads on to the goal.

Our basic revolutionary demands are:

1. *Drive out the English imperialists and their troops, fleet,
and air force from Egypt and the Sudan.*

2. *Complete, unrestricted economic and political independence
of Egypt and the Sudan.* Complete freedom of national self-determination for the Sudan. The struggle for the liberation of all the
Arab peoples from the yoke of imperialism, for an all-Arab federation of free peoples. The abolition of all the privileges of the
imperialists. The overthrow of the monarchy, the abolition of the
old bureaucracy, the 'umdah, the artificial local autonomous governments and police. Selection of judges by the people. The arming of the toilers for the defense of their national independence and
labor rights. Freedom of the press for the workers. The separation of church and state, and of the court from the church.

3. *A workers' and peasants' Soviet government. A Soviet regime.*

4. *Confiscation without compensation of all lands, draft animals,
and agricultural implements of the imperialists, landowners, usurers, the king, the top bureaucrats, and the waqf (including family*

waqf), and their division among the farm hands and the poor and middle peasants, who do not exploit the labor of others.

5. Nationalization of all irrigation projects and of *the corresponding heavy machinery (pumps, etc.).* Irrigation gratis of the lands of poor fellahin.

6. *The confiscation and nationalization of all banks and industrial enterprises of the imperialists.*

The cancellation of state debts and of all debts owing to the imperialists.

7. *The cancellation of all usurious debts and cabal schemes, cancellation of all the debts of the fellahin, abolition of all extortionate taxes levied on the toilers, a progressive income tax on the rich.*

8. *Freedom of organization of the workers and toilers, freedom of action for all their organizations.* An eight-hour working day. Equal pay for equal work for all workers, irrespective of nationality or sex. Minimum wages, a four-hour working day for teenagers, fourteen to sixteen, and six hours for teen-agers, sixteen to eighteen. Prohibition of child labor and of night work for women and teen-agers. Social insurance against sickness, old age, unemployment, and accidents. A fundamental improvement in housing. Protection of labor.

9. *Universal free education for workers and peasants.*

10. *Alliance with the U.S.S.R., with the international revolutionary proletariat, and with the toilers struggling in the colonies.*

III. *Our Partial Demands and the Tasks of the Struggle and Organization in the Immediate Future*

a. The police-bureaucratic monarchy, on the one hand, the Wafd on the other (although by various means: first, the former by means of suppression, the latter, for the most part, by way of deceit, which with the advent of the Wafd to power is accompanied by suppression of the struggling masses, as 1924 and subsequent years have shown) apply all their strength to block all efforts toward fusion and unification of the workers. For this purpose, they resort to various kinds of maneuvers, such as donning the false mask of "loving the workers." The Egyptian workers are deprived of their most elementary weapon for the defense of their vital daily interests, in the field of improvement of labor conditions. The workers' trade-unions, in most cases, are trade-unions in name only. They are controlled, either by police spies, contractors, overseers, and bosses, or by rich "protectors" from the

Wafd--lawyers and capitalists, who build their careers on the backs of the workers.

The struggle for *independence, and militant, proletarian, class-conscious trade-unions* are the tasks of primary importance before the working class. Deprived of this weapon, the Egyptian proletariat cannot struggle successfully for its most vital needs, cannot carry out strikes successfully, cannot unite, cannot wage a struggle against unemployment. Compulsory government arbitration suppresses strikes. The government gang plays with the workers, by throwing them contemptible gifts and by buying off those that are for sale. Even the hiring and firing of workers is controlled by the bloodthristy "muqawilin." The workers must organize for the struggle.

The first slogan of the workers is: *Independent* (from police and *the Wafd) class-conscious trade-unions. Freedom to strike and class-conscious workers' organizations,* freedom for the unification and struggle of the *toiling peasants,* freedom of the press for the workers and peasants. The workers must set forth their most *immediate urgent demands,* timing them with the struggle against the attacks of the exploiters. The most important of these demands are as follows:

(1) No cut whatsoever in wages, on the contrary an increase. Equal pay and identical working conditions for workers of all nations. A guaranteed minimum wage corresponding to the pay for foreigners.

(2) No wholesale layoff of workers. Compensation amounting to three months' wages to any person who is laid off. Elimination of middle men ("muqawilin") in the hiring and firing of workers. The hiring of workers must be done through employment agencies, which function under the control of the workers or under elected labor committees. The abolition of all cabal agreements and usurious deals concerning the hiring of workers.

(3) Collective bargaining with organized and class-conscious trade-union workers. A definite shortening of the working day, a struggle for an eight-hour working day. Obligatory weekly day of rest. Enactment of an effective ban on child labor, and payment of teen-agers in accordance with the amount of work done. Equal pay for equal work. A ban on night work for women and teen-agers. Leave of absence for pregnant women. Prohibition of work for women in enterprises detrimental to health. Six-hour working day for teen-agers.

(4) Immediate aid to the unemployed, by means of a levy on banks, port dispatch offices, commission offices, and concession-

aires, the stock exchange, and on the owners of industrial and transport enterprises, and top bureaucrats. Unemployment insurance at the expense of the state and employers.

(5) Bread for the unemployed and refugees. Insurance for the unemployed and refugees in the form of food and housing at the expense of the state, employers, and big business speculators. Prohibition of the expulsion of refugees without identification cards who have left the countryside.

(6) Termination of police arbitration and police interference in strikes.

(7) Free election by the workers of factory and foundry committees and recognition of them by the employers. Freedom to strike and freedom for class trade-union activities. Improvement in workers' housing.

(8) Picketing by workers during strikes and the right of workers to defend themselves against police violence.

(9) An international front of Arab workers and the workers of the national minorities. The workers must, first of all, organize themselves at their own enterprises, in order to prepare their struggle from below. For that purpose it is necessary, in the first place, to unite with the most active, and thus create a *trade-union group* at the enterprise. On their own part, it is necessary to exert every effort to organize the unemployed and refugees, by trying to create elected committees of the unemployed and refugees--fellahin and farm hands.

b. The special slogans of the struggle of the fellahin masses must be demands corresponding to their most urgent needs:

(1) Fellahin pay neither taxes nor debts.

(2) No payment of rent during a time of crisis.

(3) No confiscation of land, crops, livestock, and agricultural implements for nonpayment of taxes, rent, or debts. Not a single fellah can be driven from the land he tills.

(4) Down with the village tax collectors and usurers.

(5) No repayment of loans to the government. Division of these funds among the starving and destitute fellahin, following the same provision of "aid" extended to landowners, usurers, and the 'umdah'.

(6) Complete abrogation of the cabal treaties imposed upon the fellahin, working on the landowners' estates ("izbah"). A struggle against the forced return of fellahin who have left the landowners.

(7) A struggle for the transfer to the elected poor and middle-class committees of all means and resources (seed, fertilizers, funds), which pass through the hands of the 'umdah. A levy on

irrigation companies, banks, contractors, and bureaucrats, to aid the hungry fellahin.

(8) Independent unions of farm hands and *peasant committee organizations.*

(9) A struggle against the inventory and sale of peasant property and land at auction.

(10) Freedom of organization for farm hands, poor and middle peasants. *Freedom of action to unite and elect these committees.*

(11) The organization of farm-hand and peasant units for self-defense against the attacks of the imperialists, the government, landowners, and usurers.

The toiling and exploited peasants have more difficulty than the workers in organizing themselves. But their plight has become so horrible that they cannot help struggling to find a way out. The peasant *aktiv,* which today is openly organizing a committee for the struggle against the usurers, tomorrow will have a committee for the struggle against the sale of fellahin land at auction, etc., and it could win over the majority in the countryside if it would boldly and resolutely take up this cause. The peasants are spontaneously seeking a way out of their misery by starting conflagrations and taking matters into their own hands. It is necessary to help them organize themselves, and the city workers and farm hands must help these peasants by paralyzing the influence of the landowners, usurers, the 'umdah, and kulaks, by leading the struggle of the toiling peasants, and striving to unite them around elected peasant committees.

c. The progressive, class-conscious workers of Egypt, whom the Communist party summons to its banner, must also help the city poor and the small skilled-labor proletarians to organize themselves and to defend their interests against the usurers, forestallers, blood-sucking bosses, with the help of taxes on usurers, big foreign firms, and their agents.

To the lot of the workers falls the task of demonstrating to oppressed and exploited Egypt the revolutionary way out of the crisis. The road to revolutionary overthrow of imperialism and reactionary monarchy, the road to an agrarian peasant revolution, can be cleared only by a mass open and persistent struggle on behalf of the most urgent interests of the oppressed. The economic crisis has shattered the foundations of the reactionary regime. The urban and rural toilers, the best revolutionary elements of the student body, thirst for the struggle, and they not infrequently stray from the wide road of mass revolutionary struggle onto the road of individual and separate action. The Communists and all class-conscious revolutionary fighters must turn their attention to the work among the ranks of the army of occupation and to the armed forces of the Faud monarchy.

The working class, in alliance with the toiling and exploited peasants, must act as an instigator and organizer of the struggle for liberation. It must lead the anti-imperialist and antimonarchial movement, having tied it up with the struggle of the workers and peasants. Its slogans are clear and understandable:

(1) *Drive out the English armed forces from Egypt and the Sudan! Down with the orders and violence of English imperialism!*

(2) *Complete cessation of all state payments.*

(3) *No taxation of the toilers whatsoever. Heavy levies on imperialists, bankers, speculators, and landowners, in favor of the unemployed, starving, and refugees.*

(4) *No payments whatsoever, in the city or in the village, on debts to usurers, and no payments whatsoever on rents during the crisis.*

(5) *No cut whatsoever in wages, on the contrary an increase, termination of payments to bureaucrats and police who receive more than £20, unemployment insurance, aid to the unemployed at the expense of foreign and local parasites.*

(6) *Down with the Faud monarchy, down with the police and police spies in trade-unions and enterprises! Down with the counterrevolutionary policy of the Wafd!*

(7) *Freedom of independent, class-conscious trade-unions, peasant, and revolutionary organizations. The organization of workers' and peasants' self-defense. Freedom of the press for the toilers.*

(8) *Down with the criminal preparation for a new imperialist carnage and war against the U.S.S.R! Support of the fatherland of the toilers!*

Before the Egyptian proletariat and the toiling peasants there lies a difficult road of struggle. But this is the only road from slavery to liberation.

A united revolutionary worker-peasant front is taking shape; it grows and widens from below, against the background of the immediate repulse of the exploiters and enslavers. The revolutionary activities of the Egyptian workers for the past two years have incontestably proved that the working masses have within themselves an enormous reserve of revolutionary strength. They must turn this reserve, first of all, to the organization of a struggle for vital demands against the attacks of the imperialists, government, and capital. A united and organized struggle of the workers will swing the fellahin masses and will help to find the correct and skillful transition from economic struggle and economic strikes to demonstrations, political strikes, and to other forms of struggle which might develop.

The tasks confronting the working class demand the mobilization of all its forces for the struggle to lead all toiling and exploited Egypt.

Published in Arabic in
"Ila al-Aman" (Forward),
the organ of the Communist party of Palestine,
1931

Published in Russian in
Revolyutsionnyi Vostok,
Nos. 1-2 (1932).

3. THE TASKS OF THE COMMUNIST PARTY OF PALESTINE IN THE COUNTRYSIDE
Resolution of the VIIth congress of the Communist party of Palestine

1. Starting from the premise that, in an agrarian country such as Palestine, it is the peasant revolution that is the most significant, and considering that the basic task of the Communist movement--the national and social liberation of the country from British imperialism, from the Zionist and effendi[20] yoke--is the prerequisite for the struggle for the ultimate goal--the dictatorship of the proletariat--the Communist party must, in the first place, increase only those cadres of the revolutionary forces which could direct the peasant activities on the right road, the cadres of revolutionary Arab workers. The arabization of the Party, that is, its transformation into the real party of the Arab working masses, is thus the first and the basic condition for successful work in the countryside.

2. Together with this the Party, continuously strengthening its influence on the urban workers (industrial, transport, and unskilled labor), who constitute its main support, must begin to create durable ties with the mass of landless peasants and those with very little land. A great number of semiproletarians (seasonal workers) and agricultural workers serve in Arab countries as the vital link between the peasantry and the young urban working class. Therefore the Communist party of Palestine must direct all its efforts

----

[20]Landowner. --Ed.

toward an active struggle for *the semiproletarians and agricultural workers.*

The most important task is the creation of unions of builders, who are engaged in public construction, as well as unions of agricultural workers. The setting forth of specific demands to improve the condition of the agricultural workers, such as: the increase of their wages, etc., which, under the specific conditions prevailing in Palestine, must be accompanied by an energetic and continuous campaign against the crowding out of Arab workers by *Zionists,* and the creation of a united front of Arab and Jewish workers for the struggle against Zionist usurpation and exploitation by colonists, planters, and enterprises. The concrete demands of the agricultural workers are: an increase in wages and the equalization of the earnings of Arab and Jewish workers, abolition of feudal forms of exploitation, protection of women and child labor, etc.

3. The main slogans of the Communist party with regard to poor peasants and peasants with very little land, as well as to poor Bedouins, who comprise, in general, 35 per cent of the nonurban population of the country, are as follows: *the overthrow of British imperialism,* which is the enslaver of the peasantry and supports Zionist colonization and feudal capitalist exploitation of the peasants by Arab and Jewish landowners and planters. Only the overthrow of British imperialism will insure the solution of the central problem of the landless peasants and those with very little land--the *land* problem.

4. "The land belongs to him who tills it, and neither 'hums' or 'tult'[21] should be paid for it"; "not a single 'dunam'[22] to the imperialists and Zionist usurpers! Armed resistance of the fellahin to any attempt to expropriate fellahin crops and harat (land under cultivation)"; revolutionary seizure of land which belongs to the governments, to rich Jewish colonists, Zionist communities, big Arab landowners and planters, and its division by fellahin committees among the landless peasants and those who have very little land, and Bedouins--these are the three basic slogans of the Communist party on the land question. Along with the demand of land for the peasants and the struggle against expropriation, the Communist party must advance the slogan of the preservation of

---

[21]*Hums* or *hames*--one-fifth of the crop exacted as taxes. *Tult*--one-third of the crop. --Ed.

[22]*Dunam*--one-tenth of a ga. --Ed.

pasture for the Bedouins and oppose their being crowded out of these pastures.

5. In response to the oppression of the government, it is necessary to set forth the following slogans: *nonpayment of taxes* (ashar), *refusal to pay indemnities* levied on the villages after the August uprising, fire the police who scoff at the fellahin. However, *passive* resistance alone (nonpayment of taxes, refusal to perform compulsory labor) is not enough: the solution of all burning questions, the real liquidation of oppression, is possible only by an *armed revolt* under the leadership of the working class.

6. Various forms of feudal exploitation on the part of Arab landowners can be overcome by the fellah only through revolution: *nonpayment of taxes* to the landowner and usurer, seizure of implements and seed which are necessary to the fellah to till the land, opposition to confiscation of livestock for payment of debts, partial demands along the line of the struggle against the enslavement of the fellah by the Arab landowner, the usurer, and the waqf administration, etc.

7. Nonrecognition of deals *concerning the sale of land* at the expense of the fellahin, *a struggle against the Zionist usurpers* who steal the peasant's land; refusal to transfer to other areas, to Transjordania, Syria, or the interior of Palestine, calling upon the Jewish workers to break with the communities of Zionist robbers and colonizers and to extend aid to the expelled fellahin--these are the concrete slogans for the fellahin and Bedouins in their struggle against Zionist encroachment.

8. In contrast to the feudal and clerical forms of organization (mejlis, sheikh), the fellahin must create organizations for mutual aid, must choose peasant committees to conduct separate campaigns (a struggle against the seizure of land by the Zionists, nonpayment of the hums or taxes), must carry out mass activities, such as, for instance, nonpayment of indemnities or debts, mobilization of the peasants in neighboring villages, or even of the entire country, to aid individual villages which are subject to Zionist expropriation (Vaadi Haveres), and to government punitive expeditions (Tyre, Hebron), or to arbitrary landowners (Nablus).

9. An energetic struggle against the national reformists and all kinds of Zionist imperialist agents, and, at the same time, a struggle against any project of sham aid on the part of the government or landowners. In particular, it is necessary to sharpen this struggle in connection with the proposed Simpson project "for an agricultural bank," and various "loans" to the fellah. "No alms, but the

annulment of the hums; no new loans, no landowner-kulak bank, but down with the old debts. "[23]

10. The exposure of the traitorous leadership of the effendi, mejlis, and mufti, must occupy a prominent place in our educational work. Using the August uprising as a concrete example, it is necessary to demonstrate to the peasants that their struggle and sacrifices will bring results only when they succeed in sweeping away, not only the Zionist colonizers but also the British government and the landowners. It is necessary to contrast the execution of the three rebels in Akka with the deal of the top Arabs with the imperialists, to point out the fact that 90 per cent of the land bought up by the Zionists was sold to them by Arab landowners, who, by concentrating the fellahin lands in their own hands under the guise of "saving" this land from the Zionists, do this so they themselves can exploit the fellahin (explaining the "struggle" of the feudal lords against Zionism). Closely connected with the struggle against the landowners is the struggle against their hateful assistants and go-betweens. This struggle has to be broadened and included in the struggle against the effendi and the Zionists. However, during the work of enlightenment careful consideration must be given to the living conditions and religious factors connected with the backwardness and illiteracy of the fellahin, and at this stage, under no circumstances should the problem of the "din, " rijel-ed-din, [24] waqf, etc., be touched. The intensive propaganda by the Zionists, "histadrut, "[25] and elements of the Arab countryside who have been bribed, on behalf of the false slogan of "peace" makes it necessary to take cognizance of this agitation and to expose it mercilessly. The reply to "peace" is Vaadi Haveres, to "workers' solidarity" is Avada ivrit, [26] etc., etc.

11. Even now it is necessary to develop among the fellahin wide

---

[23]Note. The struggle against reformist slogans and plans is especially important, because these slogans create an illusion for the fellah, temporarily pacifying him, but in reality they even strengthen his enslavement (the agricultural bank and a loan are the mighty weapons of expropriation). Our slogans must have in view a revolutionary, and not a reformist solution of the agrarian question.

[24]The Muslim clergy. --Ed.

[25]The Zionist trade-union organization--a section of the Amsterdam International. --Ed.

[26]Jewish labor--a slogan by which the Zionists wage a campaign to lay off Arab workers and to replace them with Jewish workers. --Ed.

propaganda of the idea of the Soviets. Following the example of the solution of the peasant and national question in the U.S.S.R. and the new achievements of the Chinese peasants, it is necessary to instill in the peasants confidence in their own strength and to prepare the soil for the struggle for a workers' and peasants' revolutionary government, which alone is capable of solving all fellahin problems.

12. An exchange of visits of workers and peasants, not only individuals but groups in nearby villages and cities, is a very important means of contact and of the concrete realization of a workers' and peasants' bloc.

13. The Communist party must advance a number of transitional demands connected with the daily needs of the fellah and his economy: the irrigation of the fellah's land at the expense of the government, improvement of roads, reduction of railroad rates, abolition of forced labor, distribution of permanent loans, especially to the poor and to the victims of elemental calamities (locusts, mice, drought, earthquakes, etc.), the construction of schools and hospitals in the villages, abolition of arrest for debt, abolition of confiscation of property, abolition of corporal punishment, etc., etc.

14. Making extensive use of peasant gatherings (Friday in the mosque, Nabi Musa, Nabi Rubin, etc.) for propaganda for the slogans of an agrarian revolution, remembering that it is during such mass celebrations that the fighting capacity of the fellahin is appreciably aroused.

15. Propagandist literature for the fellahin must be written in the simplest language and in the form of short leaflets. The fellahin, themselves, as much as possible, should distribute them.

16. Forms of organization in the village must be as follows: the creation of fellahin committees and local unions of landless peasants and of peasants with very little land. These committees must be elected and must enjoy the complete confidence of the peasants.

17. The most important task is the creation of Party and Komsomol cells in the villages for the leadership of the work among the peasants.

Work among the Peasants and the Struggle against Zionism
(Theses approved by the secretariat of the CC of the Communist
party of Palestine)

I. The Agrarian Question in Palestine

1. The August uprising of 1929 focused the attention of the imperialist government, as well as that of all parties in the country,
on the Arab fellah. The agrarian question rose before the English
imperialists and their allies (the Zionists) in all its dimensions.
A number of very important works appeared, explaining the situation of the fellah and the agrarian movement in the country: the
Johnson-Crobie and Simpson and Vilkansky[27] investigation committees.

Once again, by concrete political example, the principle appeared
to be correct that "the national question is mainly the peasant question" (Lenin), and that a victorious revolution in the Arab countries,
at this stage, depends, in the first place, on the correct presentation by the Communist party (the party of the working class, which
is still young in these countries) of the peasant question and on the
correct policy of the Party with regard to the basic masses of the
peasantry.

2. What constitutes the Arab peasantry in Palestine?

Simpson gives the following figures, as of 1930:

Urban population . . . . ; . 340, 962
Non-urban 605, 029
Bedouins (among the above) . . . 103, 331

If we add to this the fact that there are 115, 100 Jews in the cities, and that a considerable part of the urban Arab population is
directly or indirectly connected with the countryside, it will appear that about 80 per cent of the Arab population of the country
are fellahin or semifellahin, who are engaged in agriculture. In-

---

[27]*The Johnson-Crobie and Simpson Committees* are English government committees which investigated the situation of the Palestine peasantry, 1929-30, and published corresponding reports. *Vilkansky* is a
Zionist agronomist, who published a book in 1930 on the condition of
the Arab fellahin. --Ed.

deed, according to government data, the number of Arab families engaged in agriculture amounts to 88, 980.

As regards a very important question, the problem of the social stratification of the population of the countryside, there exist no statistics whatsoever, neither government nor Zionist. Only by comparing the figures included in various journals and reports are we able to obtain the following table (usually imperialist statistics treat the peasantry as a unit, mechanically dividing the land according to the "heads" of families).

TABLE 1

Total Number of Families Engaged in Agriculture--86, 000
They have 9 Million Dunams of Land

Landless	Families	Amount of land in millions of dunams
(a) Farm hands	25, 000	-----
(b) Sharecroppers	15, 000	-----
Small fellahin economies .	46, 000	5
Landowners	250	4

Thus, at one pole there are 250 landowners, owning 4, 000, 000 dunams of land, and on the other, 25, 000 landless peasant families. Between these poles there are 46, 000 small peasant economies, with their own plots, 100 dunams per family, and 15, 000 work as tenants on the land belonging to the landowners.

3. Already, based on these figures, emerges the basic question confronting the main mass of the Palestinian peasantry: the *land* question. The imperialist and Zionist "theoreticians" allegedly maintain that the fellah has "enough land, even too much, and that the entire question boils down to its *cultivation.* " This estimate does not hold water: about 30 per cent of the peasants have no land whatsoever, more than 50 per cent have an inadequate amount, and thus from 80 to 90 per cent of the agrarian population is confronted with an urgent and immediate problem, either to get land or to augment what they have. Meanwhile, for the past ten years, the process continues, not of decreasing but of increasing the number of landless peasants and those with very little land. The English government explains this process as due to the increase of the *population* of the country. In reality, the lack of land is the result of

the continuous expropriation of peasant lands by the government, the Zionists, and the landowners.

4. *Expropriation* of the fellah constitutes the main cause of his poverty and "land hunger." It assumes various forms:

(a) *Expropriation by the government:* the British government has taken over all those lands which formerly belonged in the category of *jiftlik*,[28] and in addition, by a special law in 1928, it authorized the High Commissioner of Palestine to expropriate any land needed by the government. The expropriating activity of the government effected mainly those sections which are necessary for strategic purposes (railroads, ports, etc.), or for concessions (the Dead Sea and the lands connected with oil deposits).

(b) *Expropriation by landowners:* This long drawn-out process, which took place even under the Turks, has become particularly apparent since the English occupation. The cadastre introduced by the English government was largely instrumental in the seizure of the land by the landowners and the legalization of this robbery. Even forms of landholding peculiar to Palestine are being converted into tools of expropriation of the fellahin by the landholders. Thus, in 1928, in the Arab villages of Palestine, no less than 56 per cent of the land was held in common *("musha"),* but by 1929 this figure was only 46 per cent. By the end of the current decade the government plans to convert the entire "musha" land into *"ma-fruz"*(i.e., to divide it). But this "division" in many places amounts to camouflaged expropriation of the peasant's land by the landowner. Under present conditions, the income from the land, which he receives now from the peasant in the form of "hums", is not so important to the landowner as is the possibility of selling it or converting it into a plantation; to handle individual peasants is much easier than to deal with an entire community.

Thus, it is a false premise held by Zionist "theoreticians," the Poalei Zionists, which is also shared by certain Communists, that regards the division of the "musha" solely from the standpoint of capitalist progress: the transition from a natural to a money economy, and the creation of small peasant proprietors. In this particular situation, under imperialist and Zionist oppression and the arbitrary rule of the effendi, the partition of the "musha" is the method of expropriation of the small fellah, and it facilitates the carrying out of imperialist Zionist plans. Not infrequently the expropria-

---

[28]The term applied to land in the Turkish Empire, which originally belonged to the Sultan, but subsequently became, in fact, state lands.

tion of the peasants is being carried out by the landowners hand-in-glove with the government and the Zionists. In this connection, it is very characteristic that in 1930, under pressure of the agrarian movement, the English were compelled to pass a law limiting the sale of land to Zionists. This law was *scrapped* by the Arab landowners, who, by evading the prohibition, sold the land. The English paper, *Falestin,* for November 22, 1930, draws attention to an extraordinarily interesting fact: the Arab landowners, after the publication of the "White Paper," having found out that from the English standpoint there is a loophole in the fictitious ban on selling land inhabited by Arab peasants, began to evict the poor peasants "in advance," so that by the time of the sale the land would appear to be "vacant" and its transfer to the Zionists therefore possible.

(c) *Expropriation by Zionists:* For the fellah, Zionist expropriation is the most dangerous and cruel. Whereas, under expropriation by the government or landowners the fellah is not ordinarily driven from the land immediately, although this expropriation does provide legal grounds for such action, the Zionist societies cannot help but to drive him out.

According to statistics provided by L. Ferah, an Arab agronomist, in only one northern plain 8, 720 fellahin were evicted. If we add to this the expropriation which has taken place for the past year in other regions, the number of fellahin evicted by the Zionists will exceed twenty thousand.

The Zionist expedition is distinguished from the government and feudal lords, likewise in that it deprives the fellah of any possibility of obtaining work and thus transforms the expropriated peasants into a surplus "reserve army" of labor, into an army of homeless unemployed.

(d) *Expropriation by various religious and capitalist societies:* It is impossible to overlook also the activity of various missionary (English, French, and American) societies, as well as the capitalists of every nationality who buy up the land and often make use of the Arab bourgeois compradores (in most cases, the Christian) as a screen. The rise of the movement in 1928 (mass demonstrations in Gaza and other cities) against the missionary congress was not religious in nature, but reflected the anti-imperialist mood of the fellahin.

5. The landless peasantry, which grows continuously as a result of expropriation, is the revolutionary factor both in the village and in the city. Only an insignificant part of the landless peasantry (chiefly in the regions inhabited by Christians and Bedouins) finds

a way out through emigration. The number of Arab emigrants for the past eight years amounts to 10,575 (of whom 8,585 represent indigenous inhabitants of the country), which constitutes about 1 1/2 per cent of the aboriginal inhabitants of the population of the country, the bulk of which is made up of peasants. The dispossessed peasant, having no opportunity to find work in his own village, provides cheap labor for his exploiters, the Arab landowners and Jewish colonists in other regions. According to government reports for 1929 (Report, p. 127), "the agricultural worker, who works together with his wife and child, received, on the average, from five to twelve piasters per day."

The problem of landlessness is closely interwoven with the problem of the agrarian proletariat. It is safe to say that, as a general rule, imperialism and Zionism, which crowd out the Arab peasants from their lands, put an end to the feudal methods of exploitation of these peasants, only to leave them a prey to hunger and to create of them in a narrow and undeveloped market cheap (almost for a pittance) labor for capitalist exploitation, which appreciably lowers their living standards. The example cited by Simpson from the words of the chief engineer of the port of Haifa (Simpson Report, p. 134), is very striking: forty Arab peasants were hired to work in the Atlit stone quarry, and the next day there came from four to five hundred fellahin to ask for work. Of the general mass of workers in Palestine, the landless peasantry, the semiproletarians, and the agricultural workers are the most oppressed, the poorest stratum, and hide within themselves, as the August outbreak demonstrated, colossal revolutionary energy.

6. Closely connected with the question of the landless peasants and Arab agricultural workers is the *Bedouin* question. The number of Bedouins in Palestine, according to official data of 1922, amounts to 103,000. The plight of the Bedouins and of the semisedentary tribes beggars description. The quantity of free pasture for camels and other livestock is at a minimum, and, at the same time, the strengthening of the imperialistic political apparatus and the division of Arabia into various "mandated" territories destroys the possibility of *"rezzu."*[29]

Perpetual hunger is the source of constant discontent among the Bedouins, and this discontent is always on the verge of becoming an armed uprising. It is characteristic that up to the present time the imperialist government has not dared to disarm the Bedouin

---

[29]Raids by nomadic Bedouin tribes. --Ed.

tribes, either in Transjordania or in Palestine. The participation of the Bedouins in the August uprising proves what a great role they could play in a revolutionary revolt of the masses. At the same time, it became evident that the sheikhs and the leaders of these tribes can be bribed, as can their liaisons with the top Muslim clergy (mejlis, Islami) and with the imperialists.

The northern march begun by the Bedouins of southern Palestine was broken up due to the negotiations of the English captain, Lilar, with the sheikhs. As regards the Transjordanian Bedouins, the "Bedouin peril" (their participation in the August uprising) was prevented chiefly by the English forces (Government Report, 1929, p. 143).

The only solution of the Bedouin question is the transition of the Bedouins to a sedentary economy. But in spite of certain maneuvers of the imperialists in this direction (the allocation of thirty thousand dunams of land to the Bedouins), they are not in a position to carry out colonization in earnest, and the pauperization of the Bedouin tribes proceeds far more rapidly than their settlement on the land; the Bedouins continuously replenish the army of landless peasants and semiproletarians.

Besides the landless peasants comprising the basic masses of the Arab agrarian population, there is a large number of peasants with very little land. According to the figures of the Shaw Commission, the minimum allotment required to feed a peasant family is a section of 130 dunams, but, at the present time, the average allotment is only from 90 to 100 dunams. In addition to the constant threat to the peasant of complete expropriation, he finds himself under the yoke of a horrible exploitation, which continually lowers his living standard and transforms him into a slave.

In the Arab countries there exists *a peculiar form of feudal exploitation* of the fellahin. The most important features of this feudal slavery are as follows:

(1) *The lease system*, at the basis of which lies the unilateral contract. The land belongs to the feudal lord and the peasant, for the right of tilling it at his own *risk* and at his own *expense*, must pay the "hums" (one-fifth), which in reality is tantamount to one-third, or even to one-half of the crop. The landowners can at any moment cancel the contract without warning and evict the fellah.

(2) *The debt system:* Although in the Arab countries, officially serfdom does not exist, nevertheless the landowner can not only *evict* a peasant whenever it pleases him, but can even *affix* him to the land. The instrument of this enslavement is the peasant's indebtedness. The peasant, who has no capital turnover whatsoever

(his basic capital amounts, according to Mr. Vilkansky, to from £20 to £30, and we must also bear in mind that it is not the poor, but the middle fellah that has been taken as the basis) is forced to resort to "credit" from either the landowner or the usurer, and often from both. The interest on the loan reaches 50 per cent *("ashara hamastashar").* [30] The fellah, who never has an opportunity to free himself from his debts, is being transformed into a *serf,* continuously working for his creditor. Mr. Bowman, director of the Department of Education in Palestine, writes: "The plight of the agricultural population beggars description. There is not a single village that is not burdened with debts. . . . In certain places, money is so scarce that the fellahin cannot pay their debts without incurring new ones. 'For several years we have been in deep water, but soon the water will be over our heads, '"-- such is the typical comment of the peasants (Simpson's Report, p. 65).

(3) The third characteristic feature of feudal exploitation in Palestine is the close contact between the feudal landowners and the government. The latter, by means of taxes, plunders the peasant as much as the landowner, and its entire apparatus (police, jails, etc.) are at the disposal of the feudal lords. Not only has the English government failed to annul the glaring feudal law about imprisonment for debt, but it is being applied on such a scale that one can say without exaggeration that the majority of the Arab peasants have tasted imprisonment for being in arrears.

(4) The fourth feature is the bond between the feudal lords and the top Muslim clergy, and through it with the government. This bond was particularly strong and durable under the Sultan, who governed not only the *"vaherai"* land, but also the *"miri."* [31] This situation led certain Communists to an erroneous interpretation of the Asiatic method of production, as one which excludes feudal relations in Arab countries: in reality, the administration of the land by the Sultan was conducted through a considerable layer of feudal lords, pashas, and landowners, who applied almost the same feudal method of exploitation as Russian landowners under the Tsarist regime. English imperialism is restoring this bond. It tries

---

[30] Literally, "15 for 10," that is, for every 10 piasters the fellah borrows from the usurer or landowner at the beginning of the summer he must return 15 piasters after the harvest. --Ed.

[31] Vaherai--state or crown lands; miri-communal lands. --Ed.

to find taxes for the waqf, and in return secures for itself a decisive influence over this institution.

(5) The fifth sign of feudal relations in the Arab village is, finally, the *"hanas"*--protection, which the feudal lord extends to "his" peasants in their relations with other villages, as well as with the authorities. This "hanas" creates the illusion of a common interest between the fellah and the landowner.

(6) Of no less significance (although of secondary importance in regard to the land question, and not the main problem, as the Zionists maintain) in Arab countries are the irrigation question and the rational use of the land. Marx has already pointed out the enormous significance of irrigation in Eastern countries. Imperialism and feudalism, not being interested in the development of the country, hamper the intensification of agriculture by every possible means. The capital needed for irrigation is imported only in the proportion warranted by the expropriation of the fellahin and their transformation into capitalist hired labor (for plantations, and so on). The enrichment of certain well-to-do peasants in regions where, in the interest of capitalist planters, irrigation is introduced, is in no way characteristic of the masses of the Arab peasants, the pauperization of the majority of whom, even in those same regions, is becoming even more acute. The number of kulaks among the Arabs is very insignificant.

The amount of land possessed by the 23,573 families living in the 104 villages covered by the Simpson statistics is as follows:

TABLE 2

Number of Families		Size of Plot
16,633 have less than		100 dunams
1,463 have from	100 to 120	"
1,604 " "	120 to 140	"
3,873 " more than	140	"
23,573 families		

(7) The main forms of exploitation of the fellah by the British government (besides complete support of imperialistic Zionism and the Arab landowner) are as follows:

In the first place, the extraordinarily heavy taxes. In 1930 the government set the ashar for the population of the rural districts at £225,849, but squeezed out only £120,000, or 55 per cent; from the *verko*[32] set at £192,924 only £60,000, or 30 per cent, was received.

It is often impossible to obtain taxes without the sale of the land at auction. Even according to the opinion of the governor of Jaffa, "fifty percent of the agrarian population, in view of the small income from their economy, not exeeding £30 per year for a family of six persons, should be altogether exempt from taxation." They do not possess anything which could be sold to pay their arrears.

TABLE 3

COMPARISON OF TAXES IN CERTAIN COUNTRIES IN
PALESTINIAN POUNDS PER CAPITA OF POPULATION

Country	Total Taxes	Agricultural Tax
Turkey	1.82	1.43
Egypt	2.75	1.51
Greece	2.85	1.73
Palestine	3.05	1.92

II. Agrarian Reform or Agrarian Revolution

1. The desperate plight of the peasantry, their action in 1929, and the continuous growth of the agrarian movement--all this has brought the agrarian question sharply to the attention of the British imperialists, as well as of all Arab and Jewish parties in Palestine.

Such a situation can no longer endure; a way out is necessary. Hence, all kinds of government commissions and reports (Johnson, Crobie, Strinland, Simpson) and various demands advanced by Arab and Jewish parties and the press. All these proposals boil down to the carrying out of agrarian reforms. The "improvement" of the plight of the fellah has become the slogan of all parties. What are these programs? At whose expense must the reforms be carried out?

2. In the first place, it is necessary to consider the "agrarian program" of the British government. It is tantamount to demagogy

---

[32]A money tax per dunam, as over against the tithe (ashar), which is paid in kind. --Ed.

and deceit. The so-called reduction of taxes ("ashar") resulted in practice·*in doubling them*. Likewise, the agrarian "reforms" of the government have a single purpose: under the guise of "improving" the condition of the fellahin, they continue the pillaging policy of the government and the Zionists, strengthen the position of the effendi, and primarily guarantee the payment of taxes to the government, whose needs are increasing daily (military-strategic construction, etc.). The proposal by Miles for a loan of £2, 800, 000 serves the same purpose. It is clear that the landless peasants will derive no benefit whatsoever from this loan; their "colonization" (if it takes place at all) will become only a new system of enslavement and exploitation, whereas the debt of £2, 800, 000, plus £4, 500, 000 which has remained since 1927 will even increase still further the dependence of the country on British capital. Paltry favors to the peasants (as, for instance, the £35, 000 allocated by the government) are nothing but an attempt at temporary pacification of the countryside. But even these pitiful gifts will undoubtedly find their way, not to the poor fellahin, but to landowners and kulaks.

"The Agrarian Reform" of the government, which in no respect touches either the foundations of the Zionist policy of plunder or the landowners' lands, and which does not solve the question of irrigation and the increase of the capital turnover of the fellah, will not be able to stop the development of the agrarian movement.

3. The agrarian program of various Arab national groups, in so far as it emanates from the program of the Arab Executive Committee and from the demands of numerous "fellahin parties," amounts to a decrease in taxes, a struggle against "middle men" and Zionist purchasers of the land. The sincerity of this program is entirely suspect, since the Arab landowners represented in the Executive Committee themselves sell land to the Zionists.

However, neither the rightist nor the "leftist" Arab nationalists emphasize such basic features of the agrarian peasant question as the landlessness of the peasantry, the feudal exploitation of the village by the landowners, "the hums," peasant indebtedness, etc. Even a group, such as the Hamdi-el-Huseini, does not advance the question of *land* for the peasants. Agrarian reform, as the Arab nationalists intend to carry it out, serves only to deceive the fellah, for it does not solve the basic peasant questions. Moreover, all proposals by the nationalists on the agrarian question suffer from one and the same defect--they do not connect the solution of the agrarian question with the overthrow of imperialism. Their partial demands do not go beyond the framework of the mandate system, which is "constitutional." Therefore, not only are they incapable of organizing a peasant movement, but, in fact, they impede its development.

4. The agrarian program of the Zionists, from the revisionists to the leftist Poalei Zionists, can be formulated briefly: to carry out (it goes without saying, not against British imperialism) an agrarian *reform*, not in order to free the land for the peasants, but to free the peasants from the land and transfer it to the Jewish Zionist colonists. M. Belinson, a prominent Zionist journalist, publishes in the organ of the Histadrut a "résumé" of his thoughts on the agrarian question, as follows: "The misfortune of the fellah lies not in the inadequate supply of land, but rather in its surplus." The leftist Poalei Zionists follow the same line, regarding the expropriation of the fellah as a progressive factor in the development of capitalism.

5. All the programs of the government, the Arab nationalists, and the Zionists have one thing in common--they all see the solution of the fellah question only from "above," that is, an agrarian reform carried out in one way or another by the government. They reject the solution of the agrarian question in accordance with its internal dynamism, with the aid of the peasants, in "plebeian" fashion. The presence of the same methods of expropriation and exploitation of the peasants by imperialism, in spite of continued and repeated agrarian movements in Palestine and in other Arab lands, the peasant uprisings in Syria (1921, 1925, 1927), in Iraq (1920, 1921), in Palestine (1921 and 1929), and numerous partisan uprisings of the fellahin, the growth of peasant "banditry," demonstrates that in Palestine and in other Arab countries the solution of the agrarian question is possible in only one way--the overthrow of imperialism as a result of a victorious agrarian revolution led by the proletariat.

6. The task of the Communist party, as the vanguard of the working class, the only class whose interests at the present stage coincide basically with the interests of the masses of the peasantry, is the direction of the active peasant forces along the line of a decisive struggle against imperialism, and the destruction in this struggle of the hegemony of the Arab national bourgeoisie, and its replacement by the hegemony of the *working class*. While all other parties are interested in deceiving the peasants and in the reformist distortion of their demands, the Communist party can and must develop *revolutionary methods* of solving the agrarian question. The imperialist government demagogically interprets the solution of the agrarian question to be at the expense of the "entire population," which means at the expense of the poor peasants, at the

expense of an increase in oppression and exploitation of the peasantry; the nationalists see the solution of the question in strengthening the position of the landowners and bourgeoisie, and in toy-
ing with the struggle against the Zionists; the Zionists want to
increase the expropriation of the fellahin and they camouflage
this by talking about a struggle with the Arab landowners. The
Communist party sees that the only solution of the peasant question lies in an insurgent revolutionary struggle by the basic masses
of the peasants under the leadership of the working class led by its
Communist party against the imperialists, Zionists, and Arab landowners.

III. The Struggle with Zionism

1. "Zionism is the expression of the exploiting and great power
oppressive strivings of the Jewish bourgeoisie, which makes use
of the persecution of the Jewish national minorities in Eastern
Europe for the purpose of imperialistic policy to insure its domination" (Open Letter of the Executive Committee of the Communist International, November 26, 1930). To achieve this goal, Zionism has allied itself via the mandate and the Balfour Declaration
with British imperialism. In return for the support extended to it
by the British imperialists, Zionism has turned itself into a tool
of British imperialism to suppress the national liberation movement of the Arab masses. At the same time, it is itself making a
tool of the Jewish population of Palestine, including the semiproletarian and proletarian strata.

2. Thus, in Palestine, in addition to imperialistic oppression,
Zionism, as the militant detachment of imperialism, wages a col-
onizing struggle of annihilation against the local toiling masses.
This struggle goes through three stages:

(1) Settlement in the country of Jewish immigrants under the
protection of British bayonets. Only an insignificant part of this
immigration is spontaneous. It is, in the first place, an immigration of cadres, specially trained by means supplied by the Jewish
bourgeoisie (so-called "halutsim"), and specially prepared to seize
the country, and to create a "Jewish state." According to information supplied by the Histadrut, more than 90 per cent of the immigrants who joined it abroad are members of various Zionist parties: "Poalei Zion," "Heholuts," "Tseirei Zion," etc. Only 5 per
cent of the Jewish immigrants are workers. The majority, however, is composed of bourgeois and *petit bourgeois* elements, including counterrevolutionists exiled from the U.S.S.R., etc. The

fact remains, however, that during the first forty years of the existence of Zionism only 2000 immigrants entered Palestine, but during the past ten years, since the opening of Jewish immigration by British imperialism, 130,000 have entered (of whom 90,000 remained in the country); this shows that those who arrive in the country come not by "accident" or "spontaneously," but for the purpose of creating a Jewish state for the Zionists, that is, to win preferential rights for the Jewish bourgeoisie, as compared with the Arab bourgeoisie, to exploit the toiling masses of Palestine by expelling from the country parts of the Arab population and enslaving the rest. One of the leaders of the Jewish National Fund, in a speech made on June 28, 1930, openly declared: "If we take away the land from the Arabs in Palestine, there remains plenty of land in other Arab countries. For several thousand fellahin families, we are not going to stop the solution of the Jewish question."

(2) The second stage of Zionist occupation is the expropriation of the Arab peasants and the colonization of these regions with Jews, the crowding out of Arab workers and their replacement with Jews, the crowding out of Arab small businessmen and artisans and the strengthening of Jewish capital.

(3) In order to implement these two stages, immigration and colonization, which are the indispensable prerequisites for the creation of a "Jewish state," the Jewish bourgeoisie abroad has collected a comparatively huge fund from the broad masses of the Jewish population (Jewish *petite bourgeoisie*), by deceit and by appealing to religious feelings, and from the big Jewish bourgeoisie.

TABLE 4

Money Collected for the Jewish National Fund

Over 8 1/2 years	£3,788,952
For 10 years	£1,707,229
	£5,496,181 (Palestinian)

To this we should add about £15,000,000 (according to Gufin, a director of the Anglo-Palestinian Bank) invested by the Jewish bourgeoisie in the building of Palestine, not via "national" institutions, but directly. This relatively huge capital, considering Palestinian conditions, plus the military forces of the British imperialists, and the enormous influence of the English administrative apparatus, have produced, as compared with the Zionist plans for a Jewish state, insignificant results (6,752 colonists), but they have succeeded in exercising catastrophic influence on the Arab masses. The property of the Jewish communities has increased at the expense of rural and urban lands from 300,000 dunams in 1929 to 1,250,000 in 1930 (Simpson, p. 39). One million dunams, that is, 100,000 ga, amounts to practically nothing for mass colonization and the solution of the "Jewish question." However, the land hunger of the fellahin and Bedouins being what it is, and with the presence of thousands of landless peasants and others with very little land, the seizure of over a million dunams, or about 13 per cent of the arable land, means pauperization for the fellahin and Bedouins on an unheard of scale and tempo. The total number of fellahin families expelled from their land by the Zionists amounts to 20,000.

The prewar colonization of Palestine by the Zionists differs from that of the postwar period, when Zionism became an organic part of British imperialism, in that in the prewar era part of the expropriated peasants found work among the Jewish colonists, who *exploited* them but did not crowd them out. Since the war, however, Zionist colonization has been accompanied by a struggle for the extermination of the Arab fellahin and workers, by implementing the slogan, *"Kibush avoda."* [33] The Jewish immigrant workers not only establish themselves on lands seized from the fellahin, where they settle down with the support of Zionist societies, not only do they introduce the problem of Jewish labor in all enterprises established by Jewish capital and the exclusion of Arab labor, not only do they demand from the government an increase in the number of Jewish workers and clerks (in reality, in government institutions and enterprises Jewish immigrants not only obtain work along with the Arabs, but appreciably more than they do and usually faster), but they likewise crowd out the Arab workers from those Jewish colonies where they have been working for years. According to Zionist statistics, for instance, in Jerusalem for the past year the number of Arab construction workers decreased from 1,500 to 500, while the number of Jewish workers increased from 550 to 1,600; in the Jewish colonies, instead of 8,000 Arab workers, there remain only 4,500, and now a struggle is being waged to eliminate even those who are left.

(4) Thus Zionist activity has been detrimental to all strata of the Arab population, with the exception of the landowners. According to Dr. Rupin, 90 per cent of the lands purchased by the Zionists were sold by Arab effendi. The cost of the land has risen by

---

[33] A Zionist slogan, meaning "Seizure of Labor."--Ed.

leaps and bounds (from £0.30 per dunam prior to the war to from £3 to £4 at the present time). Zionist colonization accelerates the expropriation of the fellahin by the feudal lords, who concentrate the peasant land in their hands, in order to sell it to the Zionists. Only of late, part of the Arab landowners have begun to make use of their plots to rationalize their economy, thereby slowing down the sale of land to the Zionists. However, in the latter case, the effendi do not confine themselves to the expropriation of the small fellahin. If Zionism previously helped only to strengthen the financial position of the Arab capitalists and landowners, now it transforms them into an outright weapon of Zionist imperialist colonization, driving them to plunder the peasant lands in order to resell them to Zionist societies.

(5) The third stage of Zionist usurpation is the creation of political privileges for Jews, as compared with the Arab population. This is expressed by making it easier for Jews to obtain citizenship, by extending to the "Jewish Agency" consultative functions, by privileges for Jewish municipalities, by officially recognizing the ancient Hebrew language, etc. All this creates for the Jewish bourgeoisie an opportunity to continue the nonsensical deceit of the Jewish masses about the idea of a "Jewish state" and to increase the oppression of the Arab masses. Therefore the struggle against Zionism is such a natural and inevitable manifestation of Arab mass indignation that not one of these Arab parties, even those representing the effendi and the compradores, can refuse to make use of anti-Zionist slogans. Inasmuch as the bulk of the Jewish population of Palestine is under the direct influence and leadership of the Zionists, who conduct their imperialist policy in the name of the Jewish nation and for a Jewish state, the anti-Zionist movement emerges in the form of an anti-Jewish movement, and affords an opportunity to the English imperialists and the Jewish bourgeoisie, together with the Arab landowners, to turn the dissatisfaction of the Arab masses into the channel of a struggle against the Jewish national minority *as a whole*.

(6) However, it would be very erroneous to regard imperialism, Zionism, and the Jewish population *solely* as one organic whole (which, for the time being, they are with regard to the Arab masses), among whom there are no *internal contradictions* which undermine these oppressive forces from within. In their national and social liberation struggle the Arab masses, led by the Communist party, must give careful consideration to these internal contradictions, hostile to the colonizing forces, and must make use of them on a very wide scale. In the first place, the acute cri-

sis of imperialism and the growing weakness of the British Empire compel English imperialism to resort to various maneuvers at the expense of its alliance with Zionism. The imperialists are interested in the privileges and in the growth of the Jewish minority supported by English bayonets, but still they have no wish to create a Jewish state. Hence there is a conflict between the demands of the Jewish bourgeoisie, who want to go much too far, and British imperialism. These conflicts, however, cannot be regarded as serious, especially as signs of a breach. Nevertheless, such a clash exposes Zionist deceit to the Jewish masses of Poland, America, etc., and weakens the influence of Zionism, which is expressed in a reduction of the influx of money into Palestine. As a result of this there emerges, in the first place, a conflict between Zionist leadership and those Jewish immigrants who depend on subsidies from Zionist societies, and to whom the Zionists are often in no position to give work, or even minimum assistance (in 1926 in Palestine there were over ten thousand unemployed immigrants). Second, in order to strengthen their colonizing cause and to force the Jewish immigrants to play the role of usurpers, the Zionists cannot confine themselves to agitation and deceit, but are compelled to offer the Jewish workers certain economic benefits. For this purpose the Zionist bourgeoisie, together with the traitorous Poalei Zion party, have organized the Jewish Workers' Organization, Histadrut, whose task it is to insure the Jewish workers a privileged status in the labor market in return for including them in a "nation-wide" front. The Jewish bourgeoisie, through the so-called "National" Fund and the Histadrut, creates, in the first place, a whole net of agricultural "posts," strategically located in such a way as to facilitate the gradual seizure of the entire country.

The Jewish colonist is by no means "an oppressed peasant"--compared with the Arabs, he occupies the position of a farmer: on the average, the basic capital of the Jewish peasant (per capita) in Palestine amounts in Zionist colonies to £1000, whereas the basic capital of the fellah (together with the family) amounts to from £20 to £30. The land is bought by Zionist societies and is the property of the Jewish bourgeoisie, government clerks, etc. Often the Jewish farmer or member of a Zionist agricultural "commune," of course, is essentially a poor man; however, as compared with the Arab fellah, he is in a privileged class, which receives from the bourgeoisie schools and hospitals and which, therefore, constitutes a solid support for the Jewish bourgeoisie against the Arab toilers.

Only in those cases in which the Zionist bourgeoisie is not in a
position to fulfill its obligations and the living standards of the Jewish colonists decline sharply, the Jewish colonists are forced either
"to desert" the imperialist front, that is, to emigrate, or to go
over to the revolutionary camp. Conflicts between Jewish workers
and Jewish capitalists are one of the most important levers of the
revolutionary movement, and they cause the Jewish proletariat to
join the front of anti-imperialist struggle. The privileges of the
Jewish workers, even after they have abandoned the stage of "tutelage," and become hired laborers, are expressed as follows:
(1) preference in obtaining work in Jewish enterprises (at the huge
"Nasher" enterprise, electric power stations, etc.), (2) higher
wages, as compared with the Arabs, (3) a number of special institutions, which are closed to Arab workers, as, for instance,
a factory hospital fund, (4) better working conditions, a shorter
working day, etc.

But in proportion to Zionist expansion these privileges are gradually disappearing. There is a trend toward a decline in the wages
of Jewish workers, which, although they remain much higher than
those of Arab workers, are gradually being equalized. On this
ground, conflicts arise between the Jewish workers and the bourgeoisie. The Jewish workers, especially see clearly the instability

TABLE 5

AVERAGE WAGES OF ARAB AND JEWISH WORKERS,
BASED UPON 1929 GOVERNMENT STATISTICS (p. 27)
(in mills per day)[34]

Agricultural Workers	Jews	Arabs
Skilled	250-350	150-250
Unskilled	175-220	80-120
Women.	150-210	50-100
Children	- -	50- 80
Industrial and Construction Workers		
1st Category	350-700	350-700
2nd "	250-360	200-300
Unskilled	200-300	100-160

[34]Mill--0.01 Palestine pounds, that is approximately one kopeck.
--Ed.

of their privileges, when they are compelled to enter into an out-right struggle against a capitalist of their own nationality (the colonist manufacturer) or be thrown out in the street by him (unemployment).

(7) The process of stratification *within* the Jewish proletariat has become more and more evident in recent years. In big enterprises, there is being created a group of privileged workers, who form a stratum of Jewish "working aristocracy." These are workers in enterprises (Rutenberg, Histadrut Cooperatives, etc.). In contrast to them is the mass of unskilled labor, often unemployed, starving, and the most exploited. To the working aristocracy also belongs a part of the "oriental" workers (Georgian, Bokharan, and other Jews, who work in the colonies and at government enterprises).

(8) Besides the Histadrut, various Zionist parties, ranging from avowed Fascists to Rightist and "Leftist" Social Fascists, play no insignificant role in enslaving the Jewish workers. In spite of the fact that they are composed of petite bourgeoisie, they actually express in the most glaring fashion the great-power strivings of the Jewish bourgeoisie.

The Rightist Social Fascists (mifalaga meuhedet), who express the interests of the most privileged strata of the Jewish working class, and who carry on, in practice, the most brutal anti-Arab colonizing activity *(kibush adama, kibush avoda),* are the most loyal agents of the imperialist and Jewish bourgeoisie among the Jewish workers. They are being protected with Leftist phrases by the *"Leftist" Social Fascists* (Poalei Zion), who juggle Marxist phraseology, but in reality constitute the main obstacle to the masses of Jewish workers going over into the camp of real class struggle against the bourgeoisie (manufacturers, Zionist organizations, and colonists), into the camp of the national and social liberation movement of the Arab masses.

Published in Arabic, in *Ila al-Aman (Forward),* the organ of the Communist party of Palestine, 1931; in the Hebrew language, in a separate brochure, in 1931.

Published for the first time in Russian.

The above *Documents* undoubtedly will reinforce the views held by many scholars and statesmen as to the futility of relying on treaty arrangements concluded with the Soviet Union, the basis of which is "coexistence. " The best example is the Communist program for Turkey, an independent Muslim state, which had entered into a treaty of "friendship and fraternity" with Soviet Russia in 1921, in which each country promised to avoid interference in the internal affairs of the other. Nevertheless, the Communist program for Turkey (1931) outlines the very steps by which the regime of Kemal Pasha must be undermined, ultimately overthrown, and the country taken over by the Communists.

Likewise the programs for the Arab countries, especially for Egypt, reveal the extent of the infiltration by Communist agents in that area. It would be of great benefit for the Arabs in general, and for the Egyptians in particular, to read and study this primary source material bearing upon the future prepared for them. The Palestine program should be of equal interest to contemporary Israel. The attack on Zionism and the emphasis on the Arabization of the Communist party of Palestine clearly indicate the handwriting on the wall as far as the Jewish state is concerned. In view of their experiences in the past, the Arab peoples have been prone to question the motives of the Western powers, especially those of England and France, but also those of the United States, in the Near and Middle East. These *Documents* leave no room for doubt as to the designs of the Soviet Union. For the entire Near East, communism spells doom for Turks, Arabs, and Jews alike.

The above *Documents* also throw light on the tactics of the Third International. For instance, part of the material pertaining to Syria and Palestine was published for the first time, neither in Arabic nor in Russian, but in Japanese in 1928 in Tokyo. Although the program was designed for Arab countries, Communist leaders must have felt that, in some respects, it would be useful in Japan, especially in the agrarian areas. Although on the surface the program appeared to have nothing to do with the Japanese, since it pertained to the Arabs, it was nevertheless designed to undermine the political stability of Japan. Moreover, publication of the program in the Japanese language was less likely to attract the attention of the English and French, the League of Nations mandatory powers for Palestine and Syria respectively. Not even the Russian people were conditioned for the publication of such material in 1928, at the beginning of the first Five-Year Plan. Even the Russian edition of these programs in 1934 must have been a small one, restricted to a select group of Communists in key positions, judging by the absence of any reference to them in Soviet publications on the Near East.

Irrespective of the future course of events in the Muslim world, these programs will remain a standard text on Soviet designs for the eventual inclusion of that world in the Soviet orbit. This is further substantiated by the report of Khalid Bakdash, the leader of the Arabic Communists, to the central command of the Communist party of Syria and Lebanon in January 1951.[8] In an orgy of self-criticism, similar to that which was characteristic of Stalin's Russia in the same period, Bakdash bemoaned the general lack of theoretical knowledge of the principles of Marxism-Leninism, and admitted that the attention of the Arab Communists had been directed mainly toward the creation of "a lot of sound and fury" rather than toward the establishment of solid foundations among the workers and fellahin. His program was in substance little more than a paraphrase of the 1934 documents.

7. The Lull in Soviet-Muslim Relations, 1927-41

Leninism leads to the emancipation of the peoples of the East.
--Inscription on the Lenin Monument in Tashkent.

After Soviet expansion in the direction of the Near and Middle East was blocked in the early twenties by internal resistance on the part of Turkey, Iran, and Afghanistan, as well as by their counterattack against Soviet Russia as expressed in the *Basmatchestvo* revolt, the U.S.S.R. met with another resounding defeat in the Far East with the loss of China in 1927. The Nanking government, with Anglo-American support, broke off diplomatic relations with the Soviet Union.

Following the treaties of 1921 with Turkey, Iran, and Afghanistan, the impression was given in the Soviet press that the Soviet government was turning its attention from the Orient to Europe. Doubtful as was the prospect for European revolution, the Soviets appeared determined to continue the spread of Communist propaganda and to make enough trouble for Europeans at home that they would have no "appetite" for the renewal of intervention against the U.S.S.R. In September, 1924, however, tempted by the opportunities in China, the Soviet government sent Communist propagandists there, headed by Michael Borodin,[1] to try once again to bring about a revolution in the Orient--this time in the Far East. With their experience in the Near East, they were dubious about being able to produce in China a revolution of the 1917 Bolshevik vintage. They did hope to achieve there the equivalent of the Russian Revolution of 1905.

There is evidence in the Russian literature of the period that this sudden shift of emphasis from Europe to Asia did not meet with the unanimous approval of Soviet leaders. The best substantiation of

181

this is to be found in a cartoon published in *Pravda* (January 30, 1925), following the dispatch of Borodin to China. This cartoon depicted a compass, accompanied by the reassuring message from the Narkomindel, "The needle turns to the East. Don't worry, gentlemen. There is no anomaly here. Everything is in order." Apparently the sudden about-face in policy caught many Party members in the Soviet Union unprepared, and Party leaders took this somewhat unorthodox means of reassuring them. In spite of Soviet efforts to accomplish in the Far East what they had been unable to do in the Near and Middle East, and in spite of the millions of dollars in gold devoted to this objective at a time when the Russians could ill afford to spend it abroad, here as before the Soviet government failed to instigate a revolution.

In general, from 1927 to 1941, there was no direct Soviet action on a large scale in the Muslim countries of the Near East. Soviet activities, for the most part, were restricted to the blueprint for communism, represented by the programs presented in the previous chapter, and to instructions and guidance to local Communist groups, which were weak and inarticulate, and which, in most cases, had been driven underground.

The main reasons for the comparative lull in Soviet-Muslim relations in the Near East are as follows: the rise of Fascism, whatever our views concerning it, was the strongest deterrent to communism in Europe. Fascism represented middle-class reaction against disruptive Communist tactics in Western European countries. It likewise reflected the disillusionment of Western European Socialists and workers over Soviet treatment of Russian Social Revolutionaries and Mensheviki inside the Soviet Union. Fascism accomplished in Europe the same results in regard to the Soviet Union that Islam achieved in 1921, when it forestalled Soviet expansion in the Near and Middle East. The rise of Hitler in Germany and the expansion of Japan on the Chinese mainland in the early thirties threatened the U.S.S.R. with a possible pincer movement. The Soviet government, facing danger on two fronts, had to concentrate its efforts on defense and had little opportunity for adventures in the Muslim world. Although the Nazi brand of Fascism eventually proved more dangerous than communism, for the time being it served to divert Soviet attention from the Near East and to save the Muslim world from the Soviet orbit. In preparing to face new threats from Germany in Europe and Japan in Asia, the Soviet Union placed more and more emphasis on nonaggression pacts with neighboring countries, proceeded to normalize its relations with the United States, which recognized the U.S.S.R. in

—Стрелка поворачивается на восток. Не беспокойтесь, господа, здесь нет никакой аномалии. Все правильно.

Рис Д. Моор.

"The needle turns to the East. Don't worry, gentlemen. There
is no anomaly here. Everything is in order."

                                    --Pravda, January 30, 1925

November, 1933, joined the League of Nations in 1934, and entered into an alliance with France in 1935.

The desperate economic situation on the Soviet domestic front, with the famine that accompanied the failure of the first Five-Year Plan, and frantic Soviet efforts in the direction of industrialization, deterred the Soviet government from engaging in activities that would unduly antagonize the major colonial powers, England and France, especially in India and the Near East. The vigilance of the colonial powers themselves in the mandatory areas and in Egypt was sufficient to offset the feeble and spasmodic attempts of local Communist parties to upset the stability of established governments. Moreover, the national liberation movements against colonialism in Muslim countries, certainly among the Arabic peoples, were in the hands of the bourgeoisie and upper classes, as the Communists themselves admitted in their own programs. In Egypt, for instance, the Wafd party was a counterpart of the Kadets in Tsarist Russia.

Even as late as 1954, B. N. Zakhoder, head of the department of Near and Middle Eastern history and economics of the Institute of Oriental Studies at the Academy of Sciences of the U.S.S.R., declared that the reason why the national revolutionary struggle was successful (1949) in the Far East--the non-Muslim world--and failed in the Near and Middle East--the Muslim world--was that in the Far East it was led by the working class, which alone guaranteed victory, whereas in the Near and Middle East it was led by the national bourgeoisie, who invariably failed to take decisive action at the opportune moment.[2] Soviet historians and leaders, including Stalin, likewise attributed the failure of the Taiping Rebellion in China (1850-64) to the lack of proletarian leadership. According to Soviet thinking the view still prevails that a revolution, even in predominantly agrarian countries, to be successful must be controlled by the working class, even if it constitutes a minority.

Typical of the Soviet policy of normalizing relations with neighboring countries during this period was the alacrity with which the Soviet government responded (April 16) to the Turkish note of April 11, 1936, calling for the revision of the Lausanne Treaty of 1923, in particular for the abrogation of those clauses providing for the demilitarization of the Straits. Turkish action was a direct outgrowth of Turkish fear of the growing strength of Fascist Italy in the eastern Mediterranean and of the inability of the League of Nations to take prompt and decisive action to stop the Italian invasion of Abyssinia in 1935. At the subsequent conference at Montreux, Switzerland, June 22 to July 29, the focal point of disagreement between England and the U.S.S.R. concerned first, the right of free passage of the warships of the Black Sea powers through the Straits into the Mediterranean and second, the right of entry into the Black Sea of the fleets of non-Black Sea powers. The compromise reached was in many respects favorable to the Soviet Union.

The Montreux Convention, signed on July 20, granted complete freedom of transit through the Straits for the commercial vessels of all nations. It permitted the Russians unlimited egress for surface vessels and tankers in peacetime, subject to the proviso that warships of more than fifteen thousand tons must proceed singly through the Straits. Soviet submarines were likewise permitted to pass singly through the Straits by day when returning to their Black Sea bases or en route to dockyards located elsewhere. The control of transit for the vessels of the non-Black Sea powers was achieved by restricting the aggregate tonnage, admitting only "light warships," and limiting the length of their stay. In the event of a conflict in which Turkey remained neutral, the warships of belligerents were permitted passage to aid a victim of aggression, provided such assistance resulted from action taken under the League of Nations Covenant or under a treaty of mutual assistance signed by Turkey and concluded within the framework of the Covenant. The Convention granted Turkey complete sovereignty over the Straits, permitting her to close them to the warships of all nations in the interests of her own security when she, herself, was a belligerent or in imminent danger of war, subject to League of Nations action.

The Soviet Union was in many respects well satisfied with the Montreux Convention, which safeguarded Soviet exit to the Mediterranean and restricted the naval power of potential enemies in the Black Sea. The standard Soviet history of diplomacy as late as 1945 conceded that, "In spite of some shortcomings in the Convention, its acceptance was of great positive significance and it was a tremendous victory for Soviet diplomacy."[3] At the end of World War II, however, the Soviet government demanded the revision of the Montreux Convention on the ground that its disadvantages outweighed the advantages, due to the fact that it conferred on Turkey the exclusive right to control the Straits, to interpret the Convention, and to implement it unilaterally.[4] Since the powers concerned failed to agree on the nature of the "revision," the Montreux Convention continued to determine the use of the Straits after World War II.

The decline of Soviet influence in the Near and Middle East in this period can be measured by the fact that the very states Soviet Russia had counted upon to spread communism throughout the Muslim world--Turkey, Iran, and Afghanistan--joined with Iraq on July 8, 1937, in Teheran to conclude the Saadabad Pact,[5] the main provisions of which had been agreed upon in 1935, although the pact was held up pending the settlement of the Iran-Iraq boundary dispute. Although the Turks, who initiated proceedings for this "Near Eastern Entente," may have been impelled by fear of Italian expansion in the Mediterranean under Mussolini, the other Middle Eastern states had no immediate cause for concern from this quarter. The Soviet government viewed the pact as a British scheme to create a chain of alliances along the southern Soviet border directed against the U.S.S.R. and to insure joint action on the part of member countries to stamp out the national liberation movement in this Muslim area (Clause VII).[6] Although the Saadabad Pact remained in effect a scrap of paper, it appears to have served as a pattern for the Baghdad Pact of 1955, which was likewise intended to establish an effective barrier to Soviet expansion to the south.

In the thirties communism had still another competitor in the Near and Middle East--namely, Nazism. This was particularly true of Egypt and Iran, not to mention the growing strength of German influence in Turkey. According to Soviet sources,[7] by 1941 there were about four thousand German secret agents operating in Iran, approximately one thousand of them in Teheran. Some of these agents were located in the vicinity of the borders of Soviet Turkestan, with the alleged object of creating bases in Iran for an ultimate attack on the U.S.S.R. In Teheran and in some provincial cities, Nazi organizations were established, in many cases under the guise of tourist camps. All these Nazi activities were directed by the German ambassador, Von Ettelen, and by the German consuls in Iran, with inspection from time to time by such top Nazi leaders as Hjalmar Schacht, the financial wizard, and Baldur von Schirach, a Nazi youth leader. Extensive Nazi propaganda, aimed especially at the Soviet Union, was conducted through the press, radio, cinema, and "cultural" societies. From 1933 to 1937 the Nazis published a paper, *Irane-Bastan (Ancient Iran)* and a monthly magazine, both in the Persian language. As late as 1940 they even organized a "Brown House" in Teheran and began construction of the Nazi-Abada (Nazi city), which was to become the Nazi center in Iran.

Whereas the Bolsheviks had sought to disseminate communism in Iran, Nazi propagandists appealed to the people on the basis of their

Aryan origins, that is, on the ground of racial superiority. This approach had greater appeal for the Iranian nationalists than did Soviet propaganda, since nationalism was stronger in Iran than the *Klassenkampf*.

Because of Iran's proximity to the Soviet Union and because it was the gateway to Baku and Central Asia, the Nazis concentrated their efforts in that country over a more extended period of time. Nazi anti-Communist propaganda was likewise strong in the Arab countries, especially in Egypt and Iraq. Their emphasis among the Arabs was on Islam as the enemy of atheistic communism. Nazi propaganda appealed to the Muslim world to join forces with the Nazis under the leadership of the Führer against the Comintern. [8] As in Soviet Russia after the Baku Congress, the Germans entered upon an intensive study of the Islamic world from the standpoint of Nazi interests and possible Nazi infiltration. Just as the Communists before them had sought to identify Lenin with Mohammed and communism with the Koran, the Germans proceeded to link Hitler with Mohammed and Kemal Pasha, and Nazism with Islam. They even sought "to debunk" the Baku Congress of 1920, which had stirred up the Muslim world, by pointing out that it was run by three Jews: "Moskau hatte zu diesen Kongress drei 'Prominente' entsandt: Sinowjew [Zinoviev], damals Vorsitzender des Vollzugsausschusses der III Internationale, Bela Khun und Radek. Drei Juden!"[9]

The success of the Nazi propaganda campaign was reflected in the spectacular increase in German-Iranian trade and the parallel slump in Soviet-Iranian trade. Whereas from 1936/37 the U.S.S.R. accounted for 35.5 per cent of all Iranian foreign trade, by 1939/40 the Soviet share was only 0.5 per cent. By 1938/39 Germany, which had previously done very little business with Iran, occupied first place, with more than 40 per cent of the entire foreign trade of Iran. [10]

In spite of the strength of anti-Nazi sentiment in England at this time, British colonial authorities appear to have evinced a considerable degree of tolerance toward the Nazis under their jurisdiction and influence. The best explanation appears to be that in the colonies and mandates the British regarded the Soviet Union as a greater potential threat than the Germans and even hoped to use the Nazis as tools to rid them of communism.

Just as Turkey, Iran, and the Arab states tried to suppress the Communist movement among their peoples, in the Soviet Middle East during this period the Soviet government made every effort to counteract Western and Muslim propaganda emanating from Muslim countries outside the U.S.S.R.

The various manifestoes and appeals of the newborn Soviet regime to the Muslim peoples for national self-determination proved to be a two-edged sword. Strictly speaking, the application of self-determination to the Muslim minorities inside the Russian borders would have meant the dismemberment of Russia in the East on a scale equivalent to that effected in European Russia by the Treaty of Brest-Litovsk (1918). Like any other colonial power, the Soviet government expected to assume control of this movement, at least during its early stages. It soon discovered, however, especially during the *Basmatchestvo* revolt, that this was easier said than done. As a result, the Soviet government required time to reassert Soviet authority in this irredentist area. The Turks, Iranians, and Afghans all had claims on Soviet Central Asia, and Turkic, Iranian, and Afghan peoples were to be found on both sides of the border.

On May 1, 1918, within a few months of the establishment of the Bolshevik regime, the fifth All-Turkestan Congress of Soviets proclaimed the Turkestan Autonomous Soviet Socialist Republic (TASSR) in what was formerly Russian Turkestan. The bitter resistance of Muslim leaders to Soviet rule, together with the widespread nature of the *Basmatchi* insurrection in Central Asia, soon led the beleaguered Soviet government to divide the TASSR into a number of separate republics, thereby weakening the opposition forces. The partition of the Soviet Middle East began in August, 1921, to the tune of a high-pressure propaganda drive, emphasizing the desirability of creating independent republics along ethnic, national, and linguistic lines--the Soviet version of a national liberation movement. The effectiveness of this propaganda, even among the Muslims it was designed to weaken, was demonstrated shortly after the establishment of the Republic of Uzbekistan. On December 15, 1924, an assembly of Muslim spiritual leaders in Tashkent issued "An Appeal to All the Muslim Peoples of the East": "Turn your eyes, Muslim peoples, to the land of the Soviet Republics, where there live many free Muslim peoples. In contrast to the imperialists, who for hundreds of years have blocked the development of the native population, the Soviet Government with all its strength assists the growth of the Muslim peoples."[11]

This Soviet policy of "divide and rule," which is still in effect, has served at least a twofold purpose. As already indicated, it divided and weakened Islamic authority, the chief unifying factor in Soviet Central Asia, while at the same time the satisfaction over "national liberation" took much of the wind from the *Basmatchi* sails. In the second place, it served until World War II as an important propaganda weapon abroad, where the Muslims of the Arab world, India, and Indonesia, were still subjected to the Western "colonialism" of England, France, and the Netherlands.

Census taking in Muslim countries has always proved to be a difficult task. The same situation prevailed in Central Asiatic Russia. According to M. S. Rybakov, as of January 1, 1912 (*Mir Islama,* XI [1913], 269-71) there were in Tsarist Russia 16,226,073 Muslims, of whom 4,635,000 lived in European Russia, 7,955,000 in Central Asia, 3,335,000 in the Caucasus, and 120,000 in Siberia. [12] François de Romainville in 1947 claimed that there were 20,000,000 Muslims in the U.S.S.R.: "Avec vingt millions d'âmes, le groupe musulman constitue la minorité la plus importante de l'URSS. "[13] S. Maksudov, a member of the provisional Central Bureau of the Russian Muslims, speaking in 1917 before the Kadet Congress declared that there were 30,000,000 Muslims in Russia. [14] Today there are between 25,000,000 and 30,000,000 Muslims in the Soviet Union. [15] Although major and periodic population shifts in the U.S.S.R. do not make for stability in the location of the Muslim peoples, there are six so-called Muslim republics: Azerbaijan (capital, Baku), Uzbekistan (capital, Tashkent), Kazakhstan (capital, Alma Ata), Turkmenistan (capital, Ashkhabad), Tadjikistan (capital, Stalinabad), Kirghizia (capital, Frunze). Four other republics, the Crimean, Ingush, Chechen, and Balkar were literally liquidated in 1944.

From the standpoint of religious administration, the Sunni Muslim community has been organized since World War II, at least since 1948, under four administrative councils, each headed by a mufti, as follows: (1) Russia in Europe and Siberia; (2) Central Asia; (3) Transcaucasia; and (4) Daghestan and North Caucasia. The Shi'is in Baku have been placed under a sheikh ul-Islam.

The primary task of the Soviet government was to reconcile Soviet Muslims, who constituted from 10 to 12 per cent of the population, to the Soviet regime and to counteract the impact of the independent Muslim states of Turkey, Iran, Afghanistan, and Iraq (1936) on the Soviet frontier. Thus the Soviet government, having established the six Muslim republics, at least on paper, with a modicum of cultural and political autonomy, sought to offset the independent Muslim states of the Middle East. Likewise to counteract the Zionist homeland, it created the autonomous region of Birobidjan.

Soviet propaganda in the Muslim republics then sought to convince Soviet Muslims that they were already far ahead of foreign Muslims and could learn nothing from their experience. Soviet Muslims were assured that they were superior, culturally and economically, to their Muslim neighbors. They were told that by the establishment of the six Muslim republics, their national liberation movement was complete, that they had not only achieved political independence but had installed working-class governments. The Muslims outside the U.S.S.R., on the other hand, either remained under the domination of "the imperialist colonizers," or had achieved only the first stage of national liberation, political independence minus social revolution, and were still subject to the internal yoke--the bourgeois domestic regime.

To symbolize the leadership of Soviet Muslims among the peoples of the East, there were erected throughout Central Asia and the Caucasus monuments to Lenin, in which the Soviet leader, with his right hand uplifted, pointed to the East. On the pedestal, in Arabic and in Russian, appeared the inscription, "Leninism leads to the emancipation of the peoples of the East."[16] The Soviet government by every possible means sought to instill into the minds of Soviet Muslims that their republics were the models for the Orient.

Soviet leaders proceeded with caution to break traditional or existing cultural ties between the Soviet Muslims and those abroad. As in the case of Turkey, where Kemal Pasha had substituted the Latin for the Arabic script, the Soviet government began its attack on the Islamic character of the Muslim languages at the Congress of Turcology in Baku in 1926.[17] The decision reached at this congress to substitute the Latin instead of the Cyrillic alphabet for the Arabic was designed to prevent all semblance of "Russification" of the Muslim East. It was not until March 13, 1938, that the decree was issued making Russian the second compulsory language of the Soviet Muslim republics. The replacement of the Latin alphabet by the Cyrillic took place, beginning in 1939.

To sum up, we may safely say that during the period under consideration neither the Muslims inside the U.S.S.R. nor those outside exercised any appreciable influence upon each other. The Soviet government effectively sealed off the Soviet Muslims from contact with the outside world. Both inside and outside the U.S.S.R. the Muslim states were mainly absorbed in their own domestic problems. That these problems remained basically unsolved seems clear from the fact that Muslim states on both sides of the Soviet border were by no means immune to Nazi penetration and propaganda in World War II. In Egypt, North Africa, and Iran, Nazism constituted a major threat to the Western Allies, and it was strong

Courtesy Sovfoto

Lenin monument in Tashkent, Uzbek SSR, pointing to the Near
and Middle East

enough to bring Turkey to the brink of war with the Soviet Union during the period of German military successes. Inside the U.S. S.R., with the advance of Nazi armies to the Caucasus, many Muslims collaborated with the Germans, with the result that in 1944 the Soviet government deported the entire Muslim population of four autonomous Muslim republics--the Crimean, Ingush, Chechen, and Balkar--to unspecified destinations east of the Volga.

The comparative lull in Soviet-Muslim relations in the Near and Middle East may be attributed in large measure to the threat of Hitlerite Germany. In the thirties the Soviets, in spite of the rising Japanese menace, began to subordinate Asia to Europe in order to meet the Nazi threat. The entire regime was mobilized for this purpose. In the clash between the Red Army forces and the Japanese at Khasan in 1938 and at Nomanhan in 1939, Soviet action remained defensive, confined to the repulse of the Japanese attacks, and Soviet leaders resisted every temptation to become involved in an aggressive campaign in the Far East.

This shift in emphasis in Soviet foreign policy from the East back to the West became effective during the purges of 1936 to 1937, which revealed the existence of a fifth column in the Red Army officer corps, including Marshal Tukhatchevsky, Generals Putna, Yakir, Ulorevitch, Feldman, Kork, Primakov, Eideman, and others. Since Soviet literature and the arts are the best barometer of Soviet domestic and foreign policies, it is logical that the Soviet government should have sought to interpret the Soviet policy shift to the West and to justify it to the Soviet public through the medium of a film--the Serge Eisenstein film, *Alexander Nevsky,* produced in the record time of little more than a year. The purpose of this film was to convince the Soviet peoples that the German threat loomed larger than the Japanese, that the Germans had been in the past and still could be defeated by the Russians, and that the Russians, confronted simultaneously by invasion from the East and West, must as in the past forego retaliation in the Orient. In other words, the East must be subordinated to the West and "the Mongols can wait." Under these conditions, the Bolshevization of the Near and Middle East likewise had to wait for more propitious circumstances, soon to be provided by World War II.

8. Soviet Foreign Policy
vis-à-vis the Muslim World, 1941-58

> No matter what happens . . . peace or new con-
> cessions on the part of Russia . . . sooner or later,
> Constantinople will be ours. . . .
> --F. M. Dostoyevsky.

On June 22, 1941, breaking a ten-year nonaggression pact with
the U.S.S.R., signed on August 23, 1939, Nazi Germany invaded
the Soviet Union without a prior declaration of war. Irrespective
of the motives behind the Stalin-Hitler pact--whether it was designed to forestall an Anglo-French deal with Nazi Germany which
would have given Hitler a green light in the East, or whether it
was the product of a diabolical intent to release the forces of Nazi
Germany against the West while the U.S.S.R. remained an on-
looker--the fact remains that it was the immediate cause for the
outbreak of World War II. It likewise launched the Soviet Union on
a policy of aggressive imperialism that was to affect the destinies
of Europe and Asia.

The secret negotiations between the Germans and the Russians
during the period of Nazi-Soviet collaboration from 1939 to 1941,
in which they sought to define their respective spheres of influence,
registered the revival of Soviet designs on the Muslim world, especially with regard to Turkey and Iran. During these negotiations,
Soviet Foreign Minister Molotov insisted on the vital interest of
the Soviet Union in the Straits Question and demanded the right to
establish "a base for light naval and land forces of the U.S.S.R.
in [am] the Bosphorus and the Dardanelles by means of a long-term
lease. . . ." German intrigue in Iran notwithstanding, he likewise
pegged out a Soviet claim to an indefinite Soviet sphere "south of
Batum and Baku in the general direction of the Persian Gulf."[1]
Although the Nazi invasion of the U.S.S.R. on June 22, 1941, pre-

cluded the implementation of such a program, the Soviet government undoubtedly expected to obtain concessions from the Western Allies comparable to those demanded of the Germans.

I

Although the Iranian government formally declared its neutrality on September 4, 1939, following the outbreak of hostilities in Europe, and again on June 26, 1941, on the heels of the German attack on the U.S.S.R., the Soviet government, in view of German machinations in Iran, feared the opening up of a second German-Iranian front aimed at the Soviet Muslim areas of the Caucasus and Central Asia. In three successive notes of June 26, July 19, and August 16, 1941, it protested against German activity in Iran and called upon the Iranian government to evict German agents. The British government took parallel action. Either because Iranian leaders failed to foresee that Anglo-Soviet action was imminent or because the Germans were too well entrenched there to permit freedom of action, they failed to comply with the Anglo-Soviet ultimatums. On August 25, at four o'clock in the morning, following the presentation of their final notes to the Iranian government, Soviet and British forces invaded Iran. Encountering no appreciable resistance from the population, the Red Army entered Teheran on September 17, with the English one day behind them. On September 16, as the Red Army approached the capital, Reza Shah, founder of the Pahlevi dynasty, who successfully stemmed the tide of the Soviet advance in 1921 and reached a *modus vivendi* with the Russians the same year, abdicated in favor of his twenty-three-year-old son Muhammed Reza. Afghanistan profited by the fate of her Iranian neighbor and in October, 1941, acceded to Anglo-Soviet requests for the expulsion of Axis agents.

Foreign Minister Molotov's note of August 25, after a summation of Soviet concessions to Iran, 1918 to 1921, and of the violation of Soviet-Iranian treaty obligations resulting from German intrigue in Iran, proceeded to justify the Soviet occupation of northern Iran by citing Article VI of the Soviet-Iranian Treaty of February 26, 1921 (reaffirmed in 1927).[2] This famous article, it will be recalled, provided for Soviet entry into Iran in the event that a third country attempted to seize Iran or to make of it a base for the military invasion of Soviet Russia.

Negotiations for a Tripartite Treaty of Alliance on the part of the U.S.S.R., Great Britain, and Iran, begun in September, 1941, were concluded on January 29, 1942. By this treaty, the U.S.S.R.

and Great Britain guaranteed the territorial integrity and political independence of Iran (Article I) and provided for the withdrawal of Soviet and English forces six months after the end of the war. In order to protect the vital supply line to beleaguered Russia, Iran conceded to her allies the use and military control of the Iranian communications system. Stalin expressed his satisfaction with the provisions of this treaty in a telegram to M. A. Furuqi, prime minister of Iran (*Izvestia*, February 3, 1942). It was not until September 9, 1943, after the German retreat from Russia was well under way, that Iran declared war on Germany.

No sooner did the Red Army enter Iran than it became clear that elaborate Soviet preparations had been made for just such an eventuality.[3] The Soviet government incorporated the northern provinces within its own security zone, appropriated all available food supplies, and made every attempt to exclude British and American, not to mention Iranian, representatives from the area. Soviet propaganda was extensively and effectively organized. The Soviet embassy personnel included representatives of the Muslim peoples of Central Asia and the Caucasus, well-versed in the Persian language and in the languages of the Turkic, Armenian, and other Iranian minorities. The Soviet press representatives, under the leadership of Danil S. Komissarov, press attaché at the Soviet Embassy, by devious means obtained full coverage of *TASS* dispatches in Iranian newspapers. In Teheran the "People's Party," a Soviet front headed by Suleiman Mirza, was organized during the first month of the occupation. The amnesty which accompanied the Soviet entry released a horde of Communists and Communist sympathizers from Iranian jails to lend support to Soviet propagandist activities. The People's party established newspapers, such as *Rahbar (The Leader)*, edited by Iraj Iskandari, and *Mardom (The People)*, edited by Dr. Reza Radmanesh of well-known Communist background. During the war years political activity mushroomed. By 1944 in Teheran alone there were 103 newspapers and 29 journals reflecting widely diverse shades of opinion. Even Isfahan boasted eleven newspapers.

The Tudeh party (The Masses), officially organized in January, 1942, emanated from the People's party. Among its founders were Reza Rusta, recently released from jail; Abol Iasim Assadi, Iraj Iskandari, Dr. Morteza Yazdi, Dr. Reza Radmanesh, and Jafar Pishevari (alias Seyyid Jafar Badku Bayi and Sultan-zadeh). Pishevari, a native of Iranian Azerbaijan who lived for fourteen years in Baku (1904-18), had played a leading role in the short-lived Gilan Republic, returning to Soviet Russia following its collapse in

1921. There he remained until 1936 when, together with a band of apparently destitute refugees who claimed to have been deported by the Soviet secret police, he re-entered Iran. Released from Iranian custody by the 1941 amnesty, he became the leading instrument of Soviet tactics in Azerbaijan. The Tudeh party remained a minority, but a well-organized minority, variously estimated at from three thousand to two hundred thousand members. The hard core of this party, which in all probability never exceeded fifty thousand, included many of the Iranian Azerbaijani who crossed the border as "refugees" in 1936 and others who followed in the wake of the Red Army in 1941. Tudeh supporters infiltrated the Iranian trade-unions and scattered throughout the country, instigating strife even in the English-occupied area in the south. The Tudeh party held its first national congress in August, 1944, in which year it won eight seats in the Parliamentary elections. As a result of Soviet financial and military backing, it became for a time the largest of all the Near Eastern Communist parties.

One of the most effective Soviet propaganda organs was the Irano-Soviet Society for Cultural Relations, founded in the fall of 1943, which included in its membership many outstanding Iranian scholars and scientists, such as Professor Said Nafisy, secretary-general of the Iranian Academy of Arts and Letters; and Madame Fatima Sayah, professor at the University of Teheran and founder of a women's party, who edited the society's publication *Payam-i-No (The New Messenger)*, established in August, 1944. The society was active in the distribution of Soviet literature, newspapers, and films, held lavish parties and receptions, and through the Soviet Hospital distributed much-needed drugs and vaccines for Iranian patients. During the remaining years of the Soviet occupation, its influence was widely felt. In the winter of 1944-45 it arranged the visit of an Iranian delegation, including Professor Nafisy, to Soviet Uzbekistan to help celebrate the twentieth anniversary of that republic, and incidentally to witness the development that had occurred there under the Soviet regime.

By 1944, when Red Army victories on the Eastern front and the Allied landing in Normandy assured an early Allied victory in Europe, there were indications that Soviet interest in Iran was not confined to culture and the transport of military supplies. In September of that year a large delegation of diplomatic and technical experts headed by Sergei Kavtaradze, an assistant commissar for foreign affairs, arrived in Iran to negotiate for an oil concession. The Soviet mission was preceded in the fall of 1943 by representatives of the British Shell Company and in the spring of 1944 by those of two American companies--Standard Vacuum Oil Company and Sinclair Oil Company--likewise interested in oil concessions. Whether the Kavtaradze mission entered the picture at this particular time in order to secure for the U.S.S.R. its share of the oil resources of Iran or merely to frustrate the designs of the competing English and American companies, the announcement of a Soviet demand for an omnibus concession in the five northern provinces aroused consternation. The Iranian government on October 16, rejected all Soviet, English, and American bids for oil concessions.

Although Article V of the Tripartite Treaty of January 29, 1942, provided that the U.S.S.R. and Great Britain should withdraw their forces from Iranian territory not later than six months following the end of hostilities, that is by March 2, 1946, the Soviet Union did not comply until the beginning of May and did so then only under pressure from the United States and the United Nations organization. The Soviet government rejected both a British proposal of September 19, 1945, for joint Anglo-Soviet withdrawal from Iran by mid-December and an American proposal of November 24, for the evacuation of all American, British, and Soviet troops from Iran by January 1, 1946.[4] The United States government, which had already reduced its forces from a maximum of approximately twenty-eight thousand to fewer than six thousand, completed its unilateral withdrawal of the remainder by January 1. British troops observed the prescribed treaty deadline of March 2, 1946. Only the Red Army remained.

The main reason for Soviet violation of the Tripartite Treaty of 1942 was the situation in Iranian Azerbaijan. Of all the areas in Iran, Azerbaijan provided the most fertile soil for Soviet (Communist) activities. During the years of occupation, the Red Army had dismantled border military, customs, and police posts, virtually extending the U.S.S.R. frontier south to include Azerbaijan. The local Tudeh party, with the help of the Red Army, played a significant role in arousing the agrarian population to demand local autonomy amounting to secession and sovietization. The impression is given that the Soviets wished to accomplish as a result of World War II what they had failed to achieve in 1921--the conquest of Iran by the installment plan.

Following what appears to have been a premature effort to seize power in Azerbaijan in August, 1945, the Tudeh party in that province assumed the alias of Democratic party and intensified its activity, supported by an influx of Soviet troops. By December, 1945, preparations for the "national liberation" of Azerbaijan were complete. On December 12 the provincial "National Assembly" meeting in Tabriz proclaimed the Autonomous Republic of Azerbaijan and selected as premier none other than the veteran Communist, Jafar Pishevari. Other leaders born or trained in Russia, and under Soviet influence, included Dr. Salamollah Javid, a Communist active in Azerbaijan from 1919 to 1920; Muhammed Biriya; Sadiq Padegan; Adalat, a member of the Russian Communist party in Baku; and General Danishiyan, who, according to reports, could speak only Russian with any degree of fluency. The "People's Army" of Azerbaijan, armed with Iranian rifles produced for the Red Army at the Teheran arsenal during the war, was infested with Soviet agents of Caucasian, Armenian, and Iranian origin. Although the new regime avoided outright separation from Iran, its administration and police system were organized in the Soviet image, with Turkish rather than Persian as the official language. It undertook an extensive land distribution scheme and the nationalization of banks. Red Army troops occupying Azerbaijan prevented units of the Iranian army from entering the area to come to the rescue of the dispossessed. The spread of the revolutionary virus led to the establishment of a Kurdish People's Republic in western Azerbaijan on December 15, 1945, which entered into a military alliance with Azerbaijan the following April.

With the empire disintegrating, the Iranian government turned to the newly organized United Nations for support. On January 19, 1946, the Iranian delegate, Seyyid Hasan Taqi-zadeh, protested to the United Nations Security Council against Soviet interference in the internal affairs of Iran and called for an investigation. As in the case of the League of Nations a quarter of a century earlier, the Security Council on January 30 recommended direct negotiations between Iran and the Soviet Union. Iranian Premier Qavam Saltaneh thereupon headed an Iranian mission to Moscow, February 19 to March 11, only to find that the Soviet government demanded Iranian recognition of the autonomy of the Soviet puppet regime in Azerbaijan, the continued occupation of parts of Iran by Soviet troops, and the establishment of a Soviet-Iranian joint-stock oil company, in which the U.S.S.R. would control 51 per cent of the shares.

When the March 2 deadline for Soviet withdrawal produced no more than a Soviet announcement in *Izvestia* to the effect that the government contemplated withdrawal from certain specific areas-- Khorassan, Shahrud, and Semnan--but would remain elsewhere until the situation was "clarified," Great Britain (March 4) and the United States (March 8) joined with Premier Qavam in formally protesting this treaty violation. Since the Soviet government, instead of withdrawing dispatched additional troops and tanks to northern Iran thereby threatening a military *coup d'état*, the Iranian government through Iranian Ambassador Hussein Ala in the United States appealed a second time to the United Nations, this time about the breach of the treaty deadline. The storm of adverse publicity in the United States and throughout the Western world apparently convinced Soviet leaders of the desirability of reaching a solution. On March 26 Andrei Gromyko notified the Security Council that the Soviet government had reached an agreement with Iran providing for Soviet evacuation six weeks after March 24. The Soviet-Iranian agreement signed by Premier Qavam and Soviet Ambassador Sadtchikov on April 4 specified this deadline, announced the forthcoming establishment (seven months after March 24) of a Soviet-Iranian Joint-Stock Oil Company, subject to ratification by the Mejlis, and provided that Azerbaijan and Iran should reach a peaceful settlement.

According to Robert Rossow, Jr., who was in charge of the United States Consulate in Tabriz from December, 1945, to June, 1946, and thereafter chief of the political section of the United States Embassy in Teheran until January, 1947, the "battle of Azerbaijan" was not an isolated incident. It was rather a part of a Soviet pincer movement, aimed at the reduction of Turkey and Greece on the west and Azerbaijan on the east, which was stopped cold by United States action in a move that anticipated by precisely one year American policy under the Truman Doctrine. [5]

The sacrifice of Azerbaijan for the second time on the altar of Soviet interests was unmistakable. From the final withdrawal of Soviet troops in May, 1956, the days of the Azerbaijan and Kurdish autonomous regimes were numbered. To appease the U. S. S. R., the Teheran government reached a temporary agreement with the Azerbaijan Autonomous Republic in June, and the following August included three Tudeh members in the Iranian Cabinet. Tudeh-inspired violence in the Abadan oil refinery strike during the summer and Tudeh truculence in politics antagonized popular opinion. In late 1946 and 1947 the Iranian government of Qavam es Sultaneh suppressed the revolution in northern Iran by force of arms. As in 1921, so in 1946 the Iranian revolutionaries proved no match for the Iranian troops, once Soviet forces were withdrawn. The Iranian Mejlis, with apparent backing from the United States, on October 22, 1947, rejected the Soviet demand for a Soviet-controlled joint-stock company to prospect for oil in northern Iran.

The Soviet press gave full vent to Soviet indignation over the failure to gain access to the oil resources of northern Iran. An article in *Trud* (November 30, 1947), entitled "Representatives of the Iranian People, or American Lackeys?" by I. Belov, attributed the postponement by the Mejlis of a decision on the oil question in October, 1946, to direct intervention of the American ambassador, George Allen. It further alleged that "acting upon the orders of the American ambassador, the clause on the extension of Iranian sovereignty to the Bahrein Islands and the Persian Gulf (where the American oil concessions are to be found) was stricken from the original text of the bill. " The prospect of Iranian entry into the American orbit as the outcome of Soviet aggression in Iran was a bitter pill for Soviet leaders to swallow. Henceforth the United States replaced England as the chief butt of Soviet attacks on imperialistic colonizers.

By the Azerbaijan "adventure, " the Soviet government proved that it had not profited by its experience in Gilan following World War I. When the Red Army entered Iran in 1941, the impression was given, in spite of Soviet propagandist activities, that the U. S. S. R. wished to blot out the past, to allay Iranian fears of sovietization, and to lay the foundation for better Soviet-Iranian relations in the postwar era. During the war years, as we have seen, it did make appreciable headway among all strata of the Iranian population. By violating the treaty deadline of March 2, 1946, by actively promoting the dismemberment of Iran through the establishment of the "autonomous" republics of Azerbaijan and Kurdistan, and by seeking to grab control of the oil resources of northern Iran, the Soviet government undid everything it had accomplished previously and demonstrated to Iran and the world at large that its policy more than matched that of the so-called "imperialist" powers it was constantly denouncing. Thus vis-à-vis Iran, the Soviet Union was in the same position in 1946 as it was a quarter of a century before, in 1921. It had learned nothing and accomplished nothing. In 1946, however, it was the Americans rather than the English who played the most important part in the defeat of Soviet expansionist aims in Iran.

II

As in the case of Iran, the Soviet government expected, as a result of World War II, to advance Soviet interests in Turkey, where pro-German and anti-Soviet sentiment was sufficiently strong to prevent the Turks from joining the Allied camp until the end of the conflict was in sight on February 23, 1945. Unlike Iran, the Soviet

government did not have the advantage of Red Army occupation of
Turkish territory during the war years. Prior to the Nazi invasion
of the U.S.S.R. in 1941, while Nazi and Soviet leaders were still
drafting plans to divide the world between them, the Soviet government, as we have seen, vigorously asserted that Turkey and Bulgaria fell within the Soviet security zone and demanded a Soviet base
at the Dardanelles. It sought, first from the Germans and later
from the Allies, a decision in favor of the complete revision of the
Montreux Convention of 1936 in regard to the Straits.

On the eve of World War II, Soviet-Turkish negotiations for a
mutual assistance pact (September-October, 1939) proved fruitless,
due in part to Soviet reluctance to exempt Turkey from any obliga-
tion to participate in hostilities against England and France, to
German pressure on the Soviet Union to secure the neutralization
of Turkey, so as to insure that the latter would under no circumstances fight Germany, and Soviet pressure on the Turks for a
modification of the Straits Convention. On October 19, two days after the lapse of Soviet-Turkish negotiations, the Turks signed a
fifteen-year tripartite treaty of mutual assistance with England and
France. The Turks had wrung from them the concession that "the
obligations undertaken by Turkey in virtue of the above-mentioned
treaty cannot compel that country to take action having as its effect
or involving as its consequence armed conflict with the U.S.S.R. "
The Turks were striving to steer a neutral course in the stormy
international waters ahead of them.

During the war years, especially during the successful advance
of the German armies toward Moscow and Stalingrad, the officially
neutral Turks entered into a closer rapprochement with the Germans, under the expert guidance of Franz von Papen, Nazi ambassador in Constantinople after the death of Kemal Pasha. The
war resulted in a great increase in German-Turkish trade, under
the trade agreements of July, 1940, and October, 1941, which were
reinforced by a German-Turkish pact of "friendship and nonaggression" on June 18, 1941, four days prior to the German invasion of
the Soviet Union. The initial success of the Germans in Western
Europe, the Balkans, and the U.S.S.R. evoked a revival of Pan-
Turkism, which led many Turks to anticipate a favorable read-
justment of Soviet-Turkish boundaries, the possible establishment
of Turkish puppet regimes in the Crimea and the Caucasus, and
perhaps even the outright acquisition of Soviet Azerbaijan and Baku.

German revelation as early as March, 1941, [6] of Soviet designs
on the Straits was not calculated to dispel Turkish suspicions of the
U.S.S.R. In spite of Anglo-Soviet declarations on August 10 as to

"the scrupulous observance of the territorial integrity of Turkey, "
Anglo-Soviet occupation of Iran by the end of the same month proved
anything but reassuring to the Turks, whose fears of the revival
of the Secret Agreements of 1915 to 1916 were encouraged by the
Germans. Turko-Soviet relations were strained by the attempted
assassination on February 24, 1942, of von Papen in Constantinople, allegedly by Omer Tokat, a Muslim Macedonian Communist, and the subsequent trial and conviction by the Turkish courts
of two Russians attached to the Soviet trade mission. The services
of the British and United States ambassadors in Constantinople were
required before tension between Turkey and the Soviet Union was
alleviated.

In the fall of 1942, with the German descent upon the Caucasus
and in anticipation of the fall of Stalingrad, the Turks concentrated
considerable forces on the Caucasian boundary, and the anti-Soviet
press campaign in Turkey reached a new peak. Subsequent publication of the secret documents of the German Ministry of Foreign Affairs pertaining to Turkey lends substantiation to Soviet suspicions
that Turkish leaders were jubilant about the approaching "annihilation of the Russian colossus, " and that they were interpreting Turkish neutrality to the advantage of the Axis rather than to the advantage of the Allies. Soviet historians have contended that in the fall
of 1942 Turkey was on the brink of declaring war against the Soviet
Union. In 1947 a former member of the Turkish cabinet, writing
in the magazine *PM,* claimed that Turkish Premier Ismet İnönü
was actually on the point of announcing the Turkish decision to join
the Axis, when Franz von Papen forestalled this by revealing the
encirclement and defeat of the German armies at Stalingrad. [7]

In fact, the cautious Turks, in spite of German pressure and
German propaganda, exercised a remarkable degree of restraint,
refusing to be precipitated into war during the years of German
victory. After Stalingrad, and especially from the time of the Cairo
Conference of 1943, the Turks veered again in the direction of England and France. Although England and the Soviet Union both brought
pressure upon the Turks to abandon their neutrality, and Stalin at
the Teheran Conference in November was reported by Churchill to
be in favor of bringing them in "by the scruff of the neck if necessary, " the Turks resisted them with as much tenacity as they had
the Germans. They eventually joined the Allies in 1945 in time to
insure their participation in the San Francisco Conference.

This fortuitous Turkish about-face by no means appeased the Soviet government, which had watched with concern the occasional
use of the Straits during the war years by German and Italian war-

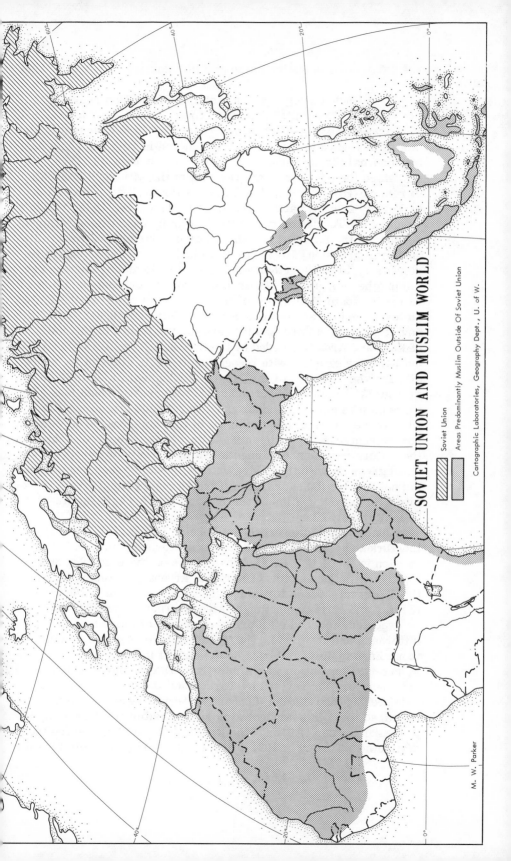

SOVIET UNION AND MUSLIM WORLD

Soviet Union

Areas Predominantly Muslim Outside Of Soviet Union

Cartographic Laboratories, Geography Dept., U. of W.

M. W. Parker

ships, in what it alleged was a violation of the Montreux Convention of 1936. [8] The United States and Great Britain were forewarned at the wartime Big-Three conferences as to subsequent Soviet tactics in regard to the Straits. At Teheran in 1943 and again during the final plenary session at Yalta on February 10, 1945, Stalin raised the question of the revision of the Montreux Convention to remove Turkey's "hand on Russia's throat," without detriment to Turkey's legitimate interests. On March 19, 1945, within a month of the Turkish entry into World War II, the Soviet government denounced the Soviet-Turkish Treaty of Friendship, Neutrality, and Nonaggression of 1925 (renewed in 1935 and due to expire November 7, 1945), together with all protocols and extensions pertaining thereto, as "no longer in accord with present conditions." At the Potsdam Conference of the three great powers--the United States, England, and the U.S.S.R. --in July and August, 1945, the Soviet government pressed its case for the return of the districts of Kars and Ardahan, ceded by the R.S.F.S.R. to Turkey in 1921, but had to be satisfied with recognition from its allies of the necessity for the revision of the Montreux Convention of 1936 on the ground that it was no longer in accord with present conditions. The three powers agreed to undertake separate and direct negotiations with Turkey toward the attainment of this objective. The Turkish government was, to all intents and purposes, prepared to discuss the Straits regime and to negotiate a new treaty of friendship and nonaggression with the Soviet Union, providing such negotiations did not involve the sacrifice of Turkish rights and Turkish integrity. [9] Soviet occupation of the Balkans had brought the Russians uncomfortably close.

In June, 1945, however, Soviet Foreign Minister Molotov notified the Turkish ambassador in Moscow that "revision" involved Turkish cession to the U.S.S.R. of a Soviet base on the Black Sea Straits, together with the districts of Kars and Ardahan, in return for which the Turks might look for compensation from Syria in the form of the city and railway junction of Aleppo. These demands, as might be expected, touched off a press campaign of more than ordinary bitterness and invective. The Turks, after consultation with Anthony Eden in July, fell back on the logical line of defense that the Montreux Convention was a multilateral agreement which could not, therefore, be revised by Turkey and the U.S.S.R. alone.

In seeking the return of Kars and Ardahan, the Soviet government appeared to be in search of a more defensible frontier along the Armenian border. Although the R.S.F.S.R. had transferred these districts to Turkey in 1921 without expressing any solicitude for

the rights of the Armenians, the Soviet press in the summer of
1945 gave extensive support to the Armenian claims, which dove-
tailed nicely with the Soviet program (announced December 2, 1945)
for the repatriation of Armenians abroad.

The basic tenets of the American recommendations for the revision of the Montreux Convention were submitted to the Turkish
government in a note of November 2, 1945. They provided: (1) that
the Straits should be open to commercial vessels at all times; (2)
that they should likewise be open at all times to warships of the
Black Sea powers; (3) that with the exception of an agreed limited
tonnage in peacetime, the passage of the Straits should be denied
to warships of non-Black Sea powers, unless with the consent of the
Black Sea powers or when acting under the U.N.; (4) the United
Nations organization should replace the League of Nations under the
Montreux Convention, and that Japan should be eliminated as a signatory. These proposals were welcomed by the Turkish government, which soon had reason to fall back upon them in its dispute
with Soviet Russia over the administration of the Straits.

Soviet activities in Iran following the termination of hostilities
in August, 1945, and the disposition of Red Army troops in Iranian Azerbaijan occasioned grave concern among the Turks. On
January 6, 1946, Prime Minister Sucru Saracoglu officially rejected Soviet claims to Kars and Ardahan, which the Soviet government
had voluntarily transferred to Turkey in 1921. Alarmed by the trend
of events and by Soviet intrigue among the Turkish Armenians and
Kurds, the Turkish government first looked to the Arab world for
support. On March 29, 1946, Turkey and Iraq signed in Ankara a
pact of mutual assistance on the question of public order, designed
to prevent further Soviet encroachment.

Blocked in its designs on Iran, from which the Red Army was
forced to retire in May, 1946, the Soviet government at once turned
its full attention to Turkey and the Straits. In a vigorous note of
August 8 (7), 1946, Soviet Foreign Minister Molotov outlined the
alleged wartime violations of the Montreux Convention, the decisions of the Potsdam Conference, and presented a five-point program for the revision of the Straits regime, designed to place that
strategic area under the control of the Black Sea powers, with Turkey and the U.S.S.R. jointly responsible for the defense of the
Straits. Well aware that such a proposition, which excluded the
other great powers from a share in the control of the Straits, would
in fact establish Soviet control at the expense of the Turks, the
Turkish government on August 22 flatly rejected this part of the
program. A second Soviet note of September 24 (*Izvestia,* Septem-

ber 28, 1946) reiterated the Soviet position in regard to the revision of the Montreux Convention and called for Soviet-Turkish talks prior to any general conference on the issue. In spite of the arrogant tone of the Soviet communications, which clearly indicated that the Russians would regard continued Turkish rejection of the Soviet program as a threat to Soviet security in the Black Sea, the Turks staunchly refused to be drawn into bilateral negotiations which would have violated the Montreux Convention. Turkish-Soviet relations had reached a new low, and the Turkish armed forces were alerted to resist a possible Soviet attack.

The Turks were undoubtedly encouraged to take a firm stand in opposition to points four and five of the Soviet program in the knowledge that their position was fully supported by the United States and England. The United States, by virtue of the Potsdam Protocol, received a copy of the Soviet note of August 7, and thereafter claimed the right to participate in any revision of the Montreux Convention. Secretary of State Dean Acheson on August 19 in no uncertain terms rejected the idea of the control of the Straits by the Black Sea powers, contending that this implied not a revision of the Montreux Convention "but rather the establishment of a new regime. . . ." He likewise objected to joint Soviet-Turkish defense of the Straits on the ground that any threat of aggression there must be a matter for action on the part of the U. N. Security Council, which the Russians had failed even to mention. [10] As if to indicate that the United States would fight to defend Turkey, Secretary of the Navy Forrestal announced on September 30 that American naval forces would remain at full strength in the Eastern Mediterranean.

The Soviet government, expecting in all probability to outflank Turkey by the establishment of a Communist regime in Greece and knowing from past experience that the Turks would fight, gave vent to its displeasure in an anti-Turkish press campaign and in military maneuvers along the Caucasian border. If it had expected that the United States and England would permit the U.S.S.R. to have a free hand at the Straits, it was already fully disillusioned on that score. As in Iran, so in Turkey, the United States took the lead in opposing Soviet expansion.

The United States government, alarmed by Communist efforts in Greece and by the prospect of early English withdrawal from that beleaguered country, as well as by Soviet designs on the Straits, on March 12, 1947, officially announced the extension of American aid to Greece and Turkey--the so-called "Truman Doctrine." The Soviet government promptly labeled the Truman pronouncement "a scarcely concealed declaration of preparation for war against the U. S. S. R. "[11] From this moment, according to I. F. Miller, a Soviet authority on Turkey, "Turkey in fact fell under the tutelage of the United States of America. "

Even prior to the enunciation of the Truman Doctrine, the United States had begun to provide aid to Turkey, including a $25,000,000 credit from the Export-Import Bank, $10,000,000 in credit for the purchase of surplus military equipment, and another $5,000,000 for the purchase of American merchant ships. Once the decision was reached, no time was lost. On March 24, Dean Acheson informed the House Committee on Foreign Affairs that $100,000,000 were required for Turkey, another $150,000,000 for Greece. On the same day the Turkish navy took over eight former United States minesweepers lent to England during World War II under the lend-lease program. The British government revealed on April 9, that some five hundred British "Spitfires," "Mosquitoes" and other types of planes had been sold to Turkey and were in the process of delivery. In May an American military mission headed by Major-General Lunsford Oliver arrived in Ankara to confer with Turkish officials. On July 12, the American and Turkish governments signed the agreement to implement Congressional authorization of the $100,000,000 for Turkish aid, of which $80,000,000 were earmarked for the modernization of the Turkish armed forces and the balance for the construction of strategic roads and ports. According to Soviet sources, which maintained a close scrunity of these unwelcome developments, during the second half of 1947, Turkey received more than twenty different American commissions, delegations, and missions to advise on all types of issues ranging from military and economic aid to press, radio, and information services.

Thus we may safely conclude that the United States not only saved Greece and Turkey from Soviet clutches, but likewise stemmed the tide of Soviet expansion throughout the Middle East. In 1921, Turkey, Iran, and Afghanistan stopped the march of communism with some help from the outside, at a time when Soviet Russia was weak and exhausted as a result of the Revolution and Civil War. In 1947, Turkey and Iran were in no position to cope alone with the victorious forces of the Red Army. They were saved only by the decisive intervention of the United States and the possibility of action by the United Nations. Since the crisis that evoked the Truman Doctrine, American relations with Turkey have been established on a firm foundation, and the United States has now superseded France and Britain in the historic role of defending Turkey from the Russians.

By reaching for a base at the Dardanelles, the return of Kars and Ardahan, and the five northern provinces of Iran, the Soviet Union lost the opportunity to secure a modification of the Straits regime. Neither by abandoning the Tsarist claims in 1917 nor by advancing its own in 1945, did the Soviet regime achieve its objectives. Contained in the Near and Middle East, the U. S.,S. R. once again turned to the Far East, where Soviet policy met with unprecedented success.

III

The alliance between the Soviet Union and Red China, signed in Moscow on February 14, 1950, upset the balance of power in the postwar world, both in Europe and Asia. It soon became clear that the further expansion of the Moscow-Peking orbit in the direction of Southeast Asia threatened to outflank the Near and Middle East, and ultimately Europe. The Sino-Soviet timetable for the achievement of this goal was undoubtedly upset by the entrance of the United States and the United Nations into the Korean War in 1950 to stem the tide of Communist aggression. Although U. N. intervention in Korea did not accomplish this objective, history will record that it temporarily retarded the Sino-Soviet advance and provided three years for the building up of Western defenses. With the signing of the Korean truce on July 26, 1953, the pace of Communist aggression in Indo-China was stepped up.

In spite of the Korean War, the treaty with Japan, and defensive pacts with Australia, New Zealand, and the Philippines, until 1953, American foreign policy subordinated the Orient to Western Europe. During the same period, in spite of our activity in Europe, Soviet foreign policy subordinated Europe to Asia. Although the Eisenhower administration made the United States Asia-conscious, with China lost, India "neutral," and Indo-China partitioned, it faced the problem of creating an effective system of Asiatic alliances to counterbalance the eight hundred million population of the Sino-Soviet axis. To make American alliances in Asia really effective, they had to be bolstered by large reserves of Asiatic manpower.

The American government soon realized that the only effective means of accomplishing this end was the extension of its system of alliances to include the countries of the Muslim world. The leading Muslim nations are strategically located along the soft underbelly of the U.S.S.R. in Asia, and they have the manpower to enable the West to balance, if not to outnumber, the thickly populated countries of the Moscow-Peking orbit. Since some Muslim peoples are still inordinately distrustful of the Western powers, it has been the task of American diplomacy to convince them that the United States does not approach them as masters or as "colonizers," but as equals, with mutual interests at stake. Conscious only of the threat of Western domination, the Arab states have often failed to realize the imminent danger of their being submerged physically and spiritually by the non-Muslim Asiatic world--a fate far worse than that imposed by the Western colonizers, under whom they have retained their national identity and religious faith, not to mention the improvement of their economic status. As Soviet policy in Iran and Turkey after World War II fully demonstrated, the Muslim world could not hope to contain non-Muslim Asiatic aggression without the United States. Likewise, without the Muslim world, the United States could not build an effective system of alliances to block the expansion of the Red axis. It was, therefore, to their mutual advantage to join forces without delay.

Many other difficulties have confronted the United States in its efforts to win the Muslim world for the Western orbit. Non-Muslim Asia, led by Red China and the Soviet Union, was growing rapidly in strength, whereas the Muslim world as yet lacked organization. It had no well-defined aims and objectives. Unfortunately, very few Muslims understood the need for Western-Muslim solidarity, and not all Western nations grasped the fact that the West must be strong in manpower as well as in technology if it were to contain the Red axis. Moreover, the majority of Americans knew little or nothing about the Muslim world and few were aware of the postwar realignment into Muslim and non-Muslim orbits in Asia. Education is a long process, but education was needed by both Muslims and Americans. Although a large part of the Muslim world had attained political sovereignty since 1917, those areas still characterized by colonial status or subject to any restrictions whatsoever in the matter of sovereignty, were a continual source of unrest, and as in the case of North Africa, served as a constant reminder to Muslims elsewhere of their own struggle for liberation from Western domination, especially that of England and France.

As we have seen, it was the Truman Doctrine (March 12, 1947) which laid the cornerstone for an American rapprochement with the Muslim world, by extending military and economic aid to save Turkey from Soviet encroachment. Subsequent to 1947 the United States continued its efforts to unite the Muslim peoples of the Arab states against the Communist menace. These efforts did not succeed, in part because of the establishment of the state of Israel in 1948, and also due to bitter rivalries among the Arab states. Had the states that comprise the Arab League--Egypt, Lebanon, Syria, Iraq, Transjordan, Saudi Arabia, and Yemen--not vacillated too long, with Egypt at the head they might have become the focal point of a Western-sponsored defensive alliance against communism. Egypt, which expected to assume the leadership of the Arab world, temporarily fell a prey to internal disunity and the struggle between General Muhammed Naguib and Lieutenant-Colonel Gamal Abdel Nasser militated against prompt and decisive action. Egyptian nationalists were more intent at that time on the control of the Sudan[12] and the Suez Canal, issues that were of more immediate concern to Egypt than the containment of the Soviet Union.

Frustrated in this direction, the United States won a major dip- lomatic and strategic victory in bringing about the Turkish-Pakis- tani Mutual Aid Agreement of April 2, 1954. To put more teeth into the pact the United States and Pakistan on May 19 signed an agree- ment providing American war materials and technical assistance to Pakistan. The Turkish-Pakistani Pact united the two strongest Muslim states, comprising about one hundred million people, or one-fourth of the Muslim world, located on the southern periphery of the U.S.S.R.

It should not be overlooked in this connection that while the Turks had been our most reliable ally in the Near and Middle East, they were far from enthusiastic about an alliance embracing the Muslim world, especially one that included the Arabs. They were appre- hensive that the Arab states might prove to be more intent on the elimination of Israel, with which Turkey carried on a thriving trade, than in concentrating on the Communist menace. The Turks also appeared to prefer a limited alliance, possibly including Iran and Afghanistan to close the gap between Turkey and Pakistan, but they did not seek closer ties with the states of the Arab League. Modern Turkey, where westernization and secularization have taken deep root, does not look with favor on any resurgence of Islam as practised in the Arab world. Nevertheless, under Western pres- sure the Turks were persuaded that Pan-Islamism offered better protection against Communist aggression than could be found in a divided Muslim world. Following the unanimous ratification of the Turkish-Pakistani Pact by the Turkish Grand National Assembly on June 11, 1954, Turkey and Pakistan announced that they would henceforth shift from a passive to an active policy in seeking to in- duce other Muslim countries of the Near and Middle East, especial- ly those in the north, to join forces with them to establish an effec- tive system of collective security.

Had the United States succeeded in implementing an Arab alliance

against communism, Soviet leaders would have displayed no great
concern, for the Arab states were divided and weak. With Turkey
and Pakistan at the helm the situation was different. The Soviet
government was fully aware that every effort would be made to create an unbroken chain of alliances from Turkey to Pakistan, which
would include Iraq and Iran, if not Afghanistan. If Iraq could be induced to break loose from the Arab League to join Turkey and Pakistan, the other Arab states might eventually conclude, no matter how reluctantly, that it was in their own interest to follow suit.
The very existence of the Turkish-Pakistani Pact, sponsored by
the United States, weakened the hold that the Soviet government still
had on Iran by virtue of the 1921 treaty.

Because the Soviet people are still impressed by man power, at
times even more than by technology, the impact on the U.S.S.R.
of the Turkish-Pakistani Agreement was therefore instantaneous.
It resulted in large-scale, strategic countermeasures involving the
status of the thirty million Muslims inside the borders of the Soviet Union. Central Asia, where the bulk of these Muslims reside,
is the bulwark for the defense of the Ural Region, the backbone of
Soviet industrial development.

Under the guise of a campaign to increase Soviet food production,
the Soviet government in the spring of 1954 instituted a program
for the reclamation of virgin and idle lands and the opening up of
new agricultural areas in Kazakhstan, West Siberia, the Ural and
Volga regions, and the North Caucasus. [13] These are highly strategic areas with reference to the Near and Middle East. One of the
principal areas selected for cultivation and reclamation was Soviet
Central Asia, known before the Revolution as Russian Turkestan,
but which now comprises the Soviet Republics of Kazakhstan, Kirghizia, Tadjikistan, Turkmenistan, and Uzbekistan.

Until the Second World War the bulk of the population in Soviet
Central Asia, in both urban and rural areas, was Muslim. The
native peoples, irrespective of current nomenclature, considered
themselves of Turkish or Iranian origin. Even under the Soviet
regime, in these republics nationalism has been associated with
Pan-Islamism, Pan-Turkism, or Pan-Iranism, all of which have
been denounced repeatedly by the Communist leadership. Together
with the Crimean Tatars, the Central Asiatic peoples proved highly unreliable in their allegiance to the U.S.S.R. during the conflict with Nazi Germany. This was proved by the aid they rendered
the Nazi armies in labor and ordnance battalions, as well as in
combat. One of their leaders, Kayum-Khan, an Uzbek exile, succeeded in organizing in Germany 180,000 men from various parts

of Central Asia into a force which became an integral part of the
Wehrmacht or the Waffen-S.S. Of these, three battalions fought
to the last man before Stalingrad. Others were destroyed in fierce
fighting in the Caucasus. Six battalions of these Muslim recruits
for a time held up the Soviet advance into Berlin in 1945. Altogether, it is estimated that they suffered the loss of fifty thousand
men.

The first step taken by the Soviet government to offset the Muslim threat in the Soviet Union was, as we have seen, the expulsion
of all Tatars from the Crimea, facing Turkey, and the resettle-
ment of the area with Slavs. Thereafter, in order to enlist wholehearted Ukrainian support for the defense of this region, the Crimea was "annexed" to the Ukrainian Republic. A second step, immediately following the Second World War was the dispatch of many
Slavs and other non-Muslim elements to the cities of the Central
Asiatic republics, to places such as Tashkent, Ashkabad, Alma
Ata, etc. By 1952, the Slavic element outnumbered the native Muslim population in these urban centers and key posts in the administration were in their hands.

The Soviet drive to cultivate "virgin and idle lands" in Central
Asia was undoubtedly designed to populate the rural areas with non-
Muslim peoples. The ultimate purpose of the Soviet government
is that both the urban and rural areas of Soviet Central Asia should
in time be largely absorbed by the Slavs, and the fate of the native
peoples in all probability will be that of the Crimean Tatars and
Kalmyks. This drastic genocidal program was launched under the
impact of the alliance between Turkey and Pakistan, two Muslim
countries strategically located on the Soviet periphery.

The extent of Soviet concern over this budding rapprochement
between Turkey and Pakistan can be gauged by the fact that the Ma-
lenkov regime sent to Soviet Central Asia, not slave laborers or
even common laborers, but members of the Komsomol (Young
Communist League), who constitute the cream of the crop of Soviet
youth, each one a trained agitator, picked for qualities of leadership and unquestioned loyalty to the Soviet regime. Judging by the
Soviet press campaign from April to June, 1956, for the extension
of this program, especially by Khrushchev's appeal for another
half million from the reservoir of 18,500,000 Komsomol members
for Kazakhstan, Siberia, and the Far East, in the near future there
may be not only a Slavic, but a Komsomol belt along this strategic
frontier of the U.S.S.R. The inclusion of the Far East in this drive
to populate Soviet Asia suggests that precautions are being taken
against any future expansionist aims on the part of Red China. The

Soviet government can safely rely on these young "agrarian pioneers" to defend Soviet Central Asia from any external Muslim
threat from the Turkish-Pakistani axis. The Komsomol will likewise provide the vanguard for future Soviet aggression in the direction of the Near East and India. Comments in the Soviet press indicate that the response of Soviet youth to this pressure campaign
in 1956 failed to meet the expectations of the government.

In addition to the Komsomol colonists, the Soviet government in
1955 dispatched whole regiments of demobilized soldiers, together
with their commanders, to the Central Asiatic republics. These
Soviet veterans serve at least three purposes: they reclaim fallow
land and thereby increase the food and cotton crops; they augment
the Slavic element in the population; and they can be mobilized at
a moment's notice for purposes of defense or offense. From the
Soviet standpoint, the strategic advantages surpass even the economic benefits.

It is important to note that in this program for the development
of "virgin and idle lands," the Soviet government stressed the establishment of *sovkhozi,* that is state-owned farms, in place of
kolkhozi, or collective farms. According to Khrushchev, secretary
of the Central Committee of the Communist party (*Pravda, Izvestia,* September 15, 1953), prior to the Soviet campaign to cultivate "virgin and idle lands" there were approximately 4, 700
sovkhozi in the U.S.S.R., in comparison with 94, 000 kolkhozi.
In January, 1956, the Soviet government revealed that since 1954
an additional 560 sovkhozi have been established, most of them in
desolate, but highly strategic, eastern areas. [14] Over the sovkhozi
the government retains more direct and rigid controls. In time of
national crisis it can carry out a more effective scorched-earth policy along the periphery. As World War II demonstrated, this was
difficult to enforce among the kolkhozi, where a modicum of private ownership prevailed.

The new sovkhozi might likewise be expected to offset in some
measure the rise of a new middle class in the U.S.S.R., which
already constitutes a problem for the Soviet regime, especially for
the Communist party. On March 9, 1956, the Soviet government
embarked upon a program aimed at the progressive reduction of
private plots and privately owned livestock on collective farms to
the point where they will merely "decorate" the life of the collective farmer, rather than constitute a threat to collective ownership.
If the international situation were not so threatening, it seems
likely that the Soviet government would have taken more drastic
action to curb the new middle class than is indicated by the cam-

paign for new state farms. Whereas the growth of new middle and upper classes remains a thorn in the flesh to the Communist party, the military element is inclined to favor this development, in the belief that those who have something at stake are more likely to fight to defend the system in the event of another conflict.

In the field of foreign affairs, the Soviet Union betrayed manifest concern over the impact of the Istanbul-Karachi agreement on the 350,000,000 Muslims beyond Soviet borders, stretching from Chinese Turkestan and Southeast Asia to Morocco and West Africa. The Soviet government immediately focused its attention upon ways and means of reducing the effectiveness of the pact by stirring up internal dissension in Pakistan. Taking advantage of the geographical division of Pakistan into two parts separated by approximately one thousand miles, and the hostility of India toward this Muslim state, Soviet propagandists fomented strikes and labor riots in the jute and other industries of thickly populated Eastern Pakistan (East Bengal) and encouraged the movement for political independence there. On May 30, 1954, Premier Muhammed Ali of Pakistan was forced to dismiss Fazlul Huq, chief minister of Eastern Pakistan and his associates for "treasonable activities" and to undertake a drastic reorganization of the government. The Communist party was banned in East Bengal on July 5 and in West Pakistan on July 24.

Even without waiting for the formal conclusion of the Turkish-Pakistani Pact, the Soviet government in an official note of protest to Turkey (*Pravda-Izvestia,* March 20, 1954) predicted that this agreement would "aggravate the situation in the Near and Middle East, and also in Southeast Asia, and would have a direct bearing on the security of the Soviet Union." It accused the United States of planning to use "the human resources" of this area to carry out American policy, and of "forging a bloc by installments" (*Pravda,* March 19).

Soviet propaganda guns have been trained on Turkey ever since the negotiation of the pact with Pakistan. The Soviet government took the stand that the pact was aggressive in design, since it came when Turkey's security was no longer threatened by any of her neighbors. No doubt this was an indirect allusion to belated Soviet action (May 30, 1953) in officially abandoning all territorial claims against Turkey. *Izvestia,* the official organ of the Soviet government, on June 15, 1954, in a lengthy analysis of the Turkish position, discussed the dispatch of Turkish troops to Korea: "It is quite obvious," commented *Izvestia,* "that Turkish ruling circles would not have sent soldiers abroad if on the Turkish borders there existed any kind of danger. . . . This consideration once again exposes the aggressive and not the defensive role assigned by Washington to the Turkish military forces. " The Soviet press tried to incite Arab opposition to the pact by frequent allegations concerning Turkey's irredentist claims on Syria, the other Arab states, and Iran. "Moreover, " continued *Izvestia*, "Turkish ruling circles do not help to mitigate the tension that exists in the areas of the Near and Middle East, as well as in the Balkan Peninsula. In spite of the fact that the Soviet government has taken numerous steps to secure good neighborly relations with Turkey, Turkish official circles are acting in such a manner as to make it appear that Turkey is less interested than the Soviet Union in such relations. " As long as Turkey receives aid and strong backing from the United States, Soviet propaganda will not have one iota of influence upon the Turkish government. This might not have been the case under circumstances prior to 1947, when Turkey faced the Soviet Union alone and without allies.

Soviet pressure, far from intimidating Turkey and Pakistan, in all probability served to facilitate and to hasten the extension of their alliance by means of a series of agreements which comprise the Baghdad Pact of 1955. On February 24, Turkey and Iraq signed an alliance, to which Great Britain adhered on April 24, at which time the British government agreed to transfer to Iraq the British air bases at Habaniya and Shaiba. Pakistan, which agreed on June 30 to join the Turkish-Iraqi Pact, formally affixed its signature on September 23. In a last-minute effort to forestall Iranian adherence to this new Middle East defense system, the Soviet Union on June 1 returned to Iran eleven tons of long-promised gold and undertook to provide compensation to the extent of £3,000,000 for Iranian supplies appropriated by the U.S.S.R. during World War II. The United States entered the picture, however, by signing with Iran a treaty of friendship, economic relations, and consular rights on August 15. Two days later the Export-Import Bank announced loans amounting to $14,000,000 to assist Iran to modernize part of its railroad equipment by shifting to diesel power. The contest for Iran was decided in favor of the United States, when on October 11 Premier Hussein Ala announced Iran's intention of adhering to the Baghdad Pact.

In November, 1955, the premiers of Iraq, Iran, Pakistan, and Turkey met with the British foreign secretary, Harold Macmillan, to establish a permanent political, military, and economic organization--in other words, a permanent secretariat--with headquarters in Baghdad. The United States, which originated the idea of the pact but was not a signatory, was represented by political and military observers. On November 22 the five powers comprising the Middle Eastern Treaty Organization (METO) announced the establishment of the "Council of the Baghdad Pact," the purpose of which was defense against "aggression or subversion." The premier of Iraq, Nuri as-Said, became the first chairman.

By the Baghdad Pact the Middle East was linked with the North Atlantic Treaty Organization (NATO) through Turkey and Great Britain, and with the Southeast Asian Treaty Organization (SEATO) through Pakistan. It marked the conclusion, at least on paper, of a United States-sponsored chain of alliances stretching from Norway to the Philippines, the object of which was to prevent further expansion on the part of the Sino-Soviet axis. In the Middle East, although the Baghdad Pact established a three thousand-mile ideological and military *cordon sanitaire* against further Soviet penetration, it still required implementation if it was to prove effective. The signatories, realizing that the effectiveness of the pact depended upon the United States, looked forward to ultimate American membership and to the inclusion of the other Arab states. The Iraq government hastened to announce, in this connection, that its adherence to the pact in no wise conflicted with its membership in the Arab League. The implication was that the pact might be used to aid any Arab state which might become the object of aggression. Nevertheless, the Baghdad Pact split the Arab world, at least temporarily.

As interpreted by the Soviet press, the Baghdad Pact was an aggressive military alliance, by means of which the United States and Great Britain hoped to saddle "a new form of colonialism" on the Middle East.[15] Soviet writers acclaimed the Arab states of Syria, Lebanon, Jordan, Saudi Arabia, and Egypt for their successful resistance to Western pressure. They likewise welcomed and no doubt helped to instigate the Jordan riots which broke out in December, 1955, as a result of British pressure on that country to join the Baghdad alliance. An *Izvestia* article (January 12, 1956) interpreted the Jordan riots as representative of the opposition of all the Arab states to further outside interference in Arab affairs. Seeking to widen the breach between Iraq and the states of the Arab League, Soviet propaganda charged that the Western powers were inciting Iraq to absorb Syria, and that Turkey intended to occupy Iranian Azerbaijan and Kurdistan. Soviet leaders were even more bitter over the failure of their efforts to keep Iran "neutral." On November 26, 1955, Soviet Foreign Minister Molotov charged Iran with violation of Article III of the Soviet-Iranian Treaty of October 1, 1927, by which both parties promised to avoid alliances or agreements directed against the other. Although it declared the Soviet frontiers to be in danger, the U.S.S.R. made no move to invoke the famous Treaty of 1921 by taking steps to occupy Iran. Nevertheless a third protest against Iran's accession to the Baghdad Pact was transmitted to the Iranian foreign minister by Soviet Ambassador Lavrentyev on February 4, 1956. The Shah's visit to the U.S.S.R. in June, 1956, was designed to convince Moscow that the Baghdad Pact is a purely defensive instrument and that its signatories have no intention of using Iran as a base for an attack on the Soviet Union. Khrushchev and his cohorts, who show no more signs of being reconciled to METO than to NATO, took advantage of the tour to continue their efforts to pry Iran loose from the Baghdad defense system.

There is still a gap in the Baghdad Pact due to the abstention of Afghanistan. Spurred into action by the Turkish-Pakistani Agreement of 1954 and by the United States-Pakistan Arms Pact, the Soviet government at once took steps to strengthen its ties with Afghanistan, regarded as the one truly "neutral" Muslim state lying athwart the U.S.S.R. and Pakistan. Soviet action took the form of economic aid--the construction of an oil pipeline from Uzbekistan to the Afghan city of Mazar-i-Sharif and of two huge wheat silos in Kabul and Pul-i-Khumr--and support of Afghan nationalist demands for a plebiscite among the Pathan tribes of Pakistan's northwest frontier province. In the fall of 1955, a Soviet-Afghan agreement for reciprocal free transit of goods through both countries relieved Afghanistan of dependence on Pakistan. With extensive atomic research reported in Soviet Kirghizia, northeast of Afghanistan, the U.S.S.R. could not afford to let its Afghan neighbors go by default into the American-sponsored Muslim alliance in the Middle East.

Following the adherence of Iraq and Iran to the Baghdad Pact and as a climax to the visit of Bulganin and Khrushchev to Kabul, the Soviet government announced on December 18, 1955, a loan of $100,000,000 to Afghanistan and a ten-year extension of the 1931 Soviet-Afghan Treaty of Neutrality and Mutual Nonaggression. Afghanistan expected to obtain arms from the Soviet orbit to offset the United States-bolstered armed strength of Pakistan and thereby to improve its prospects of "liberating" the Pathan tribes lost to Afghanistan by the treaty of 1893 with England.

Although Afghanistan remained officially "neutral" between the Soviet and Western blocs, the Soviet-Afghan rapprochement appeared to give the Soviet Union a foothold there, which served a twofold purpose. In the first place, it enabled the U.S.S.R. to maintain the gap in the METO chain of defense along the southern Soviet frontier, thereby compensating in part for the loss of Iran. In the second place, it afforded an opportunity for the Soviet Union to outflank Pakistan, one of the two major partners of the Baghdad Pact, and also to outflank Iran. It now becomes clear why the U.S. S.R. made every effort to acquire a foothold in Egypt by providing that country with arms from Czechoslovakia and by seeking a contract for the construction of the Aswan Dam. Once successful in Egypt, the Soviet government would outflank METO in the West as it does via Afghanistan in the East. It would thus hold the Middle East in a pincer grip that would constitute a direct threat to Western defense of that area.

Lenin once predicted that the film would be one of the most effective agencies for the spread of communism in the Orient. With a speed even surpassing the production of ,Alexander Nevsky, Pravda announced on January 24, 1956, the appearance of a documentary color film, In Friendly Afghanistan, recording with an appropriate background of native Afghan music the four-day visit of Bulganin and Khrushchev to various historic Afghan sites, their warm welcome in Kabul, and the signing of the Soviet-Afghan agreements concluded at that time. It is generally conceded in the West that until an agreement can be reached on the disposition of the Pathan tribes in northern Pakistan, there is little possibility of inducing Afghanistan to join the Baghdad alliance.

The Soviet Union has continued to exert every possible pressure to defeat or to delay the implementation of the American program for an effective alliance of the Muslim states against communism. It has tried, in particular, to bring about the defection of Iran by means of intimidation and economic pressure. With this in view, it has made good use of the Soviet-Iranian economic agreement of June 17, 1954, which called for a sharp increase in shipments of Soviet industrial equipment and durable goods. An Iranian parliamentary delegation, headed by Muhammed Sayed, toured the Soviet Union, including Central Asia, during the winter of 1955-56, in the interests of better Soviet-Iranian relations, and Shah Muhammed Reza Pahlevi was scheduled to pay an official visit to Moscow in May, 1956.

In February, 1956, the Soviet government intensified its propaganda for the "normalization" of Soviet-Turkish relations, in an effort to weaken Turkish adherence to the Baghdad Pact. As if in reply to a lengthy article on the subject in Pravda (February 7, 1956) a Turkish foreign ministry official on February 9 gave voice to his government's continued suspicion of Soviet motives by declaring as follows: "Turkey feels that this activity on the part of the Soviet Union proves beyond a doubt the value of the Baghdad Pact and that the Pact is doing just what it was supposed to accomplish." In spite of the Turkish rebuff, the Soviet government pursued its efforts for "normalization." Commemorating the thirty-fifth anniversary of the signing of the Soviet-Turkish Treaty of Friendship and Fraternity of 1921, *Izvestia* (March 16, 1956) called for a return to the good relations that prevailed between the two countries under Kemal Pasha and Ismet Inönü, admitted that the subsequent estrangement was a joint responsibility, and emphasized the importance of a new rapprochement for the strengthening of peace in the Near and Middle East.

Pakistan, the other major Muslim member of the Baghdad Alliance, on February 8, 1956, approved a recommendation of the Ministry of Economic Affairs for the initiation of formal negotiations for a trade pact with the Soviet Union. The only other trade contracts between the U.S.S.R. and Pakistan occurred in 1953, when a barter agreement provided for the exchange of Pakistani cotton for Soviet wheat at a time when famine threatened the new Muslim state. The decision to negotiate a trade pact was interpreted by some Western experts as an entering wedge for Soviet economic aid to Pakistan, in competition with the United States. Speaking for the press on March 24, the day following his assumption of office, Iskander Mirza, first president of the Pakistan Republic, left no room for doubt on this matter by repudiating "neutralism" and reaffirming Pakistan's determination to hold fast to the Baghdad Pact and the Southeast Asia Treaty Organization, which he regarded as "agencies for peace."

Irrespective of the outcome of Soviet efforts to undermine the Baghdad Alliance, it can be said that English membership in METO provided the Soviet government with an effective weapon to achieve such an objective. A Kukryniksy cartoon in *Pravda* (December 18, 1955) depicted the four Muslim members of the Baghdad Alliance seeking security in the open jaws of the British lion. English membership thus lent weight to Soviet claims that the pact was a ruse to inflict a new form of colonialism on the countries of the Middle East. No doubt the British government, having recently surrendered its former strategic position at Suez to Egypt, being in the process of transferring important air bases to Iraq and facing a serious challenge to British authority in Cyprus, hoped by membership in METO to compensate for its retreat elsewhere in the Near and Middle East. The fact that it still controlled the British-led and British-subsidized Arab Legion of Jordan appreciably strengthened Middle Eastern defenses. Its subsequent failure to bring Jordan into the Baghdad Alliance, followed by the abrupt dismissal on March 2, 1956, by King Hussein of Lieutenant-General John Bagot Glubb ("Glubb Pasha"), British commander of Jordan's Arab Legion, raised some doubt as to whether British membership had become more of a handicap than an asset. In retrospect, the question arises as to whether the Baghdad Alliance should not have remained exclusively a Muslim alliance, relying on the leadership of Turkey and Pakistan, with Great Britain following the American example of lending active support without becoming an active member. Unfortunately for the success of the alliance, in the minds of the Arabs and other peoples of the Muslim East, Great Britain, in spite of her genuine efforts to promote the development and stability of this area, is the country most closely associated with colonialism.

The United States has continued to offset Soviet propaganda in the Middle East by placing more and more emphasis on matters pertaining to religion and nationalism. These are still the issues which, in spite of increasing economic consciousness, are of major concern in Muslim lands, irrespective of geographical location. The Soviet press and Muslim refugees who escaped from the Soviet Union to Germany and other parts of the West during and since World War II have provided much factual material to counteract Soviet claims as to the position of Muslims in the U.S.S.R. For instance, the Soviet illustrated weekly *Ogonyok* has upon occasion published photographs of collective farmers from the Soviet republics of Central Asia, proudly displaying Soviet medals they have won for greatly exceeding their quotas in raising swine. In Soviet novels dealing with Central Asia, even elderly Muslim characters have boasted of eating pork and drinking vodka--thus defying the explicit prohibitions of the Koran. Such information, direct from Soviet sources, when made available to the theological schools and colleges of the Near and Middle East, helps to offset the propaganda of Soviet-trained mullahs about freedom of the Muslim religion inside the U.S.S.R. Writing from Tashkent, the capital of Uzbekistan, on January 3, 1956, C. L. Sulzberger of the *New York Times* (January 4) quoted Al-Hafiz Ghazi Zia-ud-Din Babahanov, son of the eighty-five-year-old Mufti of the Central Asian Muslims, to the effect that there are today in Tashkent only eighteen mosques, whereas forty years ago there were no fewer than three hundred. Outside the Soviet Union, Islamic scholars are discussing the possibility of a Muslim renaissance. In the Muslim regions of the U.S.S.R., such a renaissance is beyond the realm of possibility.

Through Muslim refugees and other sources, news of the expulsion of Muslim inhabitants from the Crimea, of the migration of approximately 450,000 members of the Young Communist League (Komsomol) to the Muslim republics of Central Asia, and the accompanying dispersal of the Muslim youth, is reaching Arab and other Muslim nationalists of the Middle East, providing them with some idea of the fate in store for the rest of the Muslim world in the event of further Soviet expansion. It helps to counteract the Communist agitators who seek to arouse nationalist aspirations in the Near East, North Africa, and Southeast Asia by extolling the autonomy of the Muslim states in the Soviet Union.

The Turks have no need to be told, but the other Muslim peoples of the Middle East, who say their countries have been occupied repeatedly by the Western powers but never by the Russians, might well ponder over the four hundred-year crusade of Russians against Muslims, dating from the capture of Kazan in 1552. That further education along these lines is needed is clear from the speech at Jakarta of President Sukarno of Indonesia at an "anticolonial" rally on January 15, 1956. This Muslim leader expressed his pleasure over the collaboration of the Communists, Nationalists, and the Muslim Union party in Indonesia. His talk was strongly reminiscent of the outlook of some of the Muslim mullahs of the postrevolutionary years, who were misled into preaching that Marxism and Leninism were in accord with the teachings of Islam. Such thinking on the part of Indonesian Muslims indicated that they still fear "colonialism" more than communism, and that they have not profited by the experience of Turkish and Iranian Muslims during the past forty years. At the Asian Prime Ministers' Conference in Colombo, Ceylon, in April, 1954, Premier Muhammed Ali, pro-American leader of Pakistan, warned his colleagues that communism is "worse than the H-bomb."

Next to the bugaboo of "colonialism," American support of the state of Israel has been and continues to be a major source of Arab and Muslim suspicion of American policy in the Near and Middle East. In spite of the bitter animosity that exists today between the Arab states and Israel, however, this problem is not so deeply rooted in the past as the problem of colonialism. Delegates to the Baghdad Conference of November, 1955, recognized the fact that an effective alliance of the Muslim world and the United States required the settlement of the Palestine problem.

Under Soviet domination there would be no room for independent

Arab or Israeli states. The U.S.S.R. and Communist China have between them more Muslims than there are Arabs in this world, yet they have not created a single sovereign Muslim state in their orbit. The fate of the thirty million Muslims and of the much-advertised Jewish autonomous region of Birobidjan inside the U.S. S.R. affords ample demonstration of that. If war should be permitted to break out between the Arabs and Israeli, it is a foregone conclusion that the Soviet Union, under the aegis of the rising military caste, would intervene to take advantage of the situation. From the standpoint of both Arabs and Jews, therefore, it is essential that a *modus vivendi* be found.

The ultimate solution appears to lie, present Arab and Jewish opposition notwithstanding, in an effective alliance between a united Muslim world and the United States. Such an alliance would provide the best possible guarantee for the Arab states against an "Israel with expansionist aims," which is what the Arabs fear most. On the other hand, the commitment of the United States to this alliance would insure the continued independence of the state of Israel, which would otherwise be submerged in a Muslim sea. Effective guarantees by the United States and the major Muslim powers, especially Turkey and Pakistan, of the independence and territorial integrity of Israel and the Arab states would reduce tension in the Middle East, greatly strengthen the Baghdad Alliance, and prove a real deterrent to further Soviet expansion. Above all, the future existence of Israel as a sovereign state and the maintenance of peace in the Near and Middle East are largely contingent upon the ability and diplomatic skill of the Israeli in winning the confidence and good will of the Arab world.

IV

Another factor in Soviet-Muslim relations in the postwar period is the resurgence of the Muslim population of Red China. The creation of new Muslim states in the Middle East, such as Pakistan, had its impact on the Muslim minority in China, which sought greater autonomy for its own members. The Soviet and Red Chinese governments have tried to organize the Muslim elements under their jurisdiction, in order to make use of them in other parts of the Muslim world, especially in the Near and Middle East. Soviet-Chinese efforts in this direction found their expression in a speech by Burhan, chairman of the Preparatory Committee of the China Islamic Association, delivered before Muslim delegates from various countries at the Peace Conference of the Asian and

Pacific Regions, October 18, 1952.[16] This Muslim conference was held concurrently with the nineteenth congress of the Communist party in Moscow, at which Stalin made his last major speech on foreign policy.

The extent of the Muslim population in China is difficult to estimate. French scholars concerned with the problem placed the figure at four million in 1911.[17] The China Islamic Association, formally inaugurated on May 9, 1953, in Peiping, declared the number to be about ten million. Another recent estimate by an American scholar, based on a Chinese population of four hundred million, suggests that 5 per cent, or around twenty million are Muslims.[18] If the census taken by the Mao Tse-tung government in 1955, which estimated the Chinese population to be in the neighborhood of six hundred million, is correct, the number of Muslims in China may reach from twenty to thirty million. Although it is extremely difficult to secure an accurate census of any Muslim population, it would appear that the number of Muslims in Red China is approximately equal to the number in the U.S.S.R. The ten organized branches of the Muslim peoples of China include the Huis, Uighurs, Kazakhs, Kirghiz, Tadjiks, Tatars, Uzbeks, Tunghsiangs, Salas, and Paoans, located for the most part in the northwest provinces of Sinkiang, Kansu, Chinghai, and Ningsia. Thus the Sino-Soviet axis has under its jurisdiction in the neighborhood of from fifty to sixty million Muslims. The stress placed on Arabic at the above-mentioned Chinese Peace Conference of 1952 should not be overlooked from the standpoint of the Middle East.

Early in 1956 it became clear that Red China and the Soviet Union were taking parallel action in the Near East and Africa, possibly as a result of the Asian-African Conference in Bandung. The most conspicuous parallels were to be seen in their diplomatic and trade overtures to Lebanon, Syria, Egypt, the Sudan, and Liberia. Thus, on January 4, one day following Soviet action, Chou En-lai, in a message to Sudanese Premier Ismail el-Azhari, announced Peiping's recognition of the Sudan as an independent state and proposed the establishment of diplomatic relations. Both the U.S.S.R. and Red China have made overtures to Liberia. On December 31, 1955, Red China signed a trade pact with Lebanon. During the previous August, the Chinese Communists signed contracts with Egypt for the purchase of fifteen thousand tons of cotton in exchange for sixty thousand tons of rolled steel. A Chinese trade mission established permanent headquarters in Cairo in February, 1956. The expansion of Chinese-Egyptian trade since the trade pact of August,

1955, and the manifest success of the Red Chinese trade fair in Cairo in April, 1956, all without benefit of diplomatic recognition, appeared to augur bigger and better "deals" to come. Egypt's recognition of Red China on May 1 6, 1956, undoubtedly accelerated the pace of Sino-Soviet collaboration in the Near East. The trek to Cairo in June by the new Soviet foreign minister, Dmitri Shepilov, to celebrate the end of three-quarters of a century of British occupation of the Suez Canal Zone was followed in July by the visit of Chou En-lai to commemorate the third anniversary of the Egyptian Revolution of 1953. Thus, no sooner did the Western powers reconcile themselves, albeit reluctantly, to the necessity for recognizing the U.S.S.R. as a factor in eastern Mediterranean affairs, than they were confronted by the sudden and unwelcome impact of Red China in that area. Just as Great Britain and the United States have cooperated on policy issues in the Middle East, we can expect Red China and the U.S.S.R. to work jointly in the future to attain Communist objectives. In doing so they are sure to make use of their own Muslims.

By 1956 it became apparent that the Baghdad Pact, far from discouraging Soviet efforts in the Near and Middle East, afforded the Soviet government a first-class opportunity to take advantage of Arab opposition to the United States-sponsored defense system for the Muslim world. Among other indications was the prompt establishment of Soviet diplomatic relations with the new Sudanese republic. On March 8, 1956, the Soviet Union followed up its treaty of friendship with Yemen (October 30, 1955) with a trade agreement, providing Soviet industrial equipment, oil products, and food in exchange for Yemenite coffee, hides, dried fruits, etc. In line with its recent challenge to the United States, the Soviet government has offered to build factories, to provide technical assistance, and possibly arms to this Arab state. The first Arab leader to undertake a "mission to Moscow" was the crown prince of Yemen, Seif al-Islam Muhammed el-Badr, who made a three-week tour of the Soviet Union in June, 1956, to strengthen "peace and cooperation" between Yemen and the U.S.S.R. In March, Soviet cultural and economic delegations were busy in Damascus, while a Syrian military mission was in Prague to negotiate for the purchase of arms. The Soviet government, in addition to providing a market for Syrian cotton, offered to construct a Syrian government oil refinery to process the oil reaching that country from Iraq. The U.S.S.R. was likewise instrumental in accelerating the issuing of a joint communiqué (March 12, 1956) by the leaders of Egypt, Saudi Arabia, and Syria for the mobilization of their defenses against Israel and for the formation of a neutral Arab bloc to counteract Western efforts to strengthen the Baghdad Pact.

The Soviet government stepped up its news coverage of Near and Middle Eastern affairs to such an extent that it vied with the Far East in importance. Using both the club and the carrot, Soviet diplomatic action and press propaganda strove to arouse opposition at home and abroad to the new Western "colonialism" envisaged in the Baghdad Alliance. Due to the four hundred-year tradition of Russian expansion at the expense of the Muslim world, it is never difficult to revive Russian interest in the Russian "mission" in that area. Anglo-American concern over renewed Soviet efforts to win friends and influence people in the Muslim world made the Middle East a topic of major consideration during the Eden-Eisenhower talks in Washington in February, 1956. [19]

In 1917 the new Soviet regime was in a position to attribute to Tsarist Russia all past aggression at the expense of the Muslim world and to profit temporarily thereby. The downgrading of Stalin in 1956 appeared to represent an attempt to wipe the slate clean of earlier Soviet mistakes and failures and to make a fresh start in the Near and Middle East, as well as elsewhere. Judging by the intensification of the Soviet diplomatic and trade campaign in that area and by Shepilov's choice of Cairo for his first major pronouncement on Soviet foreign policy, the U.S.S.R. has merely shifted its tactics and its major theater of operations.

The Bulganin-Khrushchev mission to England in April, 1956, was undoubtedly motivated by a desperate Soviet need for peace. The Soviet Union required peace in order to complete its sixth Five-Year Plan, from which Moscow hoped to emerge not only as the ideological center for Asia, but also as its technological Mecca. The indispensability of a breathing spell to the post-Stalin regime was amply demonstrated by its action on the eve of the London negotiations. In rapid succession, the U.S.S.R. joined the Western powers in admonishing the Arabs and the Israelis to maintain peace in the Near East, Molotov and Mikoyan made a further gesture in this direction by attending the independence-day celebration at the Israeli Embassy, the Kremlin announced the dissolution of the Cominform, and in the United Nations the Russians agreed to the establishment of a world-wide atoms-for-peace agency.

A careful perusal of the Soviet press appeared to indicate that with regard to the crisis in the Near and Middle East in 1956, Soviet leaders had two alternatives in mind. (1) From the standpoint of immediate Soviet security, they preferred the "neutralization" of this area, which would be tantamount to the dissolution of the Bagh-

dad Alliance. (2) Their alternative program called for increasingly
active Soviet participation in Near and Middle Eastern affairs, even
to the extent of carving out a recognized Soviet sphere of influence
there, presumably in Egypt and the Arab lands outside the Baghdad
bloc. This would amount to a modified version of partition of this
area, corresponding in some respects to the partition of Germany,
Korea, and Indo-China between the Soviet orbit and the West. In
view of the Soviet record in the past, neither "neutralization" nor
a Soviet sphere of influence in the Near and Middle East proved
acceptable to the West.

Barring the establishment of a Western *modus vivendi* with the
U.S.S.R., it is quite possible that some Muslim countries may
continue to succumb to the temptation of accepting Soviet aid and
Soviet backing, as Turkey, Iran, and Afghanistan did after the
Bolshevik Revolution and as some Muslim states are now doing,
in order to offset the power and impact of the Western orbit. Any
temptation on the part of the American government to cope with
the Sino-Soviet economic drive in the Near East by subordinating
strategic defenses to economic development inevitably will be hailed
as a Soviet victory, tantamount to the disintegration of the Baghdad Pact. This has been the primary objective of the U.S.S.R.
in the Muslim world. As long as the shadow of the Sino-Soviet
alliance continues to hover over Asia the United States, in order
to preserve peace in the Near and Middle East, has no alternative
but to strengthen its military as well as its economic ties with the
Muslim world, for which the Baghdad Alliance had already laid a
substantial foundation.

Post-Stalin Soviet policy in Asia has raised another new problem
for the West. Prior to this time the U.S.S.R. presented a challenge to the West as an ideological and as a military force. It has
now emerged, in addition, as an economic competitor. Having observed the effectiveness of the Marshall Plan in Europe, of American aid to Turkey and other underdeveloped areas, the Soviet government has adopted these tactics as its own, not only in Eastern
Europe, but in large parts of Asia and Africa.

Soviet plans to provide economic aid and technical assistance to
the peoples of the East are not in themselves new. They found expression in the years following the Revolution in the speeches and
writings of Lenin and Stalin. The Soviet oriental expert, M. Pavlovitch, envisaged the possibilities of such a program in his *Revoliutsionnyi Vostok (Revolutionary East)* in 1927. Having raised the
question as to how and where Turkey and later Persia, Afghanistan,
and China were to secure the necessary aid for the economic devel-

opment of their countries, he emphasized the need for the U.S.S.R.
to transform itself into an industrial nation, with all the essential tractors, turbines, automobiles, ships, and machines to produce this equipment. This industrialization, he contended, would
introduce in world economy "a new, important element, a mighty
new factor," which would aid the countries of the East in the process of rebirth, would save them from economic enslavement to the
capitalist world, and would prevent their use as an economic and
military base for action against the U.S.S.R. [20]

Following the Soviet neutrality and trade treaties with Turkey,
Iran, and Afghanistan in the nineteen twenties, the U.S.S.R. made
a few sporadic attempts to provide economic and technical assistance to these and other countries. Soviet engineers and technicians
began to participate in the economic development of Afghanistan.
A Soviet hospital was opened at S'ana in Yemen in 1928. After the
new Soviet-Turkish commercial treaty of 1931, two large textile
mills at Kayseri and Nazilli in Turkey were built with Soviet credits and with the aid of Soviet experts. By 1938 the U.S.S.R., as
a result of the Five-Year Plans, was ready to embark on a more
ambitious program of technical aid to the East. The socialization
of Soviet agriculture, according to the Scientific Research Institute of the Foreign Trade Monopoly "opened up the possibility of
U.S.S.R. technical aid to the countries of the East in the sphere of
agriculture," where Soviet methods could be adapted successfully
to Eastern conditions. [21] World War II forced the postponement of
the Soviet technical assistance program in the Near East.

Not until the death of Stalin did the U.S.S.R. make a determined
effort to meet the challenge of United States aid by implementing
its own program of economic assistance to the underdeveloped
countries of Asia outside the Communist orbit. This program included the dispatch of Soviet technicians to at least fourteen countries and the training of hundreds of Asian specialists in Soviet
institutions. American economists have estimated that approximately one-fourth of the $1,400,000,000 in Soviet bloc credits advanced
by the latter part of 1956 were for the purchase of arms by Egypt,
Syria, and Afghanistan. [22] Since 1953, the Soviet Union has made
available approximately $1,000,000 per annum to the United Nations
Expanded Program of Technical Assistance for equipment, fellow-
ships, study tours, economic surveys, etc. In its bilateral agreements the U.S.S.R., in contrast to the United States, has preferred
long-term, low-interest rate loans and barter deals to outright
grants, [23] has frequently accepted as payment such raw materials
as Egyptian cotton, Burmese rice, or Indian jute when these prod-

ucts were a glut on the market, and has supplied limited quantities of machine tools and industrial equipment to accelerate the industrialization of Asian countries. The object has been to render recipients of Soviet aid like Egypt, Afghanistan, Yemen, and more recently Syria, economically dependent on the Sino-Soviet orbit and to cut their ties with the West.

The Soviet program was launched in Afghanistan in 1950, with the conclusion of a four-year trade agreement which provided for the delivery of Soviet machinery and transportation equipment. In 1953, the U.S.S.R. dispatched a five-man technical mission to supervise the construction of air-conditioned wheat storage facilities in Afghanistan. Subsequent loans were applied to the construction of two large grain elevators, a flour mill, and a bread-baking plant in Kabul. The program reached a new climax with the visit of Bulganin and Khrushchev (December, 1955), with a Soviet loan to Afghanistan of $100,000,000, to be allocated to agricultural development and irrigation projects, to the reconstruction of the Kabul airport, etc. More than four hundred Soviet technicians have been reported to be actively engaged in these Afghan economic development programs.

One of the more spectacular examples of Soviet technical assistance, which created an impression in many countries of the Middle East, was the Soviet-Indian agreement of February 2, 1955, by which the Soviet Union undertook to provide India with an integrated iron and steel plant at Bhilai, as well as to furnish Soviet technicians to supervise its construction. In November, 1956, the U.S.S.R. also extended a new $126,000,000 credit to India, primarily for the purchase of heavy machinery.

Although Soviet aid to India and Afghanistan implied that it was the intention of the U.S.S.R. to outflank Pakistan economically, nevertheless the Soviet government in 1956 and 1957 made a number of gestures to this Islamic Republic, ostensibly designed to improve trade relations and undoubtedly intended to weaken Pakistan's ties with the Baghdad Alliance and SEATO. Under a 1956 trade pact, the Pakistani Batala Engineering Company arranged for the purchase of fourteen thousand tons of pig iron and steel billets. In September, 1957, a Pakistan delegation toured the U. S.S.R., Poland, Czechoslovakia, and Yugoslavia with the avowed objective of expanding its trade with the Soviet bloc.

Even Turkey, confronted in 1957 by a critical lack of foreign exchange and credits with the countries of the Western bloc, was persuaded to turn experimentally to the Soviet foreign-aid program. It was perhaps significant that Nikita S. Rijov, the U.S.S.R. ambassador in Ankara, was the Soviet engineer who supervised the construction of the Kayseri textile mill twenty-three years ago. In any event, a Turkish delegation representing the Ish Bank returned from a forty-day sojourn in Moscow with a contract for the construction in Turkey of a sheet-glass factory and a caustic-soda plant, designed to free the Turkish Republic from its dependence on foreign glass imports. In August, 1957, Himmet Olomen, a Turkish Democratic deputy in Parliament, explained that if the United States could not fulfill Turkish needs for industrialization, Turkey would have to look elsewhere (*New York Times*, August 14, 1957).

As in the case of the Pakistani and the Turks, the Iranians have been wary of Soviet trade propositions. Unable to make much headway in Iran, the Soviet regime was content for a time to provide planes, pilots, and specialists to assist Iran in combating the annual locust invasion, which destroyed crops on both sides of the Soviet-Iranian border. In April, 1957, however, a Soviet mission headed by First Deputy Foreign Minister Kuznetsov succeeded not only in settling long-standing border problems but in making a three-year trade agreement by which the U.S.S.R. would exchange machinery, cars, and sugar for Iranian minerals, agricultural products, and rugs. Another major concession won by Iran was the right of free transit through the U.S.S.R. for all commodities, irrespective of origin.

The stepped-up Soviet trade offensive in Asia has continued to include all the countries of the Soviet orbit. According to American estimates, Red China has accounted for 20 per cent of the total Sino-Soviet bloc trade. Although the Chinese drive has been directed mainly toward the countries of Southeast Asia and India, Red Chinese trade delegations have not overlooked the Middle East, especially Jordan, Egypt, and Syria. In 1957 Egypt and Syria, in particular, strengthened their economic ties with the Soviet European satellites and with Yugoslavia.

After four years of concerted effort the Soviet bloc's economic offensive is still limited in scope. It has nevertheless made significant gains in the Middle East, so much so, in fact, that the Vice-President of the United States in October, 1957, termed it a greater cause for concern than the Soviet launching of the first earth satellite (*sputnik*). In time of crisis, it has presented the countries of the Middle East with two alternatives. If the West declines to build hydroelectric plants, dams, steel plants, roads, and oil refineries, etc., there is every reason to expect that the U.S.S.R. will continue to exploit the opportunity to its own advantage. In consequence, American foreign policy in the Near and Middle East of necessity must be geared to confront this new challenge from the Soviet bloc, which has already assumed substantial proportions.

As of February 1, 1958, Soviet bloc aid in the Near East had focused on three Arab states--Egypt ($485,000,000), Syria ($294,000, 000), and Yemen ($19,000,000).[24] It is significant that the total United States aid to all Arab lands in this area was approximately one-fifth of the $798,000,000 extended by the Soviet bloc to the United Arab Republic and Yemen, now known as the United Arab States. The Arabs have contended that the Soviet Union has been much more prompt than the United States in implementing the aid it has promised, not to mention the fact that its political position has been "correct" during the Suez dispute and other recent crises in the Near and Middle East (*New York Times*, February 8, 1958). As compared with the limited amount of aid to Arab countries, the United States over the same period has advanced $283,382,000 in aid to Israel and $437,210,000 to Turkey. In 1958 the extension of foreign aid appeared to have a direct bearing on the allegiance of the states of the Near East to the Soviet and Western blocs.

A new competitor in aid to the Arab states emerged in the spring of 1958, with the announcement on May 7, that the Adenauer government had granted credits amounting to 400,000,000 Deutsche marks (about $95,000,000) to the newly established United Arab Republic of Egypt and Syria, for the purchase of industrial goods in West Germany (*New York Times*, May 8, 1958). As might be expected, Soviet reaction to this move was unfavorable.

The prospects for further Soviet encroachment in the Near East, especially in the Arab East, were enhanced by the withdrawal (July 19-20, 1956) of Anglo-American offers to help Egypt finance the building of the Aswan Dam on the Nile. President Nasser quickly retaliated on July 26, by announcing the nationalization of the Suez Canal Company twelve years prior to the end of its concession, with the avowed object of securing the revenue to finance the Aswan Dam. This action was approved without delay by the Soviet press. Without full assurance of Soviet support, it seems unlikely that Egypt would have recklessly defied the Western Powers on so crucial an issue.

Since Russia was a signatory of the Constantinople Convention of 1888, the Soviet government clearly indicated its intention to participate in any revision of that settlement and demanded the inclusion of the Arab succession states of the Ottoman Empire. Although unwilling in 1947 that Turkey should have exclusive control of the Dardanelles and Bosphorus, the U.S.S.R. now posed as the principal champion of Egyptian sovereignty over the Canal, rejecting Anglo-French plans for its internationalization. After September 12, 1956, Soviet pilots supported Nasser's efforts to keep the Canal open. On September 16, in a major pronouncement the Soviet government warned that "any disturbance of peace in the Middle East cannot but affect the security and interests of the Soviet state," and demanded a peaceful settlement through the United Nations. The "piratical" Users' Association was rejected by Moscow as an American scheme to get control of the Canal.

No sooner had the Israeli invasion of Egypt begun (October 19, 1956), closely followed by Anglo-French intervention, than Bulganin appealed to India and to Indonesia for a special session of the Asian-African bloc that comprised the Bandung Conference (*Pravda*, November 2, 1956). On November 3, Voroshilov promised Soviet aid to visiting President Shukri al-Kuwatly of Syria. Two days later the U.S.S.R. warned Britain, France, and Israel of Soviet readiness to use force "to crush the aggressors." Bulganin's call for joint United States-Soviet action to end the Egyptian war appeared to be paving the way for unilateral Soviet action, when the United States government promptly labeled the proposal "unthinkable."

Sino-Soviet intervention in the Suez crisis undoubtedly strengthened the position of President Nasser and the Arab states. Temporarily, at least, the prospect of Soviet "volunteers" in the Near East, augmented by Red China's offer of another 250,000, gave rise to near panic on the part of Egypt's invaders. Without the threat of imminent Soviet military intervention, it is doubtful whether the United Nations emergency Assembly session would have ordered and achieved a cease-fire in Egypt so quickly, that it would have proceeded so rapidly to authorize and to move into Egypt the new United Nations police force, and that England, France, and Israel would have agreed to withdraw from Egyptian territory in favor of U.N. occupation forces.

On the other hand, the second conference of the chiefs of state of the Arab League, meeting in Beirut on November 13, amid rumors of substantial Soviet arms shipments and the dispatch of Soviet technical advisers to Syria, viewed with apprehension the pro-Soviet stand of Syria and Egypt. The seven other states of the Arab League, especially Lebanon, Saudi Arabia, and Iraq, opposed the use of Soviet "volunteers." Their leaders appeared to be aware that under Soviet domination there would be no room for independent Arab or Israeli states. In spite of Anglo-French and Israeli stalling tactics in regard to the withdrawal of their forces from the

Suez Canal Zone, Nasser's Egypt appeared as reluctant to admit Soviet "volunteers" as was Kemal Pasha of Turkey in 1920. Nor did the Soviet government, handicapped by the Hungarian revolt and general unrest among its European satellites, display any haste to implement unilaterally its threats to suppress aggression at Suez, lest precipitate action might lead to a general war or force a third Soviet retreat from the Near and Middle East. As efforts to attain an early and conclusive settlement of the Suez crisis bogged down at the close of November, 1956, there were indications that the United States, which had attempted to chart an "independent" course in troubled Near Eastern waters by refusing to condone the Anglo-French-Israeli invasion of Egypt, was exerting every effort to revitalize the Baghdad Alliance as a Muslim bulwark against further Soviet penetration of the Near East via Syria and Egypt.

To prevent any possible repetition in the future of the use of Soviet "volunteers" in the Arab world, on January 5, 1957, President Eisenhower called upon Congress to authorize the use of United States armed forces against Communist or Communist-dominated aggression in the Middle East. After prolonged debate, the Senate on March 5, by a vote of 72 to 19, approved an amended version of the Eisenhower Doctrine, which limited the discretionary power of the President. On March 9, the President signed the Middle East doctrine as passed by Congress.

Following a series of articles in the Soviet press denouncing the proposed Eisenhower Doctrine (*Pravda,* January 9 and 13, 1957), the Soviet and Red Chinese governments on January 18 signed in Moscow a joint declaration condemning the doctrine and announcing their readiness to support the peoples of the Near and Middle East in order to prevent "aggression" and interference in their internal affairs. This "Sino-Soviet Doctrine," as reported in the Soviet press, met with an immediate and favorable response in some parts of the Arab world, especially in Cairo and Damascus (*Pravda,* January 22, 1957).

Since the United States government had vigorously opposed the Anglo-French-Israeli invasion of Egypt, it was perhaps unfortunate that the Eisenhower Doctrine was directed solely against the threat of "armed aggression from any country controlled by international communism." At a time when American prestige had soared to new heights in the Muslim world, and especially among the Arab states, the United States government had an opportunity to propose an ironclad guarantee of protection of the Middle East against aggression from any source, communist or noncommunist. In retrospect, it seems likely that such a guarantee would have been accepted eagerly, not only by the members of the Baghdad Alliance, but likewise by the Arab states outside the Middle East bloc, thereby healing instead of accentuating the breach in the Arab world. By uniting all the Muslim states of the Near and Middle East under United States leadership, it would have erected an effective bulwark for the preservation of world peace.

As it was, the Eisenhower Doctrine offered no protection against a repetition of the Anglo-French-Israeli invasion of Egypt, other than that offered by the temporary presence of the United Nations emergency force in the Middle East (Section 4). In the minds of Arab leaders, especially those in Cairo and Damascus, the recent invaders of Egypt constituted the real threat to peace and security in the Arab world. They rejected an American guarantee directed against the very Communist "volunteers" who ostensibly had just offered them "protection" against Anglo-French-Israeli invasion. Not only did the Eisenhower Doctrine fail to win the unanimous support of the Muslim world, but temporarily, at least, it split the Arab states, thereby providing the U.S.S.R. with still another opportunity to use the breach to secure a Soviet foothold there.

On February 11 and again on April 21, 1957, in an effort to offset the impact of the Eisenhower Doctrine, the Soviet government called upon Great Britain, France, and the United States to join with the U.S.S.R. to renounce force in the solution of the problems of the Middle East. Since the acceptance of the Soviet proposals would have been tantamount to the abandonment of the Eisenhower Doctrine and the dissolution of the Baghdad Alliance, the United States and her European partners promptly rejected it. Shortly thereafter, the United States at a conference in Karachi pledged $12,570,000 in Eisenhower Doctrine funds for financial aid to the Baghdad Pact countries. To further strengthen the Middle East treaty powers, on June 3 the United States formally joined the Baghdad Pact Military Committee. During the Syrian crisis of September-October, 1957, the Soviet government again sought to place the Western powers at a disadvantage by repeating its propaganda gesture in favor of a Big Four declaration "denouncing force" as a means of solving disputes in the Near and Middle East.

The Soviet government, pursuing its "leapfrog" tactics in the Near East, continued to provide substantial military aid to the Arab states of Egypt, Yemen, and Syria. In July, 1956, as we have seen, the Egyptians would not have had the temerity to nationalize the Suez Canal Company without assurance of Soviet backing. Likewise the landing of Egyptian troops in Syria on October 13, 1957, ostensibly to protect the Syrian border from the Turks and also to bolster the pro-Soviet Syrian regime, no doubt was undertaken as a result of assurances of the implementation of the Sino-Soviet Middle East Doctrine. It was the threat of permanent Soviet military and naval bases in Syria that precipitated the Middle East crisis of October, 1957, which in some respects amounted to a direct challenge of the effectiveness of the Eisenhower Doctrine.

Recent Soviet policy toward the Muslim world is summed up in the official record, *Afro-Asian Peoples Conference, 26 December 1957-1st January 1958,* published in Arabic, English, and French by the permanent secretariat of the conference in Cairo. This document, strictly speaking, is a blueprint of future Soviet goals in the Afro-Asian world.

The significance of the Afro-Asian Peoples' Conference, held in Cairo in December, 1957, was almost overlooked in the American press. Unlike its predecessor, the Bandung Conference of 1955, it felt the direct impact of the U.S.S.R., which played an active part in the preparation of the agenda and the drafting of the resolutions. Within a few months it became an established institution, with headquarters in Cairo. Its impact is already strong throughout Asia and Africa.

The conference program, as published by the secretariat, is strongly reminiscent of the Third International, but with nationalism instead of communism as its theme, and with emphasis on Asia and Africa. Although neither communism nor socialism is mentioned, the method of achieving nationalist goals is basically that of the Comintern. In other words, Soviet foreign policy is using nationalist tools to achieve communist objectives.

The most important person at Afro-Asian headquarters in 1958 appeared to be Abrashidov Gafour, a Soviet Muslim from Tashkent, Uzbekistan, who represents the U.S.S.R. He is the real power behind the secretariat. In brief, Soviet foreign policy toward the Arab world is being implemented in Cairo at the headquarters of the Afro-Asian Solidarity Conference.

The main tasks before the Afro-Asian organization in 1958, and indirectly the main Soviet objectives, were: (1) the promotion of Arab unity; (2) the "liberation" of the remaining dependencies in Africa and Asia from the control of the. Western "colonizers."

Among the Arab peoples there is growing recognition of the fact that small, independent nations are in a precarious position, that their independence is qualified by the need to veer in the direction of one or other of the two great power blocs--the Western or the Soviet. Many educated and politically conscious Arabs are espousing the cause of Arab unity or Arab federation, as the only effective means of terminating the endless intrigue, the divide-and-rule tactics, to which every small, independent Near Eastern state is subject under existing conditions. From Arab unity, they look for greater stability in the Near and Middle East and for an opportunity to cope with the economic, social, and political problems that override artificial political boundaries carved out by the Western powers, some of them after World War I. They vigorously oppose the imposition of any kind of outside "trusteeship," such as that proposed by some Americans, even if the trustee is the United Nations. The impression is given that the Arab peoples are sick and tired of foreign tutelage in any form, even in the guise of U.N. "observers."

At this opportune time, the Soviet Union has given its unqualified support to "the age-old aspirations of the Arab peoples for unity," to the building of the United Arab States, comprising the Arab world from the Atlantic to the Indian Ocean, from the Mediterranean to Central Africa. During the state visit of President Nasser to the U.S.S.R., April 29 to May 16, 1958, Khrushchev called for "the solidarity of the Arab people" under Nasser's leadership and promised him all the Soviet aid necessary to achieve it. In return, Nasser endorsed Soviet foreign policy objectives. Together they condemned colonialism in all its manifestations, Western military bases in the Middle East, the French war in Algeria, and the British threat to Yemen; and they heartily endorsed the resolutions of the Cairo Conference, the "legitimate rights" of the Palestine Arabs, and the progress of U.A.R.-U.S.S.R. economic and cultural collaboration.

To some experts in Cairo, it is a matter of regret that American policy has failed to support the cause of Arab unity. The very fact that its objective is the United Arab States suggests to them the impact of the American rather than the Soviet example. They regard it as a tragedy that the United States by default has enabled the U.S.S.R., a professedly atheistic and totalitarian regime, to become the champion of Arab unity in a predominantly Muslim area.

Under the aegis of the Moscow-Cairo combination, Arab leaders are working feverishly, often with manifest impatience and tactlessness, for the United Arab States. They are in such a hurry that they are willing to settle for an organic union, such as that between Egypt and Syria, which formed the United Arab Republic in February, 1958, or a loose federation comprising a monarchy and a republic, such as was established by the U.A.R. and Yemen in March, 1958. As one Arab historian and philosopher in Cairo expressed it, the Arabs need to achieve unity before any drastic change occurs in the world power balance, and while at least one of the two great international power blocs, even if it be the Soviet, is ready and willing to promote and support the realization of their objectives.

Even with Soviet support, the cause of Arab unity has met with some major setbacks. The Chamoun government in Lebanon and King Hussein of Jordan in July, 1958, summoned American and English military aid respectively in order to forestall Arab unity under the leadership of the U.A.R. In October, an open rift between Bourguiba's Tunisia and Nasser's U.A.R. in the Arab League culminated in the rupture of diplomatic relations between the two Arab states. It is nevertheless conceded, in spite of the outcome of the De Gaulle referendum in September, that Moscow and Cairo have made significant gains among students and labor unions in French Africa. Among the peoples, as distinct from the governments of the Arab states of the Middle East and North Africa, President Nasser's success ever since the Suez crisis of 1956 has created a strong sentiment in favor of Arab unity.

In the Arab world to date, the U.S.S.R. has made its greatest headway in the United Arab Republic and Yemen. There are indications, however, that all-out Soviet support for Arab independence and Afro-Asian solidarity may win for the Soviets an entering wedge in other Arab states that have hitherto rejected diplomatic relations with Communist countries and have resisted tempting Soviet offers of economic aid and closer cultural collaboration. Soviet support of the U.A.R. and Iraq during the explosive Lebanese-Iraqi-Jordanian crisis of 1958 has already paid dividends, in the renewal of Soviet diplomatic relations with Iraq, and the establishment on September 1 of Soviet diplomatic relations with Morocco. On the other hand, the Soviet line-up with the U.A.R. forced Khrushchev to sacrifice the Communist party of Syria, which Nasser has driven underground, exiling or imprisoning its leaders.

The Soviet Union has still another inducement to play an active role in behalf of Arab unity and Afro-Asian solidarity. It enables the Soviet regime to divert the attention of the U.S.S.R.'s thirty million Muslims from domestic anti-Soviet activities to pro-Soviet missionary work among the millions of Muslims beyond Soviet borders, especially in the Muslim lands of the Middle East and Africa.

For the past three years the Soviet government has exerted every effort to convince its own Muslims that they are the salt of the Muslim world, that they are the most progressive, the best educated, and that it is their mission to assume leadership of the Afro-Asian Muslims. That the Soviet regime was not entirely satisfied with the results was apparent from Radio Moscow's attack on May 22, 1958, on Islam and the Muslims of the Soviet Middle East as reactionary and fanatical. There is reason to believe, however, that Soviet efforts have not been in vain, and that many Soviet Muslims are ready and willing to substitute for the "White Man's Burden" the "Soviet Burden" in Asia and Africa. One example is Abrashidov Gafour, who is promoting the mission in Cairo. Another indication of Soviet success was provided by the "Appeal of the Muslim Spiritual Leaders of the U.S.S.R. to the Muslims of the World" against the landing in July, 1958, of American and British troops in Lebanon and Jordan respectively, and the demand for their immediate withdrawal. During the Lebanese crisis, there were hints about using Soviet Muslim "volunteers" against the Anglo-American occupation forces. To represent him on a state visit to the United Arab Republic in September, 1958, Nikita Khrushchev sent to Cairo a prominent Soviet Middle Easterner, N. A. Mukhitdinov, chairman of the Supreme Soviet's Council of Nationalities, and a member of the Central Committee of the Communist party.

It has become apparent that the U.S.S.R. is using both its own Muslims and the eager exponents of Arab unity to promote the second major objective, the "liberation" of the entire Middle East and Africa, both Arab and non-Arab, from Western hegemony. To date, Soviet intervention has been indirect, rather than direct. Soviet Muslims prod Arab Muslims, especially those of the U.A.R., to take their place in the vanguard for the elimination of the vestiges of "colonialism." Even during the Near Eastern crisis of 1958, the U.S.S.R. confined itself to pressing attacks on Anglo-American intervention, supported the U.A.R. before the United Nations Security Council and Assembly, and carefully avoided the landing of Soviet troops on Arab soil. It promptly recognized the new Iraqi regime, once it had been established as a result of Arab initiative.

A careful study of Soviet sources, such as *Sovetskoe Vostokovedenie, Sovremennyi Vostok,* and *Sovetskaya Kultura,* suggests that the ultimate Soviet objective in the Arab world is the creation of a new Middle East--one in the Soviet image. The prerequisite for this is the United Arab States, entirely divorced from the Western orbit, which will then be linked with the Soviet Middle East under Soviet Muslim leadership, that is, under the U.S.S.R. This prospect, which is present in Soviet thinking, but not spelled out for all to grasp, may well be of interest to Arab leaders who are seeking to build Arab unity with Soviet political, economic, and cultural aid.

Toward the close of 1958, there were signs of an awakening, not only in the Arab but in the Muslim world, to the danger of the Soviet "colonial" blueprint for Asia and Africa. At the Asian-African Economic Conference in Cairo in December, 1958, the climate of opinion toward the U.S.S.R. had cooled appreciably, to the extent that the head of the Indonesian delegation even questioned the right of the Soviet representatives to be there at all. There were indications that some Arab states sympathized with moves to curb Soviet influence at the conference. As the year 1959 dawned, the United States and Great Britain appeared to be taking advantage of the opportunity thus afforded to seek a better understanding with the Arab world.

9. The Soviet Cultural Impact on the Muslim World

> By turning to Asia, with our new concept of her,
> our country may experience something akin to what
> happened in Europe when America was discovered.
> For, in truth, Asia to us is like the then undiscovered
> America. With Asia as our aim, our spirit and forces
> will be regenerated . . . because the Russian is not
> only an European but also an Asiatic.
> --F. M. Dostoyevsky.

I

As a result of World War II, Soviet literature became national in form and ultranationalist in content, instead of "national in form, socialist in content." The literatures of the national minorities of the Soviet Union, as was to be expected, followed the Soviet pattern. At first the Soviet government encouraged, especially in Central Asia, works extolling the national heroes of the past and emphasizing with patriotic fervor the love and loyalty of the Central Asiatic peoples for their native lands. It hoped by this means to prevent the success of any further efforts on the part of Muslims in adjacent lands to stir up disaffection and disunity among their coreligionists in the Soviet Union.

In pursuit of this objective, the Soviet government encouraged in 1948 a nationwide celebration of the five hundredth anniversary of the birth (1441) of Alisher Navoi, the "father of Uzbek literature," whose patriotic poems called on his people to fight for family and fatherland.[1] The rehabilitation of Navoi included the popularization of his works now published in new and large editions, their introduction into the schools of Uzbekistan, and their translation into the other languages of the U.S.S.R. In the course of this celebration Navoi became not only an Uzbek hero, but a forerunner of Soviet heroes.

239

The result of this lavish build-up for Navoi and other national heroes of past ages, which was duplicated in all the national republics of Central Asia, proved unsatisfactory. Instead of producing contented Asiatic peoples detached from their coreligionists beyond their borders, it had the opposite effect. This rewriting of history renewed their ties of affinity with the outside Muslim world, and far from binding them closer to the U.S.S.R., it encouraged them to follow their neighbors in pursuit of national independence. This was by no means to Soviet liking and was directly contrary to Soviet interests. There followed a complete change in Soviet tactics.

From Uzbekistan, often heralded as "the beacon of the East," came word that the Institute of Oriental Studies of the Uzbek Academy of Sciences was "unproductive." Writing in *Pravda* (August 16, 1951) under the headline "Institute Divorced from Life," A. Shmakov claimed that the "senior scholars"--venerable old men with grey beards and black skull caps, who looked as if they came out of some theological seminary, which in reality they did, and whose Arabic manuscripts had to be translated by others into modern Uzbek--had simply buried themselves in the distant past, instead of investigating the urgent problems that confronted the contemporary Soviet man. *Pravda* clamored for the dismissal of those persons who had excluded from the Institute's 1951 research program on the social and philosophical thought of the peoples of Central Asia from the ninth to the nineteenth centuries all consideration of the age-old contacts of "progressive" Russian scholars with "progressive" figures of Central Asia and of Russian influence on the culture and peoples of the Orient. They had not unmasked Pan-Islamism and Pan-Turkism as "the ideological weapon of American imperialism" or concerned themselves about the national liberation movements in the non-Soviet East.[2] The new Soviet line required Central Asiatic writers to stress the past and present indebtedness of their peoples to the Russians and to expose the reactionary influence of Islam.

In line with the new trend, the Soviet government celebrated in 1953 the seventy-fifth anniversary of the death of Mirze Fatali Ahundov (1812-78) of Azerbaijan.[3] The tone was set by *Pravda* (April 7, 1953), which extolled him as "the first in the Near East to deal a fatal blow to the religion of Islam from the standpoint of materialism." Of decisive significance in the development of his views, according to this Communist party organ, was "his profound understanding of the enormous progressive role of Russia in the destiny of the Azerbaijanian people." Through the development of their new ties with Russia, Ahundov envisaged an auspicious future for his people, in contrast to the unhappy fate of their coreligionists in Iran and Turkey, beset by poverty and superstition. Although Ahundov was said to be indebted for his progressive outlook to the Russian revolutionary democrats, Belinsky, Herzen, Tchernyshevsky, and Dobrolyubov, *Pravda* took care to emphasize that he arrived at his criticism of Islam independently.

In similar fashion the Soviet government celebrated the two hundred and twenty-fifth anniversary of the birth of the Georgian poet, David Guramishvili (1705-92), the one hundred and fiftieth anniversary of the birth of the Armenian writer, Khatchatur Abovyan, and the fiftieth anniversary of the death of the Kazakh poet, Abai Kunanbayev. Guramishvili, whose greatest work, *The Calamites of Kartli* (Georgia), dealt with eighteenth-century Georgia, fought in the Russian armed forces for twenty-two years against Turkey, Sweden, and Prussia, following which he settled in the Ukraine. Abovyan, in his novel, *The Wounds of Armenia,* related the struggle of his people, supported by the Russians, against the Persian yoke in the first decade of the nineteenth century. The poems of Kunanbayev dealt with the struggle of the Kazakh people for national liberation from feudal and ecclesiastical overlords. In every instance, those writers whose works enjoyed a Soviet revival had looked to the Russians for aid against a foreign foe, had promoted friendship between their own peoples and the Russians, had opposed the authority of the mullahs over education and social life, and had served as propagandists for Russian culture, literature, and language.

In recent years, the Soviet government has encouraged the writers of Central Asia to produce novels, plays, and poems contrasting favorable living conditions on the Soviet side of the border with the poverty and misery prevalent in adjacent Muslim countries, and works dramatizing the successful struggle of the Soviet peoples against the *Basmatchi* during the Civil War period. Thus the Azerbaijanian poet, Suleiman Rustam, in his work *Two Banks,* portrayed the "free" progressive world on the Soviet side of the Araxes River in contrast to the "enslavement" on the Iranian bank. In *Frost in Tabriz,* which *Ogonyok* designated the finest poem of 1949, his hero was a "progressive" Iranian architect, who was imprisoned, tortured, and thrown into the Tabriz streets to die. Rustam's compatriot, Mirza Ibrahimov, chairman of the Soviet Writers' Union of Azerbaijan, in his novel *The Day Will Come* dealt with conditions on the Iranian side of the border in the years preceding the entry of Soviet and British troops into Iran in 1941. The contemporary Ar-

menian writer, Garegin Sevunts, in his novel *Teheran* covered the
period from the reaction of the thirties in Iran to the Teheran Conference of 1943, emphasizing also the activity of the "progressive"
forces. The Georgian writer, Grigol Abashidze, used as a background for his novel, *On the Southern Frontier*, the machinations
of American "imperialists" in Turkey and Iran.

In the area east of the Caspian Sea, the works of the Uzbek poet,
Hamza Hakim-zade Niyazi (1889-1929), founder of the Uzbek theater, who dealt with incidents of the Civil War struggle against the
Basmatchi, still enjoy popularity. This Uzbek patriot both wrote
and presented many of his fiery propaganda plays virtually on the
scene of the battlefield. In Tajikistan, the revered founder of modern Soviet Tajik literature, Sadriddin Aini (1878-1955) in *Pulat and
Gulru* presented the defeat of the *Basmatchi* movement in Tajikistan. The Tajik poet of the Pamirs, Mirsaid Mirshaker, author of
The Golden Kishlak, for which he won the Stalin Prize, in a later
work, *The Unvanquished Panj*, contrasted Soviet living standards
on his side of the river with those in Afghanistan and India. The
much-traveled Tajik poet, Mirzo Tursun-zade, who has visited India, Iran, and Pakistan in recent years, is dedicating his forthcoming volume *Asia* to the peoples of the East.

In addition to works revealing the reactionary influence of the
mullahs and criticizing Muslim dogma, the Soviet government has
encouraged the production of novels which demonstrate the successful defiance of Muslim rules and practices, especially the
dietary laws, in the Central Asian Republics. One such novel, *The
Millionaire*,[4] by the Kazakh writer, Gabiden Mustafin (1902-   ),
described life on a rich and successful collective farm with an income of several million rubles per annum. In this book, even elderly Muslim collective farmers violated every one of the Prophet's five prohibitions, raised pigs, ate pork, and served vodka regularly, without suffering any dire material consequences.

While new heroes have emerged, it was inevitable that some of
the old and much-revered heroes among the Asiatic peoples of the
Soviet Union should be debunked. Such was the fate of Imam Shamil (1797-1871), formerly portrayed by the Communists as a great
democrat. Born in Daghestan, where he was elected an iman in
1835, he had led the Caucasian peoples in a prolonged guerilla war
against Tsarist Russia, until he was captured at Cunib in 1859.
Whereas he was formerly lionized for his stubborn fight against
Tsarist conquest of the Caucasus, under the new historical approach he has been transformed into an agent of England and France
in their invasion of Russia during the Crimean War. Soviet his-

torians promptly criticized A. K. Kazembek's standard work, *Muridism and Shamil* (1860) for misrepresenting the social nature of Muridism, for failing to discern that Shamil's nationalist movement was "directed against the interests of the broad masses of the mountain peoples," and for ignoring the fact that behind Shamil "stood the Sultan's Turkey and England, whose interests Shamil defended with his Muridism. . . . "[5]

As a result of this high-pressure propaganda campaign directed against the writers of the Central Asiatic republics, the impact of Russian and Soviet literature in that area has been unprecedented. It amounts to a program of Russification undreamed of even by Nicholas I (1825-55). In conjunction with the influx of Slavic settlers to till "the virgin and idle lands," there appears to be little prospect, barring another shift in policy, that the Central Asiatic peoples can maintain their identity indefinitely.

Although many Russian writers of the nineteenth century and Soviet periods have influenced the literature of the Muslim republics, it was Maxim Gorky who was generally acknowledged to be the "father of the national literatures." The Gorky tradition in the Caucasus goes back to 1899, when his *Song of the Falcon* was translated into Georgian and Armenian. Gorky's literary activity began in Tiflis, Georgia, where he wrote his first story, and befriended many Georgian writers. He condemned the Armenian massacres of 1905 and Jewish pogroms. During the first decade of the twentieth century, he repeatedly urged the publication of literary collections representative of the national minorities.

One of the best tributes to Gorky came from the late Sadriddin Aini (1878-1955), founder of modern Tajik literature and former president of the Tajik Academy of Sciences. In 1954, on the eve of the second Congress of Soviet Writers in Moscow, he acknowledged his indebtedness to Gorky in *Pravda:* "The work of Gorky has taught me a great deal and I must say frankly that it has exerted a decisive influence on my development as a Soviet writer. My *Memoirs,* which have attracted the attention of Soviet readers and which were awarded a Stalin prize, were written under the direct influence of *Childhood, In the World,* and other works by the great master."[6]

Aini's *Memoirs* include the autobiographical works, *The Village,* dealing with his childhood, and *Bokhara,* the story of his adolescence as a student in the highly conservative and backward Bokhara *madrassahs.* Although the life he depicted was set against a background entirely different from that of Gorky, both works because of their artistic verity enjoyed a universal appeal. Aini acquired from Gorky, not only ideas but his method and technique of writing, especially in the matter of characterization and use of folklore. Like Gorky, Aini's realistic portrayal of sordid living conditions never sank to the level of vulgarity. In view of his basic indebtedness to Gorky and his influence in the other Muslim republics, Aini more than any other writer may be justly termed the Gorky of Central Asia.

II

It was no accident that after the Revolution of 1905 the works of Maxim Gorky received priority for translation into Near Eastern languages, and that he became more popular there than any other Russian writer. In the first place, of all Russian writers his name was more closely associated with the Revolution, especially with the Russian Social Democratic party. He was, moreover, a self-educated writer, and his stories reflected the life, not of the higher classes, but of the poor, the unemployed, and the downtrodden-- in other words, the lower depths. Although ostensibly an atheist, he was tolerant toward all religions. The works of the young Gorky indicated respect for and faith in man, which to the Muslim is an essential part of Islam. Finally, in his short stories and plays, he provided a sympathetic portrayal of the Tatars and other Muslim, Jewish, and Armenian minorities. He did for the Tatar what Turgenev did for the serf, Tolstoy for the peasant, Sholokhov for the Cossack, and what Andreyev intended to do for the Jew. This likewise explains Gorky's popularity in China and why his works were translated into more Chinese dialects than those of any other Russian writer, even prior to the Bolshevik Revolution.

As Soviet leaders turned once again to the East following World War II, they encountered some countries that were still in the pre-1905 revolutionary stage, and others that had entered upon the post-1905 revolutionary period, but were not yet ready for a revolution of the Bolshevik vintage. From the cultural point of view the Soviet government, under these circumstances, could not have chosen any better mouthpiece than Gorky, whose work is a blending of great art and revolutionary propaganda--a combination which has a strong appeal to the peoples of the Near and Middle East. His early works, especially his short stories and the play, *The Lower Depths*, which interpreted the plight of the poor and the destitute without advocating violence or retaliation, and which at times virtually appeared to accept their predicament with resignation, could win the approval of even the most conservative and orthodox Muslim. On the other hand, Gorky's novel, *Mother* (1906), the first proletarian Russian novel, begun in America immediately following the Russian Revolution of 1905, has an even stronger appeal today among the young generation of Near Eastern leaders, and among the literate workers and peasants, who demand deeds instead of words. In fact, this novel interpreted the Revolution of 1905 and explained how such a revolution was organized, with particular emphasis on strikes and demonstrations, the chief weapons of the Russian Social Democrats prior to 1917.

In view of the struggle for the minds of men in the Muslim world today, it should occasion no surprise that one of the major postwar programs of the Institute of Oriental Studies of the Academy of Sciences of the U. S. S. R. has been the preparation for publication of a large collection of studies on the general theme of "Gorky and the Literatures of the Orient, " designed to cover more than thirty countries of the East.[7] Some of these studies have already made their appearance, including articles and monographs on Gorky in the Revolution of 1905, Gorky in Iran, Turkey, the Arab world, China, and Japan, and so forth.

It is significant that of all the Muslim countries Iran has been the most consistent in resisting the introduction into Iranian literature of the works of Gorky in Persian translation.[8] Although the works of Pushkin, Tchekhov, and Tolstoy have been both tolerated and appreciated, those of Gorky were literally imposed upon Iranians under the protection of Soviet bayonets. During the years of active Soviet intervention in northern Iran following World War I, the first Gorky translation, *The Song of the Stormy Petrel,* which both predicted and invoked a revolution, was circulated among Iranian Azerbaijanians in manuscript form as a revolutionary leaflet. *The Clock* (1923) was the first work by Gorky to be published in Iran during this period. Following the withdrawal of Soviet troops from northern Iran, Gorky's works were soon banned. The only means by which his memory was perpetuated in the Persian language from 1925 to 1941 was through the works of the Persian revolutionary poet, Abdulkasim Lahuti, who as an exile in the Soviet Union wrote *To Maxim Gorky, Three Drops,* and other poems dealing with this Russian writer. The revival of Gorky in Iran came with the occupation of northern Iran by the Red Army from 1941-46. It was the Society for Cultural Relations between Iran and the U. S. S. R. which, with Soviet backing, played a significant role in the dissemination of Gorky's works in Iran. Its official organ, *The New Messenger,* from 1944 to 1945 published many of Gorky's works, including his autobiographical trilogy, *The Lower Depths,* and *Mother.* The novel

Mother, it is claimed, was the first volume of *belles lettres* from
the Persian press about the struggle of the working class. [9] After
the withdrawal of the Red Army from Iran, A. Nushin, translator
of Gorky's *The Lower Depths* and other stories, was arrested in
1950 and exiled to an island in the Persian Gulf. Nushin's play,
The First Cock, written under the influence of Gorky, was an Iranian counterpart of Gorky's *Enemies.* From his refuge in Moscow,
the venerable revolutionary poet, Lahuti, was reported in 1954 to
be engaged in translating works by Gorky, Pushkin, and Mayakovsky, as well as Griboyedov's *The Misfortune of Being Clever.*

Next to the works of Gorky, those of Tchekhov in recent years
have been the most widely disseminated of any Russian writer in
Iran, and have proved far less objectionable to the Iranian government. The characters Tchekhov portrayed, as, for instance, the
Ranevskys in *The Cherry Orchard,* were familiar to educated Iranians, for their counterparts were to be found in Iran. Although the
Persian translation of Tchekhov began in 1932 with his story *Goose-
berries,* it was in 1944, the fortieth anniversary of his death, that
over sixty of his stories appeared in Iranian periodicals, together
with translations of *The Cherry Orchard* and *The Seagull.* It is
nevertheless too early, according to Kerim Keshavarz, [10] to speak
of Tchekhov's influence on Iranian literature.

The Iranian Society for Cultural Relations with the U.S.S.R.,
which was largely responsible for the publication and distribution
of the works of Gorky and Tchekhov in Iran, likewise celebrated the
Gogol centenary in 1952 by devoting entirely to Gogol the fifty-
fifth issue of its official journal, *The New Messenger.* The Society
did not introduce Gogol to the Iranian intelligentsia, [11] for his comedy *The Revizor* was translated into Persian in 1912 and *St. Petersburg Tales* appeared during the nineteen-thirties, followed by
Mirgorod during World War II. To these were added in 1952 excerpts from *Dead Souls, Lost Certificate,* and *Old-Fashioned
Gentlefolk.* As in the case of many other translations of Russian
literature throughout the Middle East, most Iranian translations
have been made from French, English, or German, rather than
directly from the Russian.

At the beginning of the twentieth century there was a marked
interest in Russia on the part of the countries of the Near East,
especially after the Revolution of 1905. The major works of Gogol
appeared in Arabic translation in Egypt and Lebanon between 1900
and 1910. In 1907 the works of Gorky began to appear in Arabic, [12]
his first translator being Selim Kobein, a teacher and journalist,
who brought out a small collection of four works, with Gorky's

portrait. In his introduction, which reflected the mood of the Arab intelligentsia of that time, Selim Kobein wrote about Gorky as the herald of the Russian Revolution and from that standpoint attempted to reveal his significance for the Orient. The late Academician I. Y. Kratchkovsky (1883-1951) located a translation of Gorky's story *Starik*, made by Ballyan, a pedagogue of the northern Syrian schools, and published prior to World War I in a collection dedicated to Russian literature. From 1918 to 1928, the chief center for Gorky translations was Egypt. With the return of Gorky to the U.S.S.R. in 1928, new Arabic translations began to appear, chiefly in Syria and Lebanon.

Soviet literary critics have divided the leading Arab writers into two main categories--reactionaries and progressives. It stands to reason that all those writers who paid homage to Western culture and civilization were designated as reactionaries. On the other hand, those who emphasized materialism, directly or indirectly criticized Islam, stood for national liberation, and veered toward the Soviet Union, were hailed as progressives.

The "era of national renaissance" in Egypt in the 1920's produced a large number of writers and critics, such as Taha Hussein *(The Days)*;[13] Muhammed Hussein Heikal *(Zeinab);* Tewfik al-Hakim *(The Return of the Spirit, Notes of a Provincial Coroner);* M. Abbas Akkad; Abdul-Kadir al-Mazini--the Mark Twain of Egypt; Salama Musa--a Christian and a Fabian Socialist; Mahmud Taimur; Zeyat, etc. Although most of these writers were under the influence of Western European literature, especially that of France, their early works were permeated by a realism strongly reminiscent of classical Russian literature, especially of Gogol, Turgenev, and Tolstoy.

Of particular importance was the work of Taha Hussein, *The Pre-Islamic Poetry of the Arabs,* published in 1931, which amounted to an indictment of Islamic dogma. His novel *The Days* and Tewfik al-Hakim's tale *The Return of the Spirit* dealt with the life of the fellahin and the rise of the national liberation movement. In the works of these writers, however, realism soon gave way to symbolism, idealism, religious mysticism, and the advocacy of "art for art's sake." Formerly regarded as "progressives" by Soviet critics, they were promptly labeled "reactionaries." In 1953 Taha Hussein, whose work is a cross between that of Gogol and Tolstoy, was singled out for attack due to his lapse from realism. The tone and content of a letter published in the popular newspaper *Al-Misry* (March 3, 1953) by Ibrahim Amer attacking Taha Hussein was strongly reminiscent of *Belinsky's Letter to Gogol* (1847). Far from being cowed by the attacks directed against him, Taha Hussein continued to write in the same vein and in December, 1953, delivered an outstanding lecture on the problems of literature, which constituted a reply to his critics *(Al-Misry,* December 5, 1953).[14] Literature, he insisted, is above classes and social strata. Its purpose is not to feed the hungry, to clothe the naked, or to cure the sick. It is not the servant of anyone.

In contrast to Taha Hussein, however, is Haled Muhammed Haled, a young *ulema* (Muslim theologian) of Al-Azhar University, author of *We Begin from Here* and *Citizens, Not Subjects.* The former, published in 1950 in Cairo, was twice banned by the censor because the author "attacks religion and its leaders, and also instigates the poor against the capitalists." Haled was branded as an adherent of Russian communism. Even a cursory examination of his work seems to indicate that what Haled opposed was not Islam, but those ecclesiastical leaders whose actions were at variance with the spirit of Islam. Strictly speaking, he preaches Tolstoyism against an Egyptian background.

The influence of Soviet literature has been especially strong in Egyptian works published since the "revolution" of 1952. In numerous articles, short stories, and novels, Egyptian writers introduced their readers to Russian and Soviet literature--to Leo Tolstoy, Pushkin, Turgenev, Tchekhov, Gorky, Sholokhov, Simonov, Polevoi, Gorbatov, and Ehrenburg. Abdarrahman ash-Sharkavi, author of *The Land,* a novel dedicated to the struggle of the Egyptian peasant for land during the past twenty years, in the spring of 1953 published a series of articles in *Al-Misry* against "the machinations of imperialism in the East," which was strongly reminiscent of the articles that appeared in *Pravda* and *Izvestia* on the same subject. His attack on Secretary of State Dulles was likewise a repetition of arguments in the Soviet press. Other writers who appear to veer toward the Soviet orbit are Abdarrahman al-Hamisi; Mahmud Subhi, the translator of stories by Gorbatov and Leonov; Mahmud Abdulmanam Murad; Ahmed al-Badini; Dr. Abdul Azim Anis; Ibrahim al-Misry; Hairam al-Gamravi; Mahmud Kasym, Yousef Idris; and so on.

In February, 1953, two Arabic periodicals, *As-Sikafa* and *Ar-Risalya,* discontinued publication in Egypt. Critics of these magazines attributed their failure to aloofness from the common people. Their discussion of this issue recalls the controversy between the Slavophiles and the Westernizers in nineteenth-century Russia, as well as the arguments about what constitutes socialist realism typical of Soviet literature today. It is apparent that Egyptian critics are familiar with Russian and Soviet thinking along these lines. Ahmed al-Badini, apropos of the discontinuation of the above-mentioned magazines, said that the reading public would not have abandoned them had their authors taken part in the national struggle. Our literature, he wrote, "for a long time was stranded in Sufism and symbolism. . . . Realistic literature is indebted for its greatness and success to Russian literature. Even prior to the Revolution, it produced such leading representatives of realism as Turgenev, Tolstoy, Gogol, and Gorky."[15] It is the opinion of A. F. Sultanov that the "new realistic trend in Egyptian literature is developing under the direct influence of the best traditions of classical Russian literature, and of socialist realism in Soviet literature."[16]

III

Next to Egypt in importance, from the standpoint of the impact of Russian writers and translation of Russian works in the Arabic world, are Lebanon and Syria. Long before the October Revolution one of the leading Russian orientalists, I. Y. Kratchkovsky, spent two years in Syria and made a number of additional trips there and to Lebanon. According to his memoirs,[17] he frequently visited the Russian schools of the Palestinian Society in Syria and Lebanon, where the educational methods of N. I. Pirogov (1810-81) and K. D. Ushinsky (1824-70) were in vogue, and where the school libraries invariably included volumes of Turgenev and Tchekhov, the magazine *Niva*, and the reference work *Znaniye (Knowledge)*. Students at these schools were strongly influenced by Russian literature. In the words of Kratchkovsky, "many modern writers of the older generation, not only translators from Russian, but also authors in their own right who spoke to the entire Arab world, had passed through the schools of the Palestinian Society." These schools came to an end after World War I.

Kratchkovsky likewise was impressed by the influence of Russian literature on Michael Nu'ayme (Naimy), a Syrian writer who had been a seminarist in Poltava (the Ukraine) from 1905 to 1911, during which time he became immersed in Russian literature and emerged with a determination to end "literary stagnation in the entire Arabic world." After spending many years in the United States, Naimy returned to Syria in 1932. Kratchkovsky was of the opinion that his strong attachment for Russian literature was "probably unequaled among Arabic authors."[18] In recent Soviet criticism, however, Naimy has been labeled a bourgeois intellectual, detached from the people and their interests, whose writings reflect the "decadence and pessimistic culture of the contemporary West, " and who prefers to write about King Solomon and the Queen of Sheba instead of current problems. [19]

After World War II Lebanon once again became a center where the impact of Russian literature was strongly felt among writers and the intelligentsia. Two outstanding literary periodicals--*Al-Adaab (Literature)* and *Al-Adib (Writers)*--devote considerable space to Russian literary criticism and translations from Russian literature. Beirut and Damascus publishers have extensive projects for the publication of Russian literature, mainly that of the nineteenth century, in Arabic translation. One of the first such translations to be made directly from the Russian rather than from a Western European language was the Gogol classic, *The Cloak*, which appeared in the Beirut periodical, *As-Sakafa Al-Vataniya*. Commenting on these translation projects, Jalal Farouk El-Sharif summed up what Arab writers and educated Arabs in general might be expected to learn from the study of Russian literature, namely, that their engrossment in Western literature need not result in the loss of their own Arabic originality; that it is possible for them to reach the peak in art and humanity through Arabic national literature alone; that aloofness of the writer and the intelligentsia from the people results in a hybrid, sterile, shallow literature without content; and that only contact between men of letters and the people will give their art value and meaning. [20] If he accurately voices Arab reaction to Russian literature, this would seem to indicate the appearance of an Arab populist movement, a counterpart of the one which flourished in the eighteen-seventies in Russia.

IV

In Turkey, interest in Russian literature dates from the closing years of the nineteenth century when Griboyedov's *The Misfortune of Being Clever (Woe from Wit)*, together with representative works of Pushkin, Lermontov, and Leo Tolstoy appeared in Turkish translation, followed by those of Gogol and Turgenev. The Russian Revolution of 1905 which, according to Soviet interpretation, had an appreciable impact on the Young Turk movement and the Turkish Revolution of 1908, [21] greatly stimulated interest in Russian literature. The Turkish press published translations from Gorky, Tchekhov, and Garshin *(The Four Days)*. In 1908 excerpts from Gorky's *Mother* were translated from the French. This was followed in 1911 by the publication of the entire novel in two volumes.

Tolstoy's *War and Peace* and *Anna Karenina,* likewise translated from the French, were especially popular in Turkey during these years.

Unlike Iran, the Turkish government of Kemal Pasha continued to permit the publication of Russian and Soviet literary works following World War I and the October Revolution. In 1918, Rushen-Eshref, a Turkish writer and diplomat, translated Gorky's *Song of the Falcon.* From 1919 on many works by Gogol, Turgenev, Tolstoy, Tchekhov, and Pushkin appeared in Turkish editions. Among Soviet writers other than Gorky whose works proved popular in Turkey were Alexei N. Tolstoy *(Peter I),* Mikhail Sholokhov *(Virgin Soil Upturned),* and Valentin Katayev. Gorky's passage through Istanbul in 1932 renewed Turkish interest in his works and, according to V. A. Gordlevsky, his name became very prominent. After an extended visit to the Soviet Union, where he made a special study of the Soviet theater and cinema, including the Moscow Art Theater, the talented Turkish producer and actor, Ertugrul Muhsin, became director of the Istanbul Municipal Theater, where he presented stage productions of Dostoyevsky's *Crime and Punishment* and Gogol's *The Revizor* (1934), Dostoyevsky's *The Brothers Karamazov* (1935), Gorky's *The Lower Depths* (1936-37), and Tolstoy's *Anna Karenina* (1939). Although the impact of nineteenth-century Russian literature in Turkey has been greater than that of the Soviet period, among representatives of the younger generation of Turkish writers, such as Sadri Ertem, Ali Sabahattin (died 1947), Kenan Hulusi, and the Turkish novelist, Yakub Kadri *(Ankara),* Soviet influence has been felt.

Among Turkish writers, only five were sufficiently in vogue from 1918 to 1954 to merit translations of their works, totaling almost one million copies, into twelve languages of the Soviet Union. [22] Of these, by far the most important from the standpoint of Soviet ideology vis-à-vis the Soviet Muslims and the Muslim world in general was the Turkish Communist poet and dramatist, Nazim Hikmet 1902-   ), who has lived for some years in the U. S. S. R.

Son of a high Turkish official and grandson of a pasha, Hikmet achieved popularity among Turkish nationalists during the Allied occupation of Constantinople following World War I, when his poems, *Captive of the Forty Thieves* and *Anatolia,* summoned the Turks to arms against the foreign invader. In 1922, during a visit to Moscow, he fell under the influence of the Soviet revolutionary poet, Vladimir Mayakovsky. Hikmet spent twelve years in a Turkish prison, 1938-50, for spreading Communist doctrine. During these years he was a prolific writer, having produced among other

works, *Five Days of My Hunger Strike*, *Symphony of Moscow*, and
a play, *Joseph and his Brothers (Kardeslerini satan Jusuf)*. The
last-mentioned play, in which Hikmet elevated revolution to a
creed, was banned in France in 1951. Hikmet's release in 1950
and his arrival in Moscow the following year were regarded by
Soviet writers as a major ideological victory in the Cold War.
Since that time, several short studies of his work have been published by the Institute of Oriental Studies of the U.S.S.R. Academy of Sciences. [23] A recent play, *Story of Turkey*, which according to one Soviet critic follows the Gorky and Tchekhov tradition,
dealt with the struggle of the Turkish partisans of peace during the
Korean War. Due to its propaganda value, it was immediately published in Russian in the Soviet literary journal *Zvezda* (No. 7,
1952), and excerpts appeared in *Literaturnaya Gazeta* (May 1,
1952). Today he is one of the aces of Soviet propaganda, not only
in the U.S.S.R. and Turkey, but throughout the Near East.

V

Although Russian and Soviet literature has proved to be one of the
most effective means for extending Soviet influence in the Muslim
world, other forms of communication have not been neglected,
especially in recent years. Soviet radio broadcasts in Arabic did
not begin until 1943. [24] In 1946, the Moscow and Baku broadcasting stations, which were already broadcasting in Turkish and Persian, greatly expanded the Arabic phase of their program, although
little effort was made prior to 1950 to relate the programs to issues of primary concern to the Arabic world. For the Middle East,
Radio Tashkent, with its ultra-modern facilities, is second only to
Moscow in importance, for it broadcasts daily in Persian, Pashto
(Afghan), Urdu (Pakistan), Kurdish, Turkish, Armenian, Arabic,
etc., to impress the Muslim world with the political, military, and
economic might of the U.S.S.R. as the sole support of the liberation movements of the colonial and semicolonial peoples of the East.
Since 1950, the propaganda themes reiterated time and again in
Arabic broadcasts have sought to arouse suspicion of Turkey as
"the gendarme of the Middle East," to represent Israel as "a
bridgehead of American imperialism," to accentuate Anglo-American differences on Near Eastern policy issues, to arouse interest
in the Soviet-sponsored World Peace Council, to emphasize the
economic exploitation of the area by Western "imperialist" powers
and their strategic plans for transforming the Middle East into a
military base for ultimate attack on the Soviet Union. From time

to time a clandestine Azerbaijani "democratic" station has called upon the Kurds and Azerbaijanians to revolt.

The Soviet government has actively solicited Arabic and Muslim support for its propagandist World Peace Movement, apparently with a modicum of success, since the World Peace Council's first appeal for a peace pact was signed by representatives from Algeria, Egypt, Iran, Lebanon, Syria, and Tunisia. Sheikh Muhammed Al-Ashmar of Syria, head of the Syrian Peace Council, was awarded a Stalin Peace Prize in 1955, and a gold peace medal went to the Lebanon magazine *Al-Tarik (The Path)*, organ of the peace partisans of the Near East. A Soviet "cultural" delegation arrived in Damascus in March, 1956, at the very time Stalin's reputation was under fire in Moscow, to present this leading Muslim nationalist sheikh, who visited Moscow the previous year, with his Stalin peace award! The delegation included colorfully dressed Soviet ulema. In a country where the Communist party is technically outlawed, the World Peace Movement has served the Soviet cause well.

It is, of course, impossible to gauge the effectiveness of Soviet broadcasts among the Arab peoples. It is generally conceded that today, in contrast to the situation prior to World War II, the Arab intelligentsia is aware of the Soviet point of view on issues pertaining to the Middle East, and sometimes welcomes Soviet broadcasts as a means of counteracting Western influence, especially when national liberation is at stake. The history of the U.S.S.R. to date does not indicate that any Muslim regime has toppled like a house of cards due to Soviet radio or press propaganda, unless as in Iran that propaganda has been accompanied by military intimidation and outright invasion.

Wherever it has been possible to make use of Soviet films in the Muslim world, the Soviet Union, in line with the teachings of Lenin, has not neglected this basic propaganda weapon. In Algeria, the newly founded Society for Cultural Relations with the Soviet Union in 1950 introduced such Soviet films as *Conquerors of the Desert, Takhir and Zukhra,* and *Mitchurin.* The Society for Cultural Relations between Iran and the U.S.S.R., which has presented a regular schedule of Soviet film programs for adults and children, found that Soviet films appealed even to Iranians unfriendly to the Soviet Union. During the third festival of Soviet films sponsored by the Society in Iran in 1952, such films as *Unforgettable 1919, The Fall of Berlin, The Village Schoolmistress,* and *Cavalier of the Gold Star,* based on Babayevsky's novel, were shown. Even in Turkey, many of the best Soviet films have been presented. In December, 1954, a Soviet cultural delegation visiting

Afghanistan reported that two Soviet films, *Circus Arena* and *Vasilisa the Beautiful*, were running in Kabul. At the international exhibition in Damascus in the summer of 1954, where every country of the Near and Middle East was represented, the Soviet government, in addition to an elaborate exhibit of technical equipment, books, music, records, etc., carefully chose to display documentary films on the opening up of new lands in drought-ridden areas of Siberia and Central Asia, including *The First Spring, On the New Lands, The Awakened Steppe,* and *The Offensive on the Virgin Soil,* films certain to appeal to peoples from the parched lands of North Africa and Asia Minor. These films were shown likewise in Izmir, Salonika, and as far east as Jakarta, Indonesia.

Especially since World War II, the Soviet press has recorded the visits of innumerable "cultural delegations" from Asiatic countries to the Soviet Union. Long before the exchange of American and Soviet delegations was resumed in 1955, representatives from the Muslim countries of the Near and Middle East were welcomed in Moscow, and encouraged to visit such centers as Baku, Tashkent, Alma Ata, Stalinabad, etc., at a time when the Central Asiatic republics were closed to Western tourists. Since 1952 this program for "cultural exchange" has been stepped up considerably. It is significant that members of such delegations are frequently persons of considerable importance in the political and educational life of the Muslim countries they represent. The Iranian cultural delegation of 1953, the first from that country to visit the U.S.S.R. for some years, included Professor Ali Asker Hekmat; Iranian lawyer Shekhab Ferdouss; poetess Shakhnaz Aliyami; General Amanulla Djhakhanbani; and Ibrahim Nabil Samii, a top-ranking official in the Iranian Ministry of Labor, who had not visited Russia since the Revolution. The director of the Saadi Theater in Teheran, Hussein Kheirkhakh, visited the U.S.S.R. during the same year. Such delegations appeared to be particularly impressed by the success of Soviet efforts in eradicating illiteracy in a quarter of a century.

A prominent Afghan delegation which visited Moscow, Leningrad, Tashkent, Baku, and other centers in 1953, included Dr. Muhammed Anas, rector of the University of Kabul; Mir Amanuddin Ansari, dean of the Faculty of Letters; Dr. Muhammed Adram, dean of law; and Dr. Osman Anvari, professor of medicine--all of them from the same university--as well as Dr. Abdul Rakhim, chief of the Malaria Prevention Board of the Afghan Ministry of Health. This delegation was particularly interested in the Soviet educational system from the elementary to the university level, with the result that a Soviet delegation headed by Y. Velitchkovsky, director of the Moscow Institute for the Advanced Training of Teachers, paid a return visit to Afghanistan in 1954. The Soviet delegation included two experts in the Persian language and oriental culture, who were able to converse without interpreters on subjects pertaining to science, literature, and education.

The second Congress of Soviet Writers at the end of 1954 included visitors from such Muslim countries as Iran, Syria, and Lebanon, with Nazim Hikmet on hand to represent Turkish "progressives." Even on such political occasions as the thirty-sixth anniversary of the Bolshevik Revolution (1953), representatives from Tunisia, Algeria, Madagascar, Syria, and Lebanon were present. An international seminar of agricultural students in Moscow in the summer of 1955 attracted Atia Abib from Tunis. Of course, the number of delegations from the Muslim countries cannot begin to match those from Communist China and India.

The re-establishment of the Holy Synod (1943) and the partial rehabilitation of the Russian Orthodox Church during World War II afforded the U.S.S.R. an unprecedented opportunity to make use of the Church for propaganda purposes in the Near East. The election of a new Patriarch of Moscow in January, 1945, brought to the Soviet Union a galaxy of Orthodox prelates from other countries, including the Oecumenical Patriarch of Constantinople; the Patriarch of Jerusalem; the Patriarch of Antioch, who traveled from Baku to Moscow in Stalin's special train; the Patriarch of Alexandria, who is reputed to have carried back to Egypt ikons valued at £30,000 as the gift of the Soviet government; and the archbishops of Homs and of Tyre and Sidon. At the end of May the new Patriarch of Moscow, accompanied by an entourage, which included the Metropolitan of Kiev and ten leading Russian prelates, visited the Orthodox Patriarch of Jerusalem and was enthroned in the Church of the Holy Sepulcher. His tour, ostensibly a courtesy visit to those prelates who had traveled to Moscow for his election, included Cairo, Alexandria, and Beirut, but not Constantinople. That there were political implications involved in this tour was obvious from the assiduous attention afforded the prelates by Soviet diplomatic representatives in the Levant. The estrangement of the Soviet Union and Turkey over the proposed "revision" of the Montreux Convention may account for the slight to the Patriarch of Constantinople, but it likewise served to focus the limelight on the primate of Moscow as an aspirant for the leadership of Orthodoxy. Subsequent contacts between Soviet and Near Eastern Orthodox prelates have not been as close as this effusive beginning appeared to forecast, but they have been continued, especially with Syria. Although in July, 1926, a Soviet delegation of the Chief Muslim Ecclesiastical Directorate of Ufa attended the All-Muslim Congress in Mecca in support of Ibn Saud's bid for the caliphate, no more such pilgrimages occurred until the end of World War II. In the summer of 1955, however, a strong Muslim delegation comprised of delegates from Uzbekistan, Azerbaijan, Daghestan, Bashkiria, Kazakhstan, and the "Tatar Republic, " under the leadership of Imam Sapokari Alikariev of Tashkent, undertook the pilgrimage to Mecca via a special Soviet plane to Jidda, with brief stops at Ankara, Beirut, and Cairo. They issued a formal invitation to Iman Kaaba of the Chief Mosque in Mecca to visit the Soviet Union.

Following the precedent set the previous year, in 1956 a large delegation of Soviet Muslims under the leadership of Kamaretdin Salikhov, imam of the Moscow Mosque and member of the Muslim Council for the R.S.F.S.R., with Soviet blessing undertook the pilgrimage to Mecca by air. This delegation, comprising mullahs and lay Muslims, peasants and workers from Uzbekistan, Tajikistan, Turkmenia, Kirghizia, Kazakhstan, Azerbaijan, Bashkiria, Daghestan, Moscow, and the Urals, performed all the customary religious rites of the hajj at Mecca, visited Muslim shrines at Medina, and spent some time in Cairo. Most of its members were said to have children who had enjoyed the benefits of a college education. A young Uzbek doctor among them ministered to the needs of sick pilgrims unable to secure medical attention. Not only did they join with Egyptian Muslim leaders in the reading of the Koran, but they assured all who would listen that there exists freedom of religion in the U.S.S.R., that they are permitted to have their own madrassahs, to print religious literature, and that a new edition of the Koran was issued in the Soviet Union in 1956.

The role of these Soviet Muslims has not been confined to the dissemination of Soviet propaganda throughout the Muslim East. They have played host to an increasing number of Islamic and non-Islamic visitors from abroad. With this purpose in mind, the Soviet regime has created what may be termed Islamic oases in such centers as Tashkent, Samarkand, Ashkhabad, Baku, etc., in Central Asia and the Caucasus. Mirzo Tursun-Zade, perhaps the most prominent literary figure in Soviet Central Asia, who has himself traveled widely in Iran, Afghanistan, India, Pakistan, and China, claims that hundreds of foreign tourists have visited Tajikistan in recent years. It was his conclusion that "in language, music, literature, and folklore, there is close affinity between the peoples of Soviet Central Asia and India, Afghanistan, and other neighboring countries. "[25] Uzbekistan is fast becoming one of the major scientific centers of the U.S.S.R. and already serves as "Exhibit A" for Asian tourists. Indeed, according to Anvar Kutchkarov, the Uzbek minister of culture, the one hundred research institutes under the Uzbek Academy of Sciences steadily increased their contacts abroad in 1956, especially with the academies of sciences of China, India, Pakistan, Iran, Afghanistan, etc. In January, 1957, M. Abdullaev, president of the Uzbek Academy of Sciences, attended the Indian Scientific Congress.

The Congress of the Intelligentsia of Uzbekistan, which opened in Tashkent on October 11, 1956, and which included twelve hundred Uzbek representatives, as well as delegates from the other republics of Central Asia and the Caucasus, was used to lure scholars from abroad, from China, India, and Korea, and especially an important delegation of members of the Association of Egyptian Writers under the leadership of Dr. Muhammed Mandur, philologist and critic. [26] Invited to the U.S.S.R. by the Union of Soviet Writers, this delegation was primarily interested in Central Asia, in the Arab settlements in Uzbekistan on which considerable research has been in progress under the direction of Professor I. Vinnikov. [27] The Egyptian delegation, which spent five days in Tashkent and visited Samarkand and Stalinabad, included Muhammed Said al-Erian, a writer; Shauki Diaf, a professor of Arabic literature at Cairo University; Ali Bakasir, an Egyptian dramatist and poet; and Abderrakhman ash-Sharkavi, novelist and dramatist.

Soviet "religious" propaganda as we have seen, has not been confined solely to Islam. Early in 1956 there were indications that the Soviet government was trying to use the Armenian Orthodox Church as a means of spreading Soviet propaganda in the Middle East. A good example of Soviet tactics was afforded by the dispatch to Beirut in February of Vazken Baldjan, known as Catholicos Vazken I, Patriarch of Eshmiazine (Armenia), to take an active part in the election of the Patriarch of Cilicia, and thereby to gain control of the Armenian Orthodox Church, which has been split since the fifteenth century into the two above-mentioned patriarchates.

VI

Following the pattern of Soviet-Chinese cultural relations since 1950, the U.S.S.R. has worked assiduously in recent years for the conclusion of cultural exchange agreements with the countries of Asia. The opening months of 1957 witnessed the renewal or establishment of a whole series of such agreements with Red China. Vietnam, the Mongol People's Republic, and with several of the Soviet European satellites. The high watermark of Soviet success among the Arab states came on August 21, 1956, with the Egypt-Syria-Lebanon tour of Sergei Kaftanov, [28] first deputy minister of culture of the U.S.S.R. At this time he signed in Damascus a broad cultural cooperation agreement, covering Soviet-Syrian exchange in the fields of science, art, general and technical education, physical training, and sports. The Kaftanov Agreement provided for exchange visits of delegations and individuals, the pooling of cultural information, the holding of exhibits, concerts, etc., cooperation in broadcasts, the exchange of films, the establishment of university scholarships to encourage student exchange, and the staging of Soviet-Syrian sports events. Kaftanov's hopes of concluding similar agreements with Lebanon and Egypt did not advance beyond the preparatory stages. The implementation of the Kaftanov Agreement could scarcely fail to make of Syria a "cultural satellite" of the U.S.S.R. Judging by V. Borisov's report on the second Congress of Arab Writers in Damascus in the latter part of 1956, Soviet thinking in regard to the role of literature and the state has already had an impact on the outlook of a substantial part of the Arab intelligentsia. [29]

Until the Suez crisis, Soviet-Egyptian cultural contacts proceeded more slowly. Since 1955, VOKS, the Soviet Society for Cultural Relations with Foreign Countries, has maintained a permanent exhibit in Cairo, with the object of popularizing Soviet cultural achievements. In May, 1956, Intourist and Misr Travel and Shipping Company concluded an agreement for tourist exchanges. About the same time, a group of Soviet archeologists and ethnographers visited Egypt to establish contacts with Egyptian scholars, and to collaborate in preparations to safeguard Egyptian monuments located in the area due to be inundated by the construction of the projected Aswan dam. [30]

In the spring of 1956, the first delegation of Egyptian cinema specialists arrived in Moscow, their visit timed to coincide with the showing of the first Egyptian feature films in the U.S.S.R., namely, *Struggle in the Valley*, and *Blazing Sun*. It was admitted that Egyptian knowledge of Soviet films was still very slight, having included up to that time only *Sadko*, *Men of Daring*, *The Big Top*, and the Soviet-Albanian film, *Skanderbeg*. Egyptian publication of *Film Art*, by Vsevolod Pudovkin, and of a study of *The Soviet Cinema* by two Egyptian directors, Tlemseni and A. K. Musa, was regarded as an important step toward bridging this gap.

"It seems that we no longer have a job!"
--*Krokodil*, No. 1, January 10, 1956

On buildings representing Africa, the Middle East, the Near
East, and Southeast Asia, identical signs are posted:
"No Governesses Wanted"

In June, 1956, the Soviet Publishing House for Foreign Literature brought out a collection of nineteen stories, entitled *Egipetskie
Novelly*, designed to acquaint Soviet readers with "the creative
family of Egyptian writers, " namely, the "progressives. " Included
were several works by Mahmud Teimur, the so-called founder of
the Egyptian short story. Abdurrakhman ash-Sharkavi, author of
The Land, whose anti-American outlook won him a trip to the
U.S.S.R. in 1956, was also represented, as were the young Egyptian
physician, Yusuf Idris; Is Ubeid; Mahmud Bagasir; Mahmud Tahir
Lashin; and one Egyptian authoress, Bint ash-Shati. These stories
emphasized such themes as the plight of the Egyptian peasant and
the Egyptian woman, the "revolting" Muslim customs of the past,
the corrupting influence of American films on Egyptian youth, etc.
They serve as examples of the method of socialist realism in the
literature of the countries of the East.

In recent years, the U.S.S.R. Academy of Sciences has promoted
a book-exchange program, [31] not only with Red China and India but
with the Near and Middle East, including Turkey, Iran, Egypt,
Syria, and Lebanon. In all, according to the report of A. Kh. Rafikov, ten countries of the Near and Middle East have taken part
in the book exchange with the library of the U.S.S.R. Academy of
Sciences, through eighty-five institutions, including five Academies of Sciences, eleven universities, two biological, nine agricultural, and sixteen historico-philological institutes, etc. Although
this program has shown a marked increase since 1950, the visit
of the Soviet historian, V. I. Shunkov, to Cairo and Alexandrian
libraries in May, 1956, suggested that in Egypt, at least, the book-
exchange program was still in its infancy. [32] In spite of the lively
interest in things Russian, Shunkov found "almost no books in Russian" at the National Library in Cairo, and in the Music Library a
complete absence of Soviet publications on Russian music and art.

The year 1957, which from the Soviet standpoint began so aus-
piciously in January with the opening of the first Soviet industrial
exhibit in Cairo, the Soviet film festival, and the performances of
the U.S.S.R. State Ensemble of the People's Dance, almost ended
in disaster with the *première* of the Soviet film, *Mother*, on January 19. The works of Maxim Gorky, especially his novel, *Mother*,
have long been popular among left-wing industrial workers and the
intelligentsia of the Near East, who demand deeds instead of
words. [33] Although *Mother* is a blending of great art and revolutionary propaganda--a combination which appeals strongly to the
younger generation in the Near and Middle East--the Soviet film
based on this novel was shown in the wrong place at the wrong

time. [34] Its emphasis on the organization of an underground movement, methods of bribing the police, the printing and distribution
of subversive literature, and instigation of strife in factories, was
tantamount to an invitation to overthrow the Egyptian government,
which itself claims to be revolutionary.

It is an established fact that Nasser has confronted opposition,
not only from the extreme right wing but also from left-wing intellectuals who regard his regime as transitional, to be superseded
sooner or later by an authentic socialist government. [35] The in-
flammatory nature of the film, *Mother*, alarmed Egyptian leaders,
who abruptly terminated the entire Soviet festival and substituted
an American Western film. The fact that the elaborate and widely
distributed Arab-language brochure on the U.S.S.R. advertising
the Soviet industrial fair was printed backward proved to be another
blow to Soviet prestige.

Neither Egypt nor the U.S.S.R. permitted this denouement to
wreck Soviet-Egyptian relations. According to the Soviet press, the
première of *Mother* was a tremendous success, with an ovation
for the Soviet film star, V. Maretskaya, and there the matter was
dropped. [36] When Nasser visited the Soviet industrial fair on January 26, I. G. Bolshakov, deputy Soviet minister of foreign trade,
announced that a large part of the ten thousand items on exhibit
would be donated to the Egyptian government. The Soviet Dance
Ensemble directed by I. A. Moiseev, which carried out a strenuous
schedule of performances in Egypt and Syria, was reputed to be a
huge success. The mission of the Soviet Red Cross and Red Crescent Society to Egypt, bringing food, medical supplies, and am-
bulances amounting to fifteen million rubles in cost for the "victims of Anglo-French-Israeli invasion" was warmly received. Had
Soviet officials and their Egyptian sympathizers not acted so
promptly to offset the cultural crisis over *Mother*, the blunder of
presenting this revolutionary film to an Egyptian audience might
have resulted in a boomerang, strongly reminiscent of the Zinoviev debacle at the historic Baku Congress of September, 1920.

In view of what happened in Egypt, it is interesting to note that
in the Sudan, according to L. Izzeldin Ali Amer, leader of a Sudanese cultural delegation to China and the U.S.S.R. in the summer of 1956, translations of the works of Maxim Gorky enjoy top
priority among Sudanese readers. Perhaps the most significant
event in the brief history of Soviet-Sudanese relations to date was
the presence of a large delegation from the Sudan at the International Seminar on the Equality of Women in the U.S.S.R., held in
Moscow in the summer of 1956. The head of the delegation, Fat'ma

Talib Ismail, herself a teacher and the first woman in the Sudan to receive a university education, was particularly interested in the status of women in the Soviet Union. [37] Upon her return to the Sudan, she planned to write a book on the U.S.S.R.; she and her associates hoped to create a union of the women of Africa, to organize a conference of the women of Asia and Africa, and to establish a society for Sudano-Soviet friendship. Already Sudanese students have begun to go to the Soviet Union to study Russian, medicine, etc. The announced intent of the Soviet government to expand its efforts in Africa in 1957 appears to be under way in the Sudan.

Among the countries of the Baghdad Pact, the U.S.S.R. has been more successful in maintaining cultural contacts with Iran than with Turkey, Iraq, and Pakistan. Although Soviet scholars have lamented the substantial decline in these contacts since the withdrawal of the Red Army from northern Iran in 1946, both the Iranian and Soviet governments have made an effort during the past year to offset the breach created by Iranian accession to the Baghdad Pact. In addition to an exchange of Parliamentary delegations, 1956-57, designed to extend economic and cultural relations, the Shah of Iran and Queen Sorayeh visited the Soviet Union in the summer of 1956, apparently with good results.

The Congress of Scholars which opened on May 26, 1956, in Teheran, with representatives from Muslim universities and neighboring countries, afforded "a gratifying opportunity" for two of the U.S.S.R.'s Iranian specialists, Professor of History B. Zakhoder and Candidate in Historical Sciences M. N. Ivanova, to exchange ideas with scholars from Afghanistan, Egypt, India, Iraq, Lebanon, Pakistan, Syria, and Turkey. [38] Soviet writers have lamented the termination of *Payam-i-No*, the journal of the Soviet-Iranian Cultural Society, the few translations of Russian and Soviet literature into Persian, and the corresponding dearth of Soviet translations of Persian poetry and prose. The chief recent contributions, both in 1955, appear to have been a collection of contemporary Iranian short stories by leftist writers, entitled *Razkazy Persidskikh Pisateley*, and a collection of articles on literary criticism, published in *Kratkie Soobshcheniya Instituta Vostokovedeniya* (XVII [1955]), dealing with such matters as socialist realism and the "positive hero" in Iranian literature.

VII

In spite of the rapid introduction of Russian and Soviet culture into the Muslim countries of the Near and Middle East, especially since World War II, it is impossible to gauge with any degree of accuracy the extent of its influence. The Soviet impact has been not a constant, but a fluctuating factor, dependent in part on the international situation, or, as in the case of Iran, on the presence of Soviet occupation forces. Among young Arabic, Turkish, and Iranian writers, Soviet influence has often been transient and, like Taha Hussein of Egypt, they have eventually veered toward the West and Western culture. The members of the Near and Middle Eastern intelligentsia traditionally have had closer contacts with the West-- especially with France and England--where frequently they have received university training.

Nor has the West, especially the United States, been sitting idly by. American colleges, information services, student exchange programs, etc., have constituted effective propaganda for the Western world. Indeed, Western activity in this direction has been conducted on a much larger scale than anything the Soviet Union has attempted in the Near and Middle East to date. That it has proved effective is clear from the fact that Soviet writers constantly complain of meeting with obstruction and frustration as a result of American activities. Where, for example, the Soviet government provides for the translation of a mere handful of books into Turkish, a Soviet writer has reason to lament that the United States has a program for the early translation of nearly two thousand books and will, of course, have every facility available for their distribution.

More important than the translation of books into Arabic, Turkish, Persian, etc., is the program for the eradication of illiteracy under the Point Four Program, a striking example of which is to be found in Iran. Whereas in 1953 the vast majority of Iranian gendarmes were illiterate, by 1956 at least fourteen thousand out of a total number of twenty-two thousand were enrolled in literacy courses prepared by the United States Point Four Program for aid to underdeveloped nations. Following the American example with the gendarmes, the Iranian government early in 1956 launched an extensive campaign to eradicate illiteracy in the villages, the potentialities of which are tremendous. It is characteristic that people, especially Muslims, who have but recently emerged from a state of illiteracy, are inclined to worship the printed word and to be influenced most by what they read first. The Soviets themselves have had remarkable success with their own literacy programs which, however, have been confined to the Muslims under their own jurisdiction, and to participation in the programs of other countries, like China, in their own orbit. The Near and Middle

Eastern governments have been impressed by Soviet accomplishment in this respect. By assuming the initiative in their own countries, they are taking the wind out of the Soviet propaganda sails, and they have within their grasp an unprecedented opportunity to influence their own peoples through their own educational programs.

In spite of the success of our countermeasures to date, through our educational institutions, publications, literacy programs, and communications media, we should not underestimate the impact of Soviet cultural propaganda in the Muslim world of the Near and Middle East. Although the Soviet government greatly intensified its propaganda activities throughout the Muslim world early in 1956, nevertheless A. I. Mikoyan, speaking before the twentieth congress of the Communist party (*Pravda, Izvestia,* February 18, 1956), complained that whereas the entire Orient has awakened, the Oriental Institute of the Academy of Sciences of the U.S.S.R. is still asleep and fails "to meet the demands of our time." He likewise protested the liquidation of the 139-year-old Moscow Institute of Oriental Studies at the very time Soviet "economic, political, and cultural connections with the countries of the Orient have immeasurably increased the interest of Soviet public opinion in them, as well as the demand for persons who know the languages, the economy, and the culture of the Eastern countries."

Toward the close of 1956 the Presidium of the U.S.S.R. Academy of Sciences continued to express general dissatisfaction with the accomplishments to date of the Institute of Oriental Studies, including its failure to produce serious studies of contemporary conditions in the countries of the East.[39] It demanded better qualified cadres, still more contacts with research institutes abroad, the temporary employment of at least twenty specialists from the non-Soviet East, and the establishment under the Institute of a Publishing House of Eastern Literature. No doubt with these changes in mind, the Academy announced in September the appointment of B. G. Gafurov to succeed A. A. Guber as director of the Institute. Although Soviet scholars have been unable to keep pace with Soviet designs for the Middle East, in spite of the loss of such outstanding specialists as I. Y. Kratchkovsky and V. A. Gordlevsky (1956), there is a brand new crop of orientalists in the making, many of whom are already engaged in specialized studies of the literature and history of the countries of Asia.

VIII

A careful study of the Soviet program reveals no intent on the part of the U.S.S.R. to stress the Near and Middle East at the expense of the rest of Asia. In order to promote "a thorough and all-embracing study" of the experience and accomplishments of the Chinese People's Republic, the Academy of Sciences of the U.S.S.R. decided toward the close of 1956 to organize an Institute of Chinese Studies as an integral part of its historical branch. Beginning in 1957, this institute was granted permission to publish a bimonthly scientific journal, *Sovetskoye Kitayevedeniye (Soviet Chinese Studies)*.

There has been particular emphasis on the need for "solidarity" among Asian peoples as a whole. As a result of the Conference of Fifteen Asian Countries in Delhi in 1955, the U.S.S.R. established a Soviet Committee for the Solidarity of Asian Countries, with headquarters in Moscow, to promote the extension of the "Peace Zone." The most significant outcome in 1957 was the arrival in Egypt on February 9, on a goodwill mission, of the representatives of the Committees of Solidarity of the Countries of Asia, headed by Anap Singh, a member of the Indian Parliament, and including delegates from China, Japan, and the Soviet Union.[40] The delegation made tentative arrangements with President Nasser for the calling of a new conference for the solidarity of the Asian and African peoples--a second Bandung--which was held in Cairo in December, 1957. Significantly enough, although the first Asian-African Conference was held in Southeast Asia, the second was scheduled for the Near East. Whereas the U.S.S.R. was not formally represented in Bandung, the holding of a conference under the auspices of the Egyptian National Committee for the Solidarity of the Countries of Asia would practically assure Soviet participation.

With Asian solidarity in mind, the U.S.S.R. is placing great emphasis on the development of Asian studies, in the expectation of making the Soviet Union the Mecca for Asian scholars of the Near, Middle, and Far East. Out of Asian solidarity the U.S.S.R. looks for the evolution of a new society, socialist in content and largely self-sufficient economically and culturally, to be achieved by degrees in the nonsocialist Asian orbit. From this new society, needless to say, Western influence would be eliminated.

Although Cairo is still the Afro-Asian headquarters, two important cultural events were staged in Tashkent, the foremost Soviet Middle Eastern center of oriental studies, in the late summer and fall of 1958. The first was an Afro-Asian Cinema Festival, August 20 to September 2, admittedly an experiment without sufficient advance preparation, representing eight Soviet Republics

and fourteen Afro-Asian countries, including the Arab states of
the U.A.R., Tunisia, and Morocco. This was followed in October
by an Afro-Asian Writers' Conference, organized by Yussef El-
Sebai of the Cairo secretariat, where at least thirty countries of
the Afro-Asian bloc were represented. The delegates came to seek
a common ground, a common hero, and a common genre in the literatures of the Afro-Asian peoples. Judging by the Soviet press,
the real object was the mobilization of the writers for a campaign
in support of Arab unity and the independence of the remaining colonies under Western jurisdiction. It is significant that whereas
only Asian delegates attended the first writers' conference in Delhi
in 1955 and the first cinema conference in Peking in 1957, the Soviet Union, in particular, insisted on the inclusion of African representatives in 1958. The first Economic Conference of the Afro-
Asian countries was scheduled to be held in Cairo in December,
1958.

The U.A.R.-Soviet cultural agreement of April, 1958, has borne
fruit in one respect, which portends important Soviet advantages in
the Arab world in the years ahead. Beginning with the academic
year, 1958-59, the study of the Russian language was introduced in
several U.A.R. high schools and at Cairo university, with at least
ten Soviet instructors provided for the purpose. In addition, the
U.A.R., in October, 1958, admitted forty Soviet scientists and
technicians to lay the groundwork for scientific and technical education. As yet there is no Russian-speaking audience in the United
Arab Republic to facilitate Soviet instruction. There will be, however, within two or three years, when the three hundred Egyptian
students being sent to study in the U.S.S.R. return to the U.A.R.,
and when the first crop of students in Cairo is trained.

In September, 1958, the U.A.R. Ministry of Education sent a
delegation of twenty Egyptian educators to the U.S.S.R., led by
Undersecretary Ahmed Naguib, to study Soviet educational methods
with a view to the revision of the educational curriculum of the U.
A.R., to select Soviet universities where Egyptian students will
be sent to study, and to implement the other provisions of the So-
viet-U.A.R. cultural agreement. With Egyptian teachers serving
as U.A.R. political missionaries in Yemen, Saudi Arabia, and
Iraq, the early spread of Soviet educational methods to other parts
of the Arab world can be expected.

10. Conclusions

From our experience since 1917 in Asia, and particularly in the Near and Middle East, certain conclusions can be drawn. In the first place, it is clear that the Asiatic peoples have subordinated living standards to liberation from either Soviet or Western colonialism. In other words, when these peoples were confronted with a choice between better living standards and sovereignty, with but few and minor exceptions, their natural tendency was to choose independence. In the case of the Muslim countries, Islam as well as liberation took precedent over economic betterment. In fact, at times Islam and liberation from colonialism became so closely interwoven that it was difficult to draw a line of demarcation between them. They became virtually synonymous.

In retrospect, the theory advanced in Western Europe and the United States since the Bolshevik Revolution of 1917, to the effect that communism breeds in and thrives on poverty, is by no means universally true. In fact, it is actually dangerous to accept it as a maxim. Perhaps the best refutation of this tenet is to be found in the reaction of Turkey, Iran, and Afghanistan in 1921 to the Soviet program to raise agrarian living standards in regions where poverty beggared description. In these three Islamic countries two factors, political independence and the religion of Islam, proved stronger than the bait of Soviet "prosperity." When Soviet Russia in effect tried to substitute Red colonialism (sovietization) for Western colonialism and hurled invectives at the Islamic faith, these Muslim states turned thumbs down on the whole program.

In the Western world, where political sovereignty was already well established and living standards were infinitely higher than in the East, communism did indeed breed among the poverty-stricken and the unemployed, for whom security and higher living standards became the major issue. On more than one occasion following World War I, the Communists were able to convince

267

these people that the only remaining barrier to higher living standards, security, and full employment for them was the capitalist
system represented by their existing governments. In politically
independent Western Europe after World War II, when the United
States offered economic aid in the form of the Marshall Plan, the
results were strikingly successful.

Today, there can be no doubt whatsoever that if Czechoslovakia,
Poland, Hungary, as well as the former Baltic and Balkan states
now under Soviet domination, were offered a choice between improved living standards and political freedom, they would without
hesitation choose independence, even if that meant an appreciable
reduction in living standards. Even in Western Germany, it seems
clear that a bona fide unification program without Soviet strings
attached thereto would take precedence over any quantity of military and economic aid. A report from Bonn, Germany, on January 15, 1956 (*New York Times,* January 16, 1956), revealed that
propaganda based on living standards higher than those of the Russians will not suffice much longer to stave off communism. A bulletin issued by the Adenauer government predicted that unless new
spiritual values are found the only difference between the two major
protagonists will be that the Russians are "materialists in theory, "
whereas the peoples of the West are "materialists in practice. " The
bulletin called for a new ideology to resist Communist faith in col-
lectivism, one which did not depend on material things or on "the
expectation of future well-being, " but was instead based on "freedom, personal dignity, the lives of other men, the truth of religion. "

Obviously, as far as Western Germany is concerned, and perhaps the same is true for the greater part of Western Europe, our
economic and military aid program has reached the peak of possible achievement. The Germans may yet be surprised to find that
Americans have in fact an untapped reservoir of faith in freedom,
personal dignity, and religion to supplement the material aid already rendered. This may be what is needed to restore the ethical
and spiritual values crushed by Nazism, just as our economic aid
has restored the material damage wrought by Hitlerite aggression.

In their much-publicized junket through Asia in 1955 the theme
song of Bulganin and Khrushchev was "Down with Colonialism!"
Judging by the reception they were given, even in countries like
India and Burma which had already achieved their independence,
they won the attention and good will of the Asian masses. Only after these Asian peoples had shouted themselves hoarse in approval

of the Soviet denunciation of colonialism did the Soviet "ambassadors of good will" cast them a few crumbs of economic aid.

When Americans turned to Asia after World War II they began, as in Europe, with Point Four and military aid. Food, technical equipment, and arms can be purchased, even behind the Iron Curtain as we have discovered in Egypt, Syria, and Yemen, but liberation is in a different category--it must be won! The country that stands for national liberation is the one that captures the imagination of the Asian peoples, as the Bulganin-Khrushchev tour demonstrated.

In India, where political independence has been won, but where the people are still highly sensitive to any threat to its preservation, the United States action in providing military and economic aid to neighboring Pakistan resulted in the Indians veering toward Moscow. An article in the Soviet illustrated weekly *Ogonyok* (No. 48 [November, 1955], p. 5), entitled "A Window in Moscow," by Akhmad Abbas, calls to mind the well-known slogan attributed to Peter the Great about opening a window to Europe. This Indian writer appeared to be calling upon Asians to open a window to Moscow rather than to the West, thereby orienting themselves toward the U.S.S.R.

In the Near and Middle East, where the United States is heading the drive for the organization of the Muslim world against the Soviet-Chinese axis, it stands to reason that with colonialism the paramount issue there, Americans are unlikely to make appreciable headway unless they dissociate themselves completely from the policies, past and present, of the colonial powers. Today, in proportion as the Muslim countries acquire political independence, they are becoming economically minded. Once their political sovereignty rests on sure foundations and the United States is free from any aura of colonialism acquired by association with those involved in the prolongation of colonial status in that area, then and then only can we expect to make real strides with our Point Four Program, to find that it is welcomed and fully appreciated. With our technological superiority, we can outbid and outmatch the Soviet Union in any economic competition for many years to come.

The prospects for the success of American efforts in behalf of a united Muslim front would be greater if the United States were in a position to act alone, without the aid of the other Western allies. Although in Europe it is to the advantage of the Western powers to present a solid front, and for Britain and the United States to have an ironclad accord, vis-à-vis the Muslim world America's allies unfortunately have proved to be a liability. Rightly or wrong-ly, they remind the Muslim peoples of their former colonial status, even if, as is true, some of them gained their independence and improved their economic status under British or French tutelage. The action of the Muslim religious leaders in Iraq, who on August 29, 1955, asked that relations with France be broken in protest against French colonial administration in North Africa, affords just one illustration of the handicaps under which the United States operates in the Middle East. Recent French action in granting independence to Morocco and Tunis appears likely to produce even greater Muslim denunciation of French policy in Algeria. English action since World War II in abandoning the vestiges of colonialism in Egypt, the Sudan, Iraq, Burma, Malaya, and India was all but forgotten in the storm over Cyprus and the Suez invasion. Once granted a free hand by Great Britain and France, the United States could work more effectively for a united Muslim front to halt the Communist menace to the strategic Near and Middle East.

From the October Revolution (November 7, 1917, N.S.) to the end of World War II, the Soviet government regarded Great Britain as the principal exponent of imperialism (colonialism) in the Near and Middle East, and as such the chief obstacle to Soviet expansion in that area. During this period Great Britain was the main target of Soviet propaganda. Since World War II, with the progressive retreat of England and France on the colonial front, the United States has assumed the lead in resisting Soviet aggression in both Europe and Asia. Whether the Soviet government sought to expand its empire or its orbit in Iran, Turkey, Korea, Vietnam, or Syria, it confronted the military power and prestige of the United States. Thus the United States since World War II has superseded Great Britain as the chief target of Soviet propaganda, both in literature and in the press, especially vis-à-vis the Muslim world. In the postwar duel between the United States and the U.S.S.R. for the support of the Muslim world, the Soviet government, which has studied American policy as never before, has not infrequently adopted American tactics of furnishing military and economic aid and of closer personal contacts with the leaders of the Muslim states, in order to undermine American influence in the Near and Middle East.

Since World War II, the relations of the Soviet Union and the United States, with few exceptions, have been based on strategy rather than on diplomacy. Soviet efforts, direct and indirect, to acquire strategic bases in Iran, Turkey, and Greece, 1945-47, evoked the Truman Doctrine of March 12, 1947. To offset this American move in the Middle East, the U.S.S.R. won a major victory in the Far East with the culmination of the Sino-Soviet Alliance of February 14, 1950, which upset the balance of power in both Europe and Asia. To prevent a Sino-Soviet pincer movement against Asia and Europe, the United States turned to the Muslim states bordering upon the U.S.S.R., and succeeded in bringing about the Turkish-Pakistani Mutual Aid Agreement of April 2, 1954, which developed into the Baghdad Alliance of November, 1955. Confronted with this strategic victory, which was part of an overall program for the encirclement of the U.S.S.R. in Europe and Asia, the Soviet government hastily acquired a political and economic foothold in Afghanistan in the fall of 1955. By its leapfrog tactics, it outflanked the Middle East Alliance with its military and economic aid offensive in Egypt, Yemen, and Syria, 1956-57.

In the Syrian crisis of October, 1957, the implementation of the Eisenhower Doctrine was challenged by a Soviet threat to implement the Sino-Soviet "Doctrine" formulated the previous January. The crisis clearly demonstrated that the continuation of strategic moves by the United States and the U.S.S.R. could lead only to armed conflict. There appeared to be no place for either adversary to move with safety on this planet, although the launching of the first sputnik pointed the way to future competition in other spheres. This deadlock left but one alternative short of war--a return to diplomacy. The obstacles strewing the path of the United States government in making diplomatic overtures to the U.S.S.R. were manifold, but the issues at stake seemed to make another attempt imperative.

In spite of the growing Soviet impact on the Arab world, there are still no Soviet roots there. Irrespective of the fact that official Arab and American policies are often widely at variance, and in spite of hostile press and radio campaigns, there is still a substantial reserve of warm friendship for the American people among Arabs in all walks of life. To improve relations with the Arab world, and thereby steal at least some of the Soviet thunder, Americans will need to analyze and define what is meant by Arab nationalism, which, like Islam, is all-embracing, all-inclusive. The movement for Arab unity is only one aspect of it. We shall need to send trained and sympathetic representatives throughout the Arab world, not merely to establish and maintain listening posts, but to serve as ambassadors of good will.

In the final analysis, it is more important for the United States to have bases in Muslim hearts than on Muslim soil.

Appendixes

I. THE REVOLUTION OF 1905 AND THE EAST*
The Revolution of 1905. The Russo-Japanese War and the East.
Lenin on the results of the Russo-Japanese War.

In a prophetic article, "The Fall of Port Arthur," published in *Vperyod* several days prior to January 9--to be precise, on January 1, 1905--Comrade Lenin explained as follows the role of the unsuccessful war with Japan as a mighty propaganda weapon, as the greatest revolutionary factor:

The military might of autocratic Russia proved to be trumpery. Tsarism proved to be an obstacle to contemporary military organization, which was at a high level, and to which Tsarism was devoted with all its heart, of which it was more and more proud, and for which it made unlimited sacrifices, not being blocked by any popular opposition. A beautiful apple rotten at the core--that is what the autocracy proved to be in the sphere of external defence, which was, so to speak, its own particular specialty.

But why and to what extent does the fall of Port Arthur constitute a real historic catastrophe?

First of all, we are struck by the significance of this event for the course of the war. The Japanese have accomplished the main goal of the war. *A progressive and advanced Asia has inflicted an irreparable blow on a backward and reactionary Europe.* Ten years ago this reactionary Europe (with Russia at the head) became disturbed over the defeat of China by young Japan and united to deprive her of the best fruits of victory. *Europe preserved the established relations and privileges of the old world, its prerogative, hallowed by centuries, its primordial right, to exploit the Asiatic peoples.* The return of Port

---

*M. Pavlovitch, "SSSR i Vostok," *Revolyutsionnyi Vostok*, Part I (Moscow-Leningrad, 1927), pp. 21-35.

272

Arthur to Japan is a blow, inflicted on reactionary Europe. Russia held Port Arthur for six years, having spent hundreds and hundreds of millions of rubles on strategic railroads, on the construction of ports, on building new cities, on strengthening fortifications, which the whole mass of European papers, bribed by Russia, hailed as impregnable. Military writers say that in strength Port Arthur was equal to six Sevastopols. And behold, a small, hitherto universally despised Japan took possession of this citadel in eight months, whereas England and France together took a whole year to seize one Sevastopol.

And we know that events have substantiated the forecast of Lenin. The fact that little Japan could defeat gigantic Russia, up to that time the frightful enemy of all the Asiatic peoples, made the strongest impression on the inhabitants of all Asia. The little Japanese defeated the strongest military power in Europe. How did they achieve this? They took lessons from Europe itself and adopted European institutions.

The Russian Revolution of 1905 made an even greater impression on the peoples of the East. In the life of the Asiatic peoples the Russian Revolution played the same tremendous role as the great French Revolution formerly played in the lives of the Europeans.

After the Russo-Japanese War and the Russian Revolution of 1905, we see an upsurge of the liberation movement in Persia, the general strike in August 1906 in Teheran, the calling of the first Mejlis (Parliament) in October of the same year, followed by the strengthening of the Young Turk movement in Turkey, culminating in the Revolution of 1908 which broke into smithereens the foundations of the despotic power of the blood-smeared Sultan, Abdul-Hamid; and thereafter, the revolutionary movement in China, culminating in the overthrow of the Manchu Dynasty and the proclamation of the Republic in 1911.

After the Russo-Japanese War and the Russian Revolution of 1905, the national liberation movement throughout the East began to develop a stronger tempo, both as a struggle against internal reaction and the despotic regime in their own countries, as well as against the yoke of the imperialistic European powers, who transformed the entire East into a colony of world capitalism.

For many centuries the Asian looked with fear and trembling on the European, regarding the latter as an evil and perfidious, but at the same time as an invincible enemy, the scourge of God, conflict with whom was doomed to failure and accompanied by cruel punishment. Liaotung and Mukden, the retreat of the countless armies of the White Tsar, the mightiest ruler in Europe before the yellow-skinned soldiers of little Japan seemed to have opened the eyes of the Asians and demonstrated to them that the struggle with Europe was possible, and that with proper organization and persistent onslaught of the yellow masses it must lead to victory. At the very moment when the hitherto terrifying double eagle was unexpectedly defeated, and when, according to Vl. Solovyov, pieces of its banners were given to yellow children to play with, the hitherto slumbering Asia woke up forthwith to a new life.

The Political and Economic Premises of the National Liberation Movement in the Twentieth Century

The decade which preceded the Russo-Japanese War and the Russian Revolution of 1905 was an epoch of special intensification of the onslaught of the capitalist powers on the black and yellow continents. Thus, as regards the Middle Empire, the period beginning with the Sino-Japanese War of 1894, which severed from China a number of its territories, may be characterized as the period of the intensification of the dismemberment of China by the world plunderers. Germany seized the province of Kiaochow, with the port of Tsingtao; Russia--Port Arthur and Dairen; England grabbed from China Weihaiwei and the territory lying along the mainland opposite Hongkong; France added to its possessions Kwangchowan and rounded out its territory at the expense of China, in order not to be overtaken in the struggle for the partition of China by the other plunderers. The United States in 1898 declared war on Spain and seized not only Cuba, the key to the Panama Canal, the shortest route from the east coast of America to the Chinese coast on the Pacific, but also the Philippines, a base on the approaches to China. This attack of world capitalism on China evoked a rebuff from the Chinese people's masses in the form of the Boxer Rebellion of 1900-1.

Following the Spanish-American War of 1898 there began the Anglo-Boer War, 1899-1901, a war for the hegemony of England not only in South Africa and in all the eastern half of the Black Continent, but likewise in the Indian Ocean, and on the sea route along the west coast of the Black Continent into Asia. After England established its hegemony in South Africa imperialist France, in the interests of the preservation of the "balance of power" in Africa, began its attack on northwest Africa. Having signed secret treaties with Spain, Italy, and England, France secured freedom of action in Morocco and began the conquest of this region. While these events were taking place in China, in South and North Africa, Ger-

many, "establishing her sphere of influence" in West and East Africa and participating in the rape of China, vigorously pushed ahead
in Asia Minor its Baghdad railroad, which of necessity hitched
Turkey, with its tremendous natural resources, to the victorious
chariot of the German Empire, and the question of the Baghdad
railroad became one of the main pivots around which international
policy began to revolve. At the same time, Tsarist Russia continued
its drive into Persia from the north, England from the south; and
from the Turkish boundary came Germany, which created a plan
for the construction of branch lines from the Baghdad main line
(Baghdad--Haneken--Kermanshah--Hamadan), in order to subject
Persia to its economic and political influence.

It goes without saying, that along with the seizure of African and
Asian territories, the creation there of military bases, and the
building of railroads, there also occurred an intensified penetration of European and American capital into the colonial and semicolonial countries. Feverishly railroads and highways were built,
ports and quays were erected, and European goods in ever-increasing quantity penetrated into the most remote points of Persia, Turkey, India, etc., destroying local handicraft industry, *and the
countries of the East day by day were transformed more and more
into raw material and food bases, into a so-called "economic territory," into a "hinterland," on which the industrial countries depended.* In the period from 1901 to 1906 the foreign trade of British India grew from 3,081 million marks to 3,928; that of China from
1,376 million marks to 2,294; that of Persia from 149 million marks
to 251. Thus, for the first five years of the present century alone,
the trade of the three Asiatic countries increased by almost 2,000,
000,000 marks. At the same time, under the influence of financial capital, which created factories and foundries in India, China,
and Turkey, exploited coal mines, etc., in the countries of the
East, there began to come into being at first a very small, but later
an ever-increasing railroad and factory proletariat.[1] This proletariat in India, China, and Turkey naturally fell under the influence
of the opposition-minded native trade bourgeoisie, which was dis-
satisfied with the domination of foreign capital and apprehensive in

---

[1]In India we have in 1905 about 350,000 employees and workers on
railroads and railroad construction, about 300,000 in the cotton and
jute industry, about 70,000 in mining, and in general about 800,000
persons, including railroad personnel, in big enterprises, which em-
ploy more than 50 workers.

Turkey, Persia, and China of the complete destruction of the last vestiges of the independence of their countries.

Thus a base was created for the national liberation movement in the entire East. The Russo-Japanese War and the Revolution of 1905 provided the first great impetus to this movement.

Persia

Of all the countries of the East, Persia was especially closely connected with Tsarist Russia economically. As regards imports and exports, Russia occupied first place among other powers in the foreign trade of Persia. In 1886 Russian exports to Persia amounted to 6,100,000 rubles; in 1896, to 14,500,000 rubles; in 1907, to 28,300,000 rubles. Russian imports from Persia were expressed in the following figures: in 1886--10,300,000 rubles; in 1896--17,700,000 rubles; and in 1907--20,300,000 rubles. But the connection between Persia and Russia was not only expressed in the growth of trade ties from year to year. In the fifteen years prior to 1905, tens of thousands of poor people left Persia annually for the Caucasus, where they worked in the oil industries of Baku and Grozny, where at each factory, at each industrial concern in Tiflis, Erivan, Vladikavkaz, Novorossiisk, Derbent, Temir-Khan-Shura, representatives of the Persian toiling masses were to be found. And in association with Russian and Caucasian proletarians, in work under a common factory code or inside the four walls of one and the same stuffy shop, Persian toilers, as represented by their more enlightened elements, joined the great revolutionary movement, the waves of which stormed over the whole Russian Empire.

The events of the Russian Revolution--January 9, the general strike, the Moscow armed uprising--made a tremendous impression on the population of Persia. Illegal Persian literature made its way into all the cities, demonstrations took place everywhere against the Shah and his satraps, the cry of "Long live the constitution," reverberated all over the country. Finally, in August 1906, there began the famous general strike in Teheran, in which all the clergy in the city took part, all the mosques were closed, all the merchants, having closed all the shops and bazaars, and then the artisans, workers, in a word, all classes of the population participated. The general strike resulted in the promulgation of the constitution in August 1906 and the calling of the first Mejlis (Parliament) in October of the same year.

The first Persian Mejlis did not last long. But even in the short time it existed, it succeeded in accomplishing a great deal. New laws were passed, which inflicted a terrific blow on the economic domination of the *mülkadars* (big landowners). There began a radical reform of the tax and administrative systems of Persia. It seemed as if a new era was opening for the tormented country. But the prospect of the rebirth of Persia could not but frighten the Russian Black Hundreds and the English bourgeoisie.

At first, England supported the Persian national political movement.

Inasmuch as Russian political, economic, and military influence in Teheran was very strong, thanks to the gravitation of the reactionary Shah toward the Tsarist government which supported the old Persian regime with a Cossack brigade, trained and guided by Russian officers, England, in order to undermine Russian influence in Persia, entered as though into a secret alliance with the Persian people, made use of the awakening constitutional movement in the country and, by extending energetic support to the population which was struggling for freedom, raised its prestige in northern Persia to an extraordinary degree, and thereby created for itself a loyal ally in the 10,000,000 Persian population in the struggle against the aggressive policy of Russia in Central Asia. But the friendship of English diplomacy for the Persian liberation movement did not last long. England supported the constitutional movement in the northern regions of Persia as long as it was necessary to counteract Russian influence at the Shah's court, but at the same time England with all her strength suppressed the liberation movement in the southern provinces adjacent to the Indian boundary, and extended in these areas every kind of support to the Persian satraps who fought against the ideas of liberation. The growth of the revolutionary movement among the 300,000,000 population in India, as much as fear of Germany, drove England toward a rapprochement with Russia. It was precisely due to apprehension that the triumph of revolution throughout Persia would provide a strong impetus to the revolutionary movement in India that English diplomacy was forced to change its course abruptly with regard to the liberation movement in Persia. Such were the basic motives underlying the notorious Anglo-Russian agreement of 1907 on Persian affairs.

The publication of the Anglo-Russian Convention, which amounted to the virtual destruction of Persian independence and the establishment of an Anglo-Russian protectorate over Persia, greatly disturbed the enlightened strata of Persian society and introduced much confusion in the domestic life of the country, which aggravated the feeling of uncertainty for the future. Anarchy was every-

where on the increase, reaction reared its head, and the Shah with
particular energy began to prepare for a decisive attack, at the
same time waging a systematic underground war against the new
institutions.

On June 11 (24), 1908, the head of the Persian Cossack brigade,
Colonel Lyakhov, acting according to a plan worked out by him
jointly with Hartwig, Russian ambassador in Teheran, and Emir
Bohadur Djank, the head of the Persian reactionaries, with the approval of the commander of the troops of the Caucasian military
district, bombarded the Persian Mejlis. Many of the people's representatives were killed or executed (Mirza Ibrahim, Mirza Khan,
Mutaqalimin, and others), others were subjected to torture and
thrown into prison, still others were exiled or escaped.

Thus the movement to which the Russian Revolution and the Russo-Japanese War gave such a strong impetus was temporarily suppressed by a Russian colonel.

The Persian revolutionary movement was closely connected with
the workers' movement in Russia; on the other hand, the Persian
counterrevolution drew its strength from the foot of the Tsarist
throne. It is very curious *that the founder of the Persian Social
Democratic Party (Itchmayun Amiyun) was the late Comrade N.
Narimanov; and, on the other hand, the main instigator of the Persian counterrevolution was a Russian subject, S. M. Shapshal, who
aroused general animosity against himself in Persia.* Shapshal was
graduated from the oriental department of Petersburg University,
and at the recommendation of the Tsarist government was appointed
tutor of the Shah, Memed-Ali, when he was the heir apparent.
Shapshal and Lyakhov were the main instigators and leaders of the
political revolution of June 23, 1908, of the bombardment and destruction of the Persian Mejlis. At this historic moment of decisive
struggle against the Persian revolutionary movement, as N. P.
Mamontov, correspondent of one of the Russian military periodicals
wrote, there remained "with the Shah" only two loyal and honest
men--the evil irony of his fate--both Russian subjects: Sergei Mar-
kovitch Shapshal and Colonel Lyakhov, commander of His Majesty
the Shah's Cossack brigade. On the other hand, the Persian revolution found its most loyal allies in Russia. The Baku Social Democratic organization alone sent to Tabriz 22 armed workers, who
brought with them 40 Berdan rifles and 50 bombs. With one of these
bombs, Governor Maranda was killed. The Caucasian Regional
Committee sent one of its members as a leader of the Caucasian
revolutionaries in Persia in the struggle against reaction.

Comrade Gurko-Kryazhin, in a very interesting article, "Narimanov and the East" (see *Novyi Vostok*, 1925, No. 1 [7]), emphasizing the fact that Narimanov was the founder of the Persian Social Democratic Party, posed the question: "How did it happen? Why did the Transcaucasian revolutionary become the founder of the Persian political party?" To this question, Comrade Gurko-Kryazhin gave the following answer:

In order to understand this fact, it is necessary to bear in mind that the Transcaucasus in the years of the upsurge of the Russian revolutionary movement had its counterpart in the neighboring countries-- Persia and Turkey. Just as General Alikhanov-Avarskii plundered the settlements of the Guri in western Georgia and Colonel Martynov shot Tiflis workers, another Tsarist colonel, Lyakhov, dispersed and hanged Persian democrats in Teheran. This pressure of Tsarism created a solidarity of interests, evoked the need for common revolutionary action. In particular, this was felt after the suppression of the revolutionary movement of 1905-1906: the Transcaucasian revolutionaries, including Comrade Narimanov, arrived at the quite correct conclusion that it did not matter where one made a revolution, as long as it was a revolution. And thus we see how a handful of Caucasian "Fedayeens" under the leadership of the Armenian, Yefrem, overthrew Shah Memed-Ali. Another handful of Caucasian heroes endured for nine months the historic siege of Tabriz.[1] It is curious to note that the news of the Young Turk Revolution inspired them greatly. Small wonder that Russian reactionary circles, through the mouthpiece, *Novoe Vremya*, demanded "ruthless extermination of the criminal Fedayeens," on the ground that "even pure humanity demands atrocities." The threats of *Novoe Vremya*, of course, did not frighten the Caucasian revolutionaries. One after another, their detachments infiltrated Persia and took the most active part in the struggle with the Persian counterrevolution, directed by Tsarist agents.

Turkey

The Russo-Japanese War and the Russian Revolution likewise provided an impetus to the national liberation movement in Turkey. As Muliukov, in his time, was forced to admit, *the Turkish revolutionaries, while still in Paris, followed the development of the*

---

[1] In the defense of Tabriz, 22 Caucasian Social Democrats perished (Vladimir Dumbadze, Valiko Bokradze, Nakhviladze, Georgii Emushvari, Chita, and others). At the seizure of Resht in January 1909, Caucasian Social Democrats lost several comrades, among whom were two Social Democratic bomb throwers.

Revolution with great attention and drew certain conclusions (P. Miliukov, *The Balkan Crisis and the Policy of A. I. Izvolsky*. St. Petersburg, 1910). But the significance of the Russian Revolution consisted not so much, of course, in its influence on emigré circles, as *in its profound impact on the broad masses of the Turkish people and on the Turkish army*. Prior to 1906, the Turkish opposition movement seemed to be concentrated exclusively abroad among the Turkish emigrés, in Geneva, Paris, and in several other European cities. The Young Turk party, Ittihad ("Unity and Progress"), exercised the greatest influence among the Turkish emigrés in Europe. Beginning with 1905, the influence of the Young Turks in Turkey itself grew rapidly and the Ittihad party soon created a whole network of underground organizations throughout the country, especially in the army. *In 1906, the Young Turk movement assumed such an imposing character that the Party's Central Committee left Paris and moved to Salonika,* where the headquarters staff of the movement against the Sultan's government was formed. In 1907 in Paris, upon the initiative of the Dashnaktsutyun party, a congress of all the revolutionary parties and organizations against Turkey was held. At this congress, it was decided to begin a general offensive against the Sultan's government on the thirtieth anniversary of the accession of Abdul Hamid to the throne, with the object of overthrowing the bloodthirsty Sultan.

The Anglo-Russian project for Macedonian reforms, which followed the historic meeting of the English and Russian sovereigns at Reval, June 9, 1908, hastened the explosion. The Young Turk party decided not to wait longer and forthwith to raise the banner of revolt against the Sultan.

The role of the Turkish army in the liberation movement was great. It does not follow, however, that one should belittle the role of the other elements of the Turkish population in the constitutional movement, as many have done. One may regard as already fully established the fact that the Turkish liberation movement was not necessarily a movement which first and foremost seized the army, as the bourgeois writers of Europe and Tsarist Russia described the 1908 Revolution.

The Turkish Revolution was a nation-wide movement, in which all strata of the Turkish population took a most active part. And if it is true that of the first two Turkish battalions which raised the banner of revolt against the Sultan, the battalion under the command of Lt. Enver-Bey was composed to a considerable extent of soldiers, on the other hand, the second and larger detachment which advanced under the leadership of Major Niyazi-Bey, commandant of the fortress of Ren, was composed almost exclusively of *civilians*. The whole significance of this fact immediately strikes one. Thus, in the first two battalions, which began the uprising together, there were more civilians than soldiers. Thus already this initial episode of the Turkish Revolution, which represents one of those factors to which we may apply the adage: "an ounce of facts is worth more than 40 pounds of arguments, " destroys the concept of the Turkish Revolution of 1908 as a specific military *pronunciamento* (uprising, revolt).

The tiny army of Niyazi-Bey and Enver-Bey proved invincible because, first of all, the whole Muslim population of Macedonia and all the Muslim peasantry of European Turkey immediately went over to its side.

In all the Turkish villages, the peasants equipped the Fedayeens (volunteers) with provisions gratis, informed them of the movements of government detachments, gave asylum to the Fedayeens and hid them. For the head of Enver-Bey a huge sum was promised, but this enticed no one. Many villages openly refused to obey the government and to pay taxes. After the Turkish villages, the Bulgarian villages likewise went over to the side of Niyazi-Bey. It was only after the peasant masses resolutely declared their sympathy and readiness to extend support to the revolutionary plans of Niyazi-Bey, that the latter began his victorious march from one city to another. In general, the June Revolution of 1908, in its initial stage, can be safely characterized as a revolt of the Muslim peasantry of European Turkey against the old Abdul Hamid regime, rather than a military revolt.

India

In the English "Blue Book, " published in 1919 on the revolutionary movement in India for the period from 1897 to 1918, we find frequent references to the extent of the influence of the *Russian Revolution of 1905 and the Russo-Japanese War on the upsurge of the revolutionary movement in India*. To be precise, after 1905 the terrorist movement became particularly strong, in various parts of India antigovernment demonstrations took place more and more frequently, disturbances among the tribes broke out more often, the native press assumed more and more an opposition character, and the Anglo-Indian bureaucracy, frightened by the growth of the revolutionary movement in the country, took the most brutal repressive measures in order to suppress the movement for which the Russian Revolution and the Russo-Japanese War provided such a mighty impetus. First of all, the English bureaucracy descended upon the press and threw into jail the journalists who dared to raise their voices in defence of the oppressed country. Thus, in 1908 the famous Indian publicist, Tilak, was sentenced to six years in prison for his articles about the regime of terror which reigned in a country oppressed by the English government. At the same time, eight leaders of the national movement were arrested and exiled without trial by administrative order to more or less remote localities. Since that time, as substantiated by English official documents, many Indian journalists and owners of printing shops shared the fate of Tilak and were sentenced to hard labor for printing revolutionary articles. *The law of December 11. 1905, restored the exceptional state of affairs of 1818, introduced into the country by the robber British East India Company, which made it possible for the government of India to throw 130 journalists into jail.* This law destroyed freedom of the press and gave to local administrative authorities the right to confiscate all publications that were suspect.

But all these repressive measures failed to stop the movement: on November 2, 1908, antigovernment demonstrations occurred in various parts of India, in connection with the burning of the body of the Indian, Kanay, the assassin of a policeman; on November 7, there was an attempt on the life of Andrew Fraser, governor-general of Bengal; on November 9, the chief of police was assassinated; on November 25, there was an attempt to kill Omma, the attorney-general in Agarpar; on December 22, there was a second attempt on the life of the same attorney-general; on May 7, 1909, came the end of the notorious trial of the 35 Indians who, in connection with the discovery of bombs in the suburbs of Calcutta, were accused of plotting against the government, in which connection two of the accused were sentenced to death and six to hard labor for life; on June 1, the acquittal by the high court of three Indians in the case of the bomb plot in Midnapur led to a serious disturbance among the ranks of the Anglo-Indian bureaucracy, in the conservative press of the mother country, and among many members of the House of Commons; on June 5, occurred the assassination in Dacca of the Indian, Gobbesh, in connection with the delivery of members of the revolutionary society; on July 1, 1909, came the assassination in London itself of Colonel Sir Curzon Willy by a young Indian, Madar-lal-Dingra; on November 14, 1909, occurred the attempt in Amerabad on the life of the viceroy of India, Lord Minto, and his wife, under whose coach a bomb was thrown; on December 17, there was an attempt in Lahore, also by

a bomb, on the life of the government minister; on December 22,
came the assassination of Jackson, the top English official in Nasik,
in connection with which thirty Brahmins implicated in the plot
were arrested.

And acts of terrorism did not cease in India, but were repeated,
now here, now there. Scarcely a day passed but what the Anglo-
Indian papers published news about disturbances among one tribe
or another, about executions, about numerous arrests, which at
times assumed a mass character. Thus, according to the *Times* of
September 16, 1909, in the province of Patiala alone, 160 men were
arrested in a single day. And such mass arrests were not unusual
in India. Arrests likewise began among the troops. Thus, in January 1909, ten soldiers of the native Calcutta regiment were arrested. According to official information, those arrested joined
the regiment for purposes of propaganda.

China

The Russo-Japanese War and the Russian Revolution gave a
strong impetus to the reform and revolutionary movement in China.

The Russo-Japanese War, 1904-5, with its unexpected results--
the defeat of gigantic, but backward Russia and the brilliant victory
of constitutional Japan--made a strong impression on the ruling
circles of the Middle Empire. In the top bureaucracy around the
throne, there were at that time three well-defined government
parties: the Manchurian reactionary party, headed by Prince Ch'un,
the oldest representative in years of the reigning dynasty; here
were included all the obscurantist, former secret leaders of the
notorious Boxer Rebellion, all the influential Chinese Black Hundreds, etc.; the Manchurian progressive party, which included
Prince Su, Viceroy Tuan Fang, Duke Tsai-tze, and many other
influential Manchurians. This group defended the idea of destroying every barrier between the Manchurians and Chinese, insisted
on the immediate carrying out of other reforms, but pointed out
the well-known necessity for approaching this matter by degrees,
and proposed to begin the business of reform, first of all, with
the reorganization of one province, namely Manchuria. Finally,
there was the government party of the Chinese reformists, which
appeared to be carrying on the cause of Kang Yu-wei, so trag-
ically interrupted in 1898. The chief representatives of this group
were the viceroy of the two "H's" (Hupeh and Hunan), Chang Chih-
tung, viceroy of the Two Kwangs, Tsen Ch'un-hsüan, and many
other bureaucrats of pure Chinese blood. Remaining loyal to the

dynasty, these officials pointed out the necessity of introducing reforms throughout the empire, mainly in the field of education, defended the idea of universal literacy, and the introduction of compulsory military service, etc.

The aspiration for education was the basic feature of Chinese society in the period after the Russo-Japanese War.

In 1904, there were 2,406 Chinese students in Japan; in 1906, there were 8,620; and in 1907, the number already exceeded 10,000. The longing for education assumed an almost spontaneous character after 1905, and in this respect private initiative went far ahead of the government. During the "conference on the plague," German doctors said: "China, in only three or four years, has made such a stride forward intellectually as would have taken other nations several decades."

The reform government, which continued to increase after the Russo-Japanese War in the ranks of the Chinese merchants, progressive officialdom, the professors, etc., also forced the Manchu dynasty to make concessions to "the spirit of the times."

After the Japanese victories of 1904-5, when the awareness of the indispensability of reforms began to develop with particular strength even in the ruling circles of the Middle Empire, the bureaucracy focused its attention on Yuan Shih-Kai as the only statesman who could realize the great cause of the reorganization of the empire, without infringing on the privileges of the Mandarins and the entire ruling clique. Yuan Shih-Kai was not only the viceroy of an important province, he was entrusted with the command of six divisions of the reorganized Northern Army and of the administration of the Ministry of Finance and Communications. *It was precisely in 1905 that Yuan Shih-Kai directed the first great maneuvers in China to which foreign military attachés were invited,* and about which many articles and even brochures were printed in Europe and America. These maneuvers made a great impression in China, which was so much afraid of foreign enemies, and they were greatly instrumental in raising the prestige of Yuan Shih-Kai, even in those circles where he was hated for his participation in the rebellion of 1898. After these maneuvers and the glowing comments on them by European attachés, the influence of Yuan Shih-Kai at the court rose to an unusual degree. At the same time, began the short-lived era of reforms from above. First of all, the government sent to Europe and the United States two special commissions to acquaint themselves with the political structure of various states, constitutional laws, the organization of public education, the army, etc. A decree was issued to abolish torture in connection with judicial inquiry. Moreover, a decree was promulgated concerning the reform of military schools, the introduction of European uniforms for the troops, and new schools were opened in various parts of the empire. Measures were taken to combat the use of opium. For the first time, the word "constitution" began to be mentioned openly in the Chinese press in 1905, and the first imperial decree which dealt with the early introduction of a constitution was announced in September 1906. Meanwhile, the popular discontent in the country became aggravated, and more or less serious disturbances broke out everywhere. The various classes of the population were not content with half measures and demanded the immediate promulgation of a constitution. Finally, *in the spring of 1907 a huge revolt broke out in the six southern provinces.* In Kwantung province alone, a huge army of 60,000 was formed, which engaged in a whole series of battles with the imperial forces. The revolt was crushed; however, the revolutionaries succeeded, in spite of defeat, in concealing weapons and ammunition in secure places. This revolt produced great confusion in government circles and sharpened the struggle between the court party of the reactionaries and the group of "progressive" officials. The terroristic act of November 6, 1907, the assassination by a Chinese, Hsi Lin, of one governor general, who was director of a police school, the armed opposition of the future police to military power, the confession of the director of the school that he belonged to the revolutionary party and took the police post in order to achieve his revolutionary plans more quickly and easily--all this made an unusual impression on all Chinese society and produced unprecedented panic in the highest circles. The frightened Empress immediately summoned Yuan Shih-Kai to court. Again began the comedy of reform. A special decree announced the formation of a new bureaucratic institution--the "Upper Chamber, " "Administrative and Constitutional Control, " which was to draft constitutional laws; a big new mission was dispatched abroad for the study of foreign constitutions; finally, in all the provinces, "provincial diets" were organized. But, due to bribes and graft prevalent among the Chinese mandarins, any new reform served only as a new means of extortion for officials.

At the beginning of 1908 the revolutionary movement, at the head of which was Sun Yat-Sen, doubled in strength, and after a long struggle which dragged on with intermittent success, the Manchu Dynasty was overthrown and the Chinese Republic was proclaimed on 16/29 December, 1911, in Nanking. As provisional president of the republic until its complete establishment throughout the em-

pire, the ideological leader of the Chinese Revolution, the famous
agitator, Dr. Sun Yat-Sen was elected.

World Imperialism in the Struggle with the Awakening East--1905
and the October Revolution in the History of the East

Thus, the Russian Revolution of 1905 was the starting point of a
great liberation movement throughout the East. This movement of
the peoples of the East was strangled by the very same forces that
triumphed temporarily over the Russian Revolution: the alliance
of Tsarism with world imperialism. Just as the international bourgeoisie gave Tsarism an opportunity after 1905 to cope with both
the workers' movement and the opposition in the State Duma, having
supplied the Tsarist government with the necessary financial resources by permitting a loan on the Paris exchange, a loan in the
distribution of which not only the French, but also the English,
Belgian, Dutch, and other banks took part, so the very same international bourgeoisie eventually extended help in his struggle with
the republic to Yuan Shih-Kai, the future dictator of China, the pre-
tender to the throne of the Emperor, by granting the leader of the
Chinese counterrevolution a foreign loan of 25 million pounds sterling.

Having set on its feet a shaky Tsarism, which was tottering as
a result of the Russo-Japanese War and the Russian Revolution,
world imperialism acquired in the gigantic empire an ally for the
struggle against the peoples of the East. The fear of the revolutionary movement in India was much more instrumental than the
fear of Germany in forcing England to agree to a rapprochement
with Russia.

Thus, this great liberation movement of the peoples of the East,
to which the Russian Revolution of 1905 lent such a mighty impetus, was retarded in its development along with the triumph of
reaction in Tsarist Russia. Attacked from the flank by the imperialist powers of Europe and from the rear by Tsarist Russia, the
peoples of the East in their struggle for liberation were forced to
retreat before the onslaught of internal and external reaction in
their own countries. Thus, soon after the triumph of the Persian
constitutional movement, the new Persia was subjected to attack
simultaneously from Russia and England, which signed the notorious agreement of 1907 on the partition of Persia into spheres of
influence between the two powers.

Not confining themselves to the struggle against the Persian constitutional movement, imperialist England and Tsarist Russia like-

wise waged a struggle against the new Turkey. Not wishing to permit the rebirth of this country, England and Russia, with the cooperation of France, armed to the teeth the Balkan states--Bulgaria, Serbia, Montenegro, and Greece, and hurled them against the new Turkey.

The triumph of reaction in Russia, the imperialist plans of England, France, America, and Japan imperiled all the gains of the Chinese Revolution for the period from 1905 to 1912. This revolutionary movement led to the overthrow of the Manchu Dynasty and the proclamation of a republic in China in 1912. But soon Yuan Shih-Kai, head of the counterrevolution, who was energetically supported and subsidized by the world powers, including America, one of whose representatives in China, a professor at Columbia University by the name of Goodnow, was the chief adviser to Yuan Shih-Kai, dissolved Parliament, destroyed all the gains of the revolution and posed the question of the restoration of the monarchy in China.

One of the basic causes which determined both the defeat of the Russian Revolution of 1905 and the temporary defeat of the liberation movement of the peoples of the East, was the lack of serious support for these movements from the working masses of Western Europe, whereas, at the time, the bourgeoisie of the capitalist countries extended the most energetic support to the counterrevolution in Russia and in all the countries of the East to defeat the revolutionary movement.

The general strike, the Moscow armed revolt, the workers' movement in Russia in general, found a response in the East among the oppressed masses of Turkey, Persia, India, and China. *These two mighty streams of the revolutionary movement among the proletarian masses of Russia and the peasant masses of the East were undoubtedly the factors which lay at the basis of the brilliant theory of Lenin about the necessity for the creation of a united front of the industrial proletariat of the advanced industrial states with the enslaved masses of the colonial and semicolonial countries for the struggle against capitalism.*

At the time of the October Revolution the plight of the main countries of the East was profoundly tragic. Turkey after the imperialist war was already on the eve of collapse. Persia, actually divided into two zones of influence between Russia and England, eked out a miserable existence. Afghanistan sighed under the yoke of English capital. China was threatened with complete dismemberment among the members of the victorious Entente.

The triumph of the October Revolution was a turning point in the history of the East. The appeal of the Soviet government to the peoples of the East with a summons to liberation from the chains of European capitalism, the famous theses of Lenin on national and colonial questions adopted at the second congress of the Comintern, the Congress of the Peoples of the East in Baku which followed the Comintern Congress--all this played the role of an alarm bell, calling these peoples to a new struggle against the oppressors. "Peoples of the East, your rear is free. Rise for the struggle. Soviet Russia promises you its aid. "--This was the significance of the summons of the Soviet government and it was this which infused new strength in the tortured peoples. Having from now on a secure rear, freed from the fatal necessity of fighting on two fronts, having encountered since the October Revolution in multimillion, worker-peasant Russia not an enemy but, on the contrary, a friend and an ally of the entire East in the struggle against world imperialism, the oppressed peoples of the yellow and black continents rose with energy tenfold for the struggle against the oppressors. Now the entire colonial and semicolonial world from Agadir (the tiny capital of the little state of the Riffs, which fights successfully against two strong powers) to Canton, Shanghai, and Mukden, represents a united front in the huge revolt of the oppressed peoples against the yoke of world capitalism.

The great October Revolution completed in the history of the East the cause begun by the Revolution of 1905. That is why the twentieth anniversary of the Revolution of 1905 is a holiday not only for the Russian and international proletariat, but likewise a holiday for all the oppressed and exploited peoples of the East; for it was precisely after this Revolution, under the influence of the infectious example of the heroic struggle of the Russian proletariat, that they raised the banner of the struggle against all their oppressors.

II. A MANIFESTO TO THE PEOPLES OF THE EAST
Published in *Kommunisticheskii Internatsional* (Petrograd), II (December 20, 1920), 3141-50.

Peoples of the East

Six years ago, there broke out in Europe a colossal and monstrous carnage, a world war in which 35, 000, 000 human lives were lost, hundreds of big cities and thousands of villages destroyed, European countries devastated, and all the peoples were subjected to the torment of unheard-of poverty and unprecedented starvation.

Up to the present time, this colossal war has been waged in Europe, only partially affecting Asia and Africa.

This war was waged by the European peoples and the peoples of the East took a relatively small part in it: only the forces of hundreds of thousands of Turkish peasants who were deceived by their rulers and led by German capitalists, and from two to three million Indians and Negroes--slaves, bought by English and French capitalists and, as slaves, hurled to death on the far-distant, foreign battlefields of France, in defence of the foreign and to them unintelligible interests of English and French bankers and industrialists.

Although the peoples of the East remained aloof from this gigantic war, although they took only a insignificant part in it, nevertheless, this carnage was waged, not for the countries of Europe, not for the countries and peoples of the West, but for the countries and peoples of the East.

It was waged for the partition of the entire world, and mainly for the partition of Asia, for the partition of the East. It was waged in order to determine who will control the Asiatic countries, whose slaves the peoples of the East will be.

It was waged in order to determine precisely who, the English or the German capitalists, will skin the Turkish, Persian, Egyptian, and Indian peasants and workers.

The monstrous four years of carnage ended in a victory for England and France. The German capitalists were crushed, and along with them the entire German people were likewise crushed, destroyed, and doomed to death by starvation. Victorious France, where the war almost wiped out the entire adult population and destroyed all the industrialized areas, bled in the struggle and after the victory remained completely powerless. And as a result of the colossal, barbaric carnage, imperialist England emerged the sole and all-powerful master of Europe and Asia. She, alone, in all Europe was still able to muster sufficient strength, for she waged the war with foreign hands, with the hands of the peoples she had enslaved, Indians and Negroes, and at the expense of her oppressed colonies.

Having emerged the victor and the complete ruler and master of half the world, the English government began to carry out the objectives for which the war was waged: it began to consolidate its hold on all the Asiatic countries and to bring about the complete enslavement of all the peoples of the East.

With none to interfere and fearing no one, the junta of greedy bankers and capitalists at the head of the English government quite openly and brazenly put aside all shame and began to reduce to slavery the peasants and workers of the countries of the East.

Peoples of the East! You know what England has done in India; you know how she transformed the multimillion masses of Indian peasants and workers into unprivileged and dumb driven beasts.

The Indian peasant is obliged to give up to the English government so much of his crop that the remainder does not suffice him even for a few months. The Indian worker must work in the factory of the English capitalist for such a pittance that he cannot buy with it the handful of rice necessary for his daily subsistence. Millions of Indians die from starvation annually. Every year millions of Indians perish in the swamps and jungles from hard labor, undertaken by the English capitalists for their own enrichment.

Millions of Indians, having failed to obtain their daily bread in their own very rich and fertile native land, are forced to enter the English army and go away, in order to eke out for the rest of their lives a difficult soldier's existence and to wage endless wars in all corners of the world with all the peoples of the world, establishing everywhere ruthless English domination. Buying with their lives and blood an unending increase in wealth for the English capitalists, insuring them huge profits, luxury, and prosperity, the Indians themselves do not enjoy any human rights; the powers that be--the English officers, insolent sons of the English bourgeoisie which grew fat on Indian corpses--do not recognize them as people.

The Indian does not dare to sit at the same table with an Englishman, use the same quarters, travel in the same coach, study in the same school. In the eyes of the English bourgeois, every Indian is a pariah, a slave, a beast of burden, who does not dare to experience any human feelings, does not dare to make any demands. To each uprising brought about by the extremities of the Indian peasants and workers, the English retaliate with ruthless mass shootings. The streets of those Indian villages which revolted are covered with hundreds of corpses and those who remain alive are compelled by the English officers for their own amusement to crawl on their bellies and to lick the boots of their enslavers.

Peoples of the East! You know what England has done to Turkey? England has offered Turkey a peace by which three-fourths of Asia Minor, inhabited exclusively by Ottomans, including all the industrial cities, has gone to France, England, Italy, and Greece; and on the remainder of the Turkish land they have levied such taxes that the Ottomans have become perpetually insolvent, and have to pay tribute forever to England.

When the Turkish people refused to accept such a disastrous

peace, the English occupied Istanbul, sacred to the Muslims, drove out the Turkish Parliament, arrested all the people's leaders, shot the best of them, and exiled hundreds of others to the island of Malta, where they were imprisoned in the dark and damp dungeon of an old fortress. Now the English reign in Constantinople. From the Turks they have taken everything that it was possible to take. They have taken money, banks, factories and foundries, railroads and ships, and have cut off all access to Asia Minor. There is not a piece of material, not a piece of metal in Turkey. The Turkish peasant is forced to go without a shirt and he must plough the land with a wooden plough.

The English, with the aid of the Greek army, occupied the vilayet of Smyrna; with the aid of the French, Adana; and with the colonials, Bursa and Izmit. They have besieged the Turks on every side and are moving steadily into the interior of the country, attempting to bring about the complete exhaustion of the Turkish people, who, even aside from that, have been tormented and devastated by ten uninterrupted wars. And in Turkish areas already occupied by the English, the latter, true to their custom, scoff and jeer intolerably at the Turkish people. In Constantinople they occupied all the schools and universities for their own barracks, they forbade Turkish education, closed up Turkish newspapers, destroyed workers' organizations, filled the jails with Turkish patriots, and handed over the entire population to the uncontrolled jurisdiction of the English police, which regards itself as having the right, without any pretext, and in broad daylight in the streets of Constantinople to club over the head people wearing a fez. To the English bourgeois, one who wears a fez, one who is a Turk, is a creature of the lowest species, a pariah, a slave, who can be treated as a dog.

In Turkish occupied localities, the English indeed treat the Turks like dogs, sending them to forced labor, and punishing them by beating them up with a stick. By every ruse, baseness, and compulsion they strive to transform Turkey into a conquered country and to compel the Turkish people's masses to work for their enrichment.

Peoples of the East! What has England done to Persia? Having suppressed the peasant uprising against the Shah and the landowners, having shot and hanged thousands upon thousands of Persian peasants, the English capitalists have again restored the power of the Shah and the landowners who had been overthrown by the people, they have deprived the peasants of the landowners' lands which they had seized, and have again reduced them to the status of slaves, have again reduced them to *rayahs* and unprivileged slaves of the *mülkadars*.

And then, having bribed the Shah's corrupt government, the English capitalists, by means of a base and treacherous treaty, obtained complete ownership of all Persia, with the entire Persian people. They have seized all Persian wealth, stationed in all Persian cities garrisons composed of deceived Indians and Sepoys, bought into slavery, and they have begun to run Persia as a conquered country, treating the independent (in name) Persian people as a people reduced to serfdom.

Peoples of the East! What has England done to Mesopotamia and Arabia? Without any ado, she declared these independent Muslim countries to be her own colonies, drove from the land the former owners, the Arabs, deprived them of the best fertile valleys of the Tigris and Euphrates, deprived them of the best pastures indispensable to subsistence, took away the richest oil resources of Mosul and Basra, and thus depriving the Arabs of all means of subsistence, counted on starvation to make them her slaves.

What has England done to Palestine, where, at first, to please the Anglo-Jewish capitalists, she drove the Arabs from their lands in order to transfer these lands to the Jewish settlers, and then in order to provide an outlet for the discontent of the Arabs, she turned them against the very Jewish settlements she had established, sowing discord, hostility, and resentment among the various tribes, weakening both sides, in order to rule and govern herself?

What has England done to Egypt, where the entire native population already for the eighth decade is sighing under the heavy yoke of the English capitalists, a yoke even heavier and more ruinous for the people than the past yoke of the Egyptian pharaohs, who with the labor of their slaves built the huge pyramids?

What has England done to China? This enormous country she, together with her partner, imperialistic Japan, transformed into her own colony, exploiting and poisoning with opium the 300,000,000 people; and with the aid of her own and Japanese forces, she suppresses with unheard of atrocities the revolutionary ferment which is beginning. By restoring the old despots overthrown by the people, she tries with all her strength to hold the multimillion people under the yoke of despotism, oppression, and poverty, in order to exploit them more successfully.

What has England done to Korea, to this flourishing country with its thousand years of culture? She handed her over to be devoured by Japanese capitalists, who now by fire and sword subjugate the Korean people to English and Japanese capital.

What has England done to Afghanistan where, by bribing the

Emir's government, she holds the people in oppression, poverty, and ignorance, trying to make this country into something resembling a desert, and by means of this desert to fence in India, which she has oppressed, from any contact with the outside world?

What is England doing in Armenia and Georgia where, with her gold, she holds the masses of peasants and workers under the yoke of the hated and corrupt Dashnak and Menshevik governments which terrorize and oppress their own peoples and drive them to fight against the peoples of Azerbaijan and Russia, liberated from the yoke of the bourgeoisie?

Even into Turkestan, Khiva, Bokhara, Azerbaijan, Daghestan, and the Northern Caucasus, English imperialism penetrates, its agents poke their noses into everything, distribute with a generous hand English gold obtained with the blood and sweat of oppressed peoples, and everywhere they try to support tyrants and despots, khans and landlords, to fight the budding revolutionary movement, and to hold at any cost all the peoples in oppression, ruin, poverty, and ignorance.

The oppression and ruination, poverty and ignorance of the peoples of the East serve as sources of enrichment for imperialist England.

Peoples of the East! To you belong the richest, the most fertile, the most extensive lands of the entire world; these lands, once the cradle of all mankind, could feed not only their own inhabitants, but also the population of the whole world; nevertheless, every year 10,000,000 Turkish and Persian peasants and workers now find for themselves neither a crust of bread nor employment on their own most fertile and spacious lands, and are compelled to leave their native land and to seek subsistence in foreign countries.

They are forced to do that because in their native land everything--lands, money, banks, factories, and shops--all these are in the hands of the English capitalists. They are compelled to do that because in their native country they are not the masters and do not dare to give any orders; on the contrary, the foreigners-- the English capitalists--give them orders. Such was the situation formerly, such it was prior to the war, when imperialist England still had rivals in the rapacious German, French, and Russian imperialists, when she did not yet dare to clamp her paws on all the countries of the East, fearing that she might receive a blow on her extended paws from some rapacious rival.

But now, when imperialist England has crushed and weakened all her rivals, when she has become the complete master of Europe and Asia, now her ruling capitalists will give way to all their wolfish appetites and without restraint, without shame, will sink their rapacious fangs and claws into the bleeding body of the peoples of the East.

English capital is cramped in Europe, it has grown, it lacks opportunity, and European workers, enlightened by revolutionary consciousness, likewise become bad slaves; already they refuse to work for nothing, they demand good wages, good food. In order that capital may have elbow room, may produce a good profit, and may be able to throw a sop to the European workers to impede the growth of their revolutionary mood, in order that it may be able to bribe the top leaders of the working masses, English capital needs new lands and new workers--unprivileged and unenfranchised slaves.

And English capitalists have found these new lands in the Eastern countries, and the unprivileged and unenfranchised slave workers among the peoples of the East.

The English capitalists are trying to seize Turkey and Persia, Mesopotamia and Arabia, Afghanistan and Egypt, in order to take away the land from the peasants in these countries, by buying for a mere trifle all the plots of those who are ruined and deeply in debt; out of these plots they purchased they intend to create huge estates and plantations, and to drive the landless Eastern peasants onto them as farm hands and slaves. In Turkey, Persia, and Mesopotamia they want, by means of cheap labor, with the unpaid hands of the hungry Turkish, Persian, and Arab poor, to construct factories and foundries, to build railroads, and to work the mines. They want, by means of cheap production of factory products, to destroy native trades and millions of local craftsmen with whom the cities of the East are teeming, to throw them into the street, depriving them of work. By establishing huge firms, they want to ruin the small local merchants and to throw them likewise into the street, into the ranks of the proletariat who sell only their labor.

The English capitalists want to proletarianize in toto all the peoples of the East, to ruin the economy of all the peasants, of all the craftsmen, of all the merchants, and to drive them onto their plantations and into their factories, foundries, and mines, as starving slave laborers. Thereafter, by back-bending labor, by starvation wages, they want to squeeze from these enslaved Eastern peoples both sweat and blood. And to turn this labor sweat, this peasant blood, into increased value, into profit, into pure gold, into hard cash.

This is the kind of future imperialist England has in store for the peoples of the East!

England, with a population of barely forty millions, of which only one-fortieth constitutes a group of oppressors and exploiters, and the remaining 39 million belong to the oppressed and exploited workers and peasants, wants to dominate half the world, wants to hold in serfdom 800 million toilers living in the East. One English bourgeois capitalist, who already compels 39 English workers to work for him, likewise wants to force 2000 more workers and peasants from Persia, Turkey, Mesopotamia, India, and Egypt to work for him. Two thousand and forty hungry and tortured people who enjoy none of the blessings of life, must toil all their lives for one do-nothing parasite--an English capitalist. One million such parasites and exploiters, English bankers and industrialists, want to reduce to serfdom 800 million proletarians of the East! And it should be said that they know how to achieve their goal, they have neither shame, conscience, nor fear, they have nothing but savage greed and unlimited thirst for gain. Ruin, hunger, blood, torment, the sighs of 800 million people, mean nothing to them. All that counts is profit, all that counts is gain.

And, in pursuit of this profit and gain, the English imperialists have a tenacious grip on the throat of the peoples of the East, and prepare for them a dark future: complete ruin, eternal slavery, no rights, oppression, and unlimited exploitation. That is what is in store for the peoples of the East, if the present English government retains its power, if imperialist England retains its strength and consolidates its domination over the countries of the East. A pitiful handful of English bankers will devour hundreds of millions of peasants and workers of the East.

But this shall not happen!

Before the English capitalists, the rulers of imperialist England, rises the organized might of the peasants and workers of the peoples of the East, united under the red banner of the Communist International, under the red banner of the union of revolutionary workers, who have set as their goal the liberation of the entire world, of all mankind from any exploitation and any oppression.

The first Congress of the Peoples of the East throughout the whole world loudly proclaims to the capitalists who rule England:

--This shall not happen!

You dogs shall not devour the peoples of the East, your pitiful handful of oppressors shall not reduce to eternal serfdom hundreds of millions of Eastern peasants and workers! You have grabbed too big a slice, you have bitten off more than you can chew, and it will choke you.

The peoples of the East have long stagnated in darkness and ignorance under the despotic yoke of their own rulers and tyrants, under the yoke of foreign conquerors and capitalists. But the roar of the world carnage, the thunder of the Russian workers' revolution, which has cast off from the eastern Russian people the century-old chains of capitalist serfdom, has awakened them, and now, aroused from the sleep of many centuries, they are rising.

They wake up and hear a call to a holy war, to a *"gazovat."* This is our call!

This is the appeal of the first Congress of the Representatives of the Peoples of the East, united with the revolutionary proletariat of the West under the banner of the Communist International.

It is we--the representatives of the toiling masses of all the peoples of the East--India, Turkey, Persia, Egypt, Afghanistan, Baluchistan, Kashgar, China, Indo-China, Japan, Korea, Georgia, Armenia, Azerbaijan, Daghestan, North Caucasus, Arabia, Mesopotamia, Syria, Palestine, Khiva, Bokhara, Turkestan, Fergan, Tamaria, Bashkiria, Kirghizia, etc., united in an unbreakable union among ourselves and with the revolutionary workers of the West--we summon our peoples to a holy war.

We say:

Peoples of the East! Many times you have heard from your governments the summons to a holy war, you marched under the green banner of the Prophet; but all these holy wars were deceitful and false, and served the interests of your selfish rulers; but you, peasants and workers, even after these wars remained in serfdom and destitution; you won the blessings of life for others, but you yourselves never enjoyed any of them.

Now we summon you to the first genuine holy war under the red banner of the Communist International.

We summon you to a holy war for your own welfare, for your freedom, for your life.

England, the last mighty imperialist robber remaining in Europe, spreads over the Muslim countries of the East her black wings, trying to reduce the peoples of the East to her slaves and her prey.

Slavery, appalling slavery, ruination, oppression, and exploitation, she brings to the peoples of the East. Save yourselves, then, peoples of the East!

Rise, then, for the struggle against this plunderer!

Rise, all of you, as one man, for a *holy war* against the English conquerors!

Arise, Indian, exhausted by starvation and heavy slave labor!

Arise, Anatolian peasant, crushed by taxes and usurers!

Arise, Persian *rayah*, choked by the *mülkadar!*

Arise Armenian toiler, driven into the barren mountains!

Arise, Arabs and Afghans, lost in the sandy deserts and cut off by the English from the entire world!

Arise, all of you, for the struggle against the common enemy--imperialist England!

High waves the red banner of the holy war. . . .

This is a holy war for the liberation of the peoples of the East, so that mankind shall no longer be divided into oppressors and oppressed, for the complete equality of all peoples and tribes, irrespective of the language they speak, irrespective of the color of their skin, no matter what religion they confess!

A holy war to put an end to the division of countries into progressive and backward, dependent and independent, mother countries and colonies!

A holy war for the liberation of all mankind from the yoke of capitalist and imperialist slavery, for the elimination of any oppression of people by people and any exploitation of man by man!

A holy war against the last citadel of capitalism and imperialism in Europe, against the nest of robbers on sea and land, against the eternal oppressor of all the peoples of the East, against imperialist England!

A holy war for the freedom, independence, and happiness of all the peoples of the East, all the millions of peasants and workers enslaved by England!

Peoples of the East! In this holy war, all the revolutionary workers and all the oppressed peasants of the West will be with you. They will help you. They will fight and die with you.

It is the first Congress of the Representatives of the Peoples of the East that speaks to you.

Long live the union of all the peasants and workers of the East and the West, the union of all the toilers, of all the oppressed and exploited!

Long live its militant staff--the Communist International!

May the holy war of the Peoples of the East and the toilers of the whole world burn with unquenchable fire against imperialist England!

Honorary Members of the Presidium

Radek (Russia), Bela-Kun (Hungary), Rosmer (France), Quelch (England), Reed (America), Steinhart-Gruber (Austria), Janson (Holland), Shablin (Balkan Federation), Yoshiharo (Japan).

Zinoviev, Chairman of the Congress

Members of the Presidium:

Ryskulov, Abdurashidov, Karriev (Turkestan), Mustafa, Subhi (Turkey), Van (China), Karid (India), Mulabekdzhan, Rakhmanov

(Khiva), Mukhamedov (Bokhara), Korkmasov (Daghestan), Digurov
(Terek Region), Aliev (Northern Caucasus), Kostanyan (Armenia),
Narimanov (Azerbaijan), Yenikeyev (Tatar Republic), Amur-Sanan
(Kalmyk Republic), Makharadze (Georgia), Haidar Khan (Persia),
Aga-Zade (Afghanistan), Narbutabekov (Tashkent), Makhmudov
(Fergan), Takhsim-Baarri, Khaavis-Mahomed (Anatolia), Kuleyev
(Transcaspia), Niyas-Kuli (Turkmenia), Kari-Tadzhi (Samarkand),
Nazyr-Sedyki (India), Sidadzhedin, Kardash-Ogly (Daghestan),
Yelchiev, Musayev (Azerbaijan), Azim (Afghanistan), Abdulayev
(Khiva).

Ostrovsky, Secretary of the Congress*

III. THE EISENHOWER DOCTRINE ON THE MIDDLE EAST

Proposed by the President to Congress, January 5, 1957. Passed
by Congress, with some amendments, as the *Joint Resolution to
Promote Peace and Stability in the Middle East,* and signed by the
President, March 9, 1957.

Resolved by the Senate and House of Representatives of the United
States of America in Congress assembled,

That the President be and hereby is authorized to cooperate with
and assist any nation or group of nations in the general area of the
Middle East desiring such assistance in the development of economic strength dedicated to the maintenance of national independence.

Section 2. The President is authorized to undertake, in the general area of the Middle East, military assistance programs with
any nation or group of nations of that area desiring such assistance. Furthermore, the United States regards as vital to the national interest and world peace the preservation of the independence
and integrity of the nations of the Middle East. To this end, if the
President determines the necessity thereof, the United States is
prepared to use armed forces to assist any such nation or group
of such nations requesting assistance against armed aggression
from any country controlled by international communism: *Provided,*

---

*The Baku Congress approved in principle the issuing of this Mani-
festo to the Peoples of the East, the text of which was not presented
to the delegates or included in the official records of the Congress.
It leaves no room for doubt as to the real fate in store for Islam under Communist domination.

That such employment shall be consonant with the treaty obligations of the United States and with the Constitution of the United States.

Section 3. The President is hereby authorized to use during the balance of fiscal year 1957 for economic and military assistance under this joint resolution not to exceed $200, 000, 000 from any appropriation now available for carrying out the provisions of the Mutual Security Act of 1954, as amended, in accord with the provisions of such Act: *Provided,* That, whenever the President determines it to be important to the security of the United States, such use may be under the authority of section 401 (a) of the Mutual Security Act of 1954, as amended (except that the provisions of section 105 (a) thereof shall not be waived), and without regard to the provisions of section 105 of the Mutual Security Appropriation Act, 1957: *Provided further,* That obligations incurred in carrying out the purposes of the first sentence of section 2 of this joint resolution shall be paid only out of appropriations for military assistance, and obligations incurred in carrying out the purposes of the first section of this joint resolution shall be paid only of appropriations other than those for military assistance. This authorization is in addition to other existing authorizations with respect to the use of such appropriations. None of the additional authorization contained in this section shall be used until fifteen days after the Committee on Foreign Relations of the Senate, the Committee on Foreign Affairs of the House of Representatives, the Committees on Appropriations of the Senate and the House of Representatives and, when military assistance is involved, the Committees on Armed Services of the Senate and the House of Representatives have been furnished a report showing the object of the proposed use, the country for the benefit of which such use is intended, and the particular appropriation or appropriations for carrying out the provisions of the Mutual Security Act of 1954, as amended, from which the funds are proposed to be derived: *Provided,* That funds available under this section during the balance of fiscal year 1957 shall, in the case of any such report submitted during the last fifteen days of the fiscal year, remain available for use under this section for the purposes stated in such report for a period of twenty days following the date of submission of such report. Nothing contained in this joint resolution shall be construed as itself authorizing the appropriation of additional funds for the purpose of carrying out the provisions of the first section or of the first sentence of section 2 of this joint resolution.

Section 4. The President should continue to furnish facilities and military assistance, within the provisions of applicable law and es-

tablished policies, to the United Nations Emergency Force in the
Middle East, with a view to maintaining the truce in that region.

Section 5. The President shall within the months of January and
July of each year report to the Congress his action hereunder.

Section 6. This joint resolution shall expire when the President
shall determine that the peace and security of the nations in the
general area of the Middle East are reasonably assured by international conditions created by action of the United Nations or otherwise except that it may be determined earlier by a concurrent
resolution of the two Houses of Congress.

IV. JOINT SOVIET-CHINESE DECLARATION, JANUARY 18, 1957

Section (2), Pertaining to the Near and Middle East.

Both sides [the U.S.S.R. and the People's Republic of China]
note that since England, France and Israel suffered defeat in their
aggression against Egypt, American imperialism is trying to make
use of the situation in order to take the place of the colonialist
powers--England and France--in the Near and Middle East, to suppress the movement for national independence and to enslave the
peoples of these countries, and is also striving to step up the policy of aggression and war preparations in this area.

This is precisely the essence of the so-called "Eisenhower Doctrine." This colonialist policy of the United States in the Near and
Middle East creates new tensions in this area, which was recently
the arena of hostilities caused by the aggression against Egypt.

The governments of the Soviet Union and the People's Republic
of China resolutely condemn this policy of the United States and
are ready to continue rendering the necessary support to the peoples of the Near and Middle East so as to prevent aggression and
interference in the affairs of the countries of this area.

With the object of completely eliminating the consequences of
imperialist aggression in Egypt, both governments hold that it is
essential to satisfy the Egyptian government's legitimate demands
for complete compensation by England, France and Israel for the
damage caused by their aggressive acts.

Both governments resolutely oppose any imperialist machinations aimed at placing the Suez Canal under "international control"
and stand for the settlement of the question of free navigation
through the Suez Canal by way of negotiations among the countries
concerned, on the basis of complete respect for the sovereignty of
Egypt.

The governments of the Soviet Union and China fully support the countries and nations of Asia, Africa and Latin America in their efforts to struggle against colonialism, to defend and consolidate their national independence, sovereignty and freedom, to achieve industrial development and economic independence.

In the struggle against war, against colonialism, and in defence of world peace, the Socialist states and the nationally independent countries can achieve complete cooperation in conformity with the five principles of peaceful coexistence.

The facts show that such sincere cooperation has already played an important part in contemporary international affairs. The friendly cooperation of the Socialist countries with states that have won their national independence is not only in accord with their mutual national interests, but also with the interests of world peace.

Signed by: N. A. Bulganin
Chou En-lai

Notes

Chapter 1

1. See "The Tale of the Taking of the Empire of Kazan" (in Russian), *Anthology of Old Russian Literature*, ed. Ad. Stender-Petersen (New York: Columbia University Press, 1954), pp. 258-78.

2. See also George Vernadsky, *Kievan Russia* (New Haven: Yale University Press, 1948), p. 15.

3. See M. V. Fekhner, *Torgovlya russkogo gosudarstva so stranami Vostoka v xvi veke* (Moscow, 1952), pp. 137-38. For relations between Russia and the Near and Middle East prior to the sixteenth century, see B. M. Dantsing, "Iz istorii russkikh puteshestvii i izutchenia Blizhnego Vostoka v dopetrovskoi rusi," *Otcherki po istorii russkogo vostokovedenia* (Moscow: Akademiya Nauk, SSSR, 1953), pp. 185-231.

4. For an account of early Russian clashes with Muslims, especially in the Caucasus in the tenth century, see V. V. Bartold, "Arabskie Izvestiya o Rusakh," *Sovetskoe Vostokovedenie* (Leningrad-Moscow: AN, SSSR), I (1940), 31-32.

5. George Vernadsky, *A History of Russia* (New Haven: Yale University Press, 1930), p. 97.

6. Dominique Maroger (ed.), *The Memoirs of Catherine the Great* (London, 1955), p. 363.

7. See *P. A. Rumyantsev*, ed. P. K. Fortunatov (Moscow: AN, SSSR, 1953), Vol. II, *1768-75*.

8. Wm. Person, "The Russian Occupation of Beirut, 1772-1774," *Royal Central Asian Journal*, XLII (July-October, 1955), 283.

9. See Ivar Spector, *An Introduction to Russian History and Culture* (2nd ed.; New York, 1954), pp. 101-2.

10. See Philip E. Mosely, *Russian Diplomacy and the Opening of the Eastern Question in 1838 and 1839* (Cambridge, Mass.: Harvard University Press, 1934), pp. 22-23.

11. See, however, Harold Temperley, *England and the Near East: The Crimea* (London, 1936), especially chapters x-xiv.

12. G. Chicherin, "Rossiya i Aziatskie Narody," *Vestnik Narodnogo Komissariata Inostrannykh Del* (Moscow), No. 2 (August 13, 1919), p. 1.

13. See Academician V. P. Potemkin (ed.), *Istoriya Diplomatii* (Moscow, 1945), II, 30-39.

14. F. M. Dostoyevsky, "Once Again on the Subject that Constantinople, Sooner or Later, Must be Ours," *Diary of a Writer, 1877, Complete Works* (in Russian) (St. Petersburg, 1895), XI, 73-85.

15. Cited in Anatole Leroy-Beaulieu, *The Empire of the Tsars and the Russians* (New York and London, 1905), I, 238-39.

16. I. V. Lenin, *Sotchineniia* (4th ed.; Leningrad, 1950), XXXI, 11.

17. L. S. Sobotsinsky, *Persiya, Statistiko-Ekonomitcheskii Otcherk* (St. Petersburg, 1913), p. 289. See also A. M. Pankratova (ed.), *Pervaya russkaya revolyutsia i mezhdunarodnoe revolyutsionnoe dvizhenie* (Moscow, 1956), Part II, p. 284.

18. E. Bor-Ramensky, "K voprosu o roli bol'shevikov zakavkaz'ia v iranskoi revoliutsii, 1905-1911 godov," *Istorik-Marksist,* No. 11 (1940), p. 95. See also, *Krasnyi Arkhiv,* 2(105) (1941), pp. 33-70.

19. "Zhurnal Osobogo Soveshchaniya 14 Aprelya, 1907 g. po afghanskomu voprosu," *Krasnyi Arkhiv,* II-III (1935), 3-39. See also G. Chicherin, *op. cit.,* pp. 6-7.

20. See also chapter 9 for the cultural impact of the Revolution of 1905 in the Near and Middle East.

21. Jung Meng-Yüan, "Kitaiskaya pressa 1905 g. o russkoi revolyutsii," *Voprosy Istorii,* No. 6 (June, 1955), pp. 98-104. See also A. Ivin, "Kitaiskaya revolyutsia 1911 goda," *Krasnyi Arkhiv,* V (18) (1926), 49-53; T. Mandalyan, "Ot russkogo k Kitaiskomu Oktyabryu," *Krasnyi Internatsional Prophosoyuzov,* Nos. 8-9 (79-80) (1927), pp. 418-23; G. B. Erenburg, *Revolyutsia 1905-1907 godov v Rossii i revolyutsionnoye dvizhenie v Kitaye* (Seria I, No. 44, Moscow: Znanie, 1955).

22. See A. Krakovetsky, "Vostotchnyi Vopros," *Mezhdunarodnaya Zhizn',* No. 17 (135) (December 31, 1922), pp. 14-15.

23. See E. B. Price, *The Russo-Japanese Treaties of 1907-1916 Concerning Manchuria and Mongolia* (Baltimore, 1933). See also B. Nikolayevsky, "Sovetsko-Yaponskoe soglashenie 1925 goda," *Novyi Zhurnal* (New York), V (1943), 198-201.

24. M. Pavlovitch, "Zadatchi Vserossiiskoi Nautchnoi Assotsiatsii Vostokovedeniya," *Novyi Vostok,* I-II, No. 1 (1922), 4.

Chapter 2

1. *The Russian Review,* XIV, No. 2 (April, 1955), 118-20.

2. The sixteen regions, with their administrative centers, were: the Caucasus (Baku), the Crimea (Simferopol), Moscow-St. Petersburg (St. Petersburg), Lithuania (Minsk), the Lower Volga (Astrakhan), the Upper Volga (Kazan), Ufa (Ufa), Orenburg (Orenburg), Turkestan (Tashkent), Siberia (Irkutsk), the Steppe (Uralsk), Omsk (Omsk), Semipalatinsk (Semipalatinsk), Semiretchensk (Vernyi), Akmolinsk (Petropavlovsk), and the Transcaspian (Ashkhabad). See I. D. Kuznetsov, *et al.,* "Musul'manskoe dvizhenie v period revolyutsii i reaktsii," *Natsional'nye*

dvizheniya v period pervoi revolyutsii v Rossii (Tcheboksary, 1935), pp. 215-76.

3. Alexander Tamarin, *Musul'mane na Rusi* (Moscow, 1917), No. 52, pp. 5-6.

4. See E. D. Sokol, *The Revolt of 1916 in Russian Central Asia* (Baltimore: Johns Hopkins University Press, 1954).

5. Joseph Stalin, "The International Character of the October Revolution," *Pravda,* November 6-7, 1927. For the English translation, see J. Stalin, *The October Revolution* (New York, 1934), p. 159.

6. *Ibid.,* p. 161.

7. There has been considerable discrepancy in regard to the dating of this "Appeal." Kluchnikov and Sabanin dated it November 24 O.S. (December 7 N.S.). Jane Degras *(Soviet Documents on Foreign Policy* [London: Oxford University Press, 1951], I, 15) uses December 3, 1917. Some Soviet writers use December 3 and others resort to December 7. Actually, the document was published in *Izvestia TSIK i Petrogradskogo Soveta Rabotchikh i Soldatskikh Deputatov,* No. 232, November 22 O.S. (December 5 N.S.), 1917, pp. 2-3.

8. I. V. Kluchnikov and A. Sabanin (eds.), *Mezhdunarodnaya Politika noveishego vremeni v dogovorakh, notakh i deklaratsiakh* (Moscow, 1925-28), II, 94-96. See also Degras, *op. cit.,* I, 15-17.

9. See I. D. Kuznetsov, *et al., op. cit.,* p. 225. See also, A. Arsharuni and Kh. Gabidullin, *Otcherki Panslavizma i Panturkizma v Rossii* (Moscow, 1931), pp. 35-38.

10. See Sokol, *op. cit.*

11. See Richard Pipes, *The Formation of the Soviet Union* (Cambridge, Mass.: Harvard University Press, 1954), pp. 75-79.

12. See I. Levin and E. Drabkin, *Revolyutsia i Natsionalnyi Vopros* (Moscow, 1930), III, 294.

13. See Vasan-Girei Dzhabagi, "Sovetskii Soyuz i Islam," *Vestnik Instituta po izucheniyu istorii i kultury SSSR,* No. 3 (10) (1954), p. 45. See also François de Romainville, *L'Islam et l'URSS* (Paris, 1947), p. 89; and Professor Barakatullah, *Bolshevism in the Koran* (in Persian, Afghan, and Arabic), n.d.

14. Kluchnikov and Sabanin, *op. cit.,* II, 420.

15. *Izvestia Petrogradskago Soveta Rabotchikh Deputatov,* No. 84, June 6, 1917.

16. Pipes, *op. cit.,* p. 49.

17. Translated into English in J. Stalin, *The October Revolution,* p. 67.

18. See "Natsionalnye i Kolonialnye Voprosy," *Petrogradskaya Pravda,* July 28, 1920.

19. See the speech of Comrade Sultan-Zade, *ibid.,* July 30, 1920.

20. Pavlovitch, "Zadachi Vserossiiskoi Nauchnoi Assotsiatsii Vostokovedeniya," p. 11.

21. *Ibid.,* p. 9.

22. M. Pavlovitch, "Oktyabrskaya Revolyutsia i Vostochnyi Vopros,"
Novyi Vostok, XVI (1926), 3.

Chapter 3
1. The First (Socialist) International, known as the International
Workingmen's Association, was organized in London in 1864 and dissolved in New York in 1876. Its primary purpose was economic, the object being to improve the lot of the workers. The Second International,
or the World's Labor and Socialist parties, was more political in nature
than its predecessor. Moreover, it was admittedly pacifist and advocat-
ed that workers, in the event of war, should strike and refuse to fight.
The Second International collapsed when it failed to avert the war of
1914-18. The Third (Communist) International, 1919-43, was a casualty
of World War II, at which time it became clear that the workers of Germany and her satellites not only participated in the invasion of the
U.S.S.R. but committed atrocities there such as no capitalist nation
had ever perpetrated. What is usually termed a Fourth International was
formed abroad by the followers of Trotsky who became bitter enemies
of the Stalin program in the Soviet Union. In October, 1947, after relations between the Soviet Union and her allies in World War II had seriously deteriorated, Moscow proclaimed the existence of the Cominform, comprised of nine states within the Soviet orbit, most of them
Slavic. (See Spector, *An Introduction to Russian History and Culture,*
p. 296.)
2. Kuznetsov, *et al.,* "Priglashenie na Vsemusul'manskii Kongress,
Fevral' 1908," *op. cit.,* p. 242.
3. See *The Second Congress of the Communist International as Reported and Interpreted by the Official Newspapers of Soviet Russia,
Petrograd-Moscow, July 19-August 7, 1920* (Washington, D.C.: Government Printing Office, 1920). The translation is inadequate and sometimes inaccurate.
4. See *Pervyi S'ezd Narodov Vostoka, Baku, 1-8 September 1920
(Stenografitcheskie otchety)*(Petrograd, 1920).
5. *Ibid.,* p. 17.
6. Quoted in Olaf Caroe, *Soviet Empire: The Turks of Central Asia
and Stalinism* (London and New York, 1953), pp. 112-13, from Togan's
Bugunku Turkili, p. 403.
7. M. Pavlovitch, "Lenin i Narody Vostoka," *Novyi Vostok,* No. 5
(1924), p. 4.
8. J. Stalin, "K Postanovke Natsionalnogo Voprosa," *Sotchinenia,*
V, 53 *(Pravda,* May 8, 1921).
9. Pak Dinshun, "Revolyutsionnyi Vostok i Otcherednye Voprosy
Kommunistitcheskogo Internatsionala," *Petrogradskaya Pravda,* July
27, 1920.
10. See Yu. Steklov, "Novyi Mir," *Moskovskie Izvestia,* August 11,
1920.

11. *Pervyi S'ezd Narodov Vostoka,* pp. 224-25.

12. *Ibid.,* pp. 192-93.

13. N. A. Smirnov, *Otcherki Izutcheniya Islama v SSSR* (Moscow, 1954), p. 133. See also Lenin, *Works,* XXIX, 151; and J. V. Stalin, *Works,* IV, 361-62.

14. K. Troyanovsky, *Vostok i Revolyutsia* (Moscow, 1918), p. 42.

15. The liquidation of the Caliphate in Turkey took place in March, 1924. See *Izvestia,* March 6, 1924. The presence in Baku of Enver Pasha, a leading foe of Kemal Pasha, did not improve relations with the Turks, and it antagonized the Armenians, who regarded him as an instigator of the Armenian massacres. For further information on this episode, see E. H. Carr, *The Bolshevik Revolution, 1917-1923* (New York, 1953), III, 264-65.

16. See also Vasan-Girei Dzhabagi, *op. cit.,* p. 48; also N. S. Fatemi, *Diplomatic History of Persia, 1917-1923* (New York, 1952), p. 175.

17. *Kommunistitcheskii Internatsional.* See especially, No. 14, November 6, 1920. The manifestoes were published here, rather than in the stenographic record.

18. See the record of its early activity in *ibid.,* No. 15, December 20, 1920.

19. See *Pervyi sezd revolutsionnykh organizatsii Dalnego Vostoka* (Petrograd, 1922). For a summation in English of this congress, see Xenia Joukoff Eudin and Robert C. North, *Soviet Russia and the East, 1920-1927: A Documentary Survey* (Stanford, Cal.: Stanford University Press, 1957), pp. 145-47; 221-31.

20. I. P. Plyshevsky, "Konferentsiya stran Azii i Afriki v Bandunge," *Sovetskoe Vostokovedenie,* No. 3 (1955), pp. 36-45. See also George McTurnan Kahin, *The Asian-African Conference, Bandung, Indonesia, April 1955* (Ithaca, N.Y.: Cornell University Press, 1956), pp. 16, 54.

21. The funeral ceremony for the twenty-six Baku commissars, whose bodies had just been returned to Baku after being put to death by the "Whites," allegedly at the instigation of the English, caused a sensation in Baku. To commemorate the fortieth anniversary of the October Revolution, the Azerbaijanian poet, Suleiman Rustam, promised to write a poem in 1957 on the twenty-six Baku commissars. See also V. A. Gurko-Kryazhin, "Bakinsky protsess i istoriya 26 komissarov," *Novyi Vostok,* XIII-XIV, (1926), 179-84; and Mamed Kaziev, "Bessmertnye rytsari revolyutsii," *Sovetskaya Kultura,* Sept. 20, 1958.

Chapter 4

1. Yu. Steklov, "Turetskaya Revolyutsiya," *Izvestia,* April 23, 1919.

2. J. Stalin, *Sotchineniya,* V, 37. Stalin then looked forward to a general front of enslaved nations from Ireland to India.

3. See above, p. 26.

4. M. Pavlovitch, *Revolyutsionnaya Turtsiya* (Moscow, 1921), p. 57.

5. See A. F. Miller, *Otcherki Noveishei Istorii Turtsii* (Moscow-Leningrad: AN, SSSR, 1948), p. 78.

6. *Ibid.*, pp. 78-83. See also, A. Novitchev, "Antikrestyanskaya Politika Kemalistov v 1919-1922 godakh, " *Voprosy Istorii*, No. 9 (September, 1951), pp. 56-75.

7. Miller, *Otcherki Noveishei Istorii Turtsii*, p. 103.

8. See Novitchev, *op. cit.*, pp. 59-65, 72. At Baku, Subhi accused the Turkish pashas of selling the country to England. He and his friends openly organized the Turks in Baku to fight for the revolution in Turkey. The official Turkish representative in Moscow, however, said that the Turks "did not stand in need of men, but only of weapons and ammunition. " See *Sbornik Pamyati M. Subhi*, published in Moscow (in Turkish) in 1923 (microfilm in the Hoover Library, Stanford University, Stanford, Cal.).

9. See Miller, *Otcherki Noveishei Istorii Turtsii*, p. 105. See also *Noveishaya Istoria Stran Zarubezhnogo Vostoka* (Moscow: Moscow University, 1954), I *(1918-29)*, 283; and General Ali Fuat Cebesoy, *Millî Mücadele Hâtiralari* (Istanbul, 1953), pp. 506-22.

10. Novitchev, *op. cit.*, p. 60. Novitchev also includes material on the Green Army. See also, Pavlovitch, *Revolyutsionnaya Turtsiya*, p. 108. Pavlovitch admitted that the last chapter of this book on the Communist position in Turkey was written in Baku on the basis of personal conversations with many Turkish comrades and on material distributed by the Emigré Bureau of the Turkish Communist party and its head, Ismail Hakki (p. 5).

11. Kluchnikov and Sabanin, *op. cit.*, II, No. 197, 384-87. English translation in Degras, *op. cit.*, I, 164-67.

12. *A Speech Delivered by Ghazi Mustapha Kemal, President of the Turkish Republic, October 1927* (Leipzig, 1929), pp. 414-15.

13. Even by the end of 1918, Entente forces in Turkey were estimated as follows: English--41,500, French--49,000, and Italian--17,000. The figures were taken from Turkish sources by A. M. Shamsutdinov, "Natsional'no-osvoboditel'naya bor'ba turetskogo naroda v 1919-1922 gg. , " *Sovestskoe Vostokovedenie*, II (1956), 59.

14. *A Speech Delivered by Ghazi Mustapha Kemal*, p. 396.

15. Miller, *Otcherki Noveishei Istorii Turtsii*, p. 96. This note was not included in Kluchnikov and Sabanin. See also M. Tanin, *Mezhdunarodnaya Politika SSSR, 1917-1924* (Moscow, 1925), pp. 78-89.

16. See *Die Welt des Islams*, XVI (1934), 28.

17. Kluchnikov and Sabanin, *op. cit.*, I, Part III, 26-27. Dègras, *op. cit.*, I, 187-88.

18. "Diplomatitcheskie Otnosheniya SSSR, " *Diplomatitcheskii Slovar* (Moscow, 1948), I, 566; see also, A. F. Miller, "From the History of Soviet-Turkish Relations, " *International Affairs* (Moscow, February, 1956), p. 57; and *Izvestia* (editorial), June 3, 1958.

19. *A Speech Delivered by Ghazi Mustapha Kemal*, p. 396; see also,

P. Vostokov ("L'U.R.S.S. et le Proche-Orient," *Le Monde Slave* [May, 1937], pp. 353-78), who attributes the delay to General Wrangel's temporary successes in South Russia and to Kemal's preoccupation with the liquidation of unrest in Anatolia. See also General Ali Fuat Cebesoy, *Moskova Hatiralari* (Istanbul, 1955).

20. *Bulleten Narodnogo Kommissariata Inostrannykh Del*, No. 31 (September 15, 1920), p. 30, quoted from *Le Temps*, July 24, 1920. General Cebesoy stated in Istanbul in 1958 that he had never seen this particular telegram. It was his understanding, and that of his close associate, Rauf Orbay, that the Soviets sometimes changed the wording of such messages. In all probability, he said, the message was simply intended to convey the idea that, irrespective of the differences between Islam and communism, the two countries were working toward a common goal--the defeat of the English and the French.

21. *Bulleten Narodnogo Kommissariata Inostrannykh Del*, No. 37 (October 21, 1920), p. 85, quoted from the Turkish newspaper, *Istikbal*, September 1, 1920. See also, *Bulleten Narodnogo Kommissariata Inostrannykh Del*, No. 6 (124) (May 10, 1922), pp. 47-48.

22. Kluchnikov and Sabanin, *op. cit.*, I, Part III, 27-28. See N. Rubinstein, *Vneshniaya Politika Sovetskogo Gosudarstva v 1921-1925 gg.* (Moscow, 1953), pp. 61-62.

23. Stalin, "Polozhenie na Kavkaze," *Sotchineniya*, IV, 408-12. Also in *Pravda*, December 4, 1920.

24. Rubinstein, *Vneshniaya Politika Sovetskogo Gosudarstva v 1921-1925*, p. 61.

25. See Novitchev, *op. cit.*, pp. 56-75.

26. Pavlovitch, *Revolyutsionnaya Turtsiya*, pp. 108-23.

27. *A Speech Delivered by Ghazi Mustapha Kemal*, p. 524.

28. Quoted in N. Rubinstein, *Sovetskaya Rossiya i Kapitalistitcheskie Gosudarstva v Gody Perekhoda ot Voiny k Miru (1921-1922 gg.)* (Moscow, 1948), p. 68.

29. *Ibid.*

30. *Moskovskaya Pravda*, March 1, 1921.

31. See text in Degras, *op. cit.*, I, 237-42.

32. See George Lenczowski, *The Middle East in World Affairs* (Ithaca, N.Y.: Cornell University Press, 1952), p. 106.

33. M. V. Frunze, *Sobranie Sotchinenii*, ed. A. S. Bubnov (Moscow-Leningrad, 1929), I *(1905-23)*, 355-61. In his speech before the Sovnarkom and TSIK of the Ukraine, Frunze claimed that the most important military secrets of the Turkish armies were revealed to him, so that he felt he knew almost as much about the Turkish armed forces as he did about those of the Ukraine.

34. Rubinstein, *Vneshniaya Politika Sovetskogo Gosudarstva 1921-1925*, p. 73.

35. Miller, *Otcherki Noveishei Istorii Turtsii*, p. 114.

36. Donald Everett Webster, *The Turkey of Ataturk: Social Process in the Turkish Reformation* (Philadelphia, 1939), p. 93.

37. Louis Fischer, *The Soviets in World Affairs* (2nd ed.; Princeton, N.J.: Princeton University Press, 1951), I, 391, 393, 394.
38. Frunze, *op. cit.*, I, 281-82, 614.
39. Fischer, *op. cit.*, I, xv.
40. Novitchev, *op. cit.*, pp. 71-72.
41. See also the protest of the Moscow workers to the Turkish government on the persecution of Communists in Turkey, *Izvestia*, February 18, 1923.
42. "A New Stage in the Near East," *Izvestia*, November 21, 1922. See also, Pavlovitch, *Revolyutsionnaya Turtsiya*, pp. 106-8.
43. *Izvestia*, August 17, 1922.
44. Pavlovitch, *Revolyutsionnaya Turtsiya*, p. 111.
45. Kluchnikov and Sabanin, *op. cit.*, I, Part III, No. 107, 203-5.
46. G. Chicherin, "Lozanskaya Konferentsiya i Mirovoe Polozhenie," *Mezhdunarodnaya Zhizn* (Moscow), No. 2 (1923), pp. 3-5.

Chapter 5

1. Since 1935 Persia has been known officially as Iran.
2. Troyanovsky, *op. cit.*, pp. 47-48.
3. See Harold Nicolson, *Curzon: The Last Phase, 1919-1925* (London, 1934), pp. 119-48.
4. See Iranskii, "Russko-Persidskie Otnosheniya za Pyat Let," *Novyi Vostok*, III, No. 3 (1923), 94.
5. *Ibid.*
6. Degras, *op. cit.*, I, 54.
7. L. Trotsky, *Sotchineniya*, III (2), 251. English translation in Degras, *op. cit.*, I, 28-29.
8. Kluchnikov and Sabanin, *op. cit.*, II, p. 343.
9. Nicolson, *op. cit.*, pp. 128-29.
10. *Diplomatitcheskii Slovar*, II, 808-9.
11. Speech of Sultan-Zade, *Petrogradskaya Pravda*, July 30, 1920.
12. See *Noveishaya Istoriya Stran Zarubezhnogo Vostoka* (Moscow: Moscow University, 1954), I *(1918-29)*, 256. See also "Pervyi S'ezd persidskikh Kommunistov partii 'Adalyat,'" *Kommunistitcheskii Internatsional* (Petrograd), II, No. 14 (Nov. 6, 1920), 2889-92.
13. Major-General L. C. Dunsterville, "Military Mission to North-West Persia 1918," *Journal of the Royal Central Asian Society*, VIII, Part II (1921), 83.
14. *Noveishaya Istoriya Stran Zarubezhnogo Vostoka*, I, 242-53. See also Fatemi, *op. cit.*, pp. 217-43, on "The Soviet Government of Gilan"; and George Lenczowski, *Russia and the West in Iran, 1918-1948: A Study in Big-Power Rivalry* (Ithaca, N.Y.: Cornell University Press, 1949), chap. iii.
15. *Noveishaya Istoriya Stran Zarubezhnogo Vostoka*, I, 249.
16. *Diplomatitcheskii Slovar*, II, 603.
17. See Fischer, *op. cit.*, pp. i, xvi.

18. I. I. Korobeinikov, *Iran: Ekonomika i Vneshniaia Torgovlya* (Moscow, 1954), p. 10.

19. I. Levin, "Sredne-Aziatskie sovetskie respubliki i ikh mezhdunarodnoe znachenie," *Revolyutsia i Natsional'nosti*, No. 12 (58) (December, 1934), p. 4. See also, A. B. Bashkirov, *Ekspansia angliiskikh i amerikanskikh imperialistov v Irane, 1941-1953* (Moscow, 1954), pp. 15-27.

20. Helen Miller Davis, *Constitutions, Electoral Laws, Treaties of States in the Near and Middle East* (2nd ed.; Durham: Duke University Press, 1953), pp. 131-41.

21. *Ibid.*

22. *Privetstviya XIX S'ezdu Communistitcheskoi Partii Sovetskogo Souza ot Zarubezhnykh Kommunistitcheskikh i Rabotchikh Partii* (Moscow, 1952), pp. 114-15. See also Korobeinikov, *op. cit.*, p. 109.

23. Such as the *waqf* lands, previously confiscated for the benefit of the state, which were returned to the Muslims; the religious schools were reopened; the Shariat courts were brought back; and the NEP permitted the return of private trade. See Pipes, *op. cit.*, p. 259.

24. *Ezhegodnik Kominterna,* 1923 (copy in the Hoover Library, Stanford University), pp. 34, 71.

25. Karl Radek, *Vneshniaia Politika Sovetskoi Rossii* (Moscow-Petrograd, 1923), p. 74.

26. The First Afghan War occurred 1830-40. After sustaining losses of thirty thousand men out of an army of fifty-four thousand, the English were forced to withdraw from Afghanistan. See P. Botchkarev, *Afganistan* (Moscow, 1935), pp. 25-27.

27. "Sovetsko-Afganskie Dogovory i Soglasheniya," *Diplomaticheskii Slovar,* II, 694.

28. J. Stalin, "Marxism i Natsionalno-Kolonialnyi Vopros," *Sbornik izbrannykh statei i rechei* (Partizdat TSK VKP [b], 1936), p. 147. See also M. G. Reiser, *Afganistan* (Moscow, 1946), p. 27.

For a laudatory recognition of Amanullah Khan's reforms, expressed in genuine Near Eastern style, see Burkhan-ud-Din-Khan-i-Kushkeki, *Kattagan i Badakhshan* (Tashkent, 1926), pp. 1-3.

29. Fischer, *op. cit.*, I, 286. The letter was shown to Fischer from the Soviet State Archives.

30. See I. Maisky, *Vneshnyaya Politika RSFSR, 1917-1922* (Moscow, 1922), p. 147.

31. *Diplomatitcheskii Slovar,* II, 694.

32. Quoted in Rubinstein, *Sovetskaya Rossiya i Kapitalistitcheskie Gosudarstva, 1921-1922,* p. 63.

33. *RSFSR: Sbornik Deistvuyushchikh Dogovorov,* II, No. 44 (1921), 15-17. For the English version, see Degras, *op. cit.*, I, 233-37.

34. See British Blue Book, *A Selection of Papers Dealing with the Relations between His Majesty's Government and the Soviet Government, 1921-7* (London, 1927).

35. *Noveishaya Istoriya Stran Zarubezhnogo Vostoka,* I, 227.

36. See M. N. , "Pod Znakom Islama," *Novyi Vostok,* IV (1923), 72-97; S. B. Ginzburg, "Basmatchestvo V Fergane," *Novyi Vostok,* X-XI (1925), 175-202; and Vasilevsky, "Fazy basmatcheskogo dvizhenia v Srednei Azii," *Novyi Vostok,* XXIX (1930), 126-41.

Chapter 6

1. "Egipet pod Pyatoi Angliiskogo Imperializma," *Bolshevik,* No. 10 (May 31, 1928), pp. 56-57.
2. J. Stalin, "Ob Osnovakh Leninizma" (1924), *Sotchineniya,* IV (Moscow, 1947), 144.
3. *Ibid.,* VII, 71-72.
4. *Vostok i Revolyutsiya,* pp. 43-44.
5. See G. S. Akopian, *Borba Narodov Blizhnego i Srednego Vostoka za Natsionalnuyu Nezavisimost i Mir* (Series 1, Nos. 35-36 [Moscow, 1953]), p. 27.
6. Akhmet-Dzhevat, "The Communist Movement in Turkey," *Pravda,* October 26, 1922.
7. Gamal Abdel Nasser, *Egypt's Liberation* (Washington, D.C., 1955), pp. 39-40.
8. "For the Successful Struggle for Peace, National Independence, and Democracy We Must Resolutely Turn Toward the Workers and the Peasants," abr. trans. from the Arabic by Harold W. Glidden, *The Middle East Journal,* VII, No. 2 (Spring, 1953), 206-21.

Chapter 7

1. Borodin was arrested by the Soviet government in February, 1949, and died in an eastern Siberian prison camp in 1953.
2. *Voprosy Istorii,* No. 9 (September, 1954), p. 173.
3. See Potyomkin (ed.), *Istoriya Diplomatii,* III, 571.
4. A. F. Miller, *Turtsiya i Problema Prolivov* (Moscow, 1947), p. 19: see also I. Vasilyev, *O Turetskom "Neitralitete" vo Vtoroi Mirovoi Voine* (1951), especially pp. 66-71.
5. For the English text, see Davis, *op. cit.,* pp. 523-26.
6. A. F. Miller, *Otcherki Noveishei Istorii Turtsii,* pp. 184-85. Clause VII of the Saadabad Pact, obviously aimed at communism, provided: "Each of the High Contracting Parties agrees to take measures within its own sphere, against the formation or activities of armed bands, associations or organizations for the subversion of established institutions with a view to the disturbance of the order or security of any part, frontier or otherwise, of the territory of the other Party, or with a view to the disturbance of the authority of the Government of that other Party." (Davis, *op. cit.,* p. 525).
7. M. V. Popov, "Krakh Gitlerovskogo Plana Napadeniya na SSSR iz Irana," *Utchenye Zapiski Instituta Vostokovedeniya* (Moscow), VIII (1953), 7-14.
8. See especially, Paul Schmitz, *Moskau und die islamische Welt* (Munich, 1938), p. 58.

9. *Ibid.*, p. 12.

10. Korobeinikov, *op. cit.*, p. 114.

11. See Sh. F. Mukhamadyarov, "The History of the Partition of Central Asia into National States," *Sovetskoe Vostokovedenie*, No. 1 (1955), p. 52. See also A. K. Borovkov, "K Voprosu ob unifikatsii tyurskikh alfavitov v SSSR," *ibid.*, No. 4 (1956), pp. 101-10.

12. See Vincent Monteil, "Supplément à l'essai sur l'Islam en URSS," *Revue des Études Islamiques*, XXXI (1953), 1-36. See also *Statistitcheskii Ejegodnik Rossii* (January, 1914), pp. 41-74.

13. *L'Islam et L'URSS* (Paris, 1947), p. 7.

14. Levin and Drabkin, *op. cit.*, p. 287.

15. Richard Pipes, "Russian Moslems before and after the Revolution," *Soviet Imperialism: Its Origins and Tactics*, ed. W. Gurian (Notre Dame, Ind.: University of Notre Dame Press, 1955).

16. Vincent Monteil, *Essai sur l'Islam en URSS* (Extrait de la *Revue des Études Islamiques*, 1952 [Paris, 1953]), p. 126.

17. See A. Benningsen, "The Muslim Peoples of the Soviet Union and the Soviets," *The Islamic Review* (April, May, June, 1955).

Chapter 8

1. R. J. Sontag and J. S. Beddie (eds.), *Nazi-Soviet Relations, 1939-1941* (New York, 1948), pp. 258-59.

2. *Vneshniaia Politika Sovetskogo Soyuza v Period Otetchestvennoi Voiny* (Moscow, 1946), I, 150-57.

3. See Lenczowski, *Russia and the West in Iran, 1918-1948*, pp. 193-234.

4. See *The Study and Tactics of Communism* (House Committee on Foreign Affairs, report of subcommittee No. 5, Supplement 2, Official Protests of the United States Government against Communist Policies or Actions, and Related Correspondence, July 1945-December 1947 [Washington, D.C. 1948]), pp. 32-36.

5. See Robert Rossow, Jr., "The Battle of Azerbaijan, 1946," *The Middle East Journal*, X, No. 1 (Winter, 1956), 17-32.

6. Necmeddin Sadak, "Turkey Faces the Soviets," *Foreign Affairs* (April, 1949), p. 457.

7. See *Pravda*, March 27, 1947.

8. Summed up in *Izvestia*, August 13, 1946.

9. George Kirk, *The Middle East in the War (Survey of International Affairs, 1939-1946*, Vol. II [London: Oxford University Press, 1952]), pp. 464-66; George Kirk, *The Middle East, 1945-1950*, pp. 21 ff; and Sadak, "Turkey Faces the Soviets," *op. cit.*

10. See *The Study and Tactics of Communism*, pp. 90-94.

11. A. F. Miller, *Otcherki Noveishei Istorii Turtsii*, p. 228.

12. Sudan became a sovereign state on January 1, 1956. On March 24, the Soviet government appointed career diplomat Leonid Teploy to be its first ambassador to the new Sudanese republic. For official Soviet opinion about this new state, see *Izvestia*, January 5, 1956.

13. For a geographical appraisal, see W. A. Douglas Jackson, "The Virgin and Idle Lands of Western Siberia and Northern Kazakhstan: A Geographical Appraisal," *The Geographic Review*, XLVI, No. 1 (January, 1956), 1-19.

14. See especially, *Pravda*, February 6, 1956.

15. See especially, S. Kondrashov, "Manevry Storonnikov Bagdadskogo Pakta v Irane," *Izvestia*, January 18, 1956.

16. See *Moslems in China* (in Chinese, Arabic, and English), ed. the China Islamic Association (Peking, 1953).

17. See *Mission d'Ollone, 1906-1909: Recherches sur les Musulmans Chinois* (Paris, 1911).

18. *Atlas of Islamic History*, compiled by Harry W. Hazard (Princeton, N.J.: Princeton University Press, 1952), p. 42.

19. For immediate Soviet reaction to the Eden-Eisenhower talks, see *Pravda*, February 3, and especially February 5, 1956.

20. M. Pavlovitch, *Revoliutsionnyi Vostok*, p. 12.

21. See *Torgovye Otnosheniya SSSR so Stranami Vostoka* (Moscow: Nautchno-Issledovatel'skii Institut Monopolii Vneshnei Torgovli, 1938), p. 22.

22. See *Foreign Assistance Activities of the Communist Bloc and Their Implications for the United States*, a study prepared for the Special Committee to Study the Foreign Aid Program, United States Senate, by the Council for Economic and Industry Research, Inc., Study No. 8 (Washington, D.C., 1957). See also *Technical Assistance, Final Report of the Committee on Foreign Relations, United States Senate* (No. 139, including Staff Study No. 3, "Soviet Technical Assistance in Non-Communist Asia, June 10, 1955, pp. 235-67, and Staff Study No. 7, "Soviet Technical Assistance, July 12, 1956," pp. 399-462 [Washington, D.C., 1957]).

23. Exceptions to this general rule have been the Bulganin-Khrushchev presentation of a hundred-bed hospital to the Afghans and fifteen buses to the city of Kabul in December, 1955; also the gift to Pakistan of twenty thousand tons of wheat and twenty thousand tons of rice for the flood victims of East Pakistan in May, 1956.

24. *The Sino-Soviet Economic Offensive in the Less Developed Countries* (Department of State Publication, No. 6632 [Washington, D.C., 1958]).

Chapter 9

1. *Pravda*, May 15, 1943. The celebration, scheduled for 1941, was interrupted by the invasion of the Soviet Union.

2. See Ivar Spector, "The Russians Conquer Marx," *The Saturday Review*, January 31, 1953.

3. See Smirnov, *op. cit.*, p. 53.

4. *Soviet Literature*, No. 4 (1954).

5. Smirnov, *op. cit.*, pp. 71-72.

6. See K. Zelinsky, "Gor'kovskie Traditsii," *Oktyabr*, No. 3 (1955), p. 164.

7. S. G. Areshyan, "Gorkii i Literatury Vostoka," *Sovetskoe Vostokovedenie* (Moscow-Leningrad: Institut Vostokovedeniya, AN SSSR), III (1945), 181.

8. For a brief survey of Persian literature, including Russia's contribution to the study of it, see Arthur J. Arberry, "Islamic Literature: Persian," *Near Eastern Culture and Society*, ed. T. Cuyler Young (Princeton, N.J.: Princeton University Press, 1951), pp. 66-82.

9. See Z. G. Fil'shtinskaya, "Maksim Gor'kii Sovremennoi Progressivnoi Persidskoi Literature," *Kratkie Soobshcheniya Instituta Vostokovedeniya* (Moscow: AN SSSR, 1952), IV, 45-51.

10. Kerim Keshavarz, "Chekhov in Iran," *VOKS Bulletin*, No. 3(86) (1954), pp. 67-68.

11. "Earliest Foreign Translations from Gogol," *ibid.*, No. 73 (1952), p. 9.

12. Areshyan, *op. cit.*, pp. 177-82. See also, I. Y. Kratchkovsky, "Otzvuki Revolyutsii 1905 g. v Arabskoi Khudozhestvennoi Literature," *Sovetskoe Vostokovedenie*, III (1945), pp. 5-14.

13. Translated into Russian by I. Y. Kratchkovsky.

14. A. F. Sultanov, "Egipetskaya Literatura na Novom Etape," *Izvestia AN SSSR, Otdelenie Literatury i Yazyka* (Moscow), XIV, No. 1 (1955), 70.

15. *Ibid.*, p. 67.

16. *Ibid.*, p. 70.

17. I. Y. Kratchkovsky, *Among Arabic Manuscripts*, trans. Tatiana Minorsky (Leiden, 1953), pp. 54-56. A six-volume edition of Kratchkovsky's selected works is in process of publication in the U.S.S.R., after which his Russian translation of the *Koran* will appear. See Prof. V. B. Lutsky, "Arabic Studies in the U.S.S.R.," *VOKS Bulletin*, No. 2 (97) (February, 1956), pp. 12-16.

18. *Ibid.*, p. 58.

19. V. Borisov, "Novye Veyaniya v Arabskoi Literature," *Novyi Mir*, XXX, No. 5 (May, 1954), 266-69.

20. Jamal Farouk El-Sharif, "We and Russian Literature" (in Arabic), *Al-Itha'atu al-suriatu*, No. 16 (1953), p. 16.

21. Kh. M. Tsovikyan, "Vliyanie Russkoi Revolyutsii 1905 g. na Revolyutsionnoe Dvizhenie v Turtsii," *Sovetskoe Vostokovedenie*, III (1945), 15-35.

22. "Publication of Fiction in the U.S.S.R.," *Soviet Literature*, No. 11 (1954), p. 208. Six works of Ali Sabahattin were translated into two Soviet languages. In 1953 S. Oustoungel's *In Jail and in "Freedom,"* which is illegal in Turkey, was rendered into Russian.

23. V. A. Gordlevskii, "Slovo o Nazyme Hikmete"; R. G. Fish, "O Ryadovom Geroe"; and A. A. Babayev, "Borets za Mir, Demokratiyu i Natsional'nuyu Nezavisimost' Turetskogo Naroda," *Kratkie Soobshcheniya Instituta Vostokovedeniya* (Moscow, 1952), pp. 3-18.

24. Nevill Barbour, "Broadcasting to the Arab World," *The Middle East Journal,* V (Winter, 1951), 57-69; and Moshe Leshem, "Soviet Propaganda in the Middle East," *ibid.,* IV, No. 1 (January, 1953), 1-10.

25. See his article, "Bright Prospects," *New Times,* No. 2 (1956).

26. See *Literaturnaya Gazeta,* October 4, 13, 18, and 27, 1956. Articles by Dr. Mandur were published in this official organ of the Soviet writers on November 3, and December 11, 1956.

27. See A. Belov, "Tsennyi vklad v arabskoe yazykoznanie," *Literaturnaya Gazeta,* October 11, 1956.

28. See "Egypt-Syria-Lebanon," *News,* No. 20 (1956), for an interview with Sergei Kaftanov. See also, *Sovetskaya Kultura,* October 25, 1956.

29. "S'ezd v Damaske," *Novyi Mir,* No. 1 (1957), pp. 246-49.

30. B. B. Piotrovskii, "Poezdka sovetskikh arkheologov i etnografov v Egipet," *Vestnik AN, SSSR,* No. 9 (1956), pp. 67-70.

31. See A. Kh. Rafikov, "Nautchnye i kul'turnye svyazi so stranami zarubezhnogo vostoka," *ibid.,* No. 2 (1956), pp. 136-38.

32. See his article, "V bibliotekakh Kairi i Aleksandrii," *ibid.,* No. 11 (1956), pp. 83-85.

33. For a Soviet review of the film, see *Literaturnaya Gazeta,* February 25, 1956.

34. See the *New York Times,* January 23, 1957.

35. See Georges Ketman, 'Du Papier et des Fèves--Portrait de l'intelligentsia egyptienne," *Preuves* (January, 1957), p. 22.

36. *Pravda,* January 21, 1957.

37. See her article in *Literaturnaya Gazeta,* October 6, 1956.

38. See *Literaturnaya Gazeta,* June 26 and 28, 1956.

39. *Vestnik AN, SSSR,* No. 11 (1956), pp. 104-5.

40. See *Pravda,* February 9, 17, 1957; *Izvestia,* February 16, 1957.

Bibliography

I. Books in Languages Other Than Russian

al-Najjar, Hussein Fawzi. *Middle East Policy and Strategy* (in Arabic). Cairo, 1954.

Atiyah, Edward. *A Study in Loyalties* (in Arabic).

Ben-Gurion, David. *Rebirth and Destiny of Israel.* New York, 1953.

Bolitho, Hector. *Jinnah--Creator of Pakistan.* London, 1954.

Brainwood, R. J. *The Near East and the Foundation for Civilization.* 1952.

Byroade, H. A. *The Middle East.* Washington, D.C.: Government Printing Office, 1954.

Campbelle, John C. *Defense of the Middle East-Problems of American Policy.* New York, 1958.

Caroe, Olaf. *Soviet Empire: The Turks of Central Asia and Stalinism.* London-New York, 1953.

Carr, E. H. *The Bolshevik Revolution.* 3 vols. New York, 1951-53.

Cebesoy, General Ali Fuat. *Millî Mücadele Hatiralari,* Vol. I (1953); *Moskova Hatiralari,* Vol. II (1955); Vol. III, Istanbul, 1956.

Chicherin, George. *The Foreign Policy of Soviet Russia.* London, 1919.

Davis, H. M. (ed.). *Constitutions, Electoral Laws, Treaties of States in the Near and Middle East.* Rev. ed. Durham, N.C.: Duke University Press, 1953.

The Development of United States Policy in the Near East, 1945-1951. Washington, D.C.: Government Printing Office, 1952.

Eels, W. C. *Communism in Education in Asia, Africa, and the Far Pacific.* Washington, D.C., 1954.

El Sadat, Anwar. *Revolt on the Nile.* New York, 1957.

Eudin, X. J. and North, R. C. *Soviet Russia and the East, 1920-1927: A Documentary Survey.* Stanford, Cal.: Stanford University Press, 1957.

Farrukh, Omar A. *The Arab Genius in Science and Philosophy.* Washington, D.C., 1954.

Fatemi, N. S. *Diplomatic History of Persia, 1917-1923.* New York, 1952.

316

Gaudefroy-Demombynes, Maurice. *Muslim Institutions*. London, 1954.
Goitein, S. D. *Jews and Arabs--Their Contacts through the Ages*. New York, 1955.
Guillaume, Alfred. *Islam* (A Pelican Book). Harmondsworth, Middlesex, England, 1954.
Hall, Harvey. *The Evolution of Public Responsibility in the Middle East*. Washington, D.C., 1955.
Hitti, Philip K. *History of the Arabs*. 5th ed. London, 1953.
--------. *Lebanon in History from the Earliest Times to the Present*. London-New York, 1957.
Hollingworth, Clare. *The Arabs and the West*. London, 1952.
Hoskins, Halford L. *The Middle East*. New York, 1954.
Hostler, Charles W. *Turkism and the Soviets*. New York, 1957.
Hurewitz, J. C. *Diplomacy in the Near and Middle East*, Vols. I-II. Princeton, N.J., 1956.
--------. *Middle East Dilemmas*. New York, 1956.
Izzeddin, Nejla. *The Arab World*. Chicago, 1953.
Kahin, G. McTurnan. *The Asian-African Conference, Bandung, Indonesia, April 1955*. Ithaca, N.Y.: Cornell University Press, 1956.
Khadduri, M., and Liebesny, H. J. *Law in the Middle East*. Washington, D.C., 1955.
Kirk, George. *The Middle East in the War*. (*Survey of International Affairs, 1939-1946.*) New York-London: Oxford University Press, 1952.
--------. *The Middle East 1946-1950*. (*Survey of International Affairs, 1939-1946.*) New York-London: Oxford University Press, 1954.
--------. *A Short History of the Middle East*. New York, 1955.
Lacoste, Raymond. *La Russie sovietique et la question d'Orient*. Paris, 1946.
Laqueur, Walter Z. *Communism and Nationalism in the Middle East*. 2nd ed. New York, 1957.
--------. (ed.) *The Middle East in Transition*. London-New York, 1958.
Leaders of the Imperialist Gangs (in Arabic). Cairo, 1954.
Lenczowski, George. *Russia and the West in Iran, 1918-1948*. Ithaca, N.Y.: Cornell University Press, 1949.
--------. *The Middle East in World Affairs*. Ithaca, N.Y.: Cornell University Press, 1956.
Lewis, B. *The Arabs in History*. London, 1950.
Lobanov-Rostovsky, A. *Russia and Asia*. Ann Arbor: University of Michigan, 1951.
Luknitsky, Pavel. *Soviet Tajikistan*. Moscow, 1954.
The Middle East--A Political and Economic Survey. 2nd ed. London: Royal Institute of International Affairs, 1954.
Monteil, Vincent. *Essai sur l'Islam en U.R.S.S.* Paris, 1953.
--------. "Supplément à l'essai sur l'Islam en U.R.S.S.," *Revue des Études Islamiques*, XXI (1953), 1-36.

Morrison, S. H. *Middle East Tensions: Political, Social, and Religious*. New York, 1954.
Naguib, Mohammed. *Egypt's Destiny*. New York, 1955.
Nasser, Gamal Abdel. *Egypt's Liberation*. Washington, D.C., 1955.
Nuseibeh, Hazem Zaki. *The Ideas of Arab Nationalism*. Ithaca, N.Y.: Cornell University Press, 1956.
Park, Alexander G. *Bolshevism in Turkestan, 1917-1927*. New York: Columbia University Press, 1957.
Peretz, Don. *Israel and the Palestine Arabs*. Washington, D.C., 1958.
Philby, H. St. John. *Sa'udi Arabia*. London, 1955.
Pipes, Richard. *The Formation of the Soviet Union*. Cambridge, Mass.: Harvard University Press, 1954.
Price, M. Philips. *A History of Turkey: From Empire to Republic*. New York, 1956.
Ramsaur, Ernest E., Jr. *The Young Turks: Prelude to the Revolution of 1908*. Princeton, N.J.: Princeton University Press, 1957.
Romainville, François de. *L'Islam et l'U.R.S.S.* Paris, 1947.
Sand, William (ed.). *Tensions in the Middle East*. Washington, D.C., 1956.
Sarkisyanz, Emanuel. *Russland und der Messianismus des Orients*. Tübingen, 1955.
Sayegh, Fayez A. *Arab Unity: Hope and Fulfillment*. New York, 1958.
Schmitz, Paul. *Moskau und die Islamische Welt*. Munich, 1938.
Shakir, Amin. *The Truth About Communism* (in Arabic). Cairo, 1955.
The Sino-Soviet Economic Offensive in the Less Developed Countries. (Department of State Publication 6632.) Washington, D.C.: Government Printing Office, 1958.
Smith, W. C. *Islam in Modern History*. Princeton, N.J.: Princeton University Press, 1957.
Sokol, E. D. *The Revolt of 1916 in Russian Central Asia*. Baltimore: Johns Hopkins University Press, 1954.
Sukhanov, N. N. *The Russian Revolution, 1917*. New York-London: Oxford University Press, 1955.
Sumner, B. H. *Peter the Great and the Ottoman Empire*. New York-London: Oxford University Press, 1949.
Tensions in the Middle East (Composite). Washington, D.C.: The Middle East Institute, 1956.
Totah, Kahil. *Dynamite in the Middle East*. New York, 1955.
Voss, Carl H. *The Palestine Problem Today*. Boston, 1953.
Weizmann, Chaim. *Trial and Error*. New York: Harper and Brothers, 1949.
Yalman, A. E. *Turkey in My Time*. Norman, Okla.: Oklahoma University Press, 1956.
Young, T. Cuyler. *Near Eastern Culture and Society*. Princeton, N.J.: Princeton University Press, 1951.
Zander, Walter. *Soviet Jewry, Palestine, and the West*. London: V. Gollancz, 1947.

Zeine, Zeine N. *Arab-Turkish Relations and the Emergence of Arab Nationalism*. Beirut, 1958.

II. Books in Russian

Akopian, G. S. *Bor'ba Narodov Blizhnego i Srednego Vostoka za Natsional'nuyu Nezavisimost' i Mir*. Moscow, 1953.

Bashkirov, A. V. *Ekspansiya Angliiskikh i Amerikanskikh Imperialistov v Irane*. Moscow, 1954.

Deborin, G. A. *Sovetskaya Vneshniaia Politika v Pervye Gody Sushchestvovaniya Sovetskogo Gosudarstva, 1917-1920 gg*. Moscow, 1951.

Korobeinikov, I. I. *Iran: Ekonomika i Vneshniaia Torgovlya*. Moscow, 1954.

Kratchkovsky, I. Y. *Otcherki po Istorii Russkoi Arabistiki*. Moscow-Leningrad: A.N., SSSR, 1950.

Kriazhin, V. A. *Natsional'no-Osvoboditel'noe Dvizhenie na Blizhnem Vostoke*, Vol. I, *Siria i Palestina, Kilikia, Mesopotamia i Egipet*. Moscow, 1923.

Lenin i Vostok. Sbornik Statei, 2nd ed. Moscow, 1925.

Levin, I. *Podgotovka Voiny na Arabskom Vostoke*. Moscow, 1946.

Lutsky, V. B. *Angliiskii i Amerikanskii Imperializm na Blizhnem Vostoke*. Moscow, 1948.

-------. *Pervaya russkaya revolyutsia i mezhdunarodnoe revolyutsionnoe dvizhenie*, Part II. Moscow, 1956.

Miller, A. F. *Otcherki Noveishei Istorii Turtsii*. Moscow, 1948.

Milogradov, P. V. *Arabskii Vostok v Mezhdunarodnykh Otnosheniyakh*. Moscow, 1946.

Olderogge, D. A. and I. I. Potekhin (eds.). *Narody Afriki*. Moscow: A.N., SSSR, 1954.

Pavlovitch, M. (M. Veltman). *Revolyutsionnyi Vostok*. Moscow-Leningrad, 1927.

Radek, Karl. *Vneshniaia Politika Sovetskoi Rossii*. Moscow-Petrograd, 1923.

Reisner, I. M. and N. M. Goldberg. *Otcherki po Novoi Istorii Stran Srednego Vostoka*. Vol. I, *India, Afghanistan, Iran*. Moscow, 1951.

Reisner, I. M. and B. K. Rubtsov (eds.). *Noveishaya Istoria Stran Zarubezhnogo Vostoka*. Vol. I, *1918-1929*. Moscow: Moscow University, 1954.

Rubinstein, Nikolai L. *Vneshniaia Politika Sovetskogo Gosudarstva v 1921-1925*. Moscow: Gospolitizdat, 1953.

Safarov, G. *Problemy Vostoka*. Petrograd, 1922.

Smirnov, N. A. *Otcherki Izutcheniya Islama v SSSR*. Moscow: A.N., SSSR, 1954.

Strany Blizhnego i Srednego Vostoka. Moscow: Ogiz, 1944.

Sultan-Galiev, M. *Metody Antireligioznoi Propagandy Sredi Musul'man*. Moscow, 1922.

Troyanovsky, K. *Vostok i Revolyutsiya*. Moscow, 1918.

Vasiliev, I. *O Turetskom 'Neitralitete' vo Vtoroi Mirovoi Voine.* Moscow, 1951.

III. Articles in Russian

KSIV   *Kratkie Soobshcheniya Instituta Vostokovedeniya*
IAN   *Izvestiya Akademii Nauk*
SV   *Sovetskoe Vostokovedenie*
AN   *Akademiya Nauk*
M Zh   *Mezhdunarodnaya Zhizn*

Antonov, K. A. "Otcherki po Novoi Istorii Stran Srednego Vostoka (India, Afghanistan, Iran)," *IAN* (istoriya i fil.), VIII, No. 5 (1951).
Areshyan, S. G. "Gorky i Literatury Vostoka," *SV,* III (1945), 177-82.
Babayev, A. A. "Boretz za Mir, Demokratiyu i Natsional'nuyu Nezavisimost Turetskogo Naroda," *KSIV, AN, SSSR* (Moscow), II (1952), 13-18.
Barannikov, A. P. "Otcherednye Zadatchi Sovetskogo Vostokovedeniya," *SV, AN, SSSR* (1940), pp. 7-13.
Borisov, V. "Novye Veyaniya v Arabskoi Literature," *Novyi Mir,* No. 5 (1954), pp. 266-69.
Filshtinskaya, Z. G. "Maksim Gorky v Sovremennoi Progressivnoi Persidskoi Literature," *KSIV, AN, SSSR,* IV (1952), 45-51.
Gordlevsky, V. A. "Slovo o Nazime Khikmete," *KSIV, AN, SSSR,* II, pp. 3-6.
Kabulsky, S. "Sovremennaya Turtsiya," *M Zh,* No. 3 (1925), pp. 25-44.
Kratchkovsky, I. Y. "Otzvuki Revolyutsii 1905 v Arabskoi Khudozhestvennoi Literature," *SV,* III (1945), 5-14.
Miller, A. "Amerikanskii Plan Zakhvata Konstantinopolya i Prolivov v 1919," *Voprosy Istorii,* No. 3 (1951), pp. 61-79.
Petrov, M. "Ekspansiya S. Sh. A. na Sredizemnom More--Ugroza Miru i Bezopasnosti Narodov," *Kommunist,* No. 9 (June, 1954), pp. 90-102.
Savelyeva, L. O. "O Demokratitcheskom i Reaktsionnom Napravleniyakh Poslevoyennoi Turetskoi Poezii," *KSIV, AN, SSSR* (Moscow), IV, (1952), 29-38.
Sultanov, A. F. "Egipetskaya Literatura po Novom Etape," *IAN* (Literatury i Yazyka) (Moscow), XIV, No. 1 (1955), 63-72.
Tishin, I. "Borba Narodov Blizhnego i Srednego Vostoka za Mir i Nezavisimost," *Kommunist,* No. 16 (November, 1954), pp. 79-82.
Tsovikyan, Kh. M. "Vliyanie Russkoi Revolyutsii 1905 g. na Revolyutsionnoe Dvizhenie v Turtsii," *SV,* III (1945), 15-35.
Vasan-Girei Dzhabagi, "Sovetskii Soyuz i Islam," *Vestnik* Instituta po izucheniyu istorii i kultury SSSR (Munich), No. 3 (10), 1954, pp. 42-55.
Zhukov, E. "Suezkii Vopros ne mozhet bit reshon metodami Kolonializma," *Kommunist,* No. 14 (September, 1956), pp. 77-84.

IV. General Reference Works

Atlas of Islamic History. Compiled by H. W. Hazard. 3rd ed. Prince-
ton, N.J.: Princeton University Press, 1954.
The Encyclopaedia of Islam.
Encyclopaedia of Religion and Ethics. Edited by James Hastings.
The Shorter Encyclopaedia of Islam. Edited by H. A. R. Gibb and J.
H. Kramen. Leyden, 1953.

V. Periodicals

The American Slavic and East European Review.
Annuaire du Monde Musulman (Paris).
Central Asian Review (London).
The Egyptian Economic and Political Review.
International Affairs (Moscow).
The Islamic Review.
Journal of the Royal Central Asian Society.
The Middle East Journal.
Mir Islama (1913).
Le Monde Slave.
The Muslim World.
Novyi Vostok.
Revue des Études Islamiques.
Revue du Monde Musulman.
Russian Review.
Sovetskoe Vostokovedenie (Academy of Sciences, USSR, May 1955 to
date).
Soviet Press Translations (University of Washington, 1946-53).
Soviet Survey (London).
Utchennye Zapiski Instituta Vostokovedeniya.
VOKS Bulletin (Moscow).

Further references may be found in the chapter notes.

Index

Abdul Hamid II, 22
Abrashidov Gafour, 234
Abyssinia, 184
Acheson, Dean, 206-7
Adrianople. *See* Treaties
Aegean Islands, 71
Afghanistan, 10, 14, 18, 76, 82,
84, 96-103, 188, 211, 228, 255
Africa, 25, 42, 61, 73, 226, 262;
French, 235-36; North, 190,
209, 221, 254; West, 214
Afro-Asian: solidarity, 236, 265;
Writers' Conference, 266
Agadir, 25
Ahundov, Mirze Fatali, 240
Alexander II, 4, 12-13, 16
Alexander III, 18
Alexander Nevsky, 192, 218
Algeciras, 25
Al-Hafiz Ghazi Zia-ud-Din, 220
Allen, George, 200
Amanullah Khan, 97-99
Anatolia, 71, 78
Anglo-Afghan War, 97
Anglo-American intervention, (in
Lebanon and Jordan), 237
Anglo-French intervention (in
Egypt), 231
Ankara, 48, 68-69, 76, 80, 207,
229, 256
Appeals to the Muslims, 33-42,
45, 47. *See also Manifesto to
the Peoples of the East*
Arab: intelligentsia, 258; league,
210-11, 216, 231; legion, 220;
nationalism, 271; people, 3, 7,
23, 26, 52-53, 63, 82; periodi-
cals, 250; script, 190, transla-
tions, 246-47; writers, 246-50,
258. *See also* Communist pro-
grams: Arab
Aralov, 77
Ardahan, 15, 63, 75, 204-5
Armenia, Armenians, 22, 46-47,
68, 71, 198, 204; Orthodox
Church of, 257
Artvin, 75

Asia, 208, 226, 265; Minor, 9,
26, 71; non-Muslim, 209; South-
east, 214, 221; Soviet, 212. *See
also* Central Asia; Far East;
Middle East; Near East
Assad Khan, 85
Aswan Dam, 218, 230
Austria, 10, 15, 24
Azerbaijan, 22, 52, 76, 88, 92,
196-97, 200, 240
Azov, 7

Baghdad, 24
Baghdad Pact (1955). *See* Treaties
Bahrein Islands, 200
Bakdash, Khalid, 180
Baku, 20, 45-47, 52, 63-64, 70,
88, 105, 190, 193, 254; Con-
gress, 48-62, 66, 82, 89, 187,
261
Balkans, 4, 10, 14, 24-25, 201
Balkar, 192
Bandung, 61, 223, 231, 265
Bashkir, 30, 36
Basmatchestvo, Basmatchi, 31,
101, 188, 241
Batum, 16, 45, 63-64, 193
Beirut, 6-7, 231, 255
Bela Kun, 52
Berlin Congress, 15-18
Berlin-to-Baghdad railroad, 25
Bessarabia, 15
Best, 21
Bismarck, Otto von, 13
Black Sea, 4, 6, 9, 12, 63, 74,
81, 185, 205
Blok, Alexander, 28-30
Bokhara, 6, 36, 98, 100-1
Bolan Passes, 27
Bolsheviks, 21, 26, 32-33, 37,
45, 192. *See also* Communist
programs; Soviet
Borodin, Michael, 181-82
Bosnia, 14, 16
Bosphorus, 9-11, 26, 81, 193,
231
Brest-Litovsk. *See* Treaties